GEORGIA RESEARCH

GEORGIA RESEARCH

A Handbook for Genealogists, Historians, Archivists, Lawyers, Librarians, and Other Researchers

Second Edition

by
Robert S. Davis
and
Ted O. Brooke

Georgia Genealogical Society
Atlanta, Georgia

Georgia Research

© Copyright 2001, 2012 by the Georgia Genealogical Society

All rights reserved. First edition 2001

Second edition 2012

No part of this book may be reproduced in any form, by Photostat, microfilm, xerography, or any other means, or incorporated into any information retrieval system, electronic or mechanical, without the written permission of the copyright owner.

Address inquiries to:

Georgia Genealogical Society

P. O. Box 550247

Atlanta, GA 30355-2747

www.gagensociety.org

Printed in the United States of America

Library of Congress Control Number: 2012945930

ISBN-13: 978-0-9789916-3-0

ISBN-10:0-9789916-3-X

Cover photo credit: DeKalb History Center
The DeKalb County Old Courthouse on the Square was built in 1898 in the neoclassical style and still stands in the center of Decatur. It is currently used as the home of the DeKalb History Center. The Old Courthouse houses a museum and archives and is a popular venue for meetings and gala events. For more information, please see http://www.dekalbhistory.org.

Dedicated to the memory of

Jean Howard Edwards, Mae Ruth Green, Marion R. Hemperley, Leon Hollingsworth,
Frank Parker Hudson, and Merita Rozier

Contents

Maps xv
Figures xvi
Foreword xvii
Preface xix
Introduction xxi
Chapter I Federal and State Sources in Georgia 1
   The National Archives and Records Administration 1
   National Archives at Atlanta (Southeast Region) 2
      Population Census Reports 4
      Non-Population Census Reports 4
      Military Records 4
      Passenger Lists 5
      Naturalization Records 6
      Tax Records 6
      List of Postmasters 6
      Indian Records 6
      Court Records 7
      Other Federal Sources 7
   Guides and Bibliographies 7
   The Georgia Archives 11
      Government Records 11
      Supreme Court of Georgia 12
      Court of Appeals of Georgia 13
      Other Resources 13
      General Name File 14
      Miscellaneous Church and Cemetery File 15
      Microfilm Library 15
      Leon Hollingsworth Genealogical Collection 16
      Georgia Society, DAR "Genealogical Records" Collection 17
      Private Manuscript Collections 17
      Hereditary and Military Descent Organizations 17
   Other Statewide Repositories 18

Georgia Historical Society 19
Hargrett Rare Book and Manuscript Library 20
Historic Preservation Division 20
Huxford-Spear Genealogical Library 21
University of Georgia Main Library 22
Washington Memorial Library 22

Maps, Locations, and Place Names 22
Modern Maps 23
Historical Maps 23
Maps of State, County, and Militia District Boundaries 25
Maps of Federal Post Offices 25
Federal Topographical Maps 25
Sanborn Fire Insurance Maps 25
County Boundary Maps 26
Place Names 27
Forts, Ferries, Roads, and Place Names 27
Military Installations 27
Colonial and Coastal Places 29
Early Georgia Places 29
Indian Place Names 29
Civil War Locations 29
Taverns and Inns 30
American Place Names 30
Citations of Visits to Georgia 30

Biographical Source Directories 30
New Georgia Encyclopedia 32
Georgia Biography Card Catalog 32
File II and Related Sources 34
Atlanta Area Biographical and Death Records 34
Business Persons 35
Lists of Professionals and Persons of Note 35
Early Lawyers 35
Medical Professionals and Dental Professionals 36

Military Officers	36
Southern Artisans	37
Fraternal Organizations	37
Freemasons/Masons	37
Other Organizations	38
Special Resources on Women	38
Newspapers and Newspaper Indexes	39
Nationwide Collections	39
Georgia Newspapers	39
Georgia Newspaper Project	40
Cemeteries	42
Church Records	42
Georgia Baptist Convention	43
Primitive Baptist Denomination	44
Catholic Church	44
Jewish Religion	44
Methodist Denomination	45
Presbyterian Denomination	45
Religious Newspapers	45
Baptist Newspapers	45
Primitive Baptist Newspapers	46
Lutheran Newspapers	46
Methodist Newspapers	46
Presbyterian Newspapers	46
Miscellaneous General Sources	47
Internet Genealogy for Georgia	48
Chapter II Research by Time Period	51
Modern Era, 1917–Present	51
Census Records	51
Vital Records	52
Military Records—World War I	54
Federal Military Records—World War I and Later	55
Prison and Asylum Records	57

County Records	57
Immigration, Naturalization, and Passport Records	58

Pre-Modern Period, 1872–1917 58
- Census Records 58
- Tax Digests 60
- Vital Records 60
- Military Records 61

Reconstruction, 1866–1872 61
- Census Records 62
- Returns of Qualified Voters 62
- Pardons and Amnesty 64
- Civil War Claims Filed After the Civil War 64
- Federal Direct Tax Records, 1865–1873 66
- Freedman's Bank Records, 1868–1874 66
- Apprenticeship Records, 1866– 67
- Freedmen's Bureau Records, 1865–1872 67
- Racial Violence Records, 1866–1871 68
- Other Sources for African American Research 68
- Homestead Records, 1866– 69
- Relief Bills 69

The Civil War, 1861–1865 69
- General Reference & Bibliographical Sources 70
- Alphabetical Card File Index of the Confederate Pension Office 73
- Militia Enrollment Lists, 1864 73
- Confederate Compiled Service Records 74
- Photographs 75
- Confederate Rosters 76
- Confederate Unit Histories and Service Records by County 78
- Union Service Records 79
- Civilians in Confederate Georgia 83
- Cemetery, Hospital, and Monument Records 85
- Civil War Pension Records 87
- Confederate Soldiers' Home 89

    Civil War Miscellaneous 89

Antebellum Georgia, 1812–1860 92

    Federal Census 92

    State Censuses, 1786–1866 95

    Land Lotteries, 1805–1833 95

    Military Records 100

    Federal Bounty and Pension Claims 103

    Poor School and Academy Lists 105

    Original Native American (Indian) Records 105

    Slave Sources 111

    Records of Free Persons of Color 113

    Gold and Other Mining Information 113

    Records on Postmasters and Other Federal Employees 114

The Early Republic, 1783–1811 115

    Federal Census Records, 1790–1810 115

    Headright and Bounty Grants, 1755–1909 115

    Federal Bounty Grants for Revolutionary War Service 118

    Indian Depredations Claims 119

    Migration Records Including Passports by Georgia Governors 119

    Typescripts of Early Government Records 121

    Fleeing Felons 122

    Military Rosters and Commissions 122

    Federal Direct Tax Records 122

    Yazoo Land Fraud Records 123

The American Revolution, 1776–1782 123

    Basic Sources 123

    State and Continental Accounts 124

    Land Grants During The Revolution 124

    Bounty Land Certificates 124

    Revolutionary War Pension Claims 125

    DAR Records 127

    Loyalist Records 128

    Miscellaneous Records 129

  The Colonial Period, 1733–1775 and 1779–1782 130

    The First Georgians 131

    Land Grants, 1752–1775 133

    Military Records 134

    Colonial Georgia Books of Record, 1754–1782 134

    The Salzburgers 136

    Other Groups in Colonial Georgia 136

    Passenger Lists 137

    Marriage Records 138

    Cemeteries 138

    Newspapers 138

    Miscellaneous 138

Chapter III Counties, County Records, and Local History Sources 141

  Local Government Records 141

    Probate Court or Ordinary's Records 141

    Superior Court Records 143

    Other County Records 145

  County Data and Special Sources 146

  Georgia Colonial Parishes 153

  Georgia Counties 154

  Local Histories 267

  City Directories 267

  Business Directories, Gazetteers, and Almanacs 272

    Sherwood Series 274

    Late 19th Century Series 274

  Sanborn Fire Insurance Maps 275

  Photographs 282

  Sites Visited By The Vanishing Georgia Photograph Project Of The Georgia Archives 282

Chapter IV Genealogical Periodicals and Other Resources 285

  General 285

  Genealogical Societies 285

  Genealogical Periodicals 285

  Libraries and Records Repositories 289

Latter-day Saints (LDS) Branch Libraries In Georgia 289

Index 291

MAPS

Map 1 - Atlanta Area Repositories 21

Map 2 - "Hall's Map" showing the original and 1895 counties and land lot districts in Georgia .24

Map 3 - Roads and trails that existed in Georgia circa 1730 to 1850. 28

Map 4 - Configuration of Georgia counties in 1860 94

Map 5 - Areas of Georgia distributed through land lotteries between 1805 and 1832. 97

Map 6 - Parishes of Georgia between the years of 1773 and 1777 132

Map 7 - Georgia counties in 2012. 149

Map 8 - Seats of government for each of Georgia's 159 counties...150

Map 9 - Reference number map for use with county listings 151

Map 10 - Year of creation of each Georgia county. 152

FIGURES

Figure 1 - National Archives at Atlanta 3
Figure 2 - Georgia Archives 12
Figure 3 - Hodgson Hall, home of the Georgia Historical Society 19
Figure 4 - Number Codes on Georgia death certificates 53
Figure 5 - The organization of Confederate troops during the American Civil War 77
Figure 6 – The Dawes Records Work Sheet 110
Figure 7 - Warrant to issue a Headright land grant 116
Figure 8 - Certificate to issue a bounty land grant 117
Figure 9 - This affidavit certified that William Ball did his duty as a soldier prior to 1784 119

FOREWORD

The Georgia Research book was originally written and published by the Georgia Genealogical Society in 2001. Since that time, genealogical research has taken several giant steps forward, fueled in part by the Internet and the vast genealogical resources being added to it daily, as well as new resources which have come to light. Our society felt it was time for a major revision of the book and turned to a talented and knowledgeable core group of people to lead the effort. Without them, this revision would not have taken place. Special thanks go to Robert S. Davis, Ted O. Brooke, Kenneth H. Thomas Jr., Sandra J. Boling and Monica L. Hopkins for the extraordinary gifts of their knowledge of Georgia records and research and their dedication to making this project happen.

Many others worked quietly behind the scenes. I would like to thank the following people for their contributions: Mary Anne Abbe, David Brandenburg, Barbara Brown, Farris W. Cadle, Jennifer Dondero, Linda Geiger, Leah Gonzalez, Paul Graham, Judy Kratovil, Michelle Lewis, Georgette Lipford, Elizabeth Moye, Elaine Neal, Mary Nowell, Elizabeth Olson, Melody Porter, Vivian Price, Joye Quinn, Jim Roper, Susan Sloan, Joanne Smalley, Barbara Stock, and Dawn Watson.

I would also like to thank the Board of the Georgia Genealogical Society for its on-going support for this project. It truly "takes a village" to complete such an important resource for Georgia researchers, and I know I speak for the genealogical community in saying congratulations and thank you.

Linda S. Hughes

President, Georgia Genealogical Society

PREFACE

The Georgia Genealogical Society, founded in 1964, has long been active in the educational aspects of genealogy. One of the first and most popular issues of the *Georgia Genealogical Society Quarterly* was the 1967 "workshop" issue (Vol. 4, No. 2, 1967), by the late Leon Hollingsworth. The Society also co-hosted the first truly national genealogical conference in 1981. The same year, Robert Davis published *Research in Georgia,* the first comprehensive research aid for Georgia. In 1987 the Society updated the 1967 "Workshop" issue and, as a result, produced the *Georgia Genealogical Workbook* by Bob Davis and Ted Brooke.

In 2001, the Society published *Georgia Research*, a complete revision of the 1987 *Georgia Genealogical Workbook*, again co-authored by Bob Davis and Ted Brooke. This revision was designed to aid not only in biographical and genealogical research, but also in the study of Georgia history. It had several unique features which made it the premier resource for Georgia research.

Since 2001, there have been dramatic changes in the genealogy field, especially in Georgia. The Georgia Archives and the National Archives in Atlanta have both relocated into new facilities and Internet resources have escalated to unimaginable levels. Published resources continue to increase, especially in the areas of cemetery, newspaper and primary record abstracts. All of this accelerates and enhances the pace of successful genealogical research.

This 2012 edition of *Georgia Research* presents a thorough and balanced summary of research in Georgia, from Colonial times to the present. In the 45 years since the first Georgia research aid, the "workshop" issue by Mr. Hollingsworth, the scope of Georgia research has transformed so as to be barely recognizable.

Special acknowledgement is made here of the contributions by members of the Georgia Genealogical Society and others in preparing this 2012 revised edition of *Georgia Research*: Mary Anne Abbe, David Brandenburg, Barbara Brown, Farris W. Cadle, Jennifer Dondero, Leah Gonzalez, Paul Graham, Linda S. Hughes, Judy Kratovil, Michelle Lewis, Georgette Lipford, Elizabeth Moye, Elaine Neal, Mary Noel, Elizabeth S. Olson, Melody Porter, Vivian Price, Joye Quinn, Jim Roper, Susan Sloan, Joanne Smalley, Barbara Stock, Dawn Watson, and Gus Welborn, who aided in preparing the maps.

Special thanks and appreciation to Sandra J. Boling, Monica L. Hopkins, and Kenneth H. Thomas Jr., whose unselfish contributions made this book possible

We are pleased to present his new edition to our fellow laborers in the field of researching our wonderful state of Georgia.

Robert S. Davis	Ted O. Brooke
Hanceville, Alabama	Cumming, Georgia

INTRODUCTION

Georgia began at Savannah on February 12, 1733, as the thirteenth and last British colony founded on the American mainland. Until 1752, a non-profit board of trustees in England sent thousands of European Protestants to begin new lives in the province. Many of the settlers sent by the Trustees to Georgia had been debtors in England and Europe. Although most of the settlers were poor, they had the potential for bettering themselves in an environment of new opportunities.

Most of the first Georgians died or fled to more established colonies shortly after their arrival. After the Trustees turned their province over to the Crown in 1752, Georgia became a royal colony, with major settlement coming from other American colonies. The Trustees' restrictions on slaves, property ownership, lawyers, and rum became only a memory. Although the colony grew and prospered, by 1773 Georgia still had a population of only some 18,000 white and 15,000 black men, women, and children living on a long frontier with the Creek and Cherokee Indians, with whom they remained in conflict.

The majority of Georgians did not welcome the American Revolution, and most did not take an active part with either side, although Georgia had the highest percentage of Loyalists (Tories or supporters of the King) of any colony. Thousands of Virginians and Carolinians first saw the state while serving as mercenaries hired by Georgia's patriot government. The war left Georgia as one of the thirteen original states, but it was also devastated and in many places depopulated. Thousands of families moved into Georgia in the 1780s and 1790s, filling Georgia's narrow borders along the Savannah River and the Atlantic coast and creating pressure for more cessions of Indian lands to the west. Most newcomers to Georgia through 1840 would arrive from North Carolina and Virginia, coming in waves with each new opening of former Indian territory.

Officially, Georgia extended to the Mississippi River, but the state's various adventures in trying to impose its authority over the western lands came to nothing and produced no real records of genealogical value. As a result of the Yazoo Fraud of the 1790s, lands that Georgia had claimed in today's Alabama and Mississippi passed to private speculators who later sold the lands to the federal government. In response to other frauds and speculations, Georgia developed the unique system of disposing of lands acquired from the Indians by the means of land lotteries, which were conducted between 1805 and 1833.

As the state expanded westward, so followed the state capitol: from Savannah to Augusta in 1783, to Louisville in 1795, to Milledgeville in 1805, and to Atlanta in 1868. Georgians also moved west, some to participate in the various campaigns against the Indians and against Mexico, and some to settle newly opened territories in Alabama, Kentucky, and other states. Advances in water and steam power made Augusta, Columbus, and Macon major industrial cities. Railroads, begun in the 1830s, expanded the state's cotton belt. The cotton commerce of Savannah made that Georgia coastal city one of the largest, if not the largest, cotton port in the world. Albany, Atlanta, Dalton, and other cities developed as a result of the state's expanding railroad network.

Although Sherman's campaigns and famous march to the sea did relatively little damage to Georgia's records (contrary to popular myth), the Civil War did bring on massive economic and social chaos in Georgia that encouraged still further migrations to Texas and the West. The boll weevil, over-population, racial problems, depleted soil, "credit for cotton" economics, and other negatives inspired later exoduses. Today, except for Georgians, more visitors come to the Georgia Archives from Texas than any other state. For historical background on Georgia see Kenneth Coleman, et al., *A History of Georgia* (Athens: University of Georgia Press, 1977).

In records, Georgia has been blessed. Although lacking early birth and death records and Church of England parish records like those found in other regions, Georgia does have a number of unique records of genealogical value created as a result of the state's long frontier period (the last Indian removal came in 1838). Paper-intensive government existed in Georgia from the beginning. Although some significant losses of county records occurred for Baker, Burke, Cobb, Colquitt, Dade, Dooly, Echols, Heard, Lee, Lowndes, McIntosh, Twiggs, Walker, Washington, and Wilkinson counties, the records of many other counties survive largely intact (see Chapter III).

Many state records serve as substitutes and supplements for Georgia's county records and federal censuses. (The 1790, 1800, 1810, and 1890 federal censuses are lost for Georgia, and the 1820 census omits many names, as do the indexes to the censuses.) The many early military campaigns participated in by Georgia troops created a large body of genealogical sources. The mass of surviving county records is enhanced by documents resulting from the state's requiring the recording of marriage licenses, divorces, tuition paid for poor school children, etc., at an early date. Georgia began requiring birth and death certificates in 1919 although many counties ignored the law as late as 1928.

Georgia residents are also not deficient in interest in genealogy and local history. In addition to a large number of genealogical societies and their periodicals (see Chapter IV), the state has more than one hundred local historical groups, over one hundred chapters of the NSDAR, three historical journals, more than 140 records repositories of all types, and many other history-oriented organizations.

CHAPTER I
FEDERAL AND STATE SOURCES IN GEORGIA

The National Archives and Records Administration

The National Archives (website: http://www.archives.gov/) has responsibility for the historical records of the federal government of the United States and its predecessor, the Continental Congress. Local federal records are maintained at eleven regional archives centers and other regional repositories, including presidential libraries and other research facilities.

The following are important general guides to the holdings of the National Archives, including records relating to Georgia; some have been placed on their website. Other works relating to the holdings of the National Archives are cited elsewhere, under specific subject headings. Also, consult the current printed catalog of National Archives microfilms.

Bacon, Lee D. "Early Navy Personnel Records at the National Archives, 1776–1860." *Prologue: The Quarterly of the National Archives* 27 (1995): 76–80.

———. "Civil War and Later Naval Personnel Records at the National Archives, 1861–1924." *Prologue: The Quarterly of the National Archives* 27 (1995): 178–182.

Coren, Robert W., et al. *Guide to the Records of the United States Senate at the National Archives, 1789–1989: Bicentennial Edition* (Doct. No. 100–42). Washington, DC: National Archives and Records Administration, 1989.

Deputy, Marilyn, et al. *Register of Federal United States Military Records: A Guide to Manuscript Sources Available at the Genealogical Library in Salt Lake City and the National Archives in Washington, D.C.* Bowie, MD: Heritage Books, 1986.

Digested Summary and Alphabetical List of Private Claims Which Have Been Presented to the House of Representatives [1789–1851]. 1853. Reprint, Baltimore: Genealogical Pub. Co., 1970.

Guide to Genealogical Research in the National Archives. 3d ed. Washington, DC: National Archives and Records Administration, 2001.

Guide to Federal Records in the National Archives of the United States. 3 vols. Washington DC: National Archives and Records Administration, 1996.

Military Service Records: A Select Catalog of National Archives Microfilm Publications. Washington, DC: National Archives and Records Administration, 1985.

Mollan, Mark C. "Honoring Our War Dead: The Evolution of the Modern Government Policy on Headstones for Fallen Soldiers and Sailors." *Prologue: The Quarterly of the National Archives* 35 (1) (fall 2003): http://www.archives.gov/publications/prologue/2003/spring/headstones.html

Pfeiffer, David A. "Archivist's Perspective: Riding the Rails Up Paper Mountain: Researching Railroad Records in the National Archives." *Prologue: The Quarterly of the National Archives* 29 (1997): 52–61.

Schamel, Charles E. "Untapped Resources: Private Claims and Legislation in the Records of the U.S. Congress." *Prologue: The Quarterly of the National Archives* 27 (1995): 45–58.

Schamel, Charles E., et al. *Guide to the Records of the United States House of Representatives at the National Archives, 1789–1989.* 1989.

Schmitzer, Jeanne Carnnella. "Genealogy Notes: Far From Home: American Citizens in the United States Military and Territorial Census Records." *Prologue: The Quarterly of the National Archives* 29 (1997): 70–73.

Wehmann, Howard H. *A Guide to Pre-Federal Records in the National Archives.* 1989.

A useful record described in *The Genealogical and Biographical Research: A Catalog* is the group of often-autobiographical applications for federal jobs during the administrations of presidents John Adams through Ulysses S. Grant. This microfilm is available at the National Archives at Atlanta (see below).[1] The booklet accompanying the microfilm for each administration includes an alphabetical list of the applicants. Such job requests usually were made by persons of some, at least local, prominence; these records frequently mention past histories and personal connections. Applications by individuals to individual departments for employment such as Justice, State, Treasury, and War survive and must be searched in person or by mail from the National Archives and Records Administration, 8601 Adelphi Road, College Park, MD 20740-6001. Postmasters, before the advent of the civil service exams, were chosen by local political bosses, not by application to Washington.

National Archives at Atlanta (Southeast Region)

5780 Jonesboro Road
Morrow, GA 30260
Phone: 770-968-2100
Fax: 770-968-2547
Website: http://www.archives.gov/southeast/

The National Archives at Atlanta serves not only Georgia but its bordering states and Mississippi and Kentucky. For a guide to the holdings of the Atlanta Branch and other regional locations, see the book by Loretto Dennis Szucs, *The Archives: Guide to the National Archives Field Branches* (Salt Lake City: Ancestry, 1988). The guide for presidential libraries is by Dennis A. Burton, *A Guide to Manuscripts in the Presidential Libraries* (College Park, MD: Research Materials Corporation, 1985). By logging onto the National Archives website, a researcher can consult the Archival Research Catalog (ARC) and the Microfilm Catalog and specify a center to search for descriptions

---

[1] The National Archives at Atlanta has been known historically to researchers as part of a regional Federal Records Center, the National Archives Atlanta Branch, and the National Archives Southeast Region. Its original location was in East Point, Georgia.

of records and microfilms in its holdings. The website for the local branch will include up-to-date information on holdings and informative programs.

Figure 1 - National Archives at Atlanta

The National Archives at Atlanta has some holdings that cover the entire country, such as the complete collections for all states of the Railroad Retirement Board and the twenty-three million World War I draft cards, the population schedules of the federal censuses for 1790–1920 on microfilm, indexes to military records, 1775–1848, and the Revolutionary War pension claims. The complete collection for all states of World War II draft cards, including those previously at National Archives at Atlanta, has been transferred to the Military Records Branch at St. Louis, Missouri. Other holdings are more regional, such as their microfilm collection of indexes to passenger lists, Atlanta Federal Penitentiary Records (an index is on their website at http://www.archives.gov/southeast/finding-aids/atlanta-penitentiary/), federal direct tax records (Georgia, 1866–1873, 1913–1917), Native American records, Confederate service records, and Freedmen's Bureau records. The strongest areas for research at National Archives at Atlanta are Civil Rights, federal court, military, and African American history.

In addition to the printed catalogs to all of its original records and microfilm holdings, this institution offers free handouts on such topics as its holdings for genealogy and Asian, African American, Georgia, and Native American family research. A support group for National Archives at Atlanta is the Friends of the National Archives Southeast (website: http://friendsnas.org/).

The National Archives regional holdings include the United States (federal) and Confederate district and circuit court records, starting in 1790. Prior to 1860, most federal court records involved smuggling, the mail, and debt suits between parties in different states. In southern states, such as Georgia, almost all merchants did business with manufacturers and other companies in northern states. Federal court records are particularly rich in detailed bankruptcy suits in the late 1830s and 1840s. During the Civil War, a Confederate court replaced the federal court in Georgia and other southern states. The records of that court include extensive files on confiscation of locally- and northern-owned property, as well as suits by northern companies for debts owed by southern companies then under sequestration. Following the Civil War, cases involving moonshining, untaxed tobacco, and civil rights violations became common. The records of the United States and Confederate courts are well indexed for Georgia, although defendants in the pre-1860 district court are indexed in the individual minute books and not separately. For more information, consult the special regional archives and federal court records issue of *Prologue: The Quarterly of the National Archives*, 21, no. 3 (1989). Also check Loretto Dennis Szucs, *The Archives: Guide to the National Archives Field Branches* (Salt Lake City, UT: Ancestry, 1988) and Erwin C. Surrency, *The Work of the Federal Courts in Georgia Over Two Centuries* (Atlanta: Eleventh Circuit Historical Society, 2006).

The following references to topics related to Georgia are from a brochure listing microfilm genealogical holdings of the National Archives—Southeast Region. Detailed descriptions of the holdings of the National Archives at Atlanta can be found at http://www.archives.gov/southeast/finding-aids/index.html.

Population Census Reports

Population census schedules, entire United States, 1790–1930

The 1940 federal census will not be available on microfilm, just online.

Non-Population Census Reports

Non-Population Census, 1850–1880, Georgia, T1137, 27 Rolls

Military Records

Revolutionary War

General Index to . . .Military Service Records . . . of Soldiers, M860, 58 rolls

Index to . . . Service Records of . . . Naval Personnel, M879, 1 roll

Index to . . . Service Records of . . . Soldiers Who Served . . . in Georgia Military Organizations, M1051, 1 roll

Compiled Service Records of Soldiers Who Served in the American Army During the Revolutionary War, M881, 1096 rolls

Revolutionary War Pension and Bounty Land Warrant Application Files, 1800–1900, M804, 2670 rolls

Georgia Research
Chapter I: Federal and State Sources in Georgia

Revolutionary War Rolls, 1775–83 (muster rolls, other lists), M246, 138 rolls

War of 1812
Index to . . . Volunteer Soldiers Who Served in the War of 1812, M602, 234 rolls

Cherokee Disturbances, 1836–1839
Index to . . . Volunteer Soldiers . . . From the State of Georgia, M907, 1 roll

Index to . . . Volunteer Soldiers . . . From . . . Tennessee and Field and Staff [Officers] . . . of the Cherokee Nation, M908, 2 rolls

Civil War — Union
Index to . . . Volunteer Union Soldiers . . . from . . . Georgia, M385, 1 roll

1890 [Census Of] Union Veterans and Widows of Union Veterans, M123, 118 rolls

Civil War — Confederate
Index to . . . Confederate Soldiers . . . From . . . Georgia, M226, 67 rolls

Index to Confederate Soldiers Who Served in Organizations Raised Directly by the Confederate Government, M818, 7 rolls

Confederate States Army Casualties: Lists and Narrative Reports, 1861–1865, M836, 7 rolls

Register of Confederate . . . [Dead] in Federal Prisons and . . . Hospitals, M918, 1 roll

Official Battle Lists of the Civil War, 1861–1865, M823, 2 rolls

Passenger Lists

Federal passenger lists begin in the 1820s although many of the early ones do not survive and those that do frequently misspell names and/or are written in such bad handwriting as to be impossible to decipher; see *Immigrant and Passenger Arrivals: A Select Catalog of National Archives Microfilm Publications* (Washington, DC: National Archives and Records Administration,1983). Many of the passenger lists are available on the subscription web site Ancestry.com. For the few pre-1820s lists that have survived see Carl Boyer, *Ship Passenger Lists: The South, 1538-1825* (Newhall, CA: privately printed, 1979).

Passenger Lists of Vessels Arriving at Savannah, Georgia, 1906–1945, T493, 1 roll

Index to Passengers on Vessels Arriving at Ports in Alabama, Florida, Georgia, and South Carolina, 1890–1924, T517, 26 rolls

In addition, the Atlanta Branch has National Archives microfilm of passenger arrival lists for Darien, Georgia (1823–1825, M575, reel 2); Savannah, Georgia (1820–1868, M575, reel 16; 1906 and 1917–1923, T943); and various Georgia ports (index, 1890–1924, T517), as well as microfilm of passenger lists and federal court naturalization records for other southeastern states.

A helpful resource on the subject of passenger arrivals is in the Georgia Archives, which has microfilm of the passenger lists for the port of New York, January 1820–July 1854. The Georgia Archives does not have the index to this film, although the Archives does have the following, along with a subscription to Ancestry.com and its indexes to passenger lists, which could lead one to the proper passenger list:

> Filby, P. William, and Mary K. Meyer. *Passenger and Immigration Lists Index*. 3 vols. and 5 suppl. vols. Detroit: Gale Publishing Company, 1981–1986.
>
> Glazier, Ira A. *The Famine Immigrants: Lists of Irish Immigrants Arriving at the Port of New York, 1846–1851*. Baltimore: Genealogical Publishing Company, 1983.
>
> Mitchell, Brian. *Irish Passenger Lists* [1803–1839] 3 vols. Baltimore: Genealogical Publishing Company, 1989.

Other libraries have other published indexes of passenger lists for German, Italian, and Russian immigrants.

Naturalization Records

Until 1906, an immigrant could be naturalized in any court of record, including the federal courts. After 1906, naturalizations could occur only in federal courts. The Atlanta Branch has original naturalization records from federal courts of the states for its region from 1790 to 1945; see Linda Woodard Geiger and Meyer L. Frankel, comps., *Index to Georgia's Federal Naturalization Records to 1950 (Excluding Military Personnel)*, (Atlanta: Georgia Genealogical Society, 1996).

Records of Admission to Citizenship, U.S. District Court, Charleston, SC, 1790–1906, M1183, 1 roll

Tax Records

Internal Revenue Assessment Lists for Georgia, 1865–66, M762, 8 rolls

List of Postmasters

Records of Appointment of Postmasters, 1789–1832, M1131, 4 rolls

Records of Appointment of Postmasters, 1832–September 30, 1971, M841, 145 rolls

Indian Records

Census Roll [and index], 1835, of the Cherokee Indians East of the Mississippi, T496, 1 roll

Old Settler Cherokee Census Roll, 1895, and Index to Payment Roll, 1896, T985, 2 rolls

Reports of the Field Jurisdictions of the Office of Indian Affairs, 1873–1900, M1070, rolls 3 and 11

Records Relating to Enrollment of Eastern Cherokees by Guion Miller, 1908–1910, M685, 12 rolls

Census of Creek Indians Taken by Parsons and Abbott in 1832, T275, 1 roll

Enrollment Cards for the Five Civilized Tribes, 1898–1914, M1186, 6 rolls.

Final Rolls of Citizens and Freedmen of the Five Civilized Tribes in Indian Territory [on or before March 4, 1907, with supplements dated September 25, 1914], T529, 3 rolls

Indian Census Rolls, 1884–1940, M595, rolls 41–42, 183 and 486–487

Court Records

Index Book, 1789–1928, and Minutes and Bench Dockets, 1789–1870, for the District Court, Southern District of Georgia, M1172, 3 rolls

Minutes, Circuit Court of Georgia, 1790–1824, and Index to Plaintiffs and Defendants in Circuit Court, 1790–1860, M1184, 3 rolls

Other Federal Sources

Most major university libraries, including Emory University and the University of Georgia libraries, and some major public libraries are Federal Depository Libraries. These facilities can provide information on government publications, past and present, and current addresses for the publishing agencies. Among the standard holdings of these centers are legislative and executive printed documents, as well as publications of federal laws and Supreme Court decisions.

For a list of the Federal Depository Libraries in Georgia, see the U. S. Government Printing Office website at http://www.gpo.gov/libraries/. Many publications of federal laws, legislative minutes, and other legal subjects can be searched and read through such websites as Google Books (free), American Memory of the Library of Congress (free), and GenealogyBank (subscription site). Large government document centers have access to other more-complete databases that also allow word searches of historical government publications such as the U.S. Serial Set Digital Collection and Westlaw.

Guides and Bibliographies

Basic guides and bibliographies for Georgia include:

- Bryant, Pat, and Ingrid Shields. *Georgia Counties: Their Changing Boundaries.* Atlanta: Georgia Secretary of State, 1983. Clifford Dwyer also has published a chart of Georgia county creations.

- Davis, Robert S. *Research in Georgia.* Greenville, SC: Southern Historical Press, 1980.

- Davis, Robert S., and Ted O. Brooke. *Georgia Research: A Handbook.* Atlanta: Georgia Genealogical Society, 2012.

- Dorsey, James E. *Georgia Genealogy and Local History: A Bibliography.* Spartanburg, SC: The Reprint Co., 1983.

- Dorsey, James E., and Arthur Rowland. *A Bibliography for the Writing of Georgia History.* Spartanburg, SC: The Reprint Co., 1978.

- Lupold, John S. *Chattahoochee Valley Sources and Resources: An Annotated Bibliography.* 2 vols. Eufaula, AL: Historic Chattahoochee Commission, 1993. Volume two covers the Georgia counties, along the Chattahoochee River, that adjoin South Alabama.

- Robertson, David H. *Georgia Genealogical Research: A Practical Guide.* Stone Mountain, GA: privately printed, 1989.

- Schweitzer, George K. *Georgia Genealogical Research.* Rev. ed. Knoxville, TN: privately printed, 1995.

Simpson, John E. *Georgia History: A Bibliography*. Metuchen, NJ: Scarecrow Press, 1976.

Storey, J. Steven. *Resource Index*. Atlanta: Georgia Department of Natural Resources, 1976.

Warnock, Robert Holcomb. *Georgia Sources for Family History*. Atlanta: Georgia Genealogical Society, 1995.

The *Georgia Historical Quarterly*, 1981 to 1987, contains bibliographies of both genealogical and historical articles published during the previous year. Several journals, including *Georgia Baptist Viewpoints, Journal of Southern Legal History, Journal of the Georgia Association of Historians, Chattanooga Area Historical Journal, Historical Society of the Georgia National Guard Journal*, and others are not included in these lists. See the following volumes for the stated years covered.

Vol. 66 (1982): 514–46 for 1981
Vol. 67 (1983): 512–45 for 1982
Vol. 68 (1984): 569–601 for 1983
Vol. 69 (1985): 557–89 for 1984
Vol. 70 (1986): 729–55 for 1985
Vol. 71 (1987): 701–26 for 1986
Vol. 72 (1988): 712–24 for 1987

Beginning in 1988, the Georgia Historical Society bibliography continued with only historical articles. For genealogical articles published from 1988 to 1992, see the following volumes of the *Georgia Genealogical Quarterly*.

Vol. 26 (1990): 218–30 for 1988
Vol. 29 (1993): 220–39 for 1989
Vol. 30 (1994): 74–85 for 1990
Vol. 30 (1994): 223–43 for 1991
Vol. 31 (1995): 218–231 for 1992

For most of the historical articles published from 1988 to 2010, see these volumes of the *Georgia Historical Quarterly*:

Vol. 73 (1989): 828–42 for 1988
Vol. 74 (1990): 699–722 for 1989
Vol. 75 (1991): 804–20 for 1990
Vol. 76 (1992): 929–36 for 1991
Vol. 77 (1993): 823–29 for 1992
Vol. 78 (1994): 376–82 for 1993
Vol. 79 (1995): 453–65 for 1994
Vol. 80 (1996): 375–88 for 1995
Vol. 81 (1997): 750–60 for 1996
Vol. 82 (1998): 398–409 for 1997
Vol. 83 (1999): 342–53 for 1998
Vol. 84 (2000): 502–62 for 1999
Vol. 85 (2001): 278–89 for 2000
Vol. 86 (2002): 278–85 for 2001
Vol. 87 (2003): 297–304 for 2002
Vol. 88 (2004): 422–30 for 2003

Vol. 89 (2005): 402–409 for 2004
Vol. 90 (2006): 442–48 for 2005
Vol. 91 (2007): 348–53 for 2006
Vol. 92 (2008): 413–19 for 2007
Vol. 93 (2009): 307–13 for 2008
Vol. 94 (2010): 388–93 for 2009
Vol. 95 (2011): 541-45 for 2010

All of Georgia's genealogical periodicals, along with many historical journals such as the *Georgia Historical Quarterly*, except the *Chattooga County Historical Society Quarterly*, also are included in *Periodical Source Index*, or PERSI, an annual subject index to genealogical periodicals from 1847 to the present, prepared by the staff of the Allen County-Fort Wayne Public Library. References to articles not on counties or specific families are listed under "U.S." in the geographic section of PERSI. The PERSI index can be accessed on the Internet at the Ancestry.com website, the HeritageQuest subscription website, or through any member of the Allen County Public Library system.

Among the individual Georgia journals, the *Georgia Genealogical Society Quarterly* also has a separate every-name index for the issues 1964 through 1981 and for each issue thereafter, except for articles already in alphabetical order. The *Georgia Genealogical Society Quarterly* also has a subject index compiled by Janet Bryan McLendon, *Subject Index to 25 Years. . .1964–1989* (Atlanta: Georgia Genealogical Society, 1990).

The *Georgia Genealogical Magazine* has a book of annual indexes to its Volumes 1–12 and annual indexes thereafter, except for the issues of 1975; see the *Georgia Genealogical Magazine Subject Index* (Greenville, SC: Genealogical Research Group, 1996). Many of the articles from this periodical have been reprinted by geographical region in Silas Emmett Lucas Jr., *Some Georgia County Records*, 10 vols. (Easley and Greenville, SC, Southern Historical Press, 1990–2000). Other sources specifically for Georgia include "Scannings" and "Questions and Answers," regular features of the *Georgia Genealogical Society Quarterly*. The latter, beginning with Volume 20, No. 4, (1984), contains current responses and solutions to specific Georgia-related genealogical questions.

Of Georgia's historical journals, the *Georgia Historical Quarterly* has a published every-name index through 1976. The Atlanta History Center has a card catalog index to the *Atlanta Historical Bulletin* (1927–1933), *Atlanta Historical Journal* (1933–1986), and *Atlanta History: A Journal of Georgia and the South* (1987–2005).

Aside from general library book catalogs, many of which are on the Internet, several special sources exist for identifying books and for locating rare Georgia imprints, such as pamphlets. Specifically helpful for printed materials are the websites for ArchiveGrid and WorldCat, as well as such commercial sites as AbeBooks and Amazon.com. No such work is complete. Printed bibliographies include:

> Clizbee, Azalea. *Catalogue of the Wymberley Jones DeRenne Georgia Library at Wormsloe*. 3 vols. Mansfield Centre, CT: Maurizio Martino, 1995. Reprint of the 1931 first edition, which was limited to 300 copies and was privately published in Wormsloe in 1931. This set contains well-annotated descriptions of the most important collection of material relating to Georgia that exists. Over 6,500 books, documents, manuscripts,

and maps are described. The DeRenne Collection of Georgia-related books for which this is a bibliography is at University of Georgia, Hargrett Library.

Derfer, Lisa A. *Pamphlets in American History*. Sanford, NC: Microfilming Corporation of America, 1982.

"Georgia Ghosts or Where Are They Now?: One Researcher's Catalog of Georgia's Missing Historical Records." *Provenance* 8 (1990): 31–51.

Hummell, Ray O., Jr. *Southeastern Broadsides Before 1877: A Bibliography*. Richmond: Virginia State Library, 1971, 31–67.

Rowland, Arthur Ray. *Georgia Imprints*. Augusta, GA: the Augusta Genealogical Society, 2010.

Wright, A. J. *Criminal Activity in the Deep South, 1700–1930: An Annotated Bibliography*. New York: Greenwood Press, 1989.

The following works cover more than Georgia.

Bentley, Elizabeth Petty. *The Genealogist's Address Book: State and Local Resources; With Special Resources Including Ethnic and Religious Organizations*. 6th ed. Baltimore: Genealogical Publishing Company, 2009.

Bremer, Ronald A. *Compendium of Historical Sources: The How and Where of American Genealogy*. Bountiful, UT: American Genealogical Publishing Company, 1997.

Cerny, Johni, and Wendy Elliott. *The Library: A Guide to the LDS Family History Library*. Salt Lake City: Ancestry, 1988.

Davis, Robert S. *A Southern Researcher's Notebook: Essays on Research and Records from Past Issues of Heritage Quest*. Blountsville, AL.: privately printed, 1997.

Eichholz, Alice. *Ancestry's Red Book: American State, County and Town Sources*. Rev. ed. Salt Lake City: Ancestry, 1992. This book is the best guide to the sources available for each state.

Filby, P. William. *A Bibliography of American County History*. Baltimore: Genealogical Publishing Company, 1985.

———. *Directory of American Libraries with Genealogy or Local History Collections*. Wilmington, DE.: Scholarly Resources, 1988.

Greenwood, Val D. *The Researcher's Guide to American Genealogy*. 3rd ed. Baltimore: Genealogical Publishing Company, 2000. This book is the basic guide to understanding American records of genealogical value.

Hoffman, Marian. *Genealogical & Local History Books in Print*. 5th ed. 4 vols. Baltimore: Genealogical Publishing Company, 1996–1997.

Horowitz, Lois. *A Bibliography of Military Name Lists: From Pre-1675 to 1900: A Guide to Genealogical Sources*. Metuchen, NJ: Scarecrow Press, 1990.

Kirkham, E. Kay. *An Index to Some of the Family Records of the Southern States*. Logan, UT: Everton Publishers, 1979.

Meyerink, Kory. *Printed Sources: A Guide to Published Genealogical Records.* Salt Lake City: Ancestry, 1997.

Neagles, James C. *The Library of Congress: A Guide to Genealogical and Historical Research.* Salt Lake City: Ancestry, 1990.

Smith, Jessie Carney. *Ethnic Genealogy: A Research Guide.* Westport, CT: Greenwood Press, 1983.

Szucs, Loretto Dennis, and Sandra Hargreaves Luebking. *The Source: A Guidebook to American Genealogy.* 3rd. Ed.. Salt Lake City: Ancestry, 2006.

Wasserman, Paul, and Alice E. Kennington. *Ethnic Information Sources of the United States.* Detroit: Gale Research, 1983.

The Georgia Archives

5800 Jonesboro Road
Morrow, GA 30260
Phone: 678-364-3700
Website: www.GeorgiaArchives.org

The Georgia Archives[2] is the best place for Georgia family research. Hours and days of opening have been subject to change, and its website should be consulted before any plans for a visit are made (as with any library or archives facility). Group tours are arranged by appointment. Lists of persons willing to copy records or to conduct research for a fee at the Archives are available on the Georgia Genealogical Society website: http://www.gagensociety.org and the website of the Georgia Chapter of the Association of Professional Genealogists at http://www.rootsweb.ancestry.com/~gaapg/.

Government Records

Aside from the government records described below on microfilm or discussed by subject elsewhere, the Georgia Archives has many original state and county government records. The inventories to most of these records are online and can be accessed through the Georgia Archives website at http://find.sos.state.ga.us/archon/ or by word search through Google.

The General Name File, a card catalog (see below), indexes and cross-references some of the letters received by Georgia governors prior to 1860, the originals of which are in the artificial collection known as File II Names. These files are in Record Group 4-2-46 at the Georgia Archives. Various inventories of parts of these collections have been published in Robert S. Davis, comp., *Georgians Past* (Milledgeville, GA: Boyd Publishing, 1997). File II Names have been scanned with the generous support of the R.J. Taylor Jr. Foundation. They are available for free access through the Georgia Archives Virtual Vault.

---

[2] The Georgia Archives was created in 1918 by the Georgia General Assembly. Originally named the Georgia Department of Archives and History, it operated under the oversight of the State Historical Commission until its transfer to the Office of Secretary of State in 1931. In 2002 it was renamed the Georgia Division of Archives and History, with the alternate name of Georgia Archives.

Some 50,000 other official records of the governors of Georgia are in the Telamon Cuyler Collection of the Hargrett Rare Book and Manuscript Library of the University of Georgia. The Hargrett Library also has other official records in the Keith Read and Felix Hargrett Collections. Many other individual items of early Georgia governors are found in collections of other institutions across the country including the Georgia Historical Society.

The Georgia Archives has most of the official incoming letters to Georgia governors from 1861 to recent times, and some earlier materials, in Record Group 1-1-5. The Archives also has receipt books (for persons paid for expenses and salaries), letter books, minute books, and other records of Georgia's Executive Department. Some of this material has printed inventories that list selected items within the files.

The Georgia Archives has a complete collection of the published Georgia laws, legislative minutes, digests, state courts case files, etc. In most instances, the Georgia Archives also has almost all of the original records of the state's two appellate courts.

Figure 2 - Georgia Archives

Supreme Court of Georgia

The Georgia Archives has court cases appealed to the Supreme Court of Georgia, 1846–1990, in Record Group 92-1-3. Case files frequently include copies of some county records submitted as evidence, such as superior court case files and probate and other records, which may not have survived elsewhere.

The published series *Georgia Reports* contains summaries of cases, decisions, and indexes to the cases of the Supreme Court of Georgia. The surviving cases files from 1846–1917 are indexed and can be searched on the Georgia Archives website by name of the appellant, name of the appellee, or the case number at www.GeorgiaArchives.org. Some of these cases were never heard before the justices and therefore were not included in *Georgia Reports* and other publications of court decisions.

Cases from 1917–1990 are not included in the index but are at the Georgia Archives. Case files after 1990 can be accessed only by contacting the Clerk's office:

Supreme Court of Georgia
244 Washington Street
Room 572, State Office Annex Building
Atlanta, GA 30334
Phone: 404-656-3470

Court of Appeals of Georgia

The Court of Appeals of Georgia was created as an intermediate appellate court in 1906, in order to reduce the caseload of the Supreme Court, and the first judges met in January 1907. In 1916 the Supreme Court was granted power to review judgments of the Court of Appeals. In civil cases the Court of Appeals hears almost all the appeals that are taken from the superior courts and the state courts, except that the Supreme Court of Georgia has jurisdiction in cases involving title to land, equity, habeas corpus, wills, divorce, or alimony.

For cases heard before the Court of Appeals, the Georgia Archives has the original case records, 1907–1991, in Record Group 56-2-2, and a set of its official publication *Georgia Appeals Reports*. The Archives also has reference microfilm for case files 1992–2007. Case files after 2007 can be accessed only by contacting the Clerk's office:

Court of Appeals of Georgia
47 Trinity Avenue S.W., Suite 501
Atlanta, GA 30334
Phone: 404-656-3450

The history and working of all types of Georgia courts from colonial times to the present are covered in Erwin C. Surrency, *The Creation of a Judicial System: A History of Georgia Courts, 1733 to Present* (Holmes Beach, FL: Gaunt, 2001). A bound copy of this history, as an unpublished manuscript, is in the book collection of the Georgia Archives. An incomplete but word-searchable version of Georgia's published legislative journals and published laws has been included in the University of Georgia's project Galileo website and is a part of the Digital Library of Georgia: http://dlg.galileo.usg.edu/CollectionsA-Z/zlgl_information.html?Welcome.

Other Resources

Many of the manuscripts, photographs, public records, finding aids, and other materials in the Georgia Archives have been scanned and placed on its website in the Virtual Vault:

http://cdm.sos.state.ga.us/. This portal provides virtual access to some of Georgia's most important historical documents, from 1733 to the present, and it is periodically updated. The Archives has books, periodicals, microfilm, and original private and government records relating to Georgia. It also has a good Southern genealogical collection and materials for some other states of interest to Georgia researchers. Along with catalogs to microfilm and original government and private record sources and printed materials, the Georgia Archives has several resources of special interest to genealogists.

General Name File

This file is a card catalog to approximately 125,000 names, covering all counties in Georgia. The cards contain references to both primary, original sources as well as secondary, non-original sources that cover a date span of 1732 to about 1990. While the cards serve as only an index to names found in the referenced sources, the cards themselves usually contain extensive and valuable information that was extracted from the sources. Some of the sources listed on the index cards have been filmed either by the Genealogical Society of Utah, the Georgia Archives, or others; some of the sources are at the Archives, while some are not.

Included are names of Georgians found in commissions issued by the state of Georgia to state and local military and civil officials; personal notes on petitions by Georgians to the legislature, from legislative minutes; published family histories; and family folders that are part of the Genealogical Vertical File. The General Name File is available on the Internet as part of the Virtual Vault at: http://cdm.sos.state.ga.us/cdm4/gnf.php. Some cards contain references and extracts from the following record types:

- Marriage records (from original county records and other sources)
- Divorce records (from state legislative records and other sources)
- Militia and military records (service records, militia commissions, etc.)
- Obituaries (from newspapers)
- Bible records
- Church records
- Family genealogical folders, charts, and collections
- Will and probate, land, naturalization, and other court records

The General Name File also indexes the ABQ (autobiographical) and TBQ (typed biographical) questionnaires used chiefly for compiling the *Georgia Official and Statistical Register*. These were published from 1923 thru 1990 and can be found on the website at http://dlg.galileo.usg.edu/CollectionsA-Z/sreg_information.html. The questionnaires appear to have started with this series, c. 1923 and were last used in 1993. These questionnaires are exceptionally rich sources of genealogical data. For lists of these questionnaires on microfilm in Drawer 15, Boxes 1–15, at the Georgia Archives see: Robert S. Davis, comp. *Georgians Past* (Milledgeville, GA: Boyd Publishing, 1997) or *Georgia Genealogical Society Quarterly* 20 (1984): 141–70, 199–234.

A separate card catalog is maintained for African American family information. The Georgia Archives also has in Drawer 154, Boxes 16–25, microfilm of its family folders made in the 1950s that sometimes includes documents that are no longer in the collection.

The Georgia Archives accepts donations of family vertical file material and compiled family histories relating to Georgia families. Guidelines for these donations can be found on their website: http://www.GeorgiaArchives.org/InformationForGeneralPublic/policies_that_affect_the_public/donate_materials.htm.

Miscellaneous Church and Cemetery File

This is a card catalog to vertical subject files and a similar card catalog to records on microfilm that directs researchers to cemetery records. Also see Cemeteries section on page 42 below.

Microfilm Library

This area of the Georgia Archives contains collections of microfilm and microfiche and the printed indexes to the microfilm. Microfiche holdings, as well as books on microfilm, are included in the microfilm library card catalog.[3] The Microfilm Library card catalog is available on the Georgia Archives website at www.GeorgiaArchives.org, under "Virtual Vault", then link to "All Collections" and then to "County Records Microfilm Index" and enter the name of the county under "Search". The microforms include important Georgia county records to 1900 or later, some books, state records, federal documents (such as census records), church records, and private manuscripts. The microfilm library currently has two, large card-catalog cabinets, arranged as follows.

Public Records: Municipal [City], County, and State Records of Georgia, and Records of the United States Government

County Records (alphabetical by county), 11 drawers

This card catalog for county records has been scanned and added to the website of the Georgia Archives: http://cdm.sos.state.ga.us/cdm4/countycards.php

Federal Records, 2 drawers

Georgia Official [State Government] Records, 2 drawers

Municipal Records, 1 drawer

Tax Digests (alphabetical by county), 1 drawer

Non-Governmental Records

Bible Records (A–Z by family name), 3 drawers

Books (by author and by title), 1 drawer

Cemeteries (alphabetical by county), 1 drawer

---

[3] Most of the published books that have been microfilmed are also included in the online book catalog of the Georgia Archives.

Church Records (alphabetical by denomination, then by church name),[4] 2 drawers

Cities (alphabetical by name of city or town),[5] 1 drawer

County (business and church records, etc.; cross-referenced and alphabetical by county), 3 drawers

Genealogical Information (by family name), 2 drawers

Newspapers (alphabetical by town or city and then by name of newspaper), 2 drawers

Out-of-State and Foreign Material, 1 drawer

Private Papers (alphabetical by name of collection, including family name),[6] 2 drawers

Subject File (alphabetical by name of collection and/or family name), 3 drawers

Civil War materials—such as letters, diaries, and papers—are cross-referenced by regiment, battalion, battery, etc., in the subject drawer marked "Civil War Regiments." Also see David H. Slay, *Civil War Manuscripts in Georgia: An Annotated Bibliography* (Tuscaloosa: University of Alabama Press, 2011) and the catalog card entries in the Microfilm Library to the Civil War Miscellany collection of photocopies of Civil War source material. The records themselves are on microfilm in Drawer 83, Boxes 1–59.

In the main Reference Room and adjacent to the Microfilm Library, convenient three foot high shelving houses the printed census indexes to the federal censuses for Georgia and many other states, particularly those other states that are in migration patterns to and from Georgia. Abstracts and indexes of the federal census returns for individual counties are shelved in the general book collection with other books for respective Georgia counties.

Leon Hollingsworth Genealogical Collection

This is a microfilm publication of the note cards created by one of Georgia's most prominent genealogists. These cards are in the Microfilm Library in Drawer 216, Boxes 61–72, and Drawer 260, Boxes 28–30. The cards are arranged alphabetically by surname and then by subject. See R. J. Taylor Jr. Foundation, *The Leon S. Hollingsworth Genealogical Collection: Introduction and Inventory* (Spartanburg, SC: The Reprint Company, 1979). The subject cards are included in "The Other Leon Hollingsworth Collections," *Georgia Genealogical Society Quarterly* 21 (1985): 136–45.

Hollingsworth's original research files are in the Manuscripts Section of the Georgia Archives as (its identifying collection number) AC1986-0010. An inventory is available at the Archives, and these files are also frequently referenced in Hollingworth's note cards described above.

---

[4] In addition, check under Cities and County records to see if a church of interest is cross-referenced.

[5] These cards contain cross-references to other microfilm subjects by the city in which it was located.

[6] These private papers include some manuscript collections owned and housed at the Georgia Archives, but the bulk of this microfilm contains those that were filmed from private collections. The Archives cannot give permission to publish for those still in private hands, as they do not know if they survive, or were later donated to another institution.

Georgia Society, Daughters of the American Revolution "Genealogical Records" Collection

This is a book collection of 677 consecutively-numbered volumes (as of 2010) of typescripts of Georgia records of the widest variety of genealogical sources. The information has been copied, typed, compiled, indexed, and shared by DAR members throughout Georgia. The basis of the collection was two hundred twenty-three volumes of unpublished historical and genealogical records that were presented to the Georgia Archives in March 1940. Those volumes containing the three series of Family Bible Records in private hands have great significance; they were copied and notarized in the late 1930s and early 1940s, and many of the originals cannot be found today—because either of the loss of the original Bible or of the identity of its current custodian.

The finding aids in the Georgia Archives for this collection includes a four-volume subject catalog to Volumes 31 to 500: Volume 1, Bible and Family Records; Volume 2, State and County Records; Volume 3, Revolutionary Service; and Volume 4, Miscellaneous Records. Most volumes prior to Volume 500 also have individual name indexes; all volumes from 501 and later have individual name indexes.

The Georgia Archives no longer is able to accept additions to this collection and the last volume was compiled in 2010. However, all of the older volumes have been scanned and added to a database that is available for use only at the National Society DAR website; all new compilations are added to this digital collection on an on-going basis.

Private Manuscript Collections

Those manuscript collections that are not on microfilm have separate card catalogs organized by Main Entry (collection name); Subject File (excluding collection names); Geographic File (usually by county); Chronological File (time period); and Forms File (types of records such as account books, etc.). Apart from a search by family name, some valuable materials such as store account books and related records may be found by searching under the counties in the Geographic File. For background on early Southern business records, see Lewis E. Atherton, *The Southern Country Store, 1800–1860* (Baton Rouge: Louisiana State University Press, 1949). Civil War letters, diaries, papers, etc., are cross-referenced by regiment, battery, and battalion in the Subject File under "Civil War Regiments." Also see David H. Slay, *Civil War Manuscripts in Georgia: An Annotated Bibliography* (Tuscaloosa: University of Alabama Press, 2011).

Hereditary and Military Descent Organizations

The Georgia Archives has some genealogically valuable materials of various societies, particularly of Mayflower descendants, including microfilm of the 163,593 cards in "The Mayflower Register" by E. Huling Woodworth. These are located in Drawer 178, Boxes 69–79, and Drawer 189, Boxes 51–53. Other holdings include:

> Connell, Lamar L. *Georgia State Society of the National Society, Daughters of American Colonists, Rosters of Members [and] Ancestors Historical Reports.* Lakemont, GA: Copple House Books, 1985.

> Daughters of American Colonists: Thirteen volumes of typescripts of Georgia records and twenty-three volumes of lineage books.

Daughters of the American Revolution: Lineage books, Volumes 1–128, 134–140, and 150,151.

Galvin, Eleanor Stevens. *1812 Ancestor Index, 1892–1970*. Washington, DC: National Society, Daughters of the War of 1812, 1970.

National Society, Daughters of Founders and Patriots: Lineage books, Volumes 1–25.

United Daughters of the Confederacy: Typescripts and other records.

This lists some of the older publications of hereditary organizations found at the Georgia Archives. Many other groups have published works there including the Huguenot societies, and the United Daughters of the Confederacy whose Georgia Division has published many roster books, cemetery volumes, as well as over twenty volumes of letters and reminiscences. Check the library catalog for any society to determine what they may have there.

Other Statewide Repositories

For addresses and information on holdings of Georgia's other records repositories, see:

Overbeck, James A. *Historical Organizations and Resources in Georgia*. Atlanta: Georgia Historical Records Advisory Board, 1996. A current update is available at the Georgia Archives website: www.GeorgiaArchives.org.

Warnock, Robert H. *Georgia Sources for Family History*. Atlanta: Georgia Genealogical Society, 1995.

Georgia has more than one hundred thirty public libraries that have at least some form of local heritage research collections, and there are more than one hundred institutions with private manuscript collections. Many libraries and archives in other states also have significant Georgia materials and/or book collections, notably:

Birmingham [Alabama] Public Library: The Southern History Collection.

University of North Carolina at Chapel Hill: The Southern Historical Collection. .

University of South Carolina, Columbia: The South Caroliniana Library. .

Wallace State College, Hanceville, Alabama: The Family and Regional History Program.. It has a number of Cherokee Indian and Civil War microfilms cited elsewhere in this book.

William R. Perkins Library of Duke University, Durham, North Carolina: The Manuscripts Department.

All of these repositories have detailed printed catalogs of their manuscript collections as well as online catalogs of their respective printed and manuscript holdings. Also see:

Côté, Richard N. *Local and Family History in South Carolina: A Bibliography*. Greenville, SC: Southern Historical Press, 1981.

Draughon, Wallace R., and William Perry Johnson. *North Carolina Genealogical Reference: A Research Guide for All Genealogists, Both Amateur and Professional.* 2d ed. Durham, NC: Seeman Printery, 1966.

Georgia's other major statewide institutions for genealogical research are described below.

Georgia Historical Society

501 Whitaker Street
Savannah, GA 31499
Phone: 912-651-2128
Website: http://www.georgiahistory.com/

Figure 3 - Hodgson Hall, home of the Georgia Historical Society

The Georgia Historical Society has been collecting Georgia historical and genealogical materials longer than any other institution in the state. Its collections acquired before 1976 are exceptionally well cataloged and cross-referenced in its card catalog. It also has an online catalog of its books and manuscripts. The book collection includes rare works on early Georgia families.

Manuscript holdings represent the entire state, but its concentration is on materials of Savannah-Chatham County and the Georgia coastal area. The Society has many rare old genealogies, a genealogical publishing committee, and microfilm of the Leonardo Andrea Collection of South Carolina (and Georgia) genealogical notes, and many Savannah and Chatham County government records.

The Georgia Historical Society now handles Georgia's program for historical markers. Texts of recent markers should be sought on its website. Several books of texts of markers designating historic sites in Georgia have been published, including the following published by Kenneth W. Boyd through Cherokee Publishing.

Georgia Historical Markers (Atlanta, 1991)

Georgia Historical Markers: Coastal Counties (Atlanta, 1991)

Historical Markers of Metro Atlanta (Atlanta, 1996)

The Historical Markers of North Georgia (Atlanta, 1993)

Hargrett Rare Book and Manuscript Library

Richard B. Russell Building
300 S. Hull Street
University of Georgia Libraries
Athens, GA 30602-1641
Phone: 706-542-7123
Website: http://www.libs.uga.edu/hargrett/index.shtml

The Hargrett Library has the largest and most extensive collections of private manuscripts and printed materials relating to Georgia. It also has genealogical folders, biographical files, city directories, and subject vertical files.

Historic Preservation Division

Georgia Department of Natural Resources
254 Washington Street SW
Atlanta, GA 30334
Phone: 404-656-2840
Website: http://georgiashpo.org/

The Historic Preservation Division is the state's agency for, and archives of, Georgia's historic sites. Its library, files on National Register of Historic Places nominations, county-wide surveys of potential National Register nominations for most Georgia counties (many made in the 1970s and sometimes for buildings no longer standing), newspaper clippings files, etc., are open to researchers by appointment. Its website contains materials helpful to historic preservation. The LAMAR Institute has placed its numerous reports on Georgia archaeology sites online at http://www.thelamarinstitute.org/.

Georgia Research
Chapter I: Federal and State Sources in Georgia

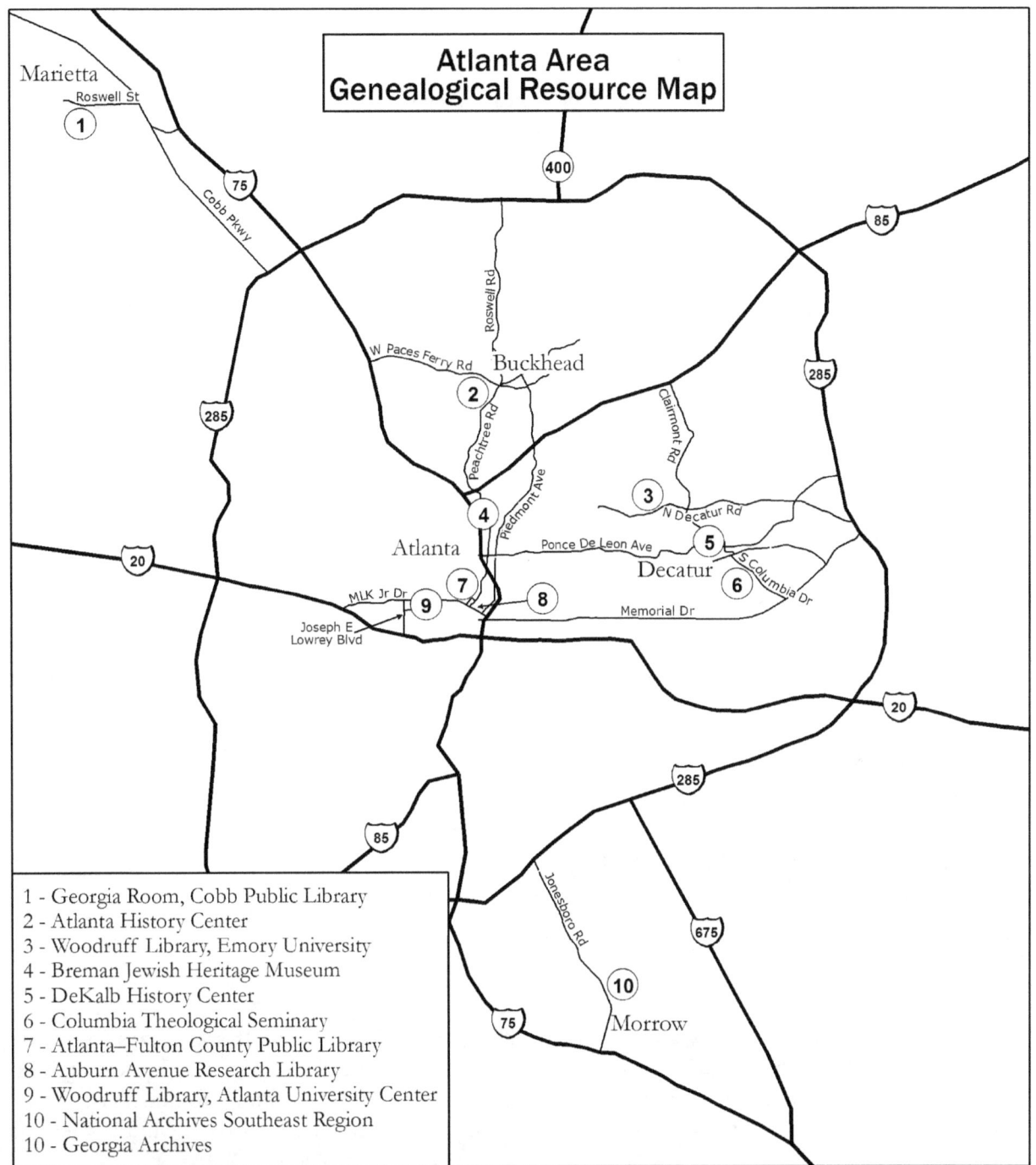

Map 1 - Atlanta Area Repositories

Huxford-Spear Genealogical Library

20 South College St., Suite F
P.O. Box 595
Homerville, GA 31634-3151

Phone: (912) 487-2310
Website: http://www.huxford.com.

The Huxford-Spear Library focuses on the southeastern United States, but has records from every state and several foreign countries. This combined library houses both the original Huxford Library collection and the Spear Library collection, resulting in over 30,000 genealogy books and other research materials. The library also has Judge Huxford's papers and maintains files of corrections and additions to these family sketches, some of which are published in its quarterly. Folks Huxford's research concerned the genealogies of families who lived south of Macon (Georgia's Wiregrass Region), see the series started by him and continued after his death, *Pioneers of Wiregrass Georgia*, 12 vols. to date (Homerville, GA: Huxford Genealogical Society, 1998–).

University of Georgia Main Library

Main Library
320 Jackson Street
University of Georgia Libraries
Athens, GA 30602-1641
Phone: 706-542-3251
Website: http://www.libs.uga.edu/

The Georgia Newspaper Project is in the main building and has a growing collection of more than eight thousand reels of microfilm of Georgia newspapers, dating from 1763 to the present. These newspapers are being added to the growing collection of genealogically and historically valuable resources on the University of Georgia's Digital Library of Georgia that includes the New Georgia Encyclopedia (which can also be accessed through search engines such as Google): http://dlg.galileo.usg.edu.

Washington Memorial Library

1180 Washington Avenue
Macon, GA 31201-1794
Phone: 478-744-0800
Website: http://www.co.bibb.ga.us/library/GH.htm

Washington Memorial is Georgia's most-extensive genealogical library. It specializes in source material on the thirteen original states, as well as Alabama, Florida, Kentucky, Tennessee, Vermont, and Great Britain. It has special finding aids to periodicals and family folders. The Genealogy Department collection area also houses the manuscript collections of the Middle Georgia Archives.

Maps, Locations, and Place Names

Georgia, the largest state east of the Mississippi River, has more counties (159) than any state but Texas, and is the largest state of the original thirteen states. It is almost unique in having such high percentages of widely-varying terrain within the same political boundaries. Many Georgia cities and towns share the same names with Georgia counties that are other than the counties where they are located. For example, the city of Macon, Georgia, is in Bibb County, not in Georgia's Macon County. For basic information on Georgia's county and state boundaries see:

>Bryant, Pat, and Ingrid Shields. *Georgia Counties: Their Changing Boundaries*. 2d ed. Atlanta: Georgia Department of Archives and History, 1983.

>Hemperley, Marion R., and Edwin L. Jackson. *Georgia's Boundaries: The Shaping of a State*. Athens, GA: Carl Vinson Institute of Government, 1993.

The Science Library of the University of Georgia Libraries has one of the world's most extensive map collections. Its Georgia maps now are placed on the Internet at: http://georgiainfo.galileo.usg.edu/gamaps.htm.

For specific maps, also see the following sources:

Modern Maps

Contemporary maps of Georgia, Georgia counties, and some Georgia cities can be purchased by mail from the Georgia Department of Transportation through its website: http://www.dot.state.ga.us/maps/Pages/default.aspx.

Historical Maps

In addition to individual county maps, the Georgia Archives also has state maps for 1780, 1818, 1839, 1847, 1854, 1859, 1877, 1883, 1889, and other years, which show the locations of early roads, water ways, post offices, communities, etc., in detail. The online catalog to maps at the Georgia Archives[7] does not include photocopies of maps although those copies are included with the original maps in three published catalogs:

>Blake, Janice Gayle. *Pre-Nineteenth Century Maps in the Collection of the Georgia Surveyor General Department*. Atlanta: State Printing Office, 1975.

>Hemperley, Marion R. *The Georgia Surveyor General Department*. Atlanta: State Printing Office, 1982.

>Johnsen, Margaret A. *Nineteenth Century Maps in the Collection of the Georgia Surveyor General Department, 1800–1849*. Atlanta: State Printing Office, 1981.

Two Internet sources for maps are the Maps section of the American Memory part of the Library of Congress website: http://memory.loc.gov/ammem/gmdhtml/gmdhome.html and the David Rumsey Map Collection website: http://www.davidrumsey.com/.

---

[7] These maps were previously in the holdings of the now discontinued Georgia Surveyor General Department.

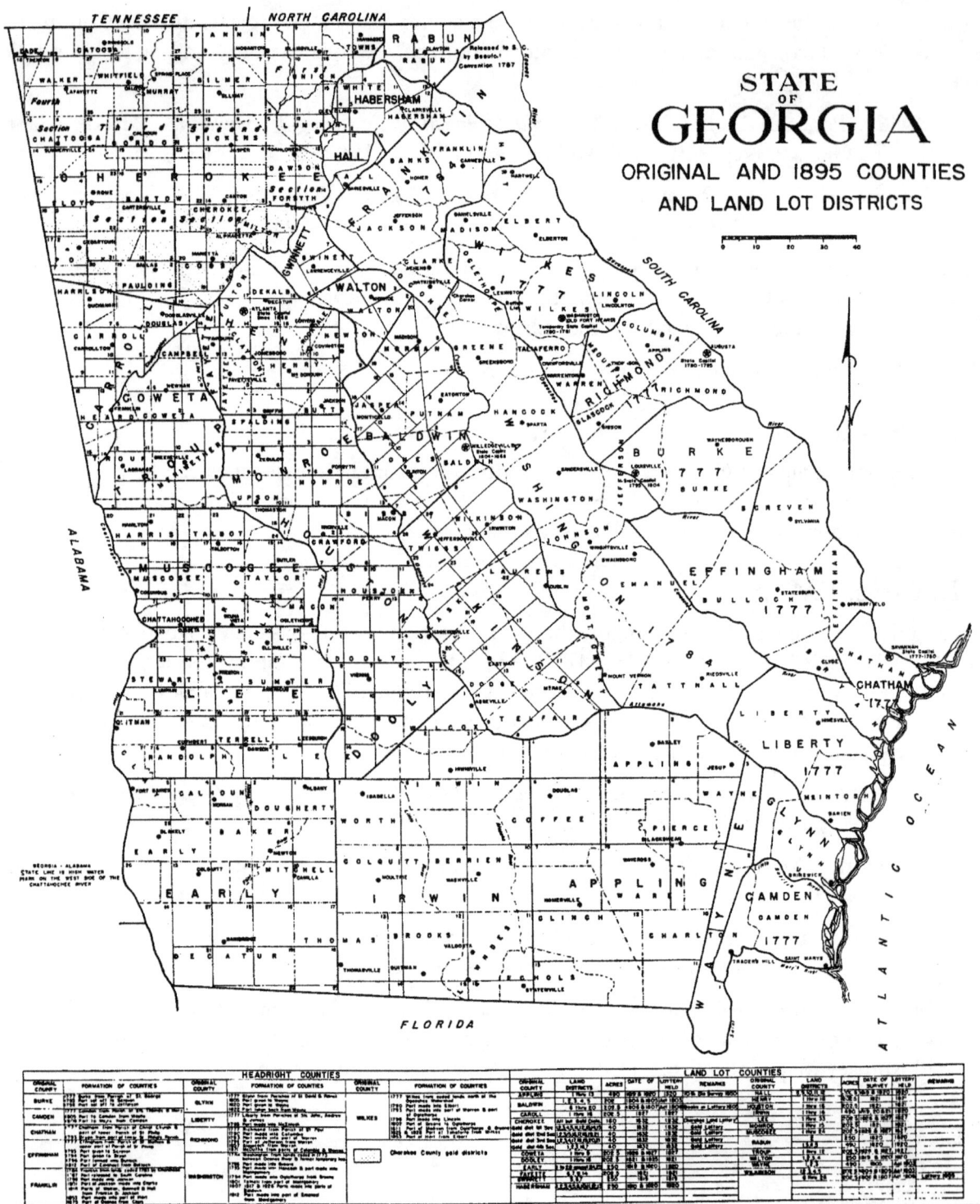

Map 2 - This map, also known as "Hall's Map," shows the original and 1895 counties and land lot districts in Georgia.

Maps of State, County, and Militia District Boundaries

The Georgia Archives, in the holdings of the Office of the Surveyor General, has files of records of Georgia's state, county, and militia district boundaries. A map of modern Georgia militia districts (GMDs) appears in Robert S. Davis *Research in Georgia* (Greenville, SC: Southern Historical Press, 1981), 77–82. A list of militia districts is in the *Georgia Official and Statistical Register* for 1971/1972, pages 1124–1140. The *Register* is available online at http://statregister.galileo.usg.edu/statregister/.

The Microfilm Library of the Georgia Archives has a binder containing lists of Georgia militia districts by name, number, and county. Those militia districts that are a part of the eastern areas of Georgia are described and accurately mapped in the publication by Paul K. Graham, *Atlas of East and Coastal Georgia Watercourses and Militia Districts* (Decatur, GA: The Genealogy Company, 2010).

Modern Georgia county road maps frequently include the modern boundaries of the Georgia militia districts. For historical background on Georgia's militia districts see Alex M. Hitz, "Georgia Militia Districts," *Georgia Bar Journal* 18 (1956): 283–91. These districts should not be confused with the numbered districts used in the western and northern three-fifths of Georgia for Georgia's land lotteries, 1805–1833. See *State of Georgia Original and 1895 Counties and Land Lot Districts* (No place: no date), a map available for sale at the Georgia Archives.

There are not any statewide compilations of information on county school or voting districts.

Maps of Federal Post Offices

The Georgia Archives has microfilm of maps of federal post offices in Georgia from the 1870s to the 1950s, arranged by county. Filed in Drawer 281, Boxes 1–25, it is a copy of the National Archives microfilm publication M1126 that is entitled *Post Office Department Reports of Site Locations*.

Federal Topographical Maps

These maps, showing buildings, elevations, creeks, roads, cemeteries, etc., are available on several websites including the free Acme Mapper: http://mapper.acme.com/ and Google Maps: http://maps.google.com/. The latter also includes the same maps in other ways including aerial photographs. Federal topographical maps past and present, as well as federal aerial photographs (beginning in the late 1930s), can be obtained for a fee from National Cartographic Information Center, U.S. Geological Survey, 507 National Center, Reston, VA 22092. A nationwide index to the current federal topographical maps has been published as *Omni Gazetteer of the United States of America* (Detroit: Omnigraphics, 1991). Volume 3 includes Georgia. A collection of the federal aerial photographs of Georgia for approximately half of the state is in the Map Room of the Science Library of the University of Georgia. Also see Charles E. Taylor and Richard E. Spurr, *Aerial Photographs in the National Archives* (Washington, DC: National Archives, 1973).

Sanborn Fire Insurance Maps

These fire insurance maps document the changing face of towns and cities, providing highly detailed information for each neighborhood and block. The Library of Congress website refers to them as "probably the single most important record of urban growth and development in the United States during the past one hundred years."

The Digital Library of Georgia includes Sanborn maps as one of its online resources. The collection is entitled Sanborn® Fire Insurance Maps for Georgia Towns and Cities, 1884–1922. See: http://dlg.galileo.usg.edu/sanborn.

The digital collection consists of 4,445 maps by the Sanborn Map Company depicting commercial, industrial, and residential areas for 133 municipalities. Originally designed for fire insurance assessment, the color-coded maps relate the location and use of buildings, as well as the materials employed in their construction. The maps indicate which city utilities—such as water and fire service—were available for the properties depicted by the maps.

For original maps, one of the most complete collections of Sanborn Maps of Georgia cities and towns is in the Map Room of the Science Library of the University of Georgia. This collection is also on microfilm in the library of Georgia State University, as is microfilm of the Library of Congress's Sanborn Map Collection. The Georgia Archives map collection also contains an edition of the Sanborn Fire Insurance Maps (1870s to 1940s) for Georgia cities, which includes some paste-on additions not found on some other surviving sets of the maps. See the section in Chapter III on Sanborn Fire Insurance Maps on page 275 for an inventory of maps for Georgia.

Many local libraries have other town maps showing buildings. For the earliest Georgia town plats, see:

>Cadle, Farris W. *Georgia Land Surveying History and Law.* Athens: University of Georgia Press, 1991.

>Sears, Joan N. *The First One Hundred Years of Town Planning in Georgia.* Atlanta: Cherokee Pub., 1976.

For a list of "bird's eye" view drawings of Georgia cities, see John W. Reps, *Views and View Makers of Urban America: Lithographs of Towns and Cities in the United States* (Columbia, MO: University of Missouri Press, 1984). A large part of this collection is also available online at the Library of Congress website for free at http://lcweb2.loc.gov/ammem/pmhtml/panhome.html.

County Boundary Maps

For county boundaries in each of the federal censuses, see: William Thorndale and William Dollarhide, *Map Guide to the U.S. Federal Censuses, 1790–1920* (Baltimore: Genealogical Publishing Company, 1987). The Georgia Archives has National Archives microfilm of boundaries used in taking the federal censuses for Georgia. Boundary descriptions for 1830–1950 are located on microfilm in Drawer 288, Boxes 64–67 (T1210 for 1900 and T1224 for 1830–1890 and 1910–1950). Useful information is also found in the following articles.

>Carpenter, Bruce. "Using Soundex Alternatives: Enumeration Districts, 1880–1920." *Prologue: The Quarterly of the National Archives* 25 (1993): 90–93.

>Parker, J. Carlyle. *City, County, Town and Township Index to the 1850 Federal Census Schedules.* Detroit: Gale, 1976.

Place Names

A number of sources exist for use in locating or identifying Georgia place-names. Among the general works are:

> Brinkley, Hal. E. *How Georgia Got Her Names*. Rev. ed. Lakemont, GA: privately printed, 1973.
>
> Goff, John H. *Place-Names in Georgia*. Athens: University of Georgia Press, 1975. Includes some early Georgia roads.
>
> Hemperley, Marion R. *Cities, Towns, and Communities in Georgia Between 1847–1962, 8500 Places and the County in Which Located*. Greenville, SC: Southern Historical Press, 1980.
>
> Krakow, Kenneth K. *Georgia Place Names*. Macon, GA: Mercer University Press, 1994. This entire book is found online at: http://www.kenkrakow.com/gpn/intro.pdf.
>
> Rowland, Arthur Ray. *Is This Your Alma Mater? Name Changes for Your College, University, Institute, Seminary, or Manual School in Georgia*. Augusta, GA: Augusta Genealogical Society, 2010.

Forts, Ferries, Roads, and Place Names

The Georgia Archives has the John H. Goff Collection, AC 1967-604, of extensive documentation on locations and origins of the names of Georgia forts, ferries, roads, and place-names. Also see Marion R. Hemperley, *Descriptive Inventory Number 2, John H. Goff Collection* (Atlanta: Georgia Surveyor General, 1971).

Also see the files of the Georgia Forts Committee, created by Goff and others for a series of articles in *Georgia Magazine* in Record Group 4-1-21 at the Georgia Archives.

Military Installations

Several sources exist for researching Georgia's military outposts and installations. A list of the fort files in the Goff Collection appears in Robert S. Davis, *A Researcher's Library of Georgia*, 2 vols. (Greenville, SC: Southern Historical Press, 1987, 1991), 2: 121–33.

The Georgia Archives has microfilm of Georgia and some records of posts in other states (Drawer 70, Boxes 38–53), made from National Archives microcopy M617—*Returns From U. S. Military Posts, 1800–1900*. This does not include National Archives microcopy M661—*Historical Information Relating to Military Posts . . . 1700–1900*, M903—*Descriptive Commentaries from the Medical Histories of Posts*, and T817—*Lists of the Adjutant General's Office of Carded Records of Military Organizations: Revolutionary War through Philippine Insurrection*. Also see:

> Davis, Robert S. *Georgia Citizens and Soldiers of the American Revolution*. Greenville, SC: Southern Historical Press, 1979, 158–66, (which includes a documented list of Revolutionary War forts in the Wilkes County area).
>
> Deeben, John P. "Coastal Bastions and Frontier Forts: Records of Military Posts, 1821–1920." *Prologue: The Quarterly of the National Archives* 41 (3) (Fall 2009): http://www.archives.gov/publications/prologue/2009/fall/frontier.html

Prucha, Frances Paul. *A Guide to Military Posts of the United States 1789–1895*. Madison, WI: State Historical Society of Wisconsin, 1964.

Map 3 - Roads and trails that existed in Georgia circa 1730 to 1850.

Colonial and Coastal Places

For colonial and coastal Georgia places, see:

Beckemeyer, Frances. *Abstracts of Colonial Conveyance Book C-1, 1750–1761.* Spartanburg, SC: The Reprint Co., 1975.

Bryant, Pat. *Entry of Claims for Georgia Landholders, 1733–1755.* Atlanta: Georgia Surveyor General, 1975.

Elliott, Daniel T. *Argyle: Historical Archaeological Study of a Colonial Georgia Fort.* Athens, GA: Lamar Institute, 1997. This book includes histories of colonial Georgia forts and communities.

Genealogical Committee. *Registers of Deaths in Savannah, Georgia, 1803–1853.* 6 vols. and composite index. Savannah: Georgia Historical Society, 1984–1989.

———. *Early Deaths in Savannah, 1763–1803: Obituaries and Legal Notices.* Savannah: Georgia Historical Society, 1993.

Index to Savannah Newspapers, 1763–1845 [typescript], which is available at the Georgia Archives, other major Georgia libraries, and on microfilm on loan through Latter-day Saints Family History centers. See the Newspapers section on page 138 for additional access to Savannah newspapers.

Early Georgia Places

Files on early Georgia places are indexed in unpublished typescripts at the Georgia Archives and the Hargrett Rare Book and Manuscript Library of the University of Georgia. These include "The Georgia Indian Depredations," "The Cherokee Indian Letters," "The Creek Indian Letters," and the indexes to Allen D. Candler's *The Revolutionary Records of the State of Georgia* and *The Colonial Records of the State of Georgia*. Various lists of Georgia place names are in Robert S. Davis, *A Researcher's Library of Georgia*. 2 vols. (Greenville, SC: Southern Historical Press, 1987, 1991), 2: 135–146, 179–93. The Georgia Archives also has various unpublished typescripts of early Georgia legislative and executive department records dating up to 1800, with indexes that include place names.

Indian Place Names

Georgia Indian place names are covered in Marion R. Hemperley, *Indian Heritage of Georgia* (Marion R. Hemperley, 1994).

Civil War Locations

For Civil War locations in Georgia, see:

Georgia Civil War Historical Markers. Atlanta: Georgia Historical Commission, 1964.

Irvine, Dallas. *Military Operations of the Civil War.* 5 fascicles in 5 vols. Washington DC: National Archives, 1977–1980.

Smedlund, William S. *Campfires of Georgia Troops, 1861–1865*. Lithonia, GA: privately printed, 1994.

The Union Army: A History of the Military Affairs in the Loyal States. 8 vols. 1908. Reprint. Wilmington, NC: Broadfoot, 1997. Volumes 7 and 8.

Also see *Military Order of the Loyal Legion of the United States,* 72 volumes, (1887–1915; reprint, Wilmington, NC: Broadfoot, 1991–1996). The several multi-volume Civil War publications of the Broadfoot Company (cited elsewhere) have indexes that include place names. In addition the Library of Congress, American Memory Collection, has Civil War maps from the Library of Congress, the Library of Virginia, and the Virginia Historical Society at http://memory.loc.gov/ammem/collections/civil_war_maps/.

Taverns and Inns

Information on some Georgia taverns and inns appears at the Georgia Archives in a typescript "Taverns and Inns of Early Georgia" by Mrs. Kirby-Smith Anderson.

American Place Names

Gilbert S. Bahn, *American Place Names of Long Ago,* rev. ed. (1898; reprint, Baltimore: Genealogical Publishing Company, 1997) includes place names from Georgia and the entire United States from the lost 1890 federal census.

Citations of Visits to Georgia

Laura Arksey, Nancy Pries, and Marcia Reed, *American Diaries,* 2 vols., (Detroit: Gale Research: 1983–1987), includes geographic indexes and citations to diaries featuring visits to many Georgia places. Also see:

Clark, Thomas D. *Travels in the Old South: A Bibliography*. 3 vols. Norman: University of Oklahoma Press. 1956.

Clark, Thomas D. *Travels in the New South: A Bibliography*. 2 vols. Norman: University of Oklahoma Press. 1962.

Coulter, E. Merton. *Travels in the Confederate States: A Bibliography*. Norman: University of Oklahoma Press, 1948.

Many compilations of travel accounts in early Georgia have been published since the above works came out, most by the Beehive Press of Savannah; also see Edward J. Cashin, comp., *Setting Out to Begin A New World: Colonial Georgia, A Documentary History* (Savannah, GA: Library of Georgia, 1995) and Cashin, *A Wilderness Still the Cradle of nature: Frontier Georgia, A Documentary History* (Savannah, GA: Library of Georgia, 1994).

Biographical Source Directories

Publications of often self-important biographical information, cynically called "mug books," became popular around 1900, and often included individuals of only local (if any) prominence. Many of these articles, however, include genealogically valuable information that survives nowhere else. Perhaps 8,000,000 individual Americans prior to 1930 had articles about their lives in biographical compilations, such as the often-reprinted volumes of the Goodspeed Company. Some 2,000,000 of these biographical sketches, nation-wide, are included in K. G. Saur's *American Biographical Archives*. Many sketches are also indexed in the series *Biography and Genealogy Master Index* (BGMI), included in the subscription website Ancestry.com. The HeritageQuest subscription website has 25,000 local and family histories that can be searched by word. The free search engine Google Books also does this for more than three million books. The Allen County-Fort Wayne Public Library has a large index to biographical sketches in local histories: Historical and Biographical Index of North-East, Mid-East, Mid-South, Mid-West, U.S.A. It can be ordered through Familysearch.org and then used at LDS Family History Centers. The Local History and Genealogy Room of the Library of Congress has a card catalog, prepared many years ago, of biographical sketches in local history works that have no indexes. Sometimes the footnotes in a scholarly biography of a prominent, even though distant, relative will lead to genealogical sources on ancestors shared with that person. The subscription website of the New England Historic Genealogical Society indexes to biographical compilations, newspapers, and genealogical periodicals for Georgia and the whole country: http://www.americanancestors.org/home.html.

Bibliographies of books for Georgia include:

> Davis, Robert S. *Research in Georgia*. Greenville, SC: Southern Historical Press, 1980, 200–202.
>
> Dorsey, James E. *Georgia Genealogy and Local History: A Bibliography*. Spartanburg, SC: The Reprint Co., 1983, 17–23.

The Hargrett Rare Book and Manuscript Library at the University of Georgia houses biographical files of prominent Georgians.

Also see:

> *Biography and Genealogy Master Index*. 19 vols. Detroit: Gale Publishing, 1986–2007.
>
> *Genealogical and Biographical Research: A Select Catalog of National Archives Microfilm Publications*. Washington, DC: National Archives, 1983. This book includes information on National Archives microfilm of letters of recommendation made to United States presidents for federal jobs.
>
> *Georgia Biographical Directory: People of All Times and Places*. St. Clair Shoals, MI: Somerset Publishers, 1994. Especially good for modern Georgians of national prominence.
>
> *Personal Name Index to The New York Times Index*. Succasunna, NJ: Roxbury Data Interface, 1976– .
>
> "Some Georgia Letters of Recommendations, 1785–1893." *Georgia Genealogical Society Quarterly* 32 (1996): 262–63.
>
> "U.S. Biography Index" and other card catalogs of the Local History and Genealogy Room of the Library of Congress, Jefferson Annex, Washington, DC

Several compilations of biographies of politicians also exist, including the following:

Biographical Directory of the American Congress, 1774–1996. Alexandria, VA: Congressional Quarterly Co., 1997.

Cook, James F. *Governors of Georgia, 1754–2004.* 1979. Macon, GA: Mercer University Press, 2005.

Gilmer, George R. *Sketches of Some of the First Settlers of Upper Georgia.* New York: D. Appleton & Co., 1855.

Jones, Charles C., Jr. *Biographical Sketches of the Delegates from Georgia to the Continental Congress.* Cambridge: Riverside Press, 1891.

Lanman, Charles. *Biographical Annals of the Civil Government of the United States.* Washington, DC: James Anglim, 1876.

Mellichamp, Josephine. *Senators from Georgia.* Huntsville, AL: Strode Pub. Co., 1976.

Ritter, Charles F., and Jon L. Wakelyn. *American Legislative Leaders, 1850–1910.* Westport, CT: Greenwood Press, 1989.

The printed indexes to Georgia newspapers and the abstracts from Georgia newspapers prepared by Tad Evans and his associates (cited elsewhere) frequently access information on politicians and elections, even in newspapers published far from the events being reported.

New Georgia Encyclopedia

The New Georgia Encyclopedia contains thousands of articles on Georgia history, culture, and current events. It also includes a number of biographical sketches. See website at http://www.georgiaencyclopedia.org.

Georgia Biography Card Catalog

The "Georgia Biography" card catalog of Special Collections at the Central Library of the Atlanta-Fulton Public Library System, 1 Margaret Mitchell Square, Atlanta, GA 30303, indexes tens of thousands of Georgia biographical articles and sketches. The index has no list of sources included, but the following was compiled from an inspection of the references on several hundreds of the cards. The "Georgia Biography" index also includes references to selected items in a "clippings file" which is located in the vertical files.

"Georgia Biography" Index (Sources by Title):

American Women—Who's Who, 1937–38

America's Young Men, 1934

Eminent Georgians

Georgia's Official and Statistical Register, 1933–37

Library of Southern Literature

Memoirs of Georgia

Pioneer Citizens . . .

Southern Editors—Book of the South

Who's Who in America

Who's Who in Colored America, 1938–40

Who's Who in the South, 1927

"Georgia Biography" Index (Sources by Author):

    Butts, Sarah Harriet, *Mothers of Some Distinguished Georgians*

    Candler, Allen Daniel, *Cyclopedia of Georgia*

    Collier, Margaret, *Biographies of Representative Women of the South, 1861–[1938]* 6 volumes

    Cooper, Walter Gerald, *Cotton States and International Exposition South*

    Cooper, Walter Gerald, *Story of Georgia*

    Fairman, Henry Clay, *Chronicles of the Old Guard*

    Glass, Dudley, *Men of Atlanta*

    Glass, Dudley, *Progressive Georgians, 1937*

    Harrison, J. P., *Georgia's General Assembly, 1880*

    Hart, Carroll, *Introduction to Georgia Writers*

    Howell, Clark, *History of Georgia*

    Knight, Lucian Lamar, *Georgia and Georgians*

    Knight, Lucian Lamar, *Georgia's Bi-Centennial Memoirs and Memories*

    Knight, Lucian Lamar, *History of Fulton County*

    Knight, Lucian Lamar, *Reminiscences of Famous Georgians*

    Lowman, George S., *Leaders in Georgia*

    Loyless, Thomas W., *Georgia Public Men, 1902–1904*

    Martin, Harold H., *Atlanta and Its Builders*

    Northen, William J., *Makers of America*

    Northen, William J., *Men of Mark in Georgia*

    Reed, Wallace Putnam, *History of Atlanta*

    Rutherford, Mildred Lewis, *South in History and Literature*

    Scott, William J., *Biographical Etchings of Ministers and Laymen of the Georgia Conferences*

    Smith, Clifford L., *History of Troup County*

Not included in the above works is the set of biographical sketches in the following:

    Gurr, C. Stephen, and Kenneth Coleman. *Dictionary of Georgia Biography*. 2 vols. Athens: University of Georgia Press, 1983.

Myers, Robert Manson. *The Children of Pride: A True Story of Georgia and the Civil War.* New Haven, Conn.: Yale University Press, 1973.

Whitehead, A. C. *Makers of Georgia's Name and Fame.* Boston, Mass.: Educational Publishing Company, 1913. This book has a large collection of anecdotal stories about Georgians that frequently appear without any citation in later published family histories, etc.

File II and Related Sources

The Georgia Archives has several special indexes to biographical information. "FILE II—Pre-1800" (on microfilm) includes many records of 1800 and later, and "FILE II—Names" includes original documents and some secondary material of biographical and genealogical value. These files are in Record Group 4-2-46. Lists of these files are at the Georgia Archives and have been published in the following:

Davis, Robert S. ed. *Georgians Past.* Milledgeville, GA: Boyd Publishing, 1997.

———. *Georgia Genealogical Society Quarterly* 33 (Summer 1997) through 34 (Winter 1998).

The Lucian Lamar Knight Scrapbooks include biographical data on many historical Georgians, although the two-drawer crude card index to the collection sometimes only lists individuals under their respective counties. The scrapbooks end in the 1930s, when Knight died. Other biographical sources at the Georgia Archives include the General Name File card catalog of public service records and biographical information, the Alphabetical Card Catalog microfilm of Confederate era records, and the various catalogs to private manuscript collections. See the section on The Georgia Archives on page 11 for more specific information on these materials.

Atlanta Area Biographical and Death Records

The *Franklin Garrett's Necrology*, 1822–1933, is a database of 163,000 entries to thirty-seven rolls of microfilm of various early records of the metropolitan Atlanta that were abstracted by Franklin Garrett. The records are primarily of white men who were deceased prior to 1932, individuals who had some connection to Fulton or DeKalb County. Researchers should be aware that not all material on the thirty-seven rolls of microfilm is included in the computer index; particularly not included are the cemetery inscriptions of Oakland Cemetery (Roll 3) and Westview Cemetery (Roll 37) in Atlanta, DeKalb County estates and death dates (Roll 4) and Fulton County estates (Rolls 4 and 5), for which the entries are alphabetically arranged and may be located by searching the microfilm. Included in the computer index are cemetery inscriptions of more than 750 cemeteries, obituaries from 1857 through 1931, estates, wills, and City of Atlanta death registers from 1888 through 1931.

The *Franklin Garrett's Necrology*, 1822–1933, is available at most large genealogical libraries, including the Georgia Archives, where it is available on the in-house computers and in the Microfilm Library, Drawer 314, Boxes 8–44 (see the catalog card inventory in the drawer marked "Private Papers A–K"). It is available online at http://Garrett.AtlantaHistoryCenter.com/.

Also see Garrett's later scrapbooks, on microfilm at the Georgia Archives (Drawer 157, Box 4) and indexed in Robert S. Davis, "Some Atlanta Obituaries, 1923–1932," *Georgia Genealogical Society Quarterly* 29 (1993): 166–73. Additional sources follow.

Austin, Jeannette Holland. *Atlanta Constitution (1868–1884, 1887, 1890)*. Fayetteville, GA: privately printed, 1987.

———. *Georgia Obituaries*. (1905–1910) Westminister, MD: Willow Bend Books, 2000.

Business Persons

Special Collections, Baker Library, Harvard University, Soldiers Field, Boston, MA 02163, has the credit reports filed by agents of the R. G. Dun & Company (one of founding firms of Dun and Bradstreet in 1933) from 1848 to the 1880s, for Georgia and the rest of the United States. These reports contain detailed information on the financial status of individual planters, businessmen, etc. These materials are not open to researchers identified as genealogists. (See Business Directories, Gazetteers, And Almanacs on page 272 for a complete explanation.) Also see John T. Smith, *Georgia Commercial Tax Digest and Directory* (Augusta, GA: Constitutionalist Press, 1851). For more information see http://www.library.hbs.edu/hc/collections/dun/

Lists of Professionals and Persons of Note

Lists of professional people, including some doctors, lawyers, peddlers, etc., appear in the following:

Davis, Robert S. *A Researcher's Library of Georgia*. 2 vols. Greenville, SC: Southern Historical Press, 1987, 1991.

Past issues of the *Georgia Genealogical Society Quarterly* and *Georgia Genealogical Magazine*.

Several similar books of "lists" of persons significant for one reason or another have been published for Georgia over the years, including:

Smith, George Gilman. *The Story of Georgia and the Georgia People*. 2d ed. 1901.

White, George. *Historical Collections of the State of Georgia*. 1855. A facsimile of the first ed. Baltimore: Genealogical Publishing Company, 1969.

———. *Statistics of the State of Georgia*. Savannah, GA: W. Thorne Williams, 1849.

Early Lawyers

Biographies of prominent early lawyers appear in Stephen F. Miller, *The Bench and Bar of Georgia*, 2 vols. (Philadelphia: J. B. Lippincott & Co., 1858). Early volumes of the *Georgia Reports*, beginning in 1846, and past issues of the *Annual Report of the Georgia Bar Association* frequently include biographical and other information on deceased prominent attorneys. A list of Georgia lawyers for 1774–1775 appears in the Loyalist claim of Attorney General Anthony Stokes on microfilm in Drawer 40, Box 47 at the Georgia Archives. Similarly, a list of lawyers qualified to practice before the Supreme Court of Georgia, 1846–1848, is in Drawer 186, Box 67. A list for the Federal District Court of Savannah, 1790–1858 and 1866–1900, is in Drawer 50, Box 77. Lists of members of the Georgia Bar Association appeared in early volumes of *Annual Report of the Georgia Bar Association*. National lists of lawyers, starting in 1868, exist. See "The Georgia Bench and Bar, 1868," *Georgia Genealogical Society Quarterly* 27 (2001): 30–44, and Emily Ann Croom, *The Genealogist's Companion and Sourcebook* (Cincinnati, OH: Betterway Books, 1994), 130. Credit reports for

Georgia attorneys, 1877–1883, are a volume in the R. G. Dun Collection, Baker Library, Harvard University. These records are not open for genealogical research.

Medical Professionals and Dental Professionals

Currently, for a fee, the National Genealogical Society will search biographical sources for individuals in the medical and dental professions. Such information may be found in the following:

> Atkinson, William B. *The Physicians and Surgeons of the United States*. Philadelphia: Charles Robson, 1878.
>
> *Biographies of the Ex-Presidents of the Georgia State Dental Association*. Atlanta: The Association, 1927.
>
> Hafner, Arthur W. *Directory of Deceased American Physicians, 1804–1929*. 2 vols. Chicago: American Medical Association, 1989.
>
> Holloway, Lisabeth M. *Medical Obituaries: American Physicians' Biographical Notices . . . before 1907*. New York: Garland Pub., 1981.
>
> Thatcher, James. *American Medical Biography*. Boston: Richardson & Lord, 1828.
>
> *Transactions of the Medical Association of Georgia*. (Past volumes).
>
> Williams, Stephen W. *American Medical Biography*. Greenfield, MA: L. Merriam, 1845.

The Georgia Secretary of State website has a current directory of Georgia doctors at www.sos.georgia.gov. The Georgia Archives has information on sources relating to medical professionals. The list of medical practitioner registers, state and county, at the Georgia Archives appears in *Georgia Genealogical Society Quarterly* 21 (1985): 39–43. Many medical colleges maintain and have published biographical information on graduates. See, for example:

> *Medical College of Georgia Alumni Directory, 1828–1984*. White Plains, NY: Bernard C. Harris, 1984. Some persons received licenses to practice medicine in Georgia by act of the legislature, although no list of these persons has been published.
>
> Young, Edwin C. and Joan Young. "Emory University Alumni: School of Medicine." *Georgia Genealogical Society Quarterly* 21 (1985): 22–24.

For historical background on Georgia medicine see Evelyn Ward Gay, *The Medical Profession in Georgia, 1733–1983* (Atlanta: Medical Association of Georgia, 1983).

Military Officers

For career information on military officers, several sources exist, including the following.

> Callahan, Edward W. *List of the Officers of the Navy of the United States and of the Marine Corps from 1775 to 1900*. New York: L. R. Hamersly & Company, 1901.
>
> Heitman, Francis B. *Historical Register of Officers of the Continental Army . . . April 1775 to December 1783*. Washington, DC: Rare Book Shop, 1914.
>
> ———. *Historical Register and Directory of the United States Army . . . September 29, 1789 to March 2, 1903*. Washington, DC: Government Printing Office, 1903.

Herbert, Sidney. *A Complete Roster of the Volunteer Military Organizations of the State of Georgia.* Atlanta: James P. Harrison & Co., 1878.

Official Register of National Guard Officers of Georgia, 1916–1917. No place: no publisher, no date.

Smith, Gordon B. *History of the Georgia Militia, 1783–1861.* 4 vols. Milledgeville, GA: Boyd Press, 2001.

Southern Artisans

The Museum of Early Southern Decorative Arts of Winston-Salem, North Carolina, has on its website the MESDA Craftsman Database: http:www.mesda.org/research_spite/mesdaCraftsmanDatabase.html, a growing index to more than 80,000 early southern artisans in 127 different trades, including even counterfeiting. At least 10,000 of these individuals were eventually Georgia residents. Bibliographies and subject catalogs to library book collections frequently lead to bibliographic/biographical compilations of members of professions and organizations such as George B. Cutten. *The Silversmiths of Georgia, Together with Watchmakers and Jewelers, 1733–1850* (Savannah, GA: Pigeonhole Press, 1958). For gun makers see Frank M. Sellers, *American Gunsmiths: A Source Book* (Highland, NJ: Gun Room Press., 2008) and for national databases of painters see Archives of American Art: http://www.aaa.si.edu/ and the Smithsonian American Art Museum: http://sirismm.si.edu/siris/saam.htm.

Fraternal Organizations

Freemasons/Masons

No statewide compilation of Masonic biographical information has been created, although some of it has survived in miscellaneous sources. See, for example:

Canaday, Barbara Bell and David Lee Canady. *Georgia Freemasons 1861–1865* (Macon : Georgia Lodge of Research, 2001).

Davis, Robert S. "Biographies of Some Georgia Knights Templar." *Georgia Genealogical Society Quarterly* 31 (1995): 113–115.

———. "Some Deceased Masons, 1874." *Georgia Genealogical Society Quarterly,* 27 (1991): 198.

Harris, Earl Douglas, David Lee Canaday, and Barbara Bell Canaday. *Outstanding Georgia Freemasons* (Macon : Grand Lodge of Georgia, 2005).

Rockwell, William S. "Ahiman Rezon." *Georgia Genealogist* (a list of Masonic officers, 1733 to 1859, referenced under "State Sources" in this work).

Rosier, William Henry and Fred Lamar Pearson, Jr. *The Grand Lodge of Georgia, Free and Accepted Masons, 1786–1980.* Macon: Masonic Home Print Shop, 1983.

Thomas, Kenneth H., Jr. "Obituaries Abstracted From the Masonic Journal, 1849–1852." *Georgia Genealogical Society Quarterly* 15 (1979): 129–133.

The Grand Lodge of Georgia, 811 Mulberry Street, Macon, GA 31201, has some records of Georgia Masons, lodge masters, and locations of surviving lodge records. Useful publications are below.

> Hughes, Jill Rueble. "Researching Masonic Records." *Heritage Quest* no. 42 (1992): 15–18.
>
> Lester, Carl F. "Information Regarding Research of Georgia Masonic Records." *Georgia Genealogical Society Quarterly* 26 (1990): 95.
>
> Yates, John S. *Researching Masonic Records*. Wichita Falls, KS: privately printed, 1995.

Other Organizations

For other organizations, see:

> Axelrod, Alan. *The International Encyclopedia of Secret Societies and Fraternal Orders*. New York: Facts on File, 1997.
>
> Bentley, Elizabeth Petty. *The Genealogist's Address Book*. 6th ed. Baltimore: Genealogical Publishing Company, 2009. Seek the most current edition.

Special Resources on Women

Several historical works are available on the history of women in Georgia and the South. The only specific bibliography of source materials is *Women's Records: A Preliminary Guide* (Atlanta: Georgia Archives, 1978). Some other Georgia source materials include:

> Blair, Ruth. *Georgia Women of 1926*. Atlanta, 1926.
>
> "Some Georgia Civil War Women." *Georgia Genealogical Magazine* 29 (1989): 104–105.
>
> "Our Women in the War." *Georgia Genealogical Society Quarterly* 31 (1995): 99.
>
> "Some Georgia Women Authors, 1870." *Georgia Genealogical Society Quarterly* 32 (1996): 114.

Also see:

> *American Women and the U.S. Armed Forces: A Guide to the Records of Military Agencies in the National Archives Relating to American Women*. Washington, DC: National Archives, 1992.
>
> Blanton, DeAnne. "Women Soldiers of the Civil War." *Prologue: The Quarterly of the National Archives* 25 (1993): 27–34.
>
> Hinding, Andrea. *Women's History Sources: A Guide to Archives and Manuscript Collections*. New York: Bowker, 1979.
>
> James, Edward T., Janet Wilson James, and Paul Boyer, eds. *Notable American Women, 1607–1950: A Biographical Dictionary*. 3 vols. Cambridge, MA: Belknap Press, 1971.

Until 1868, married women had no legal existence in Georgia except as represented by their husbands. A legislative act could authorize a married woman to conduct business on her own account, independently of her husband, as a *feme sole*. See Robert S. Davis, *Georgia Black Book, Volume II* (Greenville, SC: Southern Historical Press, 1987), 9–30.

Newspapers and Newspaper Indexes

Many Internet websites can include indexes and even the scanned images of newspapers. Millions of pages of newspapers can be instantly searched for names or combinations of words. Sometimes, however, computers fail to read images of words or misread the words, creating false leads to images. Several of these databases include Georgia newspapers and stories copied from Georgia newspapers. The list of these sources grows continuously. National bibliographies of newspaper databases include:

> Chronicling America by the Library of Congress at http://chroniclingamerica.loc.gov/
>
> International Coalition on Newspapers at http://icon.crl.edu/digitization.htm
>
> Wikipedia at http://en.wikipedia.org/wiki/List_of_online_newspaper_archives
>
> The Library of Congress at http://www.loc.gov/rr/news/oltitles.html

Nationwide Collections

America's Historical Newspapers/Early American Newspapers includes most of Georgia's colonial and Revolutionary War (Loyalist) newspapers, which are in the collections of the Library of Congress. It is a subscription database that is available for public use at the Woodruff Library of Emory University in Atlanta. This site also includes many issues from the early years of Georgia statehood.

> GenealogyBank.com (a subscription site); includes the previously described America's Historical Newspapers: http://www.GenealogyBank.com/gbnk/keyword.html
>
> Library of Congress, Chronicling America (free): http://chroniclingamerica.loc.gov/
>
> Newspaperarchive.com (a subscription site): http://newspaperarchive.com
>
> ProQuest offers digitized versions of the nation's leading modern newspapers to libraries able to afford its subscription fee (available to the public at the Woodruff Library of Emory University): http://www.proquest.com/products_pq/descriptions/pq-hist-news.shtml
>
> Thomson Gale Learning offers 19th-Century U.S. Newspapers to libraries that have purchased subscriptions, such as the Woodruff Library of Emory University and Georgia State University in Atlanta: http://gale.cengage.com. Remember to turn on the feature to search all text and not just headlines. This newspaper database can also be accessed through the subscription website of the New England Historic Genealogical Society, as can the previously mentioned America's Historical Newspapers.

Georgia Newspapers

Albany newspapers 1845–1866, 1870–1882 (access is free; newspapers were scanned by the University of Georgia as part of its Digital Library of Georgia): http://sgnewspapers.galileo.usg.edu/sgnewspapers/about

Americus newspapers 1870–1921 (access is free; newspapers were scanned by the University of Georgia as part of its Digital Library of Georgia):
http://sgnewspapers.galileo.usg.edu/sgnewspapers/about

Athens newspapers, 1827–1922 (access is free; newspapers were scanned by the University of Georgia as part of its Digital Library of Georgia):
http://athnewspapers.galileo.usg.edu/athnewspapers/search

Atlanta newspapers, 1847–1911 (access is free; newspapers were scanned by the University of Georgia as part of its Digital Library of Georgia):
http://atlnewspapers.galileo.usg.edu/atlnewspapers/search

Atlanta Constitution, 1868–1929 (access is free, but copies of newspapers are made for a fee):
http://pqasb.pqarchiver.com/ajc_historic/advancedsearch.html

Augusta newspapers, Augustaarchives.com (back issues of the *Augusta* [Georgia] *Chronicle* (a subscription site): http://augustaarchives.com

Columbus newspapers, *Columbus Enquirer*, 1828–1890 (free, one of several newspapers scanned by the University of Georgia as part of its Digital Library of Georgia):
http://enquirer.galileo.usg.edu/enquirer/search

Macon newspapers, *Macon Telegraph* (free, one of several newspapers scanned by the University of Georgia as part of its Digital Library of Georgia):
http://telegraph.galileo.usg.edu/telegraph/search

Memphis, TN newspapers, *Memphis Appeal*, 1843–1849, 1851–1894 (free, index only; includes Civil War issues published in Atlanta):
https://umdrive.memphis.edu/mckibben/www/index.html

Milledgeville newspapers, 1809–1922 (free, newspapers scanned by the University of Georgia as part of its Digital Library of Georgia): http://milledgeville.galileo.usg.edu/milledgeville/search

Thomasville newspapers, 1873–1922 (free, newspapers scanned by the University of Georgia as part of its Digital Library of Georgia): http://sgnewspapers.galileo.usg.edu/sgnewspapers/about

Valdosta newspapers 1905–1912 (free, newspapers scanned by the University of Georgia as part of its Digital Library of Georgia): http://sgnewspapers.galileo.usg.edu/sgnewspapers/about

In addition, GenealogyBank.com includes newspapers for a number of Georgia cities, including Athens, Atlanta, Augusta, Columbus, Louisville, Macon, Marietta, Milledgeville, Savannah, Sparta, and Thomasville. Often this site covers dates not covered by the Digital Library of Georgia site above.

Georgia Newspaper Project

University of Georgia Libraries, Athens, GA 30602

The Project has compiled, so far, more than 8,000 rolls of microfilm of Georgia newspapers from 1763 to the present. This collection does not include many newspapers in libraries and in private possession, such as the McGruder Collection of Northeast Georgia newspapers, largely for the 1830s and later, at the Atlanta History Center. The Georgia Newspaper Project through the Digital Library of Georgia is providing free access to digital copies of many early newspapers. So far, images are available for Athens, Atlanta, Columbus, Macon, Milledgeville, and a collection of South Georgia cities. These issues can be searched electronically. The microfilm is available for viewing at the University of Georgia Libraries. Copies are for sale, as is the *Georgia Newspaper Project Holdings List*. Also see:

Newspapers in Microfilm: United States, 1948–1972. Washington, DC: Library of Congress, 1973.

The United States Newspaper Program National Union List. 3d ed. Dublin, OH: Online Computer Library Center, 1989. This is an index, issued on microfiche, that includes many obscure newspaper issues in various repositories throughout the country.

The Georgia Archives has a substantial collection of early Georgia newspapers on microfilm. Refer to the ring binder in the Microfilm Library entitled, "Georgia Archives Index to Newspapers on Microfilm," which was compiled on June 25, 1993. This index is arranged in two formats: one is by county (coded), location, title, and dates, and groups all newspapers of each county together; the second format is by newspaper title and dates.

Information about Georgia's Civil War newspapers is found in Rabun Lee Brantley, *Georgia Journalism of the Civil War Period* (Nashville: George Peabody College for Teachers, 1929). This work gives information on 111 Georgia newspapers with histories of each. Also see:

Brigham, Clarence S. *History and Bibliography of American Newspapers, 1690–1820*. Worchester, MA: American Antiquarian Society, 1947.

Gregory, Winifred. *American Newspapers, 1821–1936: A Union List of Files Available in the United States and Canada*. New York: Wilson Company, 1937.

Marriage, death, divorce, and legal notices from Georgia newspapers are abstracted in a variety of sources. Many Georgia legal notices to 1790, for example, are listed in *Georgia Genealogist*, referenced under "State Sources" in this work. Legal notices often provide information on deaths, estates, divorces, etc., even when the original county records have been lost.

Tad Evans has abstracted many local Georgia newspapers that carried news from Georgia. For specific citations see Chapter III. Other abstracts of indexes to individual Georgia newspapers are also listed in Chapter III under the particular county where the newspaper was printed.

Statewide abstracts/indexes to Georgia newspapers include:

Austin, Jeannette H. *Georgia Obituaries, 1740–1935*. Fayetteville, GA: privately printed, 1993.

Georgia Society, Daughters of the American Revolution. "Obituaries of People Who Were Born in the 1800s." DAR Collection, Georgia Archives, 1990–1991, Volume 500.

Hodge, Robert A. *Some Georgia Reported Deaths, 1842–1848*. Fredericksburg, VA: privately printed, 1977. Includes *The Southern Banner* (Athens), *The Southern Reporter* (Milledgeville), and *The Georgia Telegraph* (Macon).

Huxford, Folks. *Genealogical Material from Legal Notices in Early Georgia Newspapers*. Greenville, SC: Southern Historical Press, 1989.

———. *Marriages and Obituaries from Early Georgia Newspapers*. Greenville, SC: Southern Historical Press, 1989.

Jarboe, Betty M. *Obituaries: A Guide to Sources*. Boston: G. K. Hall, 1982. Georgia obituaries are on pages 66–72.

Warren, Mary Bondurant. *Marriages and Deaths, 1763 to 1820, Abstracted from Extant Georgia Newspapers*. Danielsville, GA: Heritage Papers, 1968. This volume ends with 1819.

——— and Sarah Fleming White. *Marriages and Deaths, 1820 to 1830, Abstracted From Extant Georgia Newspapers*. Danielsville, GA: Heritage Papers, 1972. This volume ends with 1829.

Cemeteries

The best Internet website for grave markers and cemetery records is http://www.findagrave.com. In the summer of 2012 there were over eighty million records in this resource. Users are to be cautioned that some of the information appearing on the website is not exactly what appears on the grave markers. However, many of the records are accompanied by a photograph of the actual marker that permits verification of the transcription.

A current version of "The Georgia Cemetery Bibliography" is available on the Georgia Genealogical Society website at http://gagensociety.org/cemetery_resources.htm. This is list of all major published cemetery references of Georgia, both statewide and alphabetical by county.

Published information concerning cemeteries is found in the following.

Brooke, Ted O. *Georgia Cemetery Directory and Bibliography of Georgia Cemetery Reference Sources*. Marietta, GA: privately printed, 1985.

Dieterle, Diane. "Georgia Cemetery Records in the LDS Card File." *Georgia Genealogical Society Quarterly* 22 (1986): 14–19.

Stemmon, John and E. Diane. *The Cemetery Record Compendium*. Logan, UT: Everton Publishers, 1979: 19–28.

Van Voorhies, Christine. *Grave Intentions: A Comprehensive Guide to Preserving Historic Cemeteries in Georgia*. Atlanta: Georgia Department of Natural Resources, 2003.

Church Records

The Microfilm Library of the Georgia Archives contains a major collection of Georgia church records. The Archives in years past borrowed such records for copying onto microfilm. There are denominational records and other records that can be found with their respective congregations. For national repositories of church records, see the latest edition of Elizabeth Petty Bentley, *The Genealogist's Address Book* (Baltimore: Genealogical Publishing Company). Also see:

Carter-Walker, Fran. *Searching American Church Records*. Bountiful, UT: American Genealogical Lending Library, 1993.

Humphrey, John T. *Understanding and Using Baptismal Records*. Washington, DC: Humphrey Publications, 1996.

> Lippy, Charles H. *Bibliography of Religion in the South*. Macon, GA: Mercer University Press, 1985.

The Georgia Archives has microfilm of unpublished typescripts, "Inventory of Presbyterian Church Records in Georgia" (Drawer 186, Box 31), and similar inventories of Jewish and Baptist records, all prepared in 1941 as part of the Federal Works Progress Administration projects initiated subsequent to the Great Depression.

For church histories and published records, consult the following:

> Dorsey, James E. *Georgia Genealogy and Local History: A Bibliography*. Spartanburg, SC: The Reprint Co., 1983.

> Storey, Steven. *Resource Index*. Atlanta: Department of Natural Resources, 1976: 65.

Lists of acts incorporating Georgia churches, as well as volunteer organizations and charities, can be found in the various editions of the *Official Code of Georgia Annotated*. For example, in the 1982 edition (Charlottesville, VA: The Michie Co., 1982), these acts appear under a variety of headings, including "Religious Organizations" (pp. 762–770) and "Campgrounds" (pp. 104–105). The first Georgia church to be incorporated was in 1796. For guides on how to write a church history, see:

> Gardner, Robert. *Writing a History of Your Local Church*. Rome, GA: privately printed, 1976, which was reprinted in *Viewpoints in Georgia Baptist History* 8 (1982): 63–76.

> Smeltzer, Wallace Guy. *How to Write and Publish the History of a United Methodist Church*. Lake Junaluska, NC: Commission on Archives and History, United Methodist Church, 1969.

Researchers should be aware that most Georgians were Baptists and Methodists, denominations that seldom keep registers of births, deaths, or marriages. Their minutes, however, can sometimes prove residence, provide names of members who could be relatives, and imply migration (as well as sometimes giving explicit reasons for the migration).

Georgia Baptist Convention

The archives of the Convention (and of some of Georgia's other Baptist churches) is the Georgia Baptist Historical Collection, 1300 Edgewood Avenue, Macon, GA 31207. The records of the American Baptist Association, among other holdings, are in the Samuel Colgate Historical Library and Archives, Mercer University, 3001 Mercer University Drive, Atlanta, GA 30341-4155. The latter has nationwide holdings that include records of northern Baptist missionaries among the Southern Indians. Several collections of biographical material on Georgia Baptists exist, such as:

> Graham, B. J. W. *Baptist Biography*. 3 vols. Atlanta: Index Publishing Co., 1920.

> Hamby, Robert P. *Brief Baptist Biographies, 1707–1982*. Greenville, SC: A Press, 1983. Although Hamby identified his book as Volume 2, he never published a Volume 1.

> *History of the Baptist Denomination in Georgia with Biographical Compendium*. Atlanta: Burke, 1881. This book is downloadable on archive.org.

Primitive Baptist Denomination

Publications available for Primitive Baptist research include the following:

> "The Banner-Herald Special Birdwood College Edition," on microfilm, Drawer 187, Box 72, at the Georgia Archives.
>
> Craigmiles, Joe E., III. *Primitive Baptist Association Minutes of the United States*. Thomasville, GA: Thomas College, 1993, which contains minutes for the Alabama Association of Georgia, 1846–1941, and the Ocmulgee Association of Georgia, 1810–1947.
>
> Newsome, Jerry A. *A Modest History of Primitive Baptists in the United States*. No place: No publisher, 1976.
>
> Pittman, Reden H. *Biographical History of Primitive or Old School Baptist Ministers of the United States*. 1909. Reprint. Stone Mountain, GA: Primitive Baptist Pubs., 1984.

The Primitive Baptist Library of Carthage, Illinois, is a repository of many research resources for this denomination, including over 36,000 indexed obituaries from various primitive Baptist publications. The website is http://www.carthage.lib.il.us/community/churches/primbap/pbl.html. Another online source for Primitive Baptist research is http://www.primitivebaptist.org/.

Catholic Church

Until the creation of the Atlanta Diocese on April 11, 1937, the Roman Catholic churches in the state were served by the Savannah and Diocesan Archives, 601 East Liberty Street, Savannah, GA 31401-5196, email: http://www.diosav.org/contact. The Georgia Historical Society Library has extensive genealogical records of Savannah's Catholic community in its Walter G. Hartridge Collection.

For the churches of the Atlanta area contact the Office of Archives and Records, Archdiocese of Atlanta, 2401 Lake Park Drive, Smyrna, GA 30080, website: http://www.archatl.com/offices/archives/

Jewish Religion

For Jewish research see:

> Hertzberg, Steven. *Strangers Within the Gate City: The Jews of Atlanta, 1845–1915*. Philadelphia: Jewish Pub. Society of America, 1978.
>
> Proctor, Samuel, and Louis Schmier, editors. *Jews of the South*. Macon, GA: Mercer University Press, 1984.
>
> Rubin, Saul Jacob. *Third to None: The Saga of Savannah Jewry, 1733–1983*. Savannah, GA: privately printed, 1983.

For Georgia and Alabama as a whole there is the William Breman Jewish Heritage and Holocaust Museum, 1440 Spring Street N.W., Atlanta, GA 30309, website: http://www.thebreman.org/research-n-collections/index.html. The Georgia Historical Society maintains the Savannah Jewish Archives. For the entire South there is the Museum of Southern Jewish Experience, P.O. Box 16528, Jackson, MS 39236-6528.

Methodist Denomination

For the Methodists see:

> Lawrence, Harold A. *A Bibliography of Georgia Methodism.* Milledgeville, GA: Boyd Pub., 1981.
>
> ———. *Methodist Preachers in Georgia, 1788–1900.* Milledgeville, GA: Boyd Pub., 1984.
>
> ———. *Methodist Preachers in Georgia 1783–1900: A Supplement.* Milledgeville, GA: Boyd Pub., 1995.

Presbyterian Denomination

For Presbyterian research see:

> Scott, E. C. *Ministerial Directory of the Presbyterian Church, U.S., 1861–1941.* Austin, TX: Von Boechman Co., 1942.
>
> Wilson, John S. "The Dead of the Synod of Georgia" in *Necrology: Or Memorials of Dead Ministers Who Have Died During the First Twenty Years After Its Organization.* Atlanta: Franklin Printing House, 1869.

The Presbyterian Historical Society in Philadelphia (425 Lombard Street, Philadelphia, PA 19147) is the National Archives of the PC(USA) and has extensive library and archives holdings relating to the Presbyterian and Reformed tradition in America including congregational records. An online catalog and several online indexes are available at http://www.history.pcusa.org. Some Presbyterian seminaries, including Columbia Theological Seminary in Decatur (701 South Columbia Drive, Decatur, GA 30030), have archives that include congregation and presbytery records. Columbia Theological Seminary's library website is http://www.ctsnet.edu/Library.aspx and the archives online catalog is http://www.ctsnet.edu/Library/ArchivesOnlineCatalog.aspx. The Presbyterian Heritage Center at Montreat, P.O. Box 207, Montreat, NC 28757, is dedicated to education about the history of Presbyterian and Reformed Heritage and its worldwide missions as well as the history of Montreat. The Center provides a basic reference library and some archival materials; it does not collect congregation records. The Presbyterian Heritage Center website is http://www.phcmontreat.org/collection.htm.

Religious Newspapers

Georgia's denominational press can be a richer source of genealogical data than church records. In addition to those listed below, also see Henry Smith Stroupe, *The Religious Press in the South Atlantic States, 1802–1865: An Annotated Bibliography with Historical Introduction and Notes* (Durham, NC: Duke University Press, 1956). Major publications of newspaper abstracts from Georgia's religious press include:

Baptist Newspapers

The Christian Index, which began in 1822, has always been the organ of the main body of Baptists. Microfilm of *The Christian Index* is available at the Georgia Archives. For Baptist churches in the Georgia Baptist Convention, see:

Harwell, Jack U. *An Old Friend with New Credentials: A History of the Christian Index* (Atlanta: The Georgia Baptists Convention, 1972.

Overby, Mary. *Marriages Published in the Christian Index, 1828–1855*. Macon, GA: Georgia Baptist Historical Society, 1971.

———. *Obituaries Published in the Christian Index [1822–1899]*. 2 volumes. Macon, GA: Georgia Baptist Historical Society, 1976–1983.

Most Georgia Baptists, however, belonged to churches not in membership with the Georgia Baptist Convention.

Primitive Baptist Newspapers

For Primitive Baptists, see Fred W. McRee Jr. and Ted O. Brooke, *Southern Baptist Messenger, 1852–1862 (A Georgia Primitive Baptist Newspaper): Marriages and Obituaries.* (Lexington, GA: privately printed, 2009).

Lutheran Newspapers

For Lutherans, see Brent Holcomb, *Marriage and Death Notices from the Lutheran Observer, 1831–1861, and the Southern Lutheran, 1861–1865* (Greenville, SC: Southern Historical Press, 1979).

Methodist Newspapers

Holcomb, Brent. *Marriage and Death Notices from the Southern Christian Advocate, 1837–1867*. 2 vols. Greenville, SC: Southern Historical Press, 1979–1980.

———. *Marriage Notices from the Southern Christian Advocate, 1867–1878*. Columbia, SC: privately printed, 1994.

———. *Death and Obituary Notices from the Southern Christian Advocate, 1867–1878*. Columbia, SC: privately printed, 1993.

Presbyterian Newspapers

For Presbyterians see the following.

Holcomb, Brent. *Marriage and Death Notices from the Charleston Observer, 1827–1845*. Greenville, SC: A Press, 1980.

———. *Marriage and Death Notices from the Watchman and Observer, 1845–1855*. Greenville, SC: A Press, 1980.

———. *Marriage and Death Notices from the Southern Presbyterian, 1847–1908*. 4 vols. Columbia, SC: *South Carolina Magazine of Archives and Research*, 2009–2011.

Ware, Lowery. *Associate Reformed Presbyterian Death and Marriage Notices . . . 1843–1863*. Columbia, SC: SCMAR, 1993.

Miscellaneous General Sources

The Georgia Archives has a number of large record groups of government documents that are sometimes indexed in the sources cited below and elsewhere in this publication. Acts and minutes of the Georgia Legislature at the Georgia Archives have a wide variety of indexes and finding aids, varying widely in completeness. The website of the Digital Library of Georgia includes Georgia's legislative codes and many volumes of legislative minutes and acts for 1799–1999 that can be searched online at http://dlg.galileo.usg.edu/CollectionsA-Z/zlgl_information.html?Welcome. A thorough, personal name index to the extensive information found in Georgia laws and acts does not exist, although the acts have been arranged and abstracted in various digests over the years.

For federal laws and legislative minutes see the Library of Congress, American Memory Project: http://memory.loc.gov/ammem/browse/ListSome.php?category=Government,+Law. Also see John Corbin, *Find the Law in the Library* (Chicago: American Library Association, 1989).

For a composite index, arranged by plaintiff, to all American legal cases printed in all state reports, including Georgia, from 1658–1906, see the *1906 Decennial Edition of the American Digest* (St. Paul, MN: West Publishing Company, 1912). For information on finding abstracts of state and federal court cases, see Emily A. Croom, *The Genealogist's Companion and Sourcebook* (Cincinnati, OH: Betterway Books, 1994), 129–130.

The Georgia State Code is available on the Internet and fully word searchable. It may be found on the website: http://www.libs.uga.edu/. After going to the website, select and click on "Digital Library of Georgia." Next, scroll down to and click on "Georgia Legislative Documents." At this point, begin to search for your search keyword from the box displayed.

Several special sources cover large areas of Georgia. These works include:

    Austin, Jeannette H. *Colonial Georgians*. Riverdale, GA: J.H. Austin, 1970.

    ———. *Georgia Bible Records*. Baltimore: Genealogical Publishing Company, 1985.

    Davis, Robert S. *A Researcher's Library of Georgia*. 2 vols. Greenville, SC: Southern Historical Press, 1987, 1991.

    ———. *The Georgia Black Book* (1982) and *Georgia Black Book Volume II* (1987), both published by the Southern Historical Press, offer a collection of murder, prison, asylum, and related records.

    Hehir, Donald M. *Georgia Families: A Bibliographic Listing*. Bowie, MD: Heritage Books, 1993. This book is taken from library catalogs and lists only those references that are cataloged as pertaining to Georgia families.

    Huxford, Folks. *Pioneers of Wiregrass Georgia*. 12 vols. (to date, with comprehensive index). Adel, GA: Patten Publishing Company, 1951–1999. These volumes deal with South Georgia families.

    Jackson, Olin, *A North Georgia Journal of History*. 4 vols. (to date). Alpharetta, GA: Legacy Publications, 1989.

Lucas, S. Emmett, and LaBruce Lucas. *Some Georgia County Records*. 10 vols. (to date). Greenville, SC: Southern Historical Press, 1999.

Maddox, Joseph. *Information on Some Georgia Pioneers*. No pub., 1982. This book is based on names listed in the land lottery of 1805.

Peel, Mrs. William Lawson. *Historical Collections of the Joseph Habersham Chapter, DAR*. 3 vols. Atlanta: 1902. The first two volumes include genealogical queries from the *Atlanta Constitution, 1900–1902*.

Stewart, William C. *Gone to Georgia: Jackson and Gwinnett Counties and Their Neighbors in the Western Migration*. Washington, DC: National Genealogical Society, 1965. Much of this information is documented, but some is the author's interpretations. Also see Davidson, Alvie L., and Dianne Davidson. *Index to Gone to Georgia,* (Lakeland, FL: privately printed, 1990).

Internet Genealogy for Georgia

The Internet offers a plethora of opportunities for genealogical contacts. For those who do not have Internet service, most libraries have computers connected to the Internet available to the public. Space prohibits listing all the sites that are useful to genealogists, but below are the largest websites: Most subscription sites have some free features.

Ancestry (http://www.ancestry.com) is a growing subscription database that offers primary resources and indexes to these and other materials, which are useful with genealogical and historical research. The database can be accessed for free at many libraries and other research institutions. The institutional edition does not offer the many interactive features, such as uploading and editing personal ancestry information and messaging with other subscribers.

Archives.com (http://www.archives.com) contains original records and databases. Subscription site.

Digital Library of Georgia (http://dlg.galileo.usg.edu/) features books, maps, manuscripts, newspaper, and other resources about Georgia history and culture. Free site.

FamilySearch (http://www.FamilySearch.org) is the online presence of the Family History Library. It contains catalogs to their collection, locations of Family History Centers, and original records. Free site.

Fold3 (http://www.fold3.com) focuses mostly on military records, but some other records are available. Subscription site.

Georgia Archives (http://www.GeorgiaArchives.org) has online catalogs to much of their collection and original records available through the Virtual Vault.

HeritageQuest is no longer available to individual subscribers, but most libraries provide access from home via their individual websites. The census indexes are a useful complement to those at Ancestry. Also available are Revolutionary War pension claims, records of depositors in the Freedmans's Bank, 25,000 family and local histories, PERSI, the U. S. Serial Set, and other resources.

Library of Congress (http://www.loc.gov) features the American Memory Collection and Chronicling America Collection. Free site.

National Archives and Records Administration (http://www.archives.gov) houses federal records in Washington, DC and regional locations. This website has valuable resources about the records held by NARA and indexes to some of these records. There are not many records actually available online. Free site.

There are several books that give a basic introduction and advanced information to genealogical research on the Internet, including the following:

Lynch, Daniel M. *Google Your Family Tree: Unlocking the Hidden Power of Google*. Provo, UT: FamilyLink.com, 2008.

Morgan, George G. *How to Do Everything Genealogy*. New York: McGraw-Hill, 2012.

Porter, Pamela Boyer, and Amy Johnson Crow. *Online Roots: How to Discover Your Family's History and Heritage with the Power of the Internet*. Nashville: Rutledge Hill Press, 2003.

Georgia Internet sources will be found within many diverse Internet sites. The best option is to conduct your own Internet search for the particular items of interest.

Researcher Notes

CHAPTER II
RESEARCH BY TIME PERIOD

This chapter on records and finding aids available for Georgia research is arranged from the modern period, backward in time, to the founding of Georgia in 1733. In some instances, such as with military records, the sources often cover a broader time frame than the category. Consult the index for all references to any type of record.

Modern Era, 1917–Present

Several books and Internet websites are available for finding persons living today or who have had funeral notices or obituaries published in recent times. Many Georgia records from all periods of its history have been wrongly closed to the public or destroyed. In more modern times this occurred through the Health Insurance Portability and Accountability Act of 1996 (HIPAA) and SB205 (2001), which amended the U.S. Privacy Act of 1988.

Several of the sources described in such works are widely and commercially available, such as the Social Security Death Index (available for free at FamilySearch.org) and national telephone directories. These sources and others are also accessible through the Internet such as at the subscription website Ancestry.com. The already-extensive Georgia and genealogy resources available on the Internet grow literally by the hour.

The Social Security Death Index (SSDI) is a searchable file of over eighty million names, as of 2012, created from internal Social Security Administration (SSA) records of deceased persons who possessed social security numbers and whose deaths were reported to the Social Security Administration. Often this was done in connection with filing for SSA death benefits by a family member or other person. The SSDI can be used to obtain a copy of a Social Security application, containing the names of parents, place & date of birth, etc. given by the person while living.

Census Records

The federal census for Georgia for January 1, 1920, is available on National Archives microcopy T1262, and the Soundex index is National Archives microcopy M1557. Contrary to some printed accounts, the 1920 census seldom includes information on village and province of birth. Federal census records less than seventy-two years old are closed except to individuals seeking documented information only on themselves. This information must be requested from Bureau of the Census, P.O. Box 1545, Jeffersonville, IN 47131. The U. S. Bureau of the Census will also provide information, for a fee, on anyone in the census for censuses that have not been released, when proof is provided that the person sought is dead. Searches will be provided in census years 1910 to 2010 for a living person who requests the record for himself. The National Archives destroyed all of the original records for the 1900 through 1940 federal censuses in 1953, retaining only microfilm copies. See Kellee Green, "The Fourteenth Numbering of the People: The 1920 Federal Census," *Prologue: The Quarterly of the National Archives* 23 (1991): 140.

Federal census records for Georgia, 1820–1940, have various paper and microfilm indexes. The subscription website HeritageQuest has online indexes to all names for all surviving population schedules for 1790–1920 and partially for 1930. Ancestry.com, another subscription site, has all population schedules 1790–1940, as well as some of the mortality schedules, agricultural schedules, and slave owners (the so-called slave schedules). All of the available means of searching census records include accidental omissions and mistakes in names, including those made by the original census takers themselves.

The National Archives and Records Administration, Washington, DC 20408, has a number of related records that are open to the public, including the 1932 and 1934 manufacturers censuses; the fruit and nut growers census of 1930 (selected states); censuses of businesses for 1929 and 1933; and census schedules of local religious establishments for 1926–1928. For details see Katherine H. Davidson and Charlotte M. Ashby, *Preliminary Inventories Number 161, Records of the Bureau of the Census* (Washington, DC: National Archives, 1964).

Vital Records

Georgia began officially requiring births and deaths, including names of parents, when known, to be recorded as vital records for the first time on January 1, 1919. However, many counties were still ignoring the law as late as 1927, and many individuals did not bother with such registrations for many reasons. Also, some Georgia vital records start in the late 1918. Birth certificates are closed to the general public, but death certificates can be copied for individuals who meet the following requirements: death certificates are only issued to applicants having a direct and tangible interest, primarily family members or legal representatives of the family. They can be obtained by mail for a fee from Vital Records, 2600 Skyland Drive, Atlanta, GA 30319-3640. For information on ordering Georgia vital records, call 404-679-4702 or go to: http://health.state.ga.us/programs/vitalrecords/index.asp.

The Vital Records Branch also sells microfiche indexes, arranged alphabetically by year, to Georgia death certificates, 1919-1999; marriages, 1964-1999; and divorces, 1965-1999. The index to death certificates can also be accessed through the free website Familysearch.com and the subscription website Ancestry.com. When a death certificate may have been missed by the index, contact the county probate court or health department and request a search of the county index to death certificates.

The Georgia Archives maintains a free website named the Virtual Vault that includes images of Georgia death certificates, as the certificates become older than seventy-five years. There is an index to the certificates, 1919–1927, at http://cdm.sos.state.ga.us/cdm4/gadeaths.php.

Georgia law provides that adult adoptees should be provided the names of their biological parents, if the parents agree. For information, write to Georgia State Adoption Reunion Registry, Division of Family & Children's Services, Department of Human Services, 2 Peachtree Street NW, Suite 18-486, Atlanta, GA 30303, phone 404-657-3550 or on the Internet: http://www.ga-adoptionreunion.com/. Several books and websites are available for obtaining information on adoption research.

Georgia Research

Chapter II: Research by Time Period

Number Codes Used On Georgia Death Certificates

1 Appling	41 Dade	81 Jefferson	121 Richmond
2 Atkinson	42 Dawson	82 Jenkins	122 Rockdale
3 Bacon	43 Decatur	83 Johnson	123 Schley
4 Baker	44 DeKalb	84 Jones	124 Screven
5 Baldwin	45 Dodge	85 Lamar	125 Seminole
6 Banks	46 Dooly	86 Lanier	126 Spalding
7 Barrow	47 Daugherty	87 Laurens	127 stepehns
8 Bartow	48 Douglas	88 Lee	128 Stewart
9 Ben Hill	49 Early	89 Liberty	129 Sumter
10 Berrien	50 Echols	90 Lincoln	130 Talbot
11 Bibb	51 Effingham	91 Long	131 Taliaferro
12 Bleckley	52 Elbert	92 Lowndes	132 Tattnall
13 Brantley	53 Emanuel	93 Lumpkin	133 Taylor
14 Brooks	54 Evans	94 Macon	134 Telfair
15 Bryan	55 Fannin	95 Madison	135 Terrell
16 Bulloch	56 Fayette	96 Marion	136 Thomas
17 Burke	57 Floyd	97 McDuffie	137 Tift
18 Butts	58 Forsyth	98 McIntosh	138 Toombs
19 Calhoun	59 Franklin	99 Meriwether	139 Towns
20 Camden	60 Fulton	100 Miller	140 Treutlen
21 Candler	61 Gilmer	101 Mitchell	141 Troup
22 Carroll	62 Glascock	102 Monroe	142 Turner
23 Catoosa	63 Glynn	103 Montgomery	143 Twiggs
24 Charlton	64 Grodon	104 Morgan	144 Union
25 Chatham	65 Grady	105 Murray	145 Upson
26 Chattahoochee	66 Greene	106 Muscogee	146 Walker
27 Chattooga	67 Gwinnett	107 Newton	147 Walton
28 Cherokee	68 Hambersham	108 Oconee	148 Ware
29 Clarke	60 Hall	109 Oglethorpe	149 Warren
30 Clay	70 Hancock	110 Paulding	150 Washington
31 Clayton	71 Haralson	111 Peach	151 Wayne
32 Clinch	72 Harris	112 Pickens	152 Webster
33 Cobb	73 Hart	113 Pierce	153 Wheeler
34 Coffee	74 Heard	114 Pike	154 White
35 Colquitt	75 Henry	115 Polk	155 Whitfield
36 Columbia	76 Houston	116 Pulaski	156 wilcox
37 Cook	77 Irwin	117 Putnam	157 Wilkes
38 Coweta	78 Jackson	118 Quitman	158 Wilkinson
39 Crawford	79 Jasper	119 Rabun	159 Worth
40 Crisp	80 Jeff Davis	120 Randolph	

Age Codes Used On Georgia Death Index/Register

Code	Code Examples					
	Code	No. Of	=	Code	No. Of	=
0 = minutes	0	01	1 minute	0	59	59 minutes
1 = hours	1	01	1 hour	1	23	23 hours
2 = days	2	01	1 day	2	29	29 days
3 = months	3	01	1 month	3	11	11 months
4 = years	4	01	1 year	4	99	99 years
5 = 100 years or more	5	00	100 years	5	10	110 years

compiled by Clyde Hooks, Belvedere, S.C.

Figure 4 - Number Codes on Georgia death certificates

Military Records—World War I

The Georgia Archives in Morrow has extensive records of the veterans of World War I, both on microfilm and in Record Group 22-1-33. The latter includes World War I service records for all Georgia soldiers. The obituaries of soldiers are in Record Group 22-1-14. Also see Michael Knapp, "World War I Service Records," *Prologue: The Quarterly of the National Archives* 22 (1990): 300–303.

World War I draft registration cards taken in 1917 and 1918 for the entire United States are in the National Archives at Atlanta, arranged by state and then by draft board. These records for the whole country have been scanned onto the subscription website Ancestry.com. However, some of the draft registration cards on the Internet have the wrong reverse sides or no reverse side at all. The records also have been microfilmed by the Genealogical Society of Utah and are made available through the Latter-day Saints Family History Centers. The registrations for DeKalb, Gwinnett, and Fulton (other than City of Atlanta) Counties have been published.

Usually each county had one draft board. Cities frequently had several draft boards. The men who registered were aged seventeen to forty-five, and the cards list each man's full name, and often date of birth, address, and physical description; some cards also give place of birth and next of kin. For more information on using these records, see John J. Newman, *Uncle, We are Ready!: Registering America's Men, 1917–1918* (North Salt Lake City, Utah: Heritage Quest, 2001).

The Georgia Archives has, in the county microfilm, discharge records located in county offices. Some World War I information can also be found in published county histories. The following sources include information on Georgia World War I veterans. All of these books are found at the Georgia Archives. Also see Michael G. Knapp and Constance Potter, "Here Rests in Honored Glory: World War I Graves Registration," *Prologue: The Quarterly of the National Archives* 23 (1991): 190–193.

Some World War I sources are:

> Boss, Bert E. *The Georgia State Memorial Book*. New York: American Memorial Publishing Company, 1921. Includes service records and photographs (when available) of Georgia's WWI dead.

> Bureau of Naval Personnel. Officers and Enlisted Men of the United States Navy Who Lost Their Lives During the World War. Washington, DC: Government Printing Office, 1920.

> *Genealogical Helper*, July–August 1998 issue, has two articles on World War I research, both of which include useful bibliographies. Major Peter Belmont wrote "World War One: Documents and Basic Research for Genealogists and Historians," which covers the documents soldiers completed and where to find these and other records. Christina Schaefer wrote "Finding World War I Fighting Men," which summarizes information in her book, *The Great War: A Guide to the Service Records of All the World's Fighting Men and Women* (see below).

> Haulsee, W. M., et al. *Soldiers of the Great War*. 3 vols. Washington, DC: Soldiers Record Publishing Association, 1920. This includes the same information as the Boss book, but for the whole country.

Pilgrimage for the Mothers and Widows of Soldiers, Sailors, and Marines . . . in the Cemeteries of Europe. Washington, DC: Government Printing Office, 1930, which lists names and addresses of widows and mothers of soldiers buried in Europe. Names from this book were compiled and published by Mic Barnette and Ruth Corry in the *Georgia Genealogical Society Quarterly* 27 (1991): 219–232.

Rountree, Maude. *The Cross of Military Service.* Jackson, TN: World War Insignia Commission, 1927. Gives service records of WW I veterans with their Confederate ancestors.

Schaefer, Christina. *The Great War: A Guide to the Service Records of All the World's Fighting Men and Women.* Baltimore: Genealogical Publishing Company, 1997. This books lists, by county, how many men were conscripted, what records exist, and where to write for them. For the United States, national and state records are listed. Records listed as being in the Georgia Archives include statements of service, service record abstracts, the National Guard register, and applications for the Victory Medal and the Honor Roll.

Toomey, Joseph M. *Georgia Participation in the World War.* Macon, GA: J. W. Burke, 1936. Includes a list of Georgians decorated during the war.

Federal Military Records—World War I and Later

Records of military service from 1917 to the present must be requested by the veteran or his heirs from National Personnel Records Center, 1 Archives Drive, St. Louis, MO 63132 http://www.archives.gov/st-louis/military-personnel. A fire on July 12, 1973, destroyed eighty percent of the records for Army personnel discharged November 1, 1912, to January 1, 1960, and seventy-five percent of the records for Air Force personnel with names between "Hubbard" through "Z" discharged between September 25, 1947, and January 1, 1964. Major efforts have been made to locate replacements for the lost records, and some files are being recreated.

The National Archives and Records Administration, 700 Pennsylvania Avenue, SW, Washington, DC 20408-0001 has numerous information sheets and publications on military records by type and conflict: http://www.archives.gov/research/military/ww2/index.html; see, for example, the pamphlet "Finding Information on Personal Participation in World War II" and Norman Eisenberg, "20th-century Veterans Service Records: Safe, Secure—and Available," *Prologue: The Quarterly of the National Archives* 37 (Spring 2005). The National Archives and Records Administration has a comprehensive online index to millions of records of United States service personnel from World War II and later called AAD: http://aad.archives.gov/aad/. See David P. Kepley, "AAD: a New Tool to Search NARA Databases," *Prologue: The Quarterly of the National Archives* 35 (1) (Spring 2003): http://www.archives.gov/publications/prologue/2003/spring/spotlight-aad.html and Theodore J. Hull, "The World War II Army Records File and Access to Archival Databases," *Prologue: The Quarterly of the National Archives* 38 (1) (Spring 2006): http://www.archives.gov/publications/prologue/2006/spring/aad-ww2.html.

The Georgia Archives, however, does have microfilm of many county copies of service records for World War I and later. The Archives also has lists of Georgia's war dead from World War II, Korea, and Vietnam in the vertical files under "Georgia—War Casualties." Lists of the World War II dead can also be accessed geographically on the Internet through the National Archives website. Also see Ann Bennett Mix, *Touchstones: A Guide to Records, Rights and Resources for Families of American World War II Casualties* (Bountiful, UT: American Genealogical Lending Library, 1996). For the World War II dead of the Marines, Navy, and Coast Guard, see *State Summary of War Casualties* [Georgia] (Washington, DC: U.S. Navy, 1946). For records of German and Italian prisoners of war who died in the United States, see Kenneth S. Record, *World War I and World War II Axis Burials in the United States* (Jacksonville, FL,: privately printed, 1997).

The United States Veterans Administration maintains almost all veterans records, including the last Civil War Union pensions, for most of the twentieth century. Information on access to those records should be sought from the respective state office. The Veterans Administration has begun a National Gravesite Locator, a website for identifying persons buried in its national cemeteries: http://www.cem.va.gov/.

Each of the branches of the United States military has a historical archive open to the public. These institutions go back to the nation's founding but are particularly useful for unit and ship histories and yearbooks for World War II and later, as are websites for specific military units. These military history collections include:

    U.S. Air Force Historical Research Agency (AFHRA)
        600 Chennault Circle
        Maxwell AFB, AL 36112-6424
        http://www.afhra.af.mil/

    U.S. Air Force Historical Studies Office (AFHSO)
        3 Brookley Avenue, Box 94
        Bolling AFB, DC 20032-5000
        http://www.afhso.af.mil/

    National Museum of the United States Air Force
        1100 Spaatz Street
        Wright-Patterson AFB, OH 45433
        http://www.nationalmuseum.af.mil/

    U.S. Army Heritage and Education Center
        950 Soldiers Drive
        Carlisle, PA 17913-5021
        http://www.carlisle.army.mil/ahec

    U.S. Army Center for Military History
        Fort Lesley J. McNair
        Washington, DC 20319-5058
        http://www.history.army.mil/

    U.S. Coast Guard Historian's Office
        2100 Second Street SW
        Washington, DC 20593-0001
        http://www.uscg.mil/history

    Coast Guard Museum
        15 Mohegan Avenue

> New London, CT 06320-8511
> http://www.uscg.mil/hq/cg092/museum

Marine Corps History Division
> 3078 Upshur Avenue
> Quantico, VA 22134
> http://www.tecom.usmc.mil/HD/Home_Page.htm

American Merchant Marine Museum
> 300 Steamboat Road
> Barstow House
> Kings Point, NY 11024
> http://www.usmma.edu/about/museum

Naval Heritage and History Command
> Washington Navy Yard, DC 20374
> http://www.history.navy.mil/index.html

Many persons come to Georgia seeking information on relatives stationed in Georgia's numerous military bases in the 1950s and later. They are seldom successful working in Georgia records.

Prison and Asylum Records

Records of Georgia's penal and asylum inmates are closed when less than seventy-five years old, otherwise the records can be accessed at the Georgia Archives in Morrow. Some admission records of the Georgia Asylum have been compiled by Paul K. Graham, *Admission Register of Central State Hospital, Milledgeville, Georgia, 1842–1861* (Decatur, GA: The Genealogy Company, 2011). The Georgia Prison Historical Society, 428 Colony Farm Road, Milledgeville, GA 31061 is an affiliated chapter of the Georgia Genealogical Society.

Most state and federal court records and proceedings, kept at individual courthouses and at the National Archives at Atlanta, respectively, are open to the public. Also see Yigal Rechtman, "The FBI for Genealogy? Really? Yes," *Everton's Genealogical Helper* (November–December 1998): 42–43; and Gerald K. Haines and David A. Langbart, *Unlocking the Secrets of the FBI* (Wilmington, DE: Scholarly Resources, 1997). The National Archives at Atlanta has placed a database for the inmate case files for the Atlanta Federal Penitentiary online for 1902–1921: http://www.archives.gov/southeast/finding-aids/atlanta-penitentiary.

For the Georgia School for the Blind see *Origin and History of the Georgia Academy for the Blind: with Documents from the Beginning, 1851, to 1887* (n. p., n. d.).

County Records

The Georgia Archives and the Latter-day Saints Family History Centers have few county records on microfilm from the years after 1900. The exception to this is marriage records, which for many counties can continue to about 1950. Researchers usually must go to the individual courthouses for more recent records. The Georgia Archives, however, does have the originals of all Georgia county tax digests for most counties from 1872 to the present. These records are open to the public, although most of these tax digests have not been microfilmed.

Immigration, Naturalization, and Passport Records

Prior to 1906, naturalizations could be granted in any county, state, or federal court. After that time, federal courts assumed the responsibility for all naturalizations. For those in Georgia, see Linda Woodward Geiger and Meyer L. Frankel, *Index to Georgia's Federal Naturalization Records to 1950 (Excluding Military Petitions)* (Atlanta: Georgia Genealogical Society, 1996) and Marion R. Hemperley, "Federal Naturalization Oaths, Savannah, Georgia, 1790–1860," *Georgia Historical Quarterly* 51 (1967): 454–487.

Records of naturalizations of Irishmen brought to Georgia for early railroad construction appear in June Hart Wester, "Naturalizations of Irwin County, 1827–1847," *Georgia Genealogical Society Quarterly* 15 (1979): 117–122. Also see, among other sources, Augusta Genealogical Society, *Irish Nativities in Magnolia Cemetery, Augusta, Georgia Tombstone Inscriptions* (Augusta, GA: Augusta Genealogical Society, 1991); Alice O. Walker, comp., *Register of Signatures of Depositors in the Augusta, Georgia, Branch of the Freedman's Savings and Trust Company* [1870–1871, includes many Irish depositors] (Augusta, GA: Augusta-Richmond County Public Library, 1998); David T. Gleeson, *The Irish in the South 1815–1877* (Chapel Hill: University of North Carolina Press, 2001); Kevin J. Rich, *Irish Immigrants of the Industrial Savings Bank, 1850–1853* (3 vols., New York: Broadway-Manhattan, 1997); and Ruth-Ann M. Harris and Donald M. Jacobs, eds., *The Search for Missing Friends: Irish Immigrant Advertisements Placed in the Boston Pilot* (8 vols., Boston: New England Historic Genealogical Society, 1989).

Before World War I, most Americans traveled abroad without passports. Ancestry.com has some U.S. passports online. For information on passport records that do exist and how to access them, see:

> Colletta, John P. "U.S. Passport Applications: Leads to Immigration and Naturalization Records." *Heritage Quest*, no. 71 (September/October 1997): 9–15.
>
> National Archives microcopy M1371—*Registers and Indexes for Passport Applications, 1810–1906* and M1490—*Passport Applications, 1906–1923*.
>
> Nicastro, Kathie O., and Claire Prechtel-Kluskens. "Passport Applications." *Prologue: The Quarterly of the National Archives* 25 (1993): 390–395.

See also the section on Passenger Lists on page 5.

Pre-Modern Period, 1872–1917

Census Records

The subscription website HeritageQuest has online indexes to all names for all surviving population schedules for 1880–1910 censuses, as well as the actual pages of the census. Ancestry.com, another subscription website, which is available for free at many major libraries and other institutions such as the Georgia Archives, also has these censuses with online indexes. A nationwide transcript of the 1880 census that includes a searchable every-name index is available for free at the website Familysearch.org.

Federal census records for Georgia, 1880–1910, have various microfilm Soundex indexes available at many libraries including the Georgia Archives and the National Archives at Atlanta. The

Georgia Research
Chapter II: Research by Time Period

Soundex coding system is a coded surname (last name) index based on the way a surname sounds rather than how it is spelled. The 1880 census has a Soundex index to families with children aged ten years and younger, and the 1900 and 1910 censuses have Soundex indexes to all families. The 1910 Soundex index has a separate index for cities that includes Atlanta, Augusta, Macon, and Savannah. The original 1880 Soundex cards for Georgia are in the collection of the Gwinnett County Historical Society.

The original records of the 1880 census of Georgia and its mortality schedule are at the Georgia Archives, although the microfilm copy should be used whenever possible. Nearly all of the 1890 census was damaged in a fire in 1921 and destroyed sometime after 1933. Fragments of a few pages of the 1890 census for the city of Columbus survive and are in the Georgia Archives Microfilm Library, Drawer 165, Boxes 47–49. See Kelle Blake, "'First in the Path of the Firemen': The Fate of the 1890 Population Census," *Prologue: The Quarterly of the National Archives* 28 (1996): 64–81. The originals of the 1900–1940 census returns were destroyed by the National Archives in 1953, after microfilming them.

The 1880 federal census has extra schedules included in National Archives microcopy T1137. These records are an agriculture schedule listing each farmer and describing each farm, a mortality schedule giving information on persons who died during the census year, and a manufacturer's schedule that includes grist and saw mill operators. The 1880 census of Georgia also has a special census of persons delinquent from being confined in prisons, jails, poor farms, insane asylums, etc. as National Archives microfilm T1127, rolls 26 and 27, at the Georgia Archives Microfilm Library, Drawer 192, Boxes 61 and 62. A list of persons in Central State Hospital in Baldwin County is on pages 227–233 of Robert S. Davis, *The Georgia Black Book Volume II* (Greenville, SC: Southern Historical Press, 1987).

Some state and county copies of the 1880 census, made by the census takers, survive for use in comparing with the federal copy on National Archives microfilm. See Roger D. Joslyn, "The Short Form 1880 and 1890 Federal Censuses," *The American Genealogist* 69 (1994): 231–232. These records include, in the county records microfilm of the Georgia Archives, copies for Chattahoochee, Clarke, Columbia, Fayette, Glascock, Jefferson, Morgan, Newton, Taliaferro, Telfair, and Washington Counties. Original censuses in Record Group 44-1-2 at the Georgia Archives exist for Crawford and Franklin Counties. A county copy of the 1890 federal census has been published by the Central Georgia Genealogical Society as William R. Henry, *1890 Federal Census, Washington County, Georgia*. Several individuals and organizations have published, for specific counties, 1890 tax lists and other substitutes for the lost 1890 census.

Published census statistics survive from all of the censuses, 1790–1990, even when, as in the case of Georgia for 1790–1810, the census records themselves have not survived. The books of statistics are available at Federal Depository Libraries, such as the libraries of Emory University and the University of Georgia. For specific citations, see:

> Davidson, Katherine H., and Charlotte M. Ashby. *Preliminary Inventory of the Records of the Bureau of the Census (Record Group 29)*. Washington, DC: National Archives, 1964.
>
> Schulze, Suzanne. *Population Information in Nineteenth Century Census Volumes*. Phoenix, AZ: Oryx Press, 1983, which also covers the 1790 and 1800 censuses.

———. *Population Information in Twentieth Century Census Volumes: 1900–1940*. Phoenix, AZ: Oryx Press, 1985.

State School Census Records

As late as the 1950s, the Georgia State Vital Records Branch had the originals of the state school census records for 1908, 1913, 1918, and 1923. These records are now missing. County copies of some returns, however, are on microfilm at the Georgia Archives for the counties of Fayette (1928, 1933, and 1938), Henry (1903, 1908, 1913, and 1918), Meriwether (1898, 1903, and 1913), Tattnall (1928, 1933, and 1938), and Walton (1928, 1933, and 1938). Other school census records may still be in their counties.

Tax Digests

In addition to the tax digests on microfilm, the Georgia Archives has an almost complete set of original tax digests, starting about 1872, arranged by county. Starting in 1906, each tax digest includes a list of the Confederate pensioners residing within the county. The Georgia Archives also has county lists of liquor retailers, 1882–1888, in Record Group 8-1-26, and ledgers of individuals paying taxes as auctioneers, photographers, billiard table owners, doctors, brewers, merry-go-round operators, lightning rod dealers, meat packers, and other professions for 1889–1910 in Record Group 8-1-22. Also see "Saw Mill Operators in Central and South Georgia, 1901," *Georgia Genealogical Magazine* 36 (1996): 306–317. For more information on tax digests, see Tax Records on page 144.

Vital Records

Georgia first attempted to require vital records of births, deaths, and marriages in legislation passed in 1875. The 1875 vital records include such information as names of parents and place of birth. This effort only lasted a year. What records known to survive are on microfilm at the Georgia Archives for these counties: Carroll, Chattooga, Clarke, Clayton (no death records), Colquitt, Early, Elbert, Franklin (marriages only), Jackson, Jefferson (death records only), Lincoln (marriages only), Lumpkin, McIntosh (death records only), Miller, Muscogee (marriages only), Oglethorpe (no death records), Pulaski (birth records only), Richmond (marriages only), Sumter (no death records), Talbot (death records only), and Taliaferro (no death records). The Georgia Archives has the original 1875 vital records for Walton County in Record Group 247.

Voluntary vital records were also kept by the cities of:

Atlanta. Births start in 1896; deaths start in 1887. Order from the Fulton County Department of Health and Wellness, Vital Records Office, Room 101, 99 Jesse Hill Jr. Drive SE, Atlanta, GA 30303.

Augusta. For births, 1823–1896, see Leoda Sherry, "Richmond County Births Registry, 1823–1896," *Georgia Genealogical Society Quarterly* 4 (1968): 988–993.

Columbus. Births start in 1890; deaths start in 1890. Order from the Muscogee County Health Department, 2100 Comer Avenue, Columbus, GA 31902.

Gainesville. Births start in 1865; deaths start in 1909 (on microfilm at the Georgia Archives in Drawer 245, Box 65).

Macon. Births start in 1891; deaths start in 1882. Order from the Bibb County Department of Health, 171 Emery Highway, Macon, GA 31201.

Savannah. Births start in 1890. Order from the Chatham County Health Department, P.O. Box 6148, Savannah, GA 31405. Death records from 1803–1853 have been published by the Genealogy Committee of the Georgia Historical Society; scattered death records for later years also survive.

Many white Atlanta death records for 1888–1931 are included in the [Franklin M.] Garrett Necrology on microfilm at the Atlanta History Center, the Georgia Archives, and the Central Library of the Atlanta-Fulton Public Library System.

Military Records

Microfilm and original records of the Georgia volunteers in the National Guard, State Troops, the War with Spain (1898), the Philippines Insurrection (1898–1901), and the expedition against Poncho Villa in Mexico (1916) are at the Georgia Archives. Service cards for the War with Spain can be accessed from the Georgia Archives free website, the Virtual Vault: http://cdm.sos.state.ga.us/. These sources include records used in the incomplete Carlton J. Thaxton, et al., *A Roster of Spanish American War Soldiers from Georgia* (Americus, GA: Thaxton Company, 1984). Many men served in other units recruited in Georgia for that war; see:

- "'Ray's Immunes', Georgians who Sign up to go to Cuba, 1898." *Georgia Genealogical Society Quarterly* 37 (2001): 166–188.

- "Some Georgia Veterans of the Spanish-American War, Albany, Georgia." *Georgia Genealogical Society Quarterly* 24 (1988): 157–158.

- National Archives microcopy M871—*General Index to Compiled Service Records of Volunteer Soldiers Who Served During the War with Spain.*

- National Archives microcopy M872—*Index to Compiled Service Records of Volunteer Soldiers Who Served During the Philippine Insurrection.*

- Peterson, Clarence Stewart. *Known Military Dead During the Spanish American War and the Philippines Insurrection, 1898–1901.* Baltimore: privately printed, 1958.

The National Archives also has the pension files for all wars to 1917. The War with Spain pensions for Georgia are indexed in National Archives microcopy T289—*Organization Index to Pension Files of Veterans Who Served Between 1861 and 1900*, Reels 25 and 26. National Archives microcopy T288—*General Index to Pension Files, 1861–1934*, includes some pensions from the War with Spain, World War I, etc.

Reconstruction, 1866–1872

The end of the Civil War left Georgia in turmoil. Blacks tried to keep new rights, while whites tried to regain old ones. Forty thousand Georgians were missing, and thousands more were crippled, indigent, or homeless. Most of the individual capital was gone, while railroads, factories, and some towns and cities were in ruins. Many families dissolved at the end of the war, some without the formality of divorce, with some members moving to Texas or other states to start new lives. However, Reconstruction also generated a number of genealogically valuable records in Georgia; see Robert S. Davis, "New Ideas from New Sources: Modern Research in Reconstruction 1865–1876," *Georgia Historical Quarterly* 93 (Fall 2009): 291–306 and "Black Georgia Office Holders in Reconstruction," *Georgia Genealogical Society Quarterly* 37 (2001): 45–46.

Census Records

The population schedules for the 1870 federal census are available and searchable by every name on the commercial websites Ancestry.com and HeritageQuest. This census had a reputation, even in 1870, for being exceptionally incomplete, unreadable (in places), and for having pages bound and numbered out of order. National Archives microfilm of the June 1, 1870, census of Georgia, including the population schedule, the mortality schedule (listing persons who died during the census year, with other information), the social schedule (statistics on each county), and the agriculture schedule (listing farmers and describing farms) is at the Georgia Archives, the National Archives at Atlanta, and many other libraries and archives. The population schedule is found online with subscription websites such as Ancestry.com. The population schedule for Georgia is also indexed in Bradley W. Steuart, *Georgia 1870 Census Index* (3 volumes, Bountiful, UT: Precision Indexing, 1991), and in Ronald Vern Jackson, *Atlanta, Augusta, and Savannah, Georgia, 1870: Federal Census Index* (Salt Lake City: Accelerated Indexing Systems International, 1990).

The Georgia Archives has some county and other duplicate copies of the census of 1870, compiled by the census takers. The alternative copies, in the county records microfilm, include these counties: Camden, Cherokee, Fayette, Morgan, and Randolph; and the originals in Record Group 44-1-2 are for Cherokee, Clarke, Clay, Clayton, Clinch, Cobb, Coffee, Columbia, Coweta, Crawford, Dade, Dawson, Decatur, DeKalb, Dooly, Dougherty, Early, Echols, Effingham, Elbert, Emanuel, Fannin, Fayette, Irwin, Pike, Polk, Pulaski, Putnam, Quitman, Rabun, Richmond, Schley, Screven, Spalding, Stewart, Sumter, Talbot, Tattnall, Taylor, Telfair, Terrell, Thomas, Towns, Troup, Twiggs, Union, Upson, and Warren Counties.

Returns of Qualified Voters

Georgia and all states of the former Confederacy, with the exception of Tennessee (which reentered the Union by ratifying the Fourteenth Amendment to the U.S. Constitution), kept registrations of black and white males qualified to vote on the question of restoring each state to the Union. See "The South's 1867 Returns of Qualified Voters and Their Value in Genealogical Research," *Heritage Quest* no. 54 (1994): 62–63.

The registers (listing the returns of names of applicants) and oath books for Georgia survive for each county and major city, except Haralson County, and are at the Georgia Archives. The original oath books are on microfilm in Drawer 297, Boxes 9–145. The voter registration books created from the oath books are on microfilm in Drawer 296, Boxes 14–75, and Drawer 297, Boxes 1–8. The white men in these records are indexed in John David Brandenburg and Rita Brinkley Worthy, *Index to Georgia's 1867–1868 Returns of Qualified Voters and Registration Oath Books* (Atlanta: privately printed, 1995). Depending upon the county or city, the Georgia records give place of birth and the number of years in Georgia, the county, and the militia district. Almost all of these records contain naturalization information on foreign-born men.

Georgia Research
Chapter II: Research by Time Period

Ancestry.com has added these records to its website under this title: *Returns of Qualified Voters and Reconstruction Oath Books, 1867–1869*. They are fully searchable and can be browsed by either collection (Returns Books or Oath Books).

The following inventory shows the kinds of special genealogical data that can be found in these records. Registers with only name, race, oath, and naturalization information are not included on this list.

- COB   Country of birth is given.
- DOB   Date of birth is given for a few individuals.
- NAT   Naturalization information is provided on a large number of foreign born citizens, although this information usually can be found for at least a few persons in most of these registers.
- NOY   Number of years in Georgia, in the county, and in the militia district are provided for each individual.
- NOY?   Same as for NOY, except the years seem to be given in months.
- NOY*   Same as for NOY, except the column for number of years in the militia district is blank.
- POB   Place of birth, state or country, is given.
- POB?   Place of birth is given, but all persons listed appear to have been recorded as native Georgians.
- POB**   Place of birth is provided in one of the duplicate volumes of the register for Floyd County but not in the volume designated as the original volume.

Appling: NOY
Atlanta (City): POB, NAT
Augusta (City): NAT
Banks: POB; NOY
Berrien: POB; NOY
Bibb: POB; NOY
Bryan: POB; NOY*
Bulloch: NOY
Burke: NOY
Camden: COB
Catoosa: POB
Charlton: COB
Chatham: POB, NOY
Chattahoochee: POB
Chattooga: POB
Cherokee: NOY
Columbus (City): POB, NAT
Clay: COB
Clinch: NOY

Coffee: NOY
Columbia: COB
Dawson: COB
Decatur (County): POB
DeKalb: POB
Dooly: POB?
Echols: POB, NOY
Effingham: POB, NOY*
Fayette: POB
Floyd: POB**
Forsyth: NOY
Franklin: POB
Fulton: POB
Glynn: COB
Gwinnett: POB
Habersham: POB
Hall: NOY, POB
Hart: POB
Henry: POB

Jackson: NOY, POB
Liberty: NOY, POB
Lincoln: COB
Lowndes: NOY, POB
Lumpkin: COB
Macon (County): POB, NOY?
Macon (City): NAT
Marion: POB
McIntosh: NOY, POB, NAT
Miller: POB
Milton: NOY
Mitchell: POB
Monroe: POB, NOY
Muscogee: POB
Paulding: POB
Pierce: NOY
Pike: POB, NOY
Polk: POB
Pulaski: POB?

Quitman (County): NOY, POB
Rabun: POB
Randolph: COB
Savannah (City): POB, NAT
Schley: POB, NOY?
Screven: NOY
Spalding: POB
Stewart: POB, NOY
Sumter: POB
Tattnall: POB, NOY
Towns: POB, DOB
Union: POB, DOB
Ware: NOY
Wayne: NOY
Webster: NOY, POB
White: COB
Wilcox: POB?
Wilkes: COB

Pardons and Amnesty

Many white men found themselves disqualified from full citizenship for having substantially aided the Confederacy or for having valuable property in the Confederacy. They were required to petition the governor of their state and the president of the United States to have their full citizenship restored. From 1867 until 1898, when universal amnesty was passed, only an act of Congress could restore citizenship. A detailed explanation of this process and the persons approved by the governors of Georgia and the president is published in *Ancestoring VIII* (1984): 13–26, which is the journal of the Augusta Genealogical Society. Separate but complete lists of the presidential and the congressional pardons are published in Carolyn M. Rowe, *Index to Individual Pardon Applications from the South, 1865–1898* (Pensacola, FL: privately printed, 1996).

The petitions for pardons and amnesty through 1867, often containing personal information, are reproduced on National Archives microcopy M1003, available at the National Archives at Atlanta and, for Georgians, at the Georgia Archives on microfilm in Drawer 287, Boxes 40–48. These files have been digitized and indexed on the subscription website Fold3. Pardons files for 1868–1898 must be sought from Entry 500 40A-H21, Record Group 233, Center for Legislative Studies, National Archives and Records Administration, Washington, DC 20408.

Civil War Claims Filed After the Civil War

Many Southerners (black and white) petitioned the federal government for compensation for property destroyed or seized by the Union army and navy. Although these claims often contain genealogical data, the loyalty and credibility of the claimants is often suspect. The only comprehensive index to the claims is Entry 366, Record Group 56, General Records of the Treasury, National Archives and Records Administration, 8601 Adelphi Road, College Park, MD 20740-6001. It includes not only the Southern Claims Commission records described below but also the claims for cotton and other property seized immediately after the war by the federal military. Other claims, North and South, filed with the Quartermaster General of the U.S. Army, known as "Fourth of July Claims," must be sought from Entry 788 of Record Group 92 Records of the Quartermaster General in the National Archives and Records Administration, 700 Pennsylvania Ave. NW, Washington, DC 20408-0001. The Center for Legislative Archives at the National Archives has prepared comprehensive indexes to petitions made directly to Congress. Also see National Archives microcopy M502—*Registers of Letters Received by the Secretary of the Treasury Relating to Claims, 1864–1887*. For more information on Civil War claims, see Kenneth W. Munden and Henry Putney Beers, *The Union: A Guide to Federal Archives Relating to the Civil War* (Washington, DC: National Archives, 1986).

Southern Claims Commission

The most famous of the above claims were those brought before the Commissioners of Claims (also known as the Southern Claims Commission). These genealogically rich claims were for property lost to Union military forces by Southerners loyal to the Union. More than eighty percent of these claims were rejected from lack of evidence or from proof of attempted deceit. The claims also frequently contain information about neighbors. See, for example, the abstracts of some of the claims by Muril M. Matthews in the *Northwest Georgia Historical and Genealogical Society Quarterly*, starting Volume 26 (4) (Fall, 1994): 11 and ending with Volume 28 (4) (Fall 1996).

The various alphabetical lists of these claims contain errors and misleading identifications. In some instances for approved claims, for example, the wrong counties appeared on early lists, with those mistakes repeated on later lists. In some instances, the property taken or destroyed will be in a different county and even state from where the person filing the claim finally made his claim. Some 2,500 of the approved claims were destroyed in the nineteenth century without copies being made. The most extensive list of the claims is Gary B. Mills, *Southern Loyalists in the Civil War: The Southern Claims Commission* (Baltimore: Genealogical Pub. Co., 1994). For background on these claims, see Sarah Lawson, "Records of the Southern Claims Commission," *Prologue: The Journal of the National Archives* 12 (1980): 207–218. The approved Georgia claims, from National Archives Entry 732, Record Group 217—Records of the Accounting Office of the Department of the Treasury, are reproduced in National Archives microcopy M1658—*Approved Southern Unionist Claims for Georgia, 1871–1880*. A list of the accepted claims for Georgia is in John Hammond Moore, "Sherman's 'Fifth Column': A Guide to Unionist Activity in Georgia," *Georgia Historical Quarterly* 68 (1984): 382–409. Also see "Some Liberty and Chatham County Civil War Claims by Former Slaves," *Georgia Genealogical Society Quarterly* 27 (1991): 189–191; Miranda Booker Perry, "No Pensions for Ex-Slaves: How Federal Agencies Supressed a Movement to Aid Freedpeople," *Prologue: The Quarterly of the National Archives* 42 (Summer 2010): http://www.archives.gov/publications/prologue/2010/summer/slave-pension.html and Robert S. Davis, "Some Former Slaves and Their Masters," *Heritage Quest* no. 69 (May–June 1997): 85–87.

Most of the claims that were disapproved by the Southern Claims Commission are included in National Archives microcopy M1407—*Barred and Disallowed Case Files of the Southern Claims Commission, 1871–1880*. The reports on decisions of the disallowed claims are on microfilm at the Georgia Archives in Drawer 289, Box 63, as *U.S. Commissioners of Claims, Summary Reports of Claims (1871–1881)*. These are the "reports" referred to in the indexes to the disallowed claims.

Some, but not all, of the Southern Claims Commission files information is available on the commercial websites Fold3, GenealogyBank, and Ancestry.

When a claim is missing from any of the above, it can usually be found in the Court of Claims case files in Record Group 123 of the National Archives. To obtain the citation to such a file, write to Index Section, U.S. Court of Claims, 717 Madison Place NW, Washington, DC 20005.

Federal Direct Tax Records, 1865–1873.

The federal tax records are on microfilm at the National Archives at Atlanta for the South for 1865–1866 and as original records for 1867–1873; they also are indexed and available for 1865-1866 through the commercial website Ancestry.com. The records are arranged by state and district. The Georgia records for 1865–1866 have been microfilmed as National Archives microcopy M762. For a detailed description of these records and their background, see Cynthia G. Fox, "Income Tax Records of the Civil War Years," *Prologue: The Journal of the National Archives* 18 (1986): 250–259. The Civilian Records Branch, National Archives and Records Administration, Washington, DC 20408, has property tax evaluation records for these counties: Appling, Bibb, Bryan, Chatham, Clarke, Columbia, Crawford, Franklin, Glynn, Greene, Harris, Houston, McIntosh, Monroe, Morgan, Muscogee, Oglethorpe, Richmond, Sumter, Talbot, Taliaferro, Tattnall, Upson, Warren, and Wilkes that identifies the 1860 and 1866 owner of each piece of property taxed. The Georgia records are in Entry 882, Record Group 217—Records of the General Accounting Office. The Georgia Archives has records of attempts to refund this tax in 1891 in Bibb, Chatham, Clarke, Monroe, and Richmond Counties in Record Group 8-1-24. The Archives also has Georgia county tax maps, 1866–1871. The maps do not identify specific taxable property or taxpayers. The Georgia Archives has some county tax digests for the late 1860s through 1871, chiefly in its county records microfilm although a few such digests are originals that have not been microfilmed.

Freedman's Bank Records, 1868–1874

This agency had branches established in Atlanta, Augusta, Macon, and Savannah. Records of the Macon branch have not survived. Black depositors left detailed personal information, including parents (even if slaves), siblings, and children, useful in identifying their accounts, copied as part of National Archives microcopy M816. Sometimes this data extends decades back into slavery. These records have been transcribed, for the whole country, on the free website FamilySearch.org and have been digitized and indexed by all names on the commercial website Ancestry.com.

Crude indexes also exist for the Savannah and Augusta records as part of National Archives microcopy M817. A copy of these records is at the Georgia Archives in Drawer 159, Boxes 55–59, and Drawer 214, Box 62. See Reginald Washington, "The Freedman's Savings and Trust Company: African-American Genealogical Research," *Prologue: The Quarterly of the National Archives* 29 (1997): 170–181 and Robert S. Davis, "Documentation for Afro-American Families: Records of Freedman's Savings and Trust Company," *National Genealogical Society Quarterly* 76 (1988): 139–146. Also see Alice O. Walker, *Registers of Signatures of Depositors in the Augusta, Georgia, Branch of the Freedman's Savings and Trust Company: November 1870–June 1872* (Augusta, GA: Augusta-Richmond County Public Library, 1998).

Apprenticeship Records, 1866–

On December 8, 1866, the Georgia legislature authorized the Freedmen's Bureau to apprentice orphaned black children who were under age twenty-one. Records of these apprenticeships can be found in the county records on microfilm at the Georgia Archives.

Freedmen's Bureau Records, 1865–1872.

National Archives microfilm M798 *Records of the Assistant Commissioner for the State of Georgia, Bureau of Refugees, Freedman, and Abandoned Lands;* M799 *Records of the Superintendent of Education for the State of Georgia Bureau of Refugees, Freedmen, and Abandoned Lands 1865–1870*; and M1903 *Records of the Field Offices for the State of Georgia, Bureau of Refugees, Freedmen, and Abandoned Lands, 1865–1872* (M1903 is digitized and indexed on the commercial website Ancestry.com) include all records of the Freedmen's Bureau in Georgia. Freedmen's Bureau data contain records of various relationships between blacks and whites immediately after the Civil War and some records of confiscation of Confederate property.

Reel 36 of this microfilm M789 includes lists of black families resettled on abandoned lands of coastal Georgia, blacks contracted to work in Wilkes County, and court cases involving freedmen. Fred C. Rathbun's *Names From Georgia, 1865–1866: Freedmen's Bureau Letters, Roll 13* (Littleton, CO: privately printed, 1986) indexes 1,000 freedmen and others from Georgia. Other records are included in Jacqueline A. Lawson, *An Index of African-Americans Identified in Selected Records of the Freedman's Bureau* (Bowie, MD: Heritage Books, 1995). No Georgia records are included in National Archives microfilm M1875 *Marriage Records of the Freedmen's Bureau, 1861–1869*. See the article by Reginald Washington, "Sealing the Same Bonds of Matrimony: Freedman's Bureau Marriages," *Prologue: The Quarterly of the National Archives* 37 (1) (Spring 2005): http://www.archives.gov/publications/prologue/2005/spring/freedman-marriage-recs.html.

For information on the Freedmen's Bureau records, see:

    Cimbala, Paul A. "On the Front Line of Freedom: Freedmen's Bureau Offices and Agents in Reconstruction Georgia." *Georgia Historical Quarterly* 76 (Fall 1992): 577–611.

    ———. *Under the Guardianship of the Nation: The Freedmen's Bureau and the Reconstruction of Georgia, 1865–1870*. Athens: University of Georgia Press, 1997.

    Farmer-Kaiser, Mary. "'Are they not in some sorts vagrants?': Gender and the Efforts of the Freedmen's Bureau to Combat Vagrancy in the Reconstruction South." *Georgia Historical Quarterly* 88 (Spring 2004): 25–49.

    Guide to Genealogical Research in the National Archives. Washington, DC: National Archives and Records Administration, 1983. Pages 177, 180.

    Newman, Debra L. *Black History: A Guide to Civilian Records in the National Archives.* Washington, DC: National Archives and Records Administration, 1994.

For examples of what can be found in such records, see Barry A. Couch and Larry Madares, "Reconstructing Black Families: Perspectives from the Texas Freedmen's Bureau Records," *Prologue: The Quarterly of the National Archives* 18 (1986): 109–122.

Racial Violence Records, 1866–1871

Sometimes genealogical data can be found in reports of violence committed against African Americans in Georgia during Reconstruction. National Archives microfilm of these reports is abstracted in Robert S. Davis, *The Georgia Black Book* (Greenville, SC: Southern Historical Press, 1982), 227–270. Related information can be found in the papers of Governor Rufus Bullock in Record Group 1-1-5 at the Georgia Archives, abstracted in Robert S. Davis, *The Georgia Black Book, Volume II* (Greenville, SC: Southern Historical Press, 1987), 137–156. Similar records are also found in the papers of the Adjutant General and Justice Department described in *Black Studies: A Select Catalog of National Archives Microfilm Publications* (Washington, DC: National Archives, 1984) and in the federal court records at the National Archives at Atlanta. Also see "Georgians vs. the Ku Klux Klan," *Georgia Genealogical Society Quarterly* 31 (1995): 90–99.

Other Sources for African American Research.

Many libraries and archives, including the National Archives at Atlanta, have free brochures on their African American history sources. Also see Walter Schatz, *Directory of Afro-American Sources* (New York: Bowker, 1975). The Georgia Archives has the booklet *Microfilm Records: Black History* (no date). Debra L. Newman has published several booklets through the National Archives and Records Administration on African American historical sources. Copies of the following NARA publications can be found at the Georgia Archives:

> *Black History: A Guide to Civilian Records in the National Archives; and Selected Documents Pertaining to Black Workers Among the Records of the Department of Labor and Its Component Bureaus, 1902–1969.*

> *List of Black Servicemen From the War Department Collection of Revolutionary War Records.*

> *List of Free Black Heads of Households in the First Federal Census, 1790* (Georgia is not included, as the 1790 census of Georgia is lost).

Also see:

> Greene, Robert Ewell. *Black Defenders of America, 1775–1973.* Chicago: Johnson Publishing Company, 1973.

> The special African-American issue of *Prologue: The Quarterly of the National Archives* 29 (2) (1997).

> Woodson, Carter G. *A Century of Negro Migration.* Washington, DC: The Association for the Study of Negro Life and History, 1918.

African American researchers will find city directories, such as those listed in "City Directories," on page 267, useful in urban areas and more helpful in some ways than federal census records. Also see Barbara D. Walker, *Index to "The Journal of the Afro-American Historical and Genealogical Society Quarterly"* (Bowie, Md.: Heritage Books, 1992).

For examples of useful materials from local sources, see:

> Gardner, Oscar W. and Leroy W. Gardner. "Johnson County Freedmen and Plantation Owners, 1865–1866." *Georgia Genealogical Society Quarterly* 32 (1996): 3–19.

Ray, David Thornton. *Black Marriage Records, Hart County, Georgia.* Hartwell, GA: Savannah River Valley Genealogical Society, 1994.

Turner, Freda R. *Henry County, Georgia, 1821–1894: Marriage, Colored/Freedman, Record of Sales, Inventory and Wills.* Roswell, GA: Wolfe Pub., 1995.

Homestead Records, 1866–

Georgia had laws protecting families from debts and taxes going back decades before the Civil War. Most of the records of homestead protection, however, including detailed family information, are in county records starting with the years immediately after the Civil War. The Georgia Archives has many of these county records on microfilm.

Relief Bills

Records created from post-Civil War acts to provide aid to amputees, widows, orphans, devastated farmers, etc., are reproduced or indexed in Robert S. Davis, *Georgia Black Book, Volume II* (Greenville, SC: Southern Historical Press, 1987); and "Georgia Civil War Amputees," *Georgia Genealogical Society Quarterly* 32 (1996): 20.

The Civil War, 1861–1865

Georgia's Civil War records are exceptionally well indexed, as these records were often used to prove service for pensions and other post-Civil War veterans' benefits. Records of Civil War service can often provide information beyond military service. For example, the Alphabetical Card File Index described below can be used as a substitute census of Georgia for the Civil War years. For historical background on this period, see T. Conn Bryan, *Confederate Georgia* (Athens: University of Georgia Press, 1953); John D. Fowler and David B. Parker, eds., *Breaking the Heartland: The Civil War in Georgia* (Macon, GA: Mercer University Press, 2011); and E. N. Boney, *Rebel Georgia* (Macon, GA: Mercer University Press, 1996).

Many Civil War resources are available on the Internet, and so many more come out—including many specific to Georgia—that no bibliography can keep up; see for example, books like Alice E. Carter and Richard J. Jensen, *The Civil War on the Web: A Guide to the Very Best Sites—Completely Revised and Updated* (Wilmington, DE: SR Books, 2003). Some popular sites currently include:

The American Civil War Homepage (free): http://sunsite.utk.edu/civil-war

The Civil War Home Page (free): http://www.civil-war.net

Civil War (free): http://www.civilwar.com

Civil War Forum (free, part of the Genforum genealogical website):
    http://genforum.genealogy.com/civilwar

Information on sailors and marines (free, Library of Virginia):
    http://www.lva.lib.va.us/whatwehave/mil/connavy/search.asp

National Civil War Naval Museum (free, Columbus, Georgia):
    http://civilwarnavalmuseum.com

Naval Historical Foundation (free): http://www.navyhistory.org/photographs

Civil War Richmond (free; newspaper articles, photographs, and more on Richmond): http://www.mdgorman.com ; also see the *Richmond Daily Dispatch*, 1860–1865 (free): http://dlxs.richmond.edu/d/ddr/

General Reference & Bibliographical Sources

More books and articles have been published on the American Civil War than on any other subject in the English language. Several useful reference works are listed below. Entire books and bibliographies have been done on research and resources. The references below represent a sampling of the most notable works. So much new material appears in print that any list must also be out-of-date, even as it is being compiled.

Published Finding Aids

Union and Confederate records at the National Archives have a number of published finding aids. The best general guide is *Guide to Genealogical Research at the National Archives* (Washington, DC: National Archives, 1986). Also see:

Beers, Henry Putney. *The Confederacy*. Washington, DC: National Archives, 1986.

Military Service Records: A Select Catalog of National Archives Microfilm Publications. Washington, DC: National Archives, 1985.

Munden, Kenneth W., and Henry Putney Beers. *The Union*. Washington, DC: National Archives, 1986.

Musick, Michael. "Honorable Reports: Battles, Campaigns, and Skirmishes—Civil War Records and Research." *Prologue: The Quarterly of the National Archives* 27 (1995): 259–277.

Other Confederate Research Tools

Most of the Confederate records at the National Archives are described in detail in Elizabeth Bethel and Craig R. Scott, *Preliminary Inventory of the War Department Collection of Confederate Records (Record Group 109)* (Athens, GA: Iberian Press, 1994). There are also the following:

Current, Richard N. *Encyclopedia of the Confederacy*. 4 vols. New York: Simon and Schuster, 1993.

Noe, Kenneth W. *Reluctant Rebels; The Confederates Who Joined the Army After 1861,* Chapel Hill, University of North Carolina Press, 2010.

Jones, Charles Edgeworth. *Georgia in the War, 1861–1865*. Atlanta: Foote and Davies, 1909.

Neagles, James C. *Confederate Research Sources*. Salt Lake City: Ancestry, 1986.

Segars, J. H. *In Search of Confederate Ancestors: The Guide*. Murfreesboro, TN: Southern Heritage Press, 1993.

Private Manuscript Sources

A statewide bibliography of Civil War manuscripts in Georgia is David H. Slay, *Georgia Civil War Manuscript Collections: An Annotated Bibliography* (Tuscaloosa: University of Alabama Press, 2011). The Slay book usually does not include collections where the respective library only has copies and not the original records. Some libraries have spectacular Civil War holdings that can be searched from their individual library websites including Tulane, University of North Carolina at Chapel Hill (Southern Historical Collection), Emory University, and the William L. Clements Library. Almost all National Park Service battlefields and other Civil War sites have libraries with manuscript materials. The Atlanta History Center, Georgia Historical Society, and the Hargrett Library of the University of Georgia have received a grant to digitize and place on the Internet significant Civil War manuscript collections.

The Georgia Archives has separate catalogs to original manuscripts, typescripts, photocopies, etc., cataloged by name of soldier and by military unit. Usually the units are cataloged in subject drawers under "Civil War Regiments." The Civil War Miscellany Collection of photocopies and transcripts is on microfilm. The Georgia Archives also has fourteen volumes of indexed United Daughters of the Confederacy typescripts of Confederate records. Much of that material has been abstracted into volumes compiled by the UDC. Each of these volumes includes new manuscript material, as well as a portion of manuscripts from the previously unpublished typescripts. See: Georgia Division, United Daughters of the Confederacy, *Confederate Reminiscences and Letters, 1861–1865*, 26 vols. to date (Atlanta: Georgia Division United Daughters of the Confederacy, 1995–2010).

Confederate Biographies

For biographies of Confederate soldiers, see:

    Allardice, Bruce C. *Confederate Colonels: A Biographical Register*. Columbia, MO: University of Missouri Press. 2008.

    ———. *More Generals in Gray*. Baton Rouge: Louisiana State University Press, 1995.

    Brock, R. A. *Paroles of the Army of Northern Virginia*. New York: Antiquarian Press, 1962. Also known as the "Appomattox Roster," but incomplete.

    Clemmer, Greg S. *Valor in Gray: The Recipients of the Confederate Medal of Honor*. Staunton, VA: Heathside Publishing, 1996.

    Davis, William C. *The Confederate General*. Harrisburg, PA: National Historical Society, 1991.

    Joslyn, Mauriel. *Immortal Captives: The Story of 600 Confederate Officers and the United States Prisoner-of-War Policy*. Sharpsburg, Pa.: White Mane, 1995.

    Kerlin, Robert H. *Confederate Generals of Georgia and Their Burial Sites*. Fayetteville, GA: Americana Historical Books, 1994.

    Krick, Robert E. L. *Staff Officers in Gray: A Biographical Register of the Staff Officers in the Army of Northern Virginia*. Chapel Hill: University of North Carolina Press, 2003.

    Krick, Robert K. *Lee's Colonels: A Biographical Register of the Field Officers of the Army of Northern Virginia*. Dayton, OH: Morningside Press, 1992.

Moebs, Thomas Truxton. *Confederate States Navy Research Guide.* Williamsburg, VA: Moebs Publishing, 1991.

"Our Women and Boys in the War." *Georgia Genealogical Society Quarterly* 31 (Summer 1995): 99.

Pitts, Charles F. *Chaplains in Gray.* Nashville, TN: Boardman Press, 1957.

Sifakis, Stewart. *Who Was Who in the Civil War.* 2 volumes. New York: Facts On File, 1988.

Wakelyn, Jon L. *Biographical Dictionary of the Confederacy.* Westport, CT: Greenwood Press, 1977.

Warner, Ezra J. *Generals in Gray.* Baton Rouge: Louisiana State University Press, 1959.

Welsh, Jack D. *Medical Histories of Confederate Generals.* Kent, OH: Kent State University Press, 1996.

Confederate biographical source books, reprinted by the Broadfoot Company of Wilmington, North Carolina, with detailed indexes of personal name, place name, and military unit, include *Confederate Military History* (more than six hundred biographies and family histories of Georgia Confederate veterans); *Confederate Veteran*; *Southern Historical Society Papers*; and *Southern Bivouac*; also see "Some Georgia Confederate Veterans in 1907," *Georgia Genealogical Society Quarterly* 43 (Summer 2007): 165–169.

Some special lists of Georgians, are as follows:

Cornell, Nancy Jones. *Georgia Confederate Soldiers Volume 1—Unusual References to Confederate Information.* Riverdale, GA: privately printed, 1987.

"Georgia Rebels Remember Antietam." *Georgia Genealogical Society Quarterly* 30 (1994): 119–120.

"Some Georgia Rebels Buried in Colorado." *Georgia Genealogical Society Quarterly* 40 (2004): 218–219.

"Who's Who of the Confederacy." *Georgia Genealogical Society Quarterly* 36 (2000): 236.

Union Biographies

For biographical information on leaders of the Union side, see:

Hubbell, John T., and James W. Geary. *Biographical Dictionary of the Union: Northern Leaders of the Civil War.* Westport, CT: Greenwood Press, 1990.

Hunt, Roger D., and Jack R. Brown. *Brevet Brigadier Generals in Blue.* Gaithersburg, MD: Olde Soldier Books, 1990.

"Prominent Georgians in the Union." *Georgia Genealogical Society* Quarterly 26 (1990): 178.

"Some Georgia Federal Civil War Soldiers." *Georgia Genealogical Society Quarterly* 38 (2002): 233–235.

"Some Federal Civil War Pension Applications." *Georgia Genealogical Society Quarterly* 38 (2002): 236–239.

"Some Federal Civil War Pension Applications for Georgia Service." *Northwest Georgia Historical and Genealogical Society Quarterly* 30 (4) (1999): 3–6.

Warner, Ezra J. *Generals in Blue*. Baton Rouge: Louisiana State University Press, 1977.

Welsh, Jack D. *Medical Histories of Union Generals*. Kent, OH: Kent State University Press, 1996.

Alphabetical Card File Index of the Confederate Pension Office

The Georgia Roster Commission (1903–1930) created this card catalog in the early 1900s to index records that could help old soldiers and widows to document Civil War service for purposes of acquiring pensions. This card catalog indexes a wide variety of records used as evidence of service for Confederate pension claims, although not the pensions themselves. This microfilm documents Civil War-era activities for hundreds of Georgians for whom no other service records exist. It is on microfilm at the Georgia Archives in Drawer 253, Boxes 1–73. Among the records indexed are the following:

Rosters compiled by the Georgia Roster Commission, including, for most units, the county where enlisted

Letters received by Governor Joseph E. Brown and Adjutant General Henry C. Wayne, 1861–1865

Militia lists

Some copies and transcripts of private papers

Militia enrollment lists, 1864, or "Joe Brown Census" (see below)

Available at the Georgia Archives, but not included in the Alphabetical Card File, are the five volumes of Allen D. Candler, *The Confederate Records of the State of Georgia* (Atlanta: Charles P. Byrd, 1909) and the twenty-seven indexed typescripts of the letter books of the Adjutant General, 1861–1864. (Some volumes have indexes in the beginning of each volume, and others have the indexes bound in the back.)

Militia Enrollment Lists, 1864

A census, referred to in the above Alphabetical Card File as the senatorial district militia, and popularly known as the "Joe Brown Census," was made of all men eligible for military service in Georgia but who were not serving in the Confederate or Georgia state forces. Often a county return will give each man's age, occupation or reason for exemption, place of birth, and weapons owned. Returns do not exist for these counties: Burke, Catoosa, Chattooga, Dade, Dooly, Emanuel, Irwin, Johnson, Laurens, Montgomery, Pulaski, Telfair, and Wilcox. However, for the following counties, not only the state but county of birth is sometimes given: Bartow, Brooks, Butts, Calhoun, Cherokee, Clarke, Fayette, Floyd, Forsyth, Franklin, Gordon, Gwinnett, Habersham, Henry, Milton, Murray, Newton, Stewart, Thomas, Walker, Walton, Warren, and Whitfield.

These records are on microfilm at the Georgia Archives in Drawer 245, Boxes 4–10, and have been published and are included on the Georgia Archives free website the Virtual Vault:

http://cdm.sos.state.ga.us. See Nancy J. Cornell, *1864 Census for Re-Organizing the Georgia Militia*, (Baltimore: Genealogical Publishing Company, 2000). A scanned version of this book is available on the subscription website Ancestry.com.

Confederate Compiled Service Records

The Confederate service records compiled for almost all Georgia soldiers who have records today at the National Archives are arranged by unit in National Archives Microfilm M266 *Compiled Service Records of Confederate Soldiers Who Served in Organizations from the State of Georgia* (available at the Georgia Archives in Morrow) or in National Archives Microfilm 258 *Compiled Service Records of Confederate Soldiers Who Served in Organizations Raised Directly by the Confederate Government.* When a soldier appears in the indexes but his unit cannot be found, check the miscellaneous service records on the reels at the end of these respective microfilms.

The most complete index for Confederate Civil War soldiers for the nation as a whole is the National Park Service's Civil War database: http://www.itd.nps.gov/cwss/. It is free and provides the National Archives microfilm reel number for each soldier listed, as well as a link to a detailed history of his (and in some instances her) unit. This database and related databases are also accessed through the subscription website Ancestry.com. The Georgia Archives also has on microfilm in Drawer 290, Boxes 17–19, an alphabetical compilation of Confederate service records found in the holdings of the Georgia Historical Society.

The compiled service records can contain almost any information, but typically give each soldier's date and place of enlistment, circumstances of absences, and final discharge. Sometimes found in service records are special orders, petitions for final payment by next of kin, prisoner of war records, proof of joining the Union Army, and genealogically valuable medical discharges. This type of record often contains county and state of birth that could be the same for the soldier's siblings. The Georgia Archives has National Archives microfilm of Georgia and Confederate government compiled service records and the indexes to the same. The National Archives at Atlanta has the indexes to the compiled service records for all of the Southern states. Janet B. Hewett has published *The Roster of Confederate Soldiers, 1861–1865,* 16 vols. (Wilmington, NC: Broadfoot Company, 1995–1996), which is a printed version of National Archives microcopy M253—*Consolidated Index to Compiled Service Records of Confederates*. None of the above includes the thousands of records filed alphabetically in National Archives microcopy M347—*Unfiled Papers and Slips Belonging to Confederate Compiled Service Records*, and M260—*Records of the Confederate States Navy and Marines*. Also see Ralph W. Donnelly, *Service Records of Confederate Enlisted Marines* (Wilmington, NC: privately printed, 1979), Trevor K. Plante, "Researching Confederate Marines in the Civil War," *Prologue: The Quarterly of the National Archives* 33 (4) (Winter 2001): http://www.archives.gov/publications/prologue/2001/winter/confederate-marines-in-the-civil-war.html and DeAnne Blanton, "Confederate Medical Personnel," *Prologue: The Quarterly of the National Archives* 26 (1994): 80–84.

The Virtual Vault website of the Georgia Archives has access to a number of Georgia Civil War records including enlistment records in the state army.

For information on a Confederate soldier or civilian held as a prisoner of war, start with the information found in his service record, then search National Archives microcopy M598—*Selected Records of the War Department Relating to Confederate Prisoners of War* (records are arranged by prison camp, although there are some general indexes on Reels 1 to 6). Most, but not all, of the records on that microfilm are on and indexed in the subscription website Ancestry.com. For Confederates who died in federal custody see National Archives microcopy M918 *Confederate P.O.W.s: Soldiers & Sailors Who Died in Federal Prisons and Military Hospitals in the North*. National Archives microfilm M416 *Union Provost Marshal's File of Papers Relating to Two or More Civilians* ends with several microfilm reels of records relating to military and civilian prisoners arranged by geographic location but apparently with no index.

All of the major federal prison camps that held Confederates now have printed histories, also see:

> Gillispie, James M. *Andersonvilles of the North: The Myths and Realities of Northern Treatment of Civil War Confederate Prisoners*. Denton, TX: University of North Texas Press, 2008.
>
> Pickenpaugh, Roger. *Captives in Gray: The Civil War Prisons of the Union*. Tuscaloosa: University of Alabama Press, 2009.
>
> Speer, Lonnie R. *Portals to Hell: Military Prisons of the Civil War*. Mechanicsburg, PA: Stackpole Books, 1997.

Some National Archives microfilms relating to Southerners in the Civil War include the following, and also see "Reading the Lost Letters of the Confederate Government," *Heritage Quest* no. 73 (January/February 1998): 91–92:

> M409—Index to Letters Received by the Confederate Secretary of War, 1861–1865.
>
> M410—Index to Letters Received by the Confederate Adjutant, Inspector General, and the Confederate Quartermaster General.
>
> M686—Index to General Correspondence of the [Federal] Record and Pension Office, 1889–1920.
>
> M797—Case Files of Investigations of [Washington Federal Detectives] Levi C. Turner and Lafayette C. Baker.

Photographs

A collection of photographs of Civil War soldiers is in Anne J. Bailey and Walter J. Fraser Jr., *Portraits of Conflict: A Photographic History of Georgia in the Civil War* (Little Rock: University of Arkansas Free Press, 1997). Photographs of Confederate soldiers of all states are included in the following:

> Albaugh, William A. III. *Confederate Faces*. Salona Beach, CA: no publisher, 1970.
>
> ———. *More Confederate Faces: Photographs of Confederates*. Washington, DC: ABS Printers, 1972.
>
> Serrano, D. A. *Still More Confederate Faces*. Bayside, NY: Metropolitan Co., 1992.
>
> Turner, William A. *Even More Confederate Faces*. Orange, VA: Moss Publications, 1983.

The U.S. Army History Institute, Carlisle Barracks, Carlisle, Pennsylvania, copies photographs of Civil War soldiers on loan to the institute. It also accepts donations of information on all American veterans.

The following sources provide Civil War photographs over the Internet:

Civil War Photos, Library of Congress (high quality copies can be downloaded for free): http://www.loc.gov/pictures/collection/cwp

CivilWarPhotos.Net: http://www.civilwarphotos.net

Digital History: http://www.digitalhistory.uh.edu/timeline/timelineN.cfm

Picture History: http://www.picturehistory.com

Confederate Rosters

Many Confederate rosters did not survive the war, and for some soldiers documentation must be found in other sources such as the salt distribution to wives and widows of Confederate soldiers and other records discussed in this chapter. An incomplete copy of "Persons Exempt from Conscription under Confederate Act of 2/17/1864," is in Record Group 193-12-14 at the Georgia Archives in Morrow.

Rosters on Microfilm

The Georgia Archives has microfilm of the rosters from the National Archives upon which the above Georgia service records were compiled in Drawer 279, Boxes 61–93, and Drawer 290, Box 3. The Georgia Archives also has some original Confederate muster rolls in Record Groups 22 and 58, some arranged by county.

Compiled Rosters by County

A resolution of the Georgia Legislature in 1862 called for the compilation of a roster of the state's Confederate soldiers in 1863, but that effort was unsuccessful. In 1868 individual counties compiled rosters of their respective soldiers, listing places of residence since the war. Only a few of these rosters have been found, although some were published in local newspapers. See, for example:

"Hancock County Civil War Soldiers." *Georgia Genealogical Magazine* 97 (1985): 201–205.

"Notes on Some Chatham County Veterans of the Civil War." *Georgia Genealogical Society Quarterly* 31 (1995): 233–34.

Roster Committee Records

In 1898 the state of Georgia appointed a local roster committee of Confederate veterans in each county. The rosters they compiled, when the rosters survive, are found in their respective courthouses. The few rosters that have been microfilmed are in the county records microfilm collection at the Georgia Archives, filed by county and usually on the same reel as the annual pension lists.

Most Georgia county histories include rosters of local Confederate units, almost always from the work of these 1898–1899 roster committees. As these rosters were based in memories, these records consequently document the service of many men for whom no original records survive. These local roster committees also overlooked thousands of individuals, including some entire companies. The committees frequently were confused on names and even recorded two or more men of a similar name as the same person.

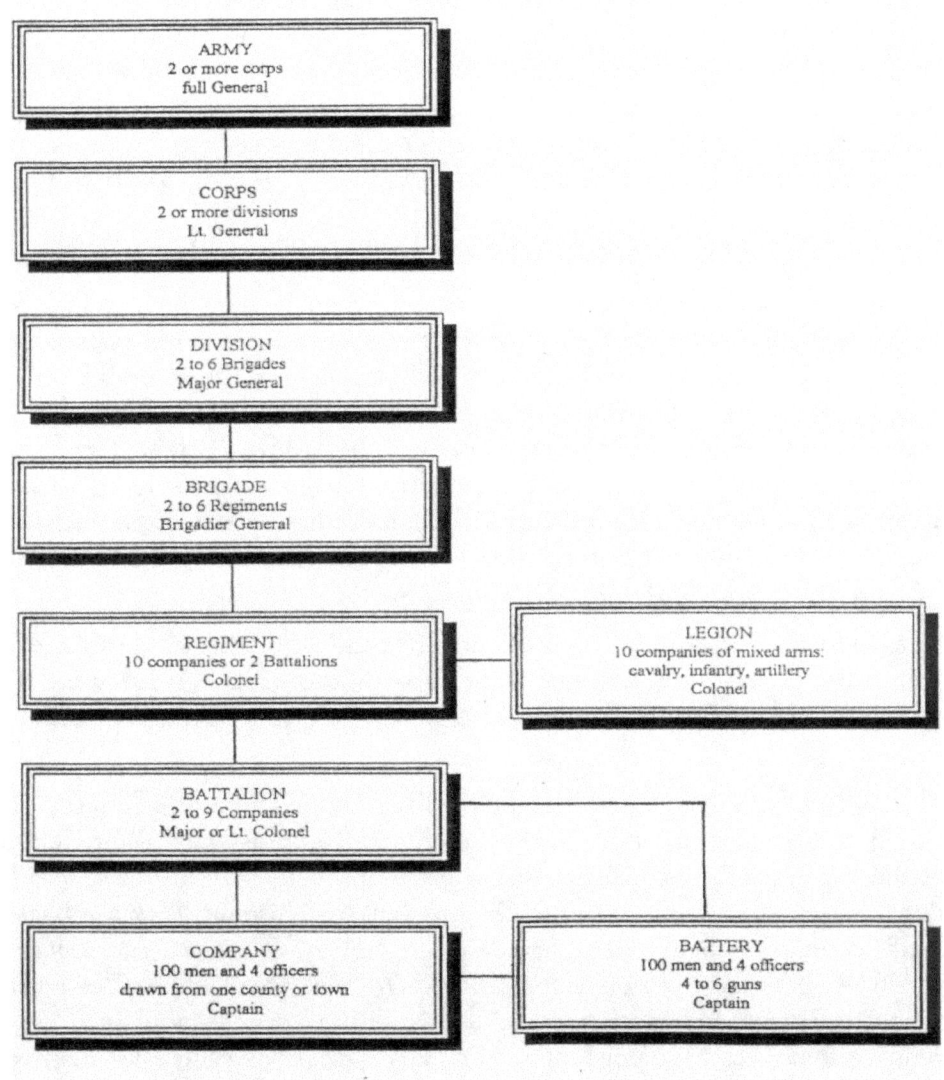

Figure 5 - The organization of Confederate troops during the American Civil War.

Published Rosters

The most complete published roster for Georgia is *Georgia Confederate Soldiers*, 4 vols. (Wilmington, NC: Broadfoot Pub. Co., 1998). This is an index to all National Archives compiled service records of Georgia Confederate infantry, artillery, cavalry, and state units. The other statewide publication of Georgia Civil War rosters is Lillian Henderson, *Roster of the Confederate Soldiers of Georgia,* 6 vols., and a cumulative index, (various state publishers, 1959–1964). This series represents the work of the Georgia State Roster Commission (1903–1930). The commission compiled rosters from Confederate pension rolls, some original rosters now at the Georgia Archives, and some of the records now at the National Archives. These books only include Confederate volunteer infantry regiments and not cavalry, artillery, legions, state troops, militia, etc., although these other units are included in the previously mentioned Alphabetical Card File catalog of the Georgia Archives. Rosters of the Georgia State Line during the Civil War are published in William Harris Bragg, *Joe Brown's Army: The Georgia State Line, 1862–1865* (Macon, GA: Mercer University Press, 1987). Rosters of the Georgia Militia during the war are published in William R. Scaife and William Harris Bragg, *Joe Brown's Pets: The Georgia Militia in the Civil War* (Cartersville, GA: Civil War Publications, 1999.) For the Home Guard companies see "A Partial Roster of the Georgia Confederate Home Guards," *Georgia Genealogical Society Quarterly* 31 (1995): 146–155.

Confederate Unit Histories and Service Records by County

Many unit histories of Georgia Civil War companies, regiments, etc., which include rosters, have been and are being published. Some Civil War rosters are also included in back issues of Georgia's genealogical periodicals. Karen Thompson Ledford has published books on Confederate rosters and cemetery records for the Northeast Georgia counties of Banks, Franklin, Habersham, Hart, Jackson, Rabun, Stephens, and White, in her *These Men Wore Grey* series. Also see William S. Smedlund's book of Confederate camp sites, *Camp Fires of Georgia Troops, 1861–1865,* rev. ed. (Atlanta: R. J. Taylor, Jr., Foundation, 1995) and a list of newspaper articles relating to various Georgia Civil War units is "Some Notes on Georgia and Georgians in the War Between the States," *Georgia Genealogical Magazine* 36 (1996): 213–219.

Several sources exist for background on a Confederate unit. For the whole Confederacy, there are Joseph H. Crute, *Units of the Confederate States Army* (Midlothian, VA: Derwent Books, 1987) and Stewart Sifakis, *Compendium of the Confederate Armies,* 10 vols. (New York: Facts On File, 1992).

The Georgia Archives has a rough and incomplete list of units by Georgia county on microfilm in Drawer 71, Box 80, and in a binder in the Reference Room as "Civil War Reference Information on Units." The Archives also has a free brochure, *Tracing the Activities of a Georgia Civil War Unit at the Georgia Archives.* Also see the Georgia Capitol Museum, *Hallowed Banners* (Atlanta, GA: Office of Secretary of State, 2005) and William F. Fox, *Regimental Losses of the Civil War, 1861–1865* (Albany, NY: Albany Publishing, 1889). The Georgia Archives has an unpublished list of Georgia Confederate unit designations. The National Archives and Records Administration, 700 Pennsylvania Ave., SW, Washington DC 20408 also has such a list in Boxes 6 and 7, Entry 459, Record Group 109—War Department Collection of Confederate Records.

At the beginning of the National Archives microfilm of each Civil War unit's compiled service records can be found "locality" or service summary cards that give something of the unit's history and organization. These cards have also been microfilmed separately as "Compiled Records Showing Military Service," National Archives microfilm M861 for the Confederates and M594 for the Union. Broadfoot Publishing has published these records in book form as part of its new supplement to the *War of the Rebellion* series.

Union Service Records

Records of Georgians, black and white, in the United States service during the Civil War are difficult to locate. A Georgian who reached the Union lines might have worked as a scout, forager, spy, contractor north of the Ohio River, sailor in the Navy, or as a soldier in any Union unit that happened to be present (particularly Tennessee units, but even units from Illinois and New York).

Records of Service

Unlike the Confederate records, the records of Union service frequently are not centralized, lack comprehensive indexes, and are not on microfilm. The most complete index for Union Civil War soldiers, black and white, for the nation as a whole is the National Park Service's Soldiers and Sailors Civil War database: http://www.itd.nps.gov/cwss/. It is free and for each soldier listed, a link is provided to a detailed history of (and in some instances her) unit. This database and related databases are also accessed through the subscription website Ancestry.com.

No guides like the Neagles and Segars books on Confederate sources exist for Union soldiers. For detailed descriptions of the records for Union soldiers at the National Archives see Inventory No. 1: *Records of the Headquarters of the Army*; Inventory No. 17: *Records of the Adjutant General's Office*; Inventory No. 187: *General Records of the Department of the Treasury*; and Inventory No. 17: *Inventory of the Records of the Accounting Offices of the Department of the Treasury*.

Compiled Service Record

Federal compiled service records for soldiers, black and white, at the National Archives frequently give such valuable genealogical information as county of birth and age. These records can be searched and copies ordered from Military Records, National Archives and Records Administration, Washington, DC 20408. Many soldiers of one state enlisted in regiments raised by or in other states. For example, more than 2,000 Georgians enlisted in Tennessee federal units. Filed at the end of the last roll of the Union service records microfilm for a particular unit can be found miscellaneous additional records, arranged alphabetically by soldier. Some of these papers refer to men not found in the unit's compiled service records. For the 1st Georgia Infantry Battalion, see *A North Georgia Journal of History*, 4 vols. to date (Alpharetta, GA: Legacy Publications, 1989–), 1: 299–300.

A comprehensive index to Union compiled service records is the *Roster of Union Soldiers, 1861–1865*, 33 vols. (Wilmington, NC: Broadfoot Pub. Co., 1997). The National Archives at Atlanta, however, has all of the available indexes by state for the Union and Confederate forces. The subscription website Fold3 is copying this index from the original indexes in the National Archives and Records Administration.

The Broadfoot Company has published an index to the compiled service records at the National Archives of the African American soldiers, *U.S. Colored Troops in the Civil War*. It includes the

21st, 33rd, 34th, 42nd, 44th, 136th, 137th, and 138th United States Colored Troops, units that included most of the 3,486 African Americans recruited in Georgia. The compiled service records of African American Union troops are being included on the commercial website Ancestry.com and Fold3. Special records of the 44th and other African American federal units are included in Record Group 249—Records of the Commissioner of Prisoners (Commutation of Rations Claims); Record Group 105—Records of the Bureau of Refugees, Freedmen, and Abandoned Lands (Entry 224); and Record Group 94—Records of the Adjutant General (Bureau for Colored Troops). Some of the former owners of members of the 44th USCT are identified in "Some African American Soldiers of the Civil War and Their Former Masters," *Georgia Genealogical Society Quarterly* 39 (2003): 170–171 and "Some Former Georgia Slaves and Their Masters," *Georgia Genealogical Society Quarterly* 40 (2004): 2–17. Also see E. Raymond Evans, *Contributions by United States Colored Troops (USCT) of Chattanooga & North Georgia* (Chattanooga: B. C. M. Foster, 2003), Jeannette Braxton Secret, *Guide to Tracing Your African-American Civil War Ancestor* (Bowie, MD: Heritage Books, 1997), and Clarence L. Mohr, *On the Threshold of Freedom: Masters and Slaves in Civil War Georgia* (Athens: University of Georgia Press, 1986), 86–92.

Lists of federal Civil War officers have been published. See U.S. Adjutant General's Office, *Official Army Register of the Volunteer Force of the United States Army for the Years 1861, '62, '63, '64, and '65* (Washington, DC: Government Printing Office, 1867). The modern reprint includes a comprehensive index. Also see William H. Powell and Edward Shippen, *Officers of the Army and Navy (Regular) Who Served in the Civil War* (Philadelphia, PA.: L. R. Hamersley and Company, 1892).

One sometimes successful way of locating an ancestor in the Union service, no matter what his regiment, is to have a search made for a pension record. A list of federal pension records for the Civil War is National Archives microcopy T288—*General Index to Pension Files, 1861–1934*. This index is also accessible on the Internet at the Ancestry.com website. Pension and service records can be searched and copies obtained for a fee from Military Records Branch, National Archives and Records Administration, Washington, DC 20408 and from the National Archives website.

The original rosters of federal units include place of residence for almost every soldier, information not included on microfilm of the compiled service records. These rosters are available for research at the National Archives in Washington, DC.

White Georgians in the Federal Forces

Several publications of white Georgians serving in the federal forces are available. A list of the men in the 1st Georgia Battalion of the United States Army, the only official Georgia unit, is published in June Hart Wester, "List of Volunteer Union Soldiers of Georgia," *Georgia Genealogical Society Quarterly* 15 (1979): 83–86. The records of these men, from National Archives microcopy M385, are also on microfilm at the Georgia Archives in Drawer 279, Box 34.

Guerrillas

Several Georgians served in the federal forces but have no records included in the above. See for example, "Forgotten Union Army Guerrillas," *A North Georgia Journal of History,* 4 vols. to date (Alpharetta, GA: Legacy Communications, 1989–), 1: 270–300.

Galvanized Yankees

Many Confederates left the horrors of federal prison camps by becoming "Galvanized Yankees," former Confederates in the Union army. An index to these records is on Rolls 23 to 26 of National Archives microcopy M1290—*Index to Compiled Service Records of Volunteer Union Soldiers Not Enlisted by State*. The service records of the former Confederates in the 1st through 6th U.S. Volunteers are in National Archives microcopy M1017. For historical background, see Dee Brown, *The Galvanized Yankees* (Lincoln: University of Nebraska Press, 1963).

Medical Records

The Military Records Branch of the National Archives also has, in addition to the compiled service records by state and then by unit, a separate collection of medical records for the Civil War. See "Medical Records of Georgia Union Soldiers, 1864–1865," *Northwest Georgia Historical and Genealogical Society Quarterly* 26 (4) (1994): 6–10, created from a microfilm copy at the Georgia Archives in Drawer 309, Box 98.

Spies, Guides, Detectives, and Scouts

Record Group 94 — Records of the Adjutant General, at the National Archives in Washington, has fragmentary records of spies, guides, detectives, and scouts working for the Union in Entries 3 and 92. See "Union Spies, Guides, Scouts, Railroad Operatives and Other Personnel, 1862–1865," *Georgia Genealogical Magazine* 33 (1993): 165–175, created from a list on microfilm in Drawer 289, Box 74, of the Microfilm Library of the Georgia Archives. Some reports (Entry 36) and pay receipts (Entry 95) of federal spies and scouts are found in the National Archives in Record Group 110—Records of the Provost Marshal. However, as most intelligence people were employed by whatever means by individual generals and bureaucrats, no complete set of their records survive. See also "Some Federal Spies in Civil War North Georgia," *Georgia Genealogical Society Quarterly* 35 (1999): 180.

Prisoners of the Confederacy

Records of people held prisoner by the Confederate States of America are fragmentary, consisting in some camps of only lists of the dead. For records of specific camps, see Henry Putney Beers, *The Confederacy* (Washington, DC: National Archives, 1986). Also, in Entry 10 of Record Group 249—Records of the Commissary General of Prisoners, at the National Archives can be found letters written about missing, captured, or released Union soldiers of the Civil War. The indexes, arranged by year and then alphabetically, are in Entry 9.

For information on how to research the members of the administration, guards, and prisoners at Camp Sumter (Andersonville) Confederate prison in today's Macon County see "Researching Andersonville Prisoners, Guards, and Others" in Robert S. Davis, *Ghosts and Shadows of Andersonville* (Macon, GA: Mercer University Press, 2010), 249–53. For federal prisoners held by the Confederates see: www.civilwarprisoners.com

Other Record Groups.

The National Archives has a number of other scattered record groups that relate to federal Civil War service including correspondence received by the paymaster, the quartermaster claims, and the crudely indexed records of correspondence relating to volunteer soldiers (V. S.) See Kenneth W. Munden and Henry Putney Beers, *The Union* (Washington, DC: National Archives, 1986).

Letters and Other Information

Several National Archives micro-publications lead to letters and information on federal service in the Civil War. These include the following:

- M495—Indexes to Letters Received by the Secretary of War, 1861–1870.
- M502—Registers of Letters Received by the Secretary of the Treasury Relating to Claims, 1864–1887.
- M725—Indexes to Letters Received by the Office of the [Federal] Adjutant General Main Series.
- M1064—Letters Received by the Commission Branch of the Adjutant General's Office, 1863–1870.
- M1105—Registers of the Records and Proceedings of the U.S. Army General Courts-Martial, 1809–1890.
- M1290—Index to Compiled Service Records of Volunteer Union Soldiers Not Enlisted by State.

Federal Unit Histories

For the history of Union units, black and white, in Georgia see Robert S. Davis, "White and Black in Blue: The Recruitment of Federal Units in Civil War North Georgia," *Georgia Historical Quarterly* 85 (2001): 348–374. For other histories of the official federal units, see:

- Bahn, Gilbert S. *Infestation of Yankees: Reference Guide to Union Troops in Confederate Territory.* Baltimore: Clearfield, 1998.
- Dyer, Frederick H. *Compendium of the War of the Rebellion.* Des Moines, IA: Dyer Publishing, 1908.
- Fox, William F. *Regimental Losses of the Civil War, 1861–1865.* Albany, NY: Albany Publishing, 1889.
- Welcher, Frank J. *The Union Army, 1861–1865: Organization and Operations.* 2 vols. Bloomington: Indiana University Press, 1989.
- *The Union Army: A History of the Military Affairs in the Loyal States.* 8 vols. 1908. Reprint Wilmington, NC: Broadfoot Pub., 1997. This work does not include Georgia or the African American units, although it does include the Tennessee regiments (Volume 4) in which some 2,000 Georgians served. The Navy is included in Volume 7.

Federal Veterans Organization

Many Civil War veterans who had served in the Union Army moved to Georgia after the war. The Grand Army of the Republic (GAR) was a veterans' organization of men who served in the federal military during the Civil War and who never took up arms against the United States. Most of the annual proceedings of the Georgia Division of the GAR, including obituaries of members and other biographical information, are in the holdings of the Library of Congress and the Minnesota State Historical Society. See Albert E. Smith Jr., *The Grand Army of the Republic: A Guide to Resources in the General Collections of the Library of Congress* (Washington, DC: Library of Congress, 1996). The only known copy is in the Local History and Genealogy Department of the Library of Congress. The Library of Congress also has an 1894 roster of the Georgia posts of the GAR.

Civilians in Confederate Georgia

Many civilians, as well as soldiers, appear in previously-cited indexes such as the Alphabetical Card File catalog of the Georgia Archives and the National Archives microfilm of indexes to letters received by the Confederate Secretary of War and Adjutant General. See, for example, "Some Georgia Civil War Women," *Georgia Genealogical Magazine* 29 (1989): 104–105; "Civilians Held Prisoner in Atlanta, 1865–1866," *Georgia Genealogical Society Quarterly* 38 (2002): 36–38; "Federal Records of Civilians in North Georgia," *Heritage Quest* 16 (3) (2000): 112–113; and "Georgians With Federal Court Martial, 1861–1865," *Georgia Genealogical Society Quarterly* 37 (2001): 117–121. A list of soldiers and civilians held by the Union Army in Georgia after the war and before the restoration of civil authority appears in Record Group 393—Records of U.S. Continental Commands, Part 1, at the National Archives in Washington, DC. Also see Vicki Bett's site on newspaper articles from throughout the country (1861–1865) on social history (particularly women) during the Civil War (free): http://www.uttyler.edu/vbetts.

The National Archives microcopy M345—*Union Provost Marshal's File of Papers Relating to Individual Civilians* indexes by every name thousands of miscellaneous records of all sorts on southern soldiers and civilians found in that file and also in M416—*Union Provost Marshal's File of Papers Relating to Two or More Civilians*. See, for example, "Some North Georgians During the Civil War," *Northwest Georgia Historical and Genealogical Society Quarterly* 26 (Winter 1994): 2–3. A list of families allowed to remain within three miles of the federal railroad in Northwest Georgia in 1864 appears in Record Group 393, Entry 2671, at the National Archives in Washington, DC. Also see "The General Sherman Census of Atlanta, September 1864," *Georgia Genealogical Magazine* 31 (1991): 132–141. The original of this record is "The Book of Exodus," item 561/562, Record Group 393 Records of Continental Commands, part I, Entry 2584, Letters Received Department of Mississippi, Box 2, National Archives and Records Administration, 701 Pennsylvania Ave. NW, Washington, DC 20408-0001.

Civilians Doing Business with the Confederacy

The National Archives and Records Administration in Washington, DC, has indexed quartermaster records of Confederate civilian workers, free and slave, in Entry 58, Record Group 109 War Department Collection of Confederate Records. A list of the major Georgia contractors is in "Georgia Suppliers to the Confederacy," *Georgia Genealogical Society Quarterly* 21 (1985): 144–48. The records of these companies and individuals are found on National Archives microcopy M346—*Confederate Papers Relating to Citizens or Business Firms*, available from Latter-day Saints Family History Centers as Reels 1664682 through 1665838. These records have been copied onto the subscription website Fold3. Correspondence between private contractors and the state of Georgia during the Civil War is indexed under "Miscellaneous" on microfilm in Drawer 253,

Box 71, at the Georgia Archives as a separate part of the Alphabetical Card Index File of the Confederate Pension Office.

Quartermaster Records

The National Archives and Records Administration in Washington, DC has quartermaster records of Confederate civilian workers, free and slave, in Entries 56, 57, and 60 of Record Group 109—*War Department Collection of Confederate Records*. The index, Entry 58, will be searched by mail. For historical background on African American services to the Confederacy, see Charles Kelly Barrow, et al., *Forgotten Confederates: An Anthology About Black Southerners* (No place: Southern Heritage, 1995).

Ordnance Works Records

The Georgia Archives (Drawer 142, Box 25; Drawer 288, Boxes 69–76; and Drawer 289, Boxes 1–3, 18), the Washington Memorial Library in Macon, and the University of Georgia Libraries have a special microfilm copy of the surviving records of the Confederate ordnance works of Atlanta, Augusta, Dalton, Macon, and Savannah, as well as Nashville, Tennessee. This microfilm is taken from Chapter IV, Record Group 109—War Department Collection of Confederate Records, at the National Archives in Washington, DC. Buried within these records are lists and other documentation of workers in the ordnance works.

Maps of Georgia

The Library of Congress American Memory Collection includes Civil War-era maps from the Library of Congress, Library of Virginia, and Virginia Historical Society: http://lcweb2.loc.gov/ammem/collections/civil_war_maps.

Civil War maps of Georgia, especially along the route of Sherman's campaigns, show individual farms and communities. See, for example, George B. Davis, et al., *The Official Military Atlas of the Civil War* (Washington, DC: Government Printing Office, 1891–1895). Confederate maps of northwest Georgia, identifying major farms and other localities are in the National Archives, as described in *A Guide to Civil War Maps in the National Archives* (Washington, DC: National Archives, 1986); the William T. Sherman Papers of the Library of Congress; and the Henry D. Clayton Collection of the Alabama Department of Archives and History. For the latter, also see "Every Crossroads and Farm: Confederate General Henry DeLamar Clayton's Civil War Maps of Northwestern Georgia," *Georgia Historical Quarterly* 82 (Spring 1998).

Refugees North of the Ohio River

Thousands of Georgians traveled north of the Ohio River voluntarily to escape the war. They left no official records of their migration, although many of them lived in the already established communities of southerners in the southern counties of Illinois and Indiana, especially around Jeffersonville, Indiana. Some remained in the North as late as the 1870 census.

Federal soldiers sent other civilians north as "political prisoners." Records of some of them are found in the records of the Louisville, Kentucky, prison camp on Reel 95 of National Archives microcopy *M598—Selected Records of the War Department Relating to Confederate Prisoners of War* (largely available on the Internet subscription website Ancestry.com). Information on the reason for the arrest of some of these individuals can be found in the previously mentioned papers of the Union Provost Marshall in National Archives microfilms M345 and 416. No list of the approximately four hundred women and other textile workers sent from Roswell and Sweetwater to Louisville, Kentucky, by General Sherman has been found. See Michael D. Hitt, *Charged With Treason: Ordeal of 400 Mill Workers During Military Operations in Roswell, Georgia, 1864–1865* (Monroe, NY: Library Research Associates, 1991). Also see Mary Deborah Petite, *The Women Will Howl, the Union Army Capture of Roswell and New Manchester, Georgia, and the Forced Relocation of Mill Workers.* (Jefferson, NC: McFarland & Co., Inc, 2008).

Sequestration and Confiscation of Property

Records of Confederate sequestration and confiscation of property in Georgia are found among the Confederate court records in the National Archives at Atlanta. For information on records of federal confiscations, see "Without Right of Conquest: The Civil War Occupation and Restoration of the Findlay Foundry of Macon, Georgia," *Prologue: The Quarterly of the National Archives* 29 (1997): 301–315. The National Archives and Records Administration, 8601 Adelphi Road, College Park, MD, 20740-6001 has records of the United States permits to trade in occupied South in Record Group 56 Records of the Department of the Treasury. Those files cannot be searched by mail. For more information see Ludwell H. Johnson, "Northern Profit and Profiteers: The Cotton Rings of 1864–1865," *Civil War History* 12 (March 1966): 101–115.

Cemetery, Hospital, and Monument Records.

For Confederate soldiers, including Georgians, who are buried in Virginia cemeteries see Thomas M. Spratt, *Men in Gray Interments: Virginia Cemetery Series,* 15 vols. (Lovettsville, VA: Willow Bend Books, 1996). Confederates buried in Georgia and Georgia Confederates buried in other states during or after the war are included in Georgia Division, United Daughters of the Confederacy, *Roster of Confederate Graves,* 9 vols. (Atlanta: privately printed, 1995–1998, 2004). Also see Robert E. Zaworski, *Headstones of Heroes: The Restoration and History of Confederate Graves in Atlanta's Oakland Cemetery* (Paducah, KY: privately printed, 1998). Mississippi burials are listed in Betty Couch Wiltshire, *Mississippi Confederate Grave Registrations,* 2 vols. (Bowie, MD: Heritage Books, 1989). The *Georgia Genealogical Society Quarterly* also has published many Civil War cemetery records of Georgia "rebels" and also "Unreported Georgia Losses in the Civil War," in Volume 23 (1987): 188–191. The Georgia Archives has Confederate cemetery records for Georgia and some other states in the Church and Cemetery Vertical File.

More than forty years after the end of the Civil War, permanent, uniform markers were authorized for the graves of Confederate soldiers buried in national cemeteries. In accordance with an act of March 9, 1906, Congress adopted the same size and material for Confederate headstones as for Union deceased but altered the design to omit the shield and give the stones a pointed rather than rounded top. In 1929 the authorization was extended to graves in private cemeteries. On May 26, 1930, the War Department implemented regulations for Confederate headstones that also authorized the inscription of the Confederate Cross of Honor in a small circle on the front face of the stone above the standard inscription of the soldier's name, rank, company, and regiment.

Records of these headstones should be sought from the National Archives and Records Administration in Washington, DC. NARA has headstone application files, which may include Confederate headstone applications, in a number of separate series described below.

RECORD GROUP 92 (Records of the Office of the Quartermaster General)

    Carded Records of Headstone Contracts, 1879–1903 (available as National Archives Microfilm Publication M1845, Card Records of Headstones Provided for Deceased Union Civil War Veterans, ca. 1879–1903)

    Applications for Headstones in Private Cemeteries, 1879–1924 (arranged by state, county and cemetery).

    Applications for Headstones in Soldiers Homes, 1909–1923 (arranged by state, and name of soldier's home).

    Applications for Headstones, 1925–1963 (arranged by state, county and cemetery).

RECORD GROUP 15 (Records of the Office of Veterans Affairs)

    Applications for Headstones and Markers, FY 1965–1985 (need to know fiscal year of application)

Federal soldiers buried in national cemeteries are included in the federal government's series, *The Roll of Honor*, in twenty-seven volumes, expanded, reprinted, and indexed by the Genealogical Publishing Company, which has also made these volumes available on CD. See "North Georgia Soldiers on the *Roll of Honor*," *Northwest Georgia Historical and Genealogical Society Quarterly* 27, no. 4 (1995): 9 and Mimi Jo Butler, *Cobb County, Georgia, Cemeteries, Volume III: Marietta National Cemetery* (Marietta, GA: Cobb County Genealogical Society, 1994). A list of the first headstones provided to any federal veteran, wherever buried, is in National Archives microcopy M1845—*Card Records of Headstones Provided for Deceased Union Civil War Veterans, 1879–1903*. Also see National Archives microcopy M2014—*Burial Registers for Military Posts, 1768–1921*. The United States Department of Veterans Affairs provides a free service of identifying the location of graves of veterans of all wars through the Grave Locator: http://gravelocator.cem.va.gov/.

Many Confederate hospital records were not seized by the federal government at the end of the Civil War. These records document service for hundreds of Confederates where no other records exist and provide additional information such as date of death. Records not duplicated in the holdings of the National Archives concerning the patients of the Atlanta and some other Georgia Confederate hospitals are in the Stout Collection of the University of Texas in Austin. These records have recently been made available on microfilm. The Alabama Department of Archives and History has the patient register for the Confederate hospital in Selma. The register is indexed for Confederate and Union patients, by state and then alphabetically, in the Archives card catalog of "Confederate" records.

The Georgia Archives has microfilm of the records of the Confederate hospital in Columbus, Georgia, in Drawer 290, Box 3. The patient register of the Wayside Hospital, Highpoint, North Carolina, which gives county and state of birth, place of residence, and other information, is in microfilm Drawer 21, Box 43, at the Georgia Archives. See the abstracts of the Georgians by Pat Collins in the *Georgia Genealogical Society Quarterly* 14 (1978): 22–29 and the Private Manuscripts Section, AC 1973-0251 for Dr. Charles Hall's book of records of examinations of 1,500 Georgians found unfit for the Confederate draft. The latter record gives county and state of birth. The Hall materials are published in *Georgia Genealogical Society Quarterly* 36 (2000) 241–255. Also see the CD-ROM, *Two Confederate Hospitals & Their Patients* which includes a searchable database of Confederate Hospitals #1 and #2 in Atlanta.

Records of deaths and burials of Confederate and Union soldiers also appear in many other sources such as Georgia's genealogical periodicals. An incomplete but indexed reprint has been made of a federal government publication, now entitled *Confederate P.O.W.s: Soldiers & Sailors Who Died in Federal Prisons and Military Hospitals in the North* (St. Louis, MO: Ingmire Publications, 1984). The original record is on National Archives microcopy M918. Also see Rhoda Anne Bowen and Freda R. Turner, *Georgia Confederate Soldier Obituaries: Henry, Newton, and Rockdale Counties* (McDonough, GA: Henry County Genealogical Society, 1992). For information on Georgia's Confederate monuments, see Frank M. McKenney, *The Standing Army: History of Georgia's County Confederate Monuments* (Alpharetta, GA: privately printed, 1993) and Georgia Division, UDC, *Confederate Monuments and Markers in Georgia* (Fernandino Beach, FL: Wolfe Publishing Company, 2002). Also see Civil War monuments: http://www.civilwarmonumentsofthesouth.com.

Civil War Pension Records

The pension records for Confederate service and Union service are very different. However, both provide information for the war and sometimes for the years before and after. The 1910 federal census indicates survivors of the Confederate and Union armies but not which persons are pensioners. Letters from many pension applicants from many wars, but chiefly for Union and Confederate pensions, are indexed in National Archives microcopy *M686—Index to General Correspondence of the Record and Pension Office, 1889–1920*. Earlier correspondence is found in the records of the Volunteer Service Division, Bureau for Colored Troops, etc., of Record Group 94—Records of the Adjutant General at the National Archives in Washington, DC.

Federal Service Disability Pensions

General federal service disability pensions began in 1890, although severely disabled war injury veterans, widows and orphans of federal soldiers killed in the war, and impoverished parents of federal soldiers killed in the war received pensions earlier. For pensioners based on federal service, including black soldiers, see National Archives microcopy T288—*General Index to Pension Files, 1861–1934*; T289—*Organization Index to Pension Files* (Georgia is on Reels 25 and 26); and M1785—*Index to Pension Application Files of Remarried Widows Based on Service in the Civil War and Later Wars*, available through Latter-day Saints Family History Centers. An 1883 list of federal pensioners for the Civil War and the War of 1812 was published as *U.S. Senate Executive Document 84, Part 1, 47th Congress, 2nd Session, Serial Number 2078* (Washington, DC: Government Printing Office, 1883). The Georgia pensioners have been published from this list several times, including in *Georgia Genealogical Society Quarterly* 15 (1979): 169–200. Also see National Archives Microcopy M1749—*Historical Register of National Homes for Disabled Soldiers, 1866–1938*.

Federal Civil War pension files must be requested from Military Records, National Archives and Records Administration, Washington, DC 20408. When ordering a pension file, insist on having copies made of all of the contents of the file. Some Union widows pensions have been copied onto the subscription website Fold3. A list of pensions for service by white Georgians in the 1st Georgia Battalion, USA, is "Some Federal Civil War Pension Applications for Georgia Service," *Northwest Georgia Historical and Genealogical Society Quarterly* 30 (2) (1998): 5–8. Records from the pensions of many of these men are found in the Robert Barker Collection of the McClung Collection, Knoxville, Tennessee, (also on microfilm at the University of Georgia Libraries). Some Confederate veterans and widows of Confederate veterans mistakenly thought that the federal government offered pensions to them prior to 1953. Their rejected claims are in the National Archives and are indexed in the same microfilmed indexes listed above.

Pensions for Injured and Destitute Confederate Veterans

The State of Georgia provided money for artificial limbs to Confederate veterans in 1877, war injury pensions in 1886, pensions to impoverished Confederate veterans in 1894, pensions to widows of veterans in 1900, and pensions to Confederate veterans and widows of veterans with property worth less than $1,500 in 1907. The property restrictions were lifted in 1919. See James R. Young, "Confederate Pensions in Georgia, 1886–1929," *Georgia Historical Quarterly* 66 (1982): 47–52. The pensions went to resident honorably-discharged veterans, and their widows, of the Southern cause and to Georgia Confederate veterans and widows living in states that did not give Confederate pensions. All of the files for Confederate pensions at the Georgia Archives have been scanned onto its website: http://cdm.sos.state.ga.us/cdm4/pension.php.

These pension files are also on microfilm at the Georgia Archives in Drawers 271 to 277, with the index to veterans, widows, and witnesses in Drawer 261, Boxes 13 to 51. This index has been published as Virgil D. White, *Index to Georgia Civil War Confederate Pension Files* (Waynesboro, TN: National Historical Pub. Co., 1997).

The regular Georgia pension files also have two supplements, both included in the Georgia Archives Virtual Vault: http://cdm.sos.state.ga.us/cdm4/pension.php. Supplement 1 to the pension files is on microfilm in Drawer 277, Boxes 13–18. Supplement Two at the Georgia Archives has never been microfilmed. It is in Record Group 58-1-1, Boxes 591–630. These two supplements contain papers previously misfiled and also a few pension files of persons accused of falsifying pension applications. An index to these two supplements has been published as Ted O. Brooke and Linda Geiger, *Index to Georgia's Confederate Pension Supplements* (Cumming, GA: privately printed, 1999).

Related Pension Records

Other related records of Georgia Confederate pensioners from Record Group 58 at the Georgia Archives include the following:

    Record Group 58-1-2—Excerpts from Soldiers' Applications by Name, Unit, and State

    Record Group 58-1-3—Lists of Pensioners by County

    Record Group 58-1-5—Reports of Removals, Deaths, and Transfers, 1908–1932

    Record Group 58-1-5—General Correspondence, 1905–1961. From this there has been published "Genealogical Letters about Georgia Confederates, 1917–1937," *Georgia Genealogical Society Quarterly* 30 (1994): 218–22

    Record Group 58-1-6—Pension Payrolls, 1908–1967

    Record Group 58-1-8—Final Settlements of Pension Payments

The Georgia Archives has microfilm of county copies of many of the annual local pension lists.

Other State Confederate Pension Records

Each of the former Confederate states and the states of Kentucky, Missouri, and Oklahoma eventually offered some form of pensions to their respective resident Confederate veterans and widows, including Georgians who had moved there; see for example, F. W. Weatherbee Jr., comp., *Georgia Veterans and Their Widows who Applied for Confederate Pensions in Alabama* (Montgomery, AL: privately printed, 1991) and see Desmond Walls Allen, *Where to Write for Confederate Pension Records* (Bryant, AR: privately printed, 1991). Indexes have been published for the pension files of Arkansas, Florida, Georgia, Kentucky, Mississippi, Missouri, Oklahoma, South Carolina, Tennessee, and Texas.

The records created by these states frequently contain a great deal of personal information. For example, the resident Confederate pension records of the state of Alabama include a 1907 and a 1921 census of Confederate veterans (many of whom served in Georgia but had moved to Alabama after the war) that, for each soldier, gives his county, state, and date of birth.

In 1911, Arkansas sent questionnaires to its Confederate veterans, hundreds of whom had Georgia roots. The questionnaires asked each veteran for his respective genealogies for three generations back. The responses have been published as Bobbie J. McLane and Capitola Glazner, *Arkansas 1911 Census of Confederate Veterans,* 3 vols. (Hot Springs, AR: Hot Springs National Park, 1977). Also see "Some Arkansas Confederate Veterans with Georgia Roots," *Georgia Genealogical Society Quarterly* 38 (2002): 160–180. Tennessee has similar published questionnaires of Confederate and Union veterans for 1915–1922. See Gustavus W. Dyer and John T. Moore, *The Tennessee Civil War Veterans Questionnaires,* 5 vols. (Greenville, SC: Southern Historical Press, 1985).

Confederate Soldiers' Home

The Confederate Soldiers' Home of Georgia opened to veterans in Atlanta in 1901 and later housed widows of Confederate veterans. Residency in the Soldiers' Home was available in place of pension payments. Some 1,200 people resided there at different times until it closed in 1967. See R. B. Rosenburg, "The House That Grady Built: The Fight for the Confederate Soldiers' Home of Georgia," *Georgia Historical Quarterly* 74 (1990): 399–432. The original records of this institution are at the Georgia Archives in Record Group 24–16. See "Records of Confederate Soldiers Home of Georgia," *Georgia Genealogical Society Quarterly* 27 (1991): 103. For historical background, see R. B. Rosenberg, *Living Monuments: Confederate Soldiers' Homes in the New South* (Chapel Hill: University of North Carolina Press, 1993). The register book is on microfilm at the Georgia Archives in Drawer 252, Boxes 2, 3, and 5. A list of the biographies of the veterans of Georgia's Soldiers' Home was published in *Georgia Genealogical Society Quarterly* 23 (1987): 1–6. Also see "Applications by Veterans and Widows of Confederate Veterans to the Georgia Soldier's Home," *Georgia Genealogical Society Quarterly* 27 (1991): 99–101 (veterans) and 102 (widows). A book is in process of abstracts from the three registers of all Confederate veterans admitted to the Georgia Soldiers Home, 1901–1941.

Civil War Miscellaneous

Other sources for information from the Civil War include:

Brinsfield, John W., et al. *Faith in the Fight: Civil War Chaplains* (Mechanicsburg, PA: Stackpole Book, 2006) and Gerald J. Smith, *Smite them hip and thigh! Georgia Methodist Ministers in the Confederate Military* (n.p., 2010).

Cole, Garold L. *Civil War Eyewitnesses: An Annotated Bibliography of Books and Articles, 1955–1986.* Columbia, SC: University of South Carolina Press, 1980.

Dornbush, Charles Emil. *Military Bibliography of the Civil War.* 4 vols. New York: New York Public Library, 1961–1987.

Garman, James Edward. "Materials for Writing Histories of Georgia Confederate Regiments: A Bibliographical Study." Master's thesis, Emory University, 1961.

Murdock, Eugene Converse. *The Civil War in the North.* New York: Garland, 1987. This book is not indexed by unit; the table of contents provides better access to this valuable book than its crude indexes.

Sellars, John R. *Civil War Manuscripts: A Guide to Collections in the Library of Congress.* Washington, DC: Library of Congress, 1986.

Smith, Albert E. *Civil War Diaries and Personal Narratives, 1960–1994: A Select Bibliography of Books in the General Collections of the Library of Congress.* Washington, DC: Library of Congress, 1997.

War Department, Office of the Chief of Staff. *Bibliography of State Participation in the Civil War, 1861–1866.* Washington, DC: Government Printing Office, 1913.

Wiley, Bell I., et al. *Civil War Books: A Critical Bibliography.* Baton Rouge: Louisiana State University Press, 1967. This book is not indexed by unit.

Wright, John H. *Compendium of the Confederacy: An Annotated Bibliography.* Wilmington, NC: Broadfoot, 1989.

The War of the Rebellion and Related Works

The most extensive collection of Civil War material ever created was compiled and published under the auspices of the U.S. War Department, with the initial title of *Official Records of the War of the Rebellion* (1881–1901). The set later was renamed *The War of the Rebellion: A Compilation of the Official Records of the Union and Confederate Armies,* but it frequently is called the *Official Records* or "the O.R." The collection is assembled into 128 books that are organized into seventy volumes in four series. Most of the volumes were issued in multiple parts, resulting in the large number of books. Volumes fifty-four and fifty-five, which were intended as a special index to Series I, were never published. Documents in the *Official Records* are the official letters and reports of the two military forces during the Civil War, and even obscure incidents are covered. Many persons are named in the *Official Records,* for the widest variety of reasons. However, the original printers are known to have had difficulty reading the manuscripts and also corrected "errors" and frequently changed the spellings of proper names.

The *Official Records* can be found in many large research libraries, in either its originally issued set or a reprint edition. However, there are two major websites that offer free digital access to the materials. The Cornell University Library features the *Official Records* and the *Official Records of the Union and Confederate Navies* series as a part of its Making of America project at:

http://ebooks.library.cornell.edu/m/moawar/waro.html. The *Official Records* were scanned using optical character recognition. The Department of History at Ohio State University hosts www.ehistory.osu.edu and provides free access to the *Official Records* as a part of its Primary Sources section. This version of the records features PDF files of the pages, so they can be viewed as published.

The original indexes are invaluable for identifying persons referred to only by surnames in the records. They refer the reader to the series number and the volume number. The "volume" referred to can be one to six physical books and the reader will have to check the index in the back of each book in the "volume."

Also of help in sorting out which volumes to read is the five-volume publication by the National Archives, *Military Operations of the Civil War: A Guide Index to the Official Records of the Union and Confederate Armies, 1861–1865* (Washington, DC: National Archives, 1986). Volume 1 of *Military Operations* has been microfilmed by the National Archives, with additional material, as microcopy M1036. Volumes 2 through 5 are on microfilm M1815. Also see Ronald A. Mosocco, *The Chronological Tracking of the American Civil War in the Official Records of the War of the Rebellion* (Williamsburg, Va.: James River Pubs., 1993) and Alan C. and Barbara A. Aimone, *A User's Guide to the Official Records of the War of the Rebellion* (Shippensburg, Md.: White Mane, 1993).

Broadfoot Publishing Company, Wilmington, North Carolina, has published a well-indexed 100-volume supplement to the *Official Records*. Material for these additional volumes has been obtained from the National Archives, Civil War newspapers, and private manuscript collections.

The Broadfoot Company has also reprinted several compilations of Civil War material while adding detailed indexes to battles, personal name, place name, and military unit, including Confederate works cited elsewhere, and: *History of Pennsylvania Volunteers, Medical and Surgical History of the Civil War, Military Order of the Loyal Legion of the United States, Papers of the Military Historical Society of Massachusetts*, and *Report on the Conduct of the War.*

The Library of Congress, as part of its free Chronicling America database includes the *National Tribune* from 1877 through 1917 (the newspaper ceased publication in 1927), the newspaper for Union Civil War veterans. It includes letters, reminiscences, articles, etc., on the Civil War that can be searched by name: http://chroniclingamerica.loc.gov/. For records of national Civil War veterans organizations see "From the Ashes of War: Some Little Known Black and White Civil War Organizations," *Heritage Quest* no. 57 (May–June 1995): 11–12. Women who served as soldiers in the Civil War are discussed in such works as DeAnne Blanton and Lauren M. Cook, *They Fought Like Demons: Women Soldiers in the American Civil War* (Baton Rouge: Louisiana State University Press, 2002).

Daily Events During the War

To learn about events of any day during the Civil War, see the following:

> Bishop, Chris, and Ian Drury. *1400 Days: The Civil War Day by Day.* New York: Gallery Books, 1990.
>
> Denny, Robert E. *The Civil War Years: A Day-by-Day Chronicle of the Life of a Nation.* New York: Sterling Publishing, 1992.

Navy History Division. *Civil War Naval Chronology, 1861–1865*. Washington, DC: Navy Department, 1971.

Terms, Tactics, and Equipment

For information on Civil War terms, tactics, and equipment, etc., consult Philip Katcher, *The Civil War Source Book* (New York: Facts On File, 1992); Francis A. Lord, *Civil War Collector's Encyclopedia* (Edison, NJ: Blue & Grey Press, 1991); or a similar work.

Antebellum Georgia, 1812–1860

Federal Census

Federal censuses were taken every ten years, starting in 1790. The censuses reflected the population on the first Monday of August for the censuses of 1790 through 1820 and on June 1 for the censuses of 1830 through 1900. The federal census records have been indexed and scanned onto the subscription websites Ancestry.com and HeritageQuest.

Through 1840, these censuses consisted of only the names of the heads of free households, with statistical descriptions of the members of the households, including non-family members. Georgia is missing all of the 1820 census for Franklin, Rabun, and Twiggs Counties. Many families were missed in returns or appear in microfilm for the wrong counties. On the Internet digitization of the 1820 census some pages and parts of pages are omitted but this does not affect the indexing. The 1820 census also has a list of manufacturers, by county, which is on microfilm (from National Archives microcopy M279—*Records of the 1820 Census of Manufactures*) in Drawer 331, Box 6, at the Georgia Archives. See "What You Should Know About the 1820 Census of Georgia," *Georgia Genealogical Society Quarterly* 26 (1990): 115–116.

The 1840 federal census has several unique features. Some pages of the 1840 census were reversed when bound and were thus microfilmed out of order, as reflected by the totals for each household. The City of Savannah was compiled and microfilmed separately from the rest of Chatham County. This census also has a special column for listing Revolutionary War pensioners (and all Revolutionary soldiers in some counties.) However, *A Census of Pensioners for Revolutionary or Military Services; With Their Names, Ages, and Places of Residence* (Washington, DC: Blair and Rives, 1841) does not include the Revolutionary War veterans incorrectly listed in the 1840 census as pensioners. The Georgia Archives also has statistical descriptions of agriculture, manufacturing, mining, etc., for Georgia counties in 1840 in microfilm Drawer 331, Boxes 30–31, copied from records at the National Archives.

Statewide indexes to Georgia census records in print for 1820–1840 include the following:

> Bradley, Homer H. II. "Georgia Cherokee Strip [Counties of Northwest Georgia]: 1840 U.S. Census," *Georgia Genealogical Society Quarterly* 5 (1969): 1–82.

> Georgia Historical Society. *Index to United States Census of Georgia for 1820,* rev. ed. Baltimore: Clearfield Company, 1989. The earlier edition used microfilm that omitted some of Lincoln County.

Jackson, Ronald Vern. *Georgia 1820 Census Index.* Bountiful, UT: Accelerated Indexing Systems International, 1976. Some references to Irwin County are actually to Jasper County.

———. *Georgia 1830 Census Index.* Bountiful, UT: Accelerated Indexing Systems International, 1976.

———, and Gary Ronald Teeples. *Georgia 1840 Census Index.* Bountiful, UT: Accelerated Indexing Systems International, 1977. Many of the Carroll County references are actually to Cass County.

Register, Alvaretta Kenan. *Index to the 1830 Census of Georgia.* Baltimore: Genealogical Publishing Company, 1974.

Sheffield, Eileen and Barbara Woods. *1840 Index to Georgia Census.* Baytown, TX: privately printed, 1969. This index does not give page numbers.

Woodson, Carter G. *Free Negro Heads of Families in the United States in 1830.* Washington, DC: The Association for the Study of Negro Life and History, 1925. A copy of this work is in the Southern History Collection of the Birmingham Public Library.

Beginning with the 1850 federal census, each free member of each household is named, with such information as age, sex, race, etc. All of the 1850 census of Georgia has been published on a county-by-county basis, and frequently county publications of census records prove to be more complete and accurate than the lists of names published as statewide indexes. Places of birth are usually given only as state or country; although, in the 1850 census for Muscogee, Tattnall, and Telfair Counties, county of birth is given for native Georgians, and in the 1850 census of Jefferson County the county of birth is given for everyone. The 1860 federal census of Camden, Pulaski, and Tattnall Counties gives county of birth for persons born in America, and the 1860 census of Chatham and Dougherty Counties gives this information for everyone.

The federal census records also have special schedules for events that occurred during the twelve months preceding the respective census day of June 1. The 1850, 1860, 1870, and 1880 censuses have agriculture schedules listing each farmer and describing each farm (except for the counties of Quitman through Wilkinson in the 1850 census) and a mortality schedule listing persons who died during the twelve months previous to June 1. The National Archives microfilm of the mortality schedules for 1850, 1860, and 1870 includes indexes to persons who died in those census years. These indexes for 1850 and 1860 include supplemental indexes to slave owners whose slaves had died. The 1850 and 1860 censuses also have slave schedules listing each slave owner or estate with a description of the slaves, but no names of slaves. The federal censuses for 1850 and 1860 also have social schedules providing statistical information (but no names) on each county. All of these extra schedules for Georgia are on microfilm at the Georgia Archives and the National Archives at Atlanta, which also has all population schedules for the whole country, taken from National Archives microcopy T1137.

The Georgia Archives has some county copies, made by the census takers, of the 1850 and 1860 censuses that can be used for comparison with the federal copies on National Archives microfilm. These county copies include, in the county records microfilm, Camden (1860), Clarke (1850, 1860), Crawford (1850), Decatur (1850, 1860), Franklin (1850, 1860), Lumpkin (1860), Marion (1860), Rabun (1860), and Taliaferro (1850, 1860) Counties. The Georgia Archives has a contemporary copy of the 1850 and 1860 federal censuses of Franklin County in Record Group 44-1-2. Luke Tate published a county copy of the 1860 census of Pickens County in *History of Pickens County* (Atlanta: W. W. Brown, 1934).

BASE MAP SOURCE: J. R. Butts, 'Map of the State of Georgia. 1859'.

Map 4 - The configuration of Georgia counties in 1860.

The following statewide indexes for Georgia, 1850–1860, are in book form:

    Acord, Arlis, and Martha S. Anderson. *An Index to the 1860 Georgia Federal Census.* LaGrange, GA: Family Tree, 1986.

    Cox, Jack F. *The 1850 Census of Georgia Slave Owners.* Baltimore: Clearfield, 1998.

    Hawes, Frank Mortimer. *New Englanders in Georgia Census of 1850.* Salt Lake City: Genealogical Society of Utah, 1946. A copy is at the Georgia Archives.

    Jackson, Ronald Vern. *Mortality Schedule: Georgia, 1850.* Bountiful, UT: Accelerated Indexing Systems International, 1979.

    ———. *Georgia 1860 Mortality Schedule.* Bountiful, UT: Accelerated Indexing Systems International, 1983.

    Jackson, Ronald Vern, et al. *Georgia 1850 Census Index.* Bountiful, UT: Accelerated Indexing Systems International, 1976. References to Upson County are actually to Richmond County and vice versa.

    Jackson, Ronald Vern, et al. *Georgia 1860 Census Index.* Bountiful, UT: Accelerated Indexing Systems International, 1986.

    Shaw, Aurora C. *1850 Georgia Mortality Schedules or Census.* Jacksonville, FL.: privately printed, 1971.

State Censuses, 1786–1866

Only a few scattered returns have survived of Georgia's state censuses, and these are usually little more than fragmentary lists of heads of households. For a list of the locations of the currently known state census records for Georgia see "Colonial and State Census Records of Georgia," *Georgia Genealogical Society Quarterly* 28 (1992): 260–263. These records include, by county, Bartow (1834), Bulloch (1865), Camden (fragment, 1786), Cass (1834), Chatham (1845, 1852), Cherokee (1834), Cobb (1834), Columbia (1859), Dooly (1845), Forsyth (1834, 1845), Gilmer (1834), Glynn (fragment, 1786), Greene (1798), Jasper (fragment, 1852), Laurens (1838), Liberty (fragment, 1786), Lumpkin (1834, 1838), Morgan (1852, 1853), Murray (1834), Newton (1838), Oglethorpe (1800), Paulding (1838), Richmond (City of Augusta only, 1852), Taliaferro (1827), Tattnall (1838), Terrell (1859), Union (1834) and Warren (1845) Counties. A pre-1859 undated census for Gilmer County is among the poor school records in Record Group 161-2-7 and an 1865 census of needy families is in the Gilmer County Inferior Court minutes (1865–1868) in microfilm reel 130-18, Georgia Archives, Morrow. Some national publications list other state censuses as having survived for Georgia that are actually only tax lists. For a detailed list of state censuses with published sources given, see Ann S. Lainhart, *State Census Records* (Baltimore: Genealogical Publishing Company, 1992), 33–35.

Land Lotteries, 1805–1833

Starting in 1805, Georgia dispensed lands acquired from the Indians to Georgia residents through lotteries. The statewide registration has survived for the 1805 lottery, but, except for a few scattered county lists of registrants, only the names of the winners are known for the 1807, 1820, 1821, 1827, 1832, and 1833 lotteries. These records supplement census records for Georgia and in the later lotteries can show migration across the state; military service in the American Revolution, the War of 1812 (the "late war with Great Britain and the Indians"), and the 1784–1797 Indian Wars; and other information. For the qualifications for the lotteries, see Robert S. Davis, *Research in Georgia* (Greenville, SC: Southern Historical Press, 1980), 183–195. **Important note:** In the nineteenth century, an orphan was someone (usually a minor) who has lost one or both of his or her parents. In the land lottery records, the term "orphans" refers only to persons under age twenty-one and not to adults. For detailed information on land lottery records see Paul K. Graham, *Georgia Land Lottery Research* (Atlanta: Georgia Genealogical Society, 2010).

The petitions of obvious genealogical value for land lots, filed by heirs of land lottery winners, are abstracted in Robert S. Davis, *The Georgia Land Lottery Papers, 1806–1914* (Greenville, SC: Southern Historical Press, 1979). The originals of the surviving petitions are arranged roughly by lottery and district in the Georgia Archives.

The state records of Georgia's land lotteries and grants are in the Georgia Archives. Additionally, the Georgia Archives has, on microfilm, county deed books containing thousands of deeds from the land lotteries of persons who won land lots, or their heirs, and also county lists of registrants for the land lotteries. Deeds for land lots won in the lotteries, like any other deeds, are almost always recorded in the county where the land lies at the time of the recording of the deed and not necessarily where the owner (or winner in the case of the land lotteries) resided. Sometimes the laws requiring the recording of a deed in its county of location went ignored. (However, in the 1805 and 1807 lotteries some of the first sales of land lots were recorded in the county of residence of the owner.) Most Georgians never saw the land lots that they won but sold their lots to land speculators who, in turn, sold the lots to families that migrated to Georgia from other states.

This situation was particularly true for the 1832 lotteries in Northwest Georgia. Many fortunate drawers in the lotteries often did not claim the lots that they won because the lots were not considered worth even the fee to have the lots granted. Unclaimed lots reverted to the state of Georgia and were sold at auction, along with fractional lots (lots withheld from the lotteries because they were less than the standard size). Winners found guilty of lying to obtain chances in the lotteries lost the lots that they won, with half of each lot reverting to the state for sale at auction and half going to the informant. Proven cases of persons winning lots by wrongly obtaining chances in the land lotteries are included in Robert S. Davis, *The Georgia Black Book: Morbid, Macabre, and Sometimes Disgusting Records of Genealogical Value* (Greenville, SC: Southern Historical Press, 1982), 15–48.

Contrary to some published claims, the land lotteries were open to Georgia's general public and not only to Revolutionary War veterans and their widows. A list of the men who won land lots on extra chances given them as Revolutionary War veterans is published in Alex M. Hitz, *Authentic List of All Land Grants Made to Veterans of the Revolutionary War by the State of Georgia* (Atlanta: Georgia Secretary of State, 1966). Revolutionary War veterans only had to be Georgia residents at the time of the lotteries to qualify for their extra chances. They were also not required to make any statements as to specifically where or when they served in the American Revolution.

Georgia's statewide land lottery lists are published in the books described in the following categories. As with almost all published sources, names are sometimes misprinted or omitted from the original records at the Georgia Archives.

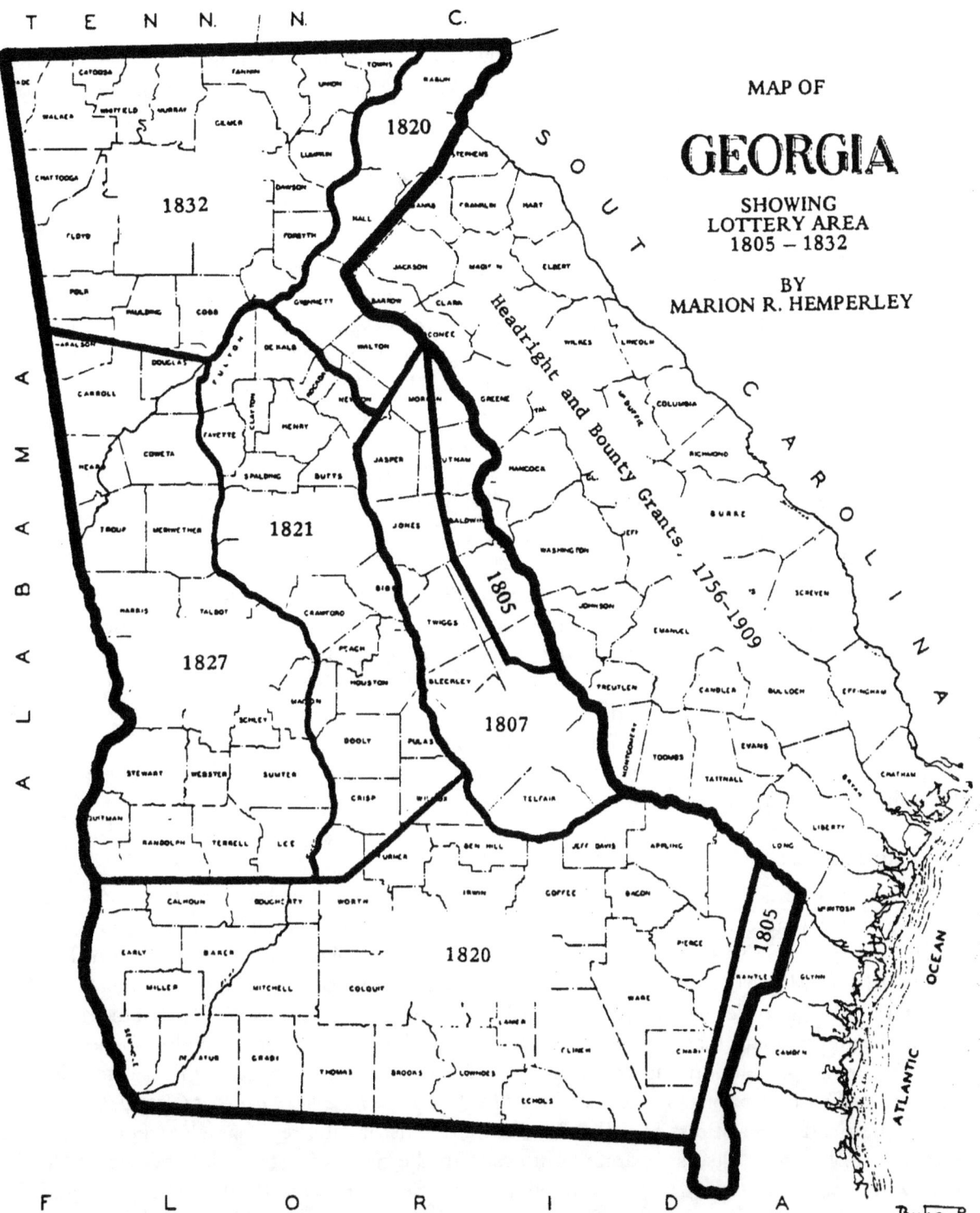

Map 5 - Areas of Georgia distributed through land lotteries between 1805 and 1832.

1805 Land Lottery

This lottery was established to dispense the 202 ½-acre land lots in original Baldwin and Wilkinson Counties and the 490-acre lots in original Wayne County. Registration occurred within four months after the act of May 11, 1803, but was later extended to March 1, 1804. A person had to be a resident of Georgia since May 11, 1802, to qualify for chances in the 1805 land lottery. The participants in this lottery (single males, heads of households, and orphans) are published in Paul K. Graham as *1805 Georgia Land Lottery Fortunate Drawers and Grantees* (Decatur, GA: The Genealogy Company, 2004) and *1805 Georgia Land Lottery: Persons Entitled to Draws* (Decatur, GA: The Genealogy Company, 2005). The incomplete Virginia S. and Ralph V. Wood, *1805 Georgia Land Lottery* (1964), does not indicate whether or not the fortunate drawer took up his lot, where it was located, or where the grant was recorded; the numbers printed beside each name were for clerical purposes in 1805 and are largely meaningless. The grants for lots won are available at the Georgia Archives in microfilm Drawer 291, Boxes 71–77. The original list of registrants of the lottery is in Drawer 90, Box 42. Also see "Land Lots Granted to Heirs of Winners in the 1805 Land Lottery," *Georgia Genealogical Society Quarterly* 29 (1993): 41–44. For historical background, see Frederick B. Gates, "The Georgia Land Act of 1803: Political Struggle in a One-Party State," *Georgia Historical Quarterly* 82 (1998): 1–21.

1807 Land Lottery

This lottery was established to dispense additional 202 ½-acre lots in original Baldwin and Wilkinson Counties. Registration for this lottery was held between June 26 and September 26, 1806. Registrants had to be residents of the state of Georgia since June 26, 1806, to qualify for the 1807 lottery. Qualifications were the same as for the 1805 land lottery except that single women and widows without children could participate. A list of the winners in this lottery is Paul K. Graham, *1807 Georgia Land Lottery Fortunate Drawers and Grantees* (Decatur, GA: The Genealogy Company, 2011); also see S. Emmett Lucas, *The Second or 1807 Land Lottery of Georgia* (Easley, S.C.: Southern Historical Press, 1986).

1820 Land Lottery

This lottery was established to dispense 490-acre lots in original Appling, Irwin, and Rabun Counties and 250-acre lots in original Early, Gwinnett, Habersham, Hall, Rabun, and Walton Counties. Registration was held from December 15, 1818, to March 15, 1819, and from December 13, 1819, to May 31, 1820. Registrants had to be residents of the state of Georgia since December 15, 1815, in order to qualify for the 1820 lottery. Qualifications were the same as for the 1805 land lottery, except that extra chances were allowed to some veterans, widows, and orphans of the American Revolution and the War of 1812. A list of the winners of this lottery is contained in the first part of Silas E. Lucas Jr., *The 1820 and 1821 Land Lotteries of Georgia* (Greenville, SC: Southern Historical Press, 1973). The Southern Historical Press has also republished the 1820 and 1821 lottery lists as separate volumes with the names in strict alphabetical order: *The Third or 1820 Land Lottery of Georgia* (Greenville, SC: Southern Historical Press, 1986) and *The Fourth or 1821 Land Lottery of Georgia* (Greenville, SC: Southern Historical Press, 1986).

1821 Land Lottery

This lottery was established to dispense the 202 ½-acre lots in original Dooly, Fayette, Henry, Houston, and Monroe Counties. Registration was within two months after the act of May 16, 1821. Registrants had to be residents of the state of Georgia since May 15, 1818. Qualifications were the same as for the 1820 lottery, and the list of winners is published as explained in the 1820 Land Lottery above.

1827 Land Lottery

This lottery was established to dispense the 202 ½-acre lots of original Carroll (5th Section), Coweta (4th Section), Lee (1st Section), Muscogee (2nd Section), and Troup (3rd Section) Counties. Registration for this lottery was held within two months after passage of the act of December 7, 1824, although some registrations continued as late as February 15, 1827. Registrants for the 1827 land lottery had to be residents of the state of Georgia since January 1, 1824. Qualifications were the same as for the 1820 lottery except that the physically and mentally handicapped were given extra chances. Abandoned wives and children were given the same extra chances as widows and orphans, respectively. The winners are published in Martha Lou Houston, *Reprint of the Official Register of the 1827 Land Lottery of Georgia* (1928; Reprint with index, Baltimore: Clearfield Company, 1975). Contrary to what is stated in the introduction of this volume, there is no missing volume of the 1827 lottery. This "missing" volume was the original publication of the 1832 Cherokee Land Lottery list.

1832 Cherokee Land Lottery

This lottery was created to dispense the land lots of 100 to 160 acres, each in the four sections of original Cherokee County, in what is today northwest Georgia. Registration was within four months after the Governor's proclamation of February 20, 1832, and was held concurrently with the 1832 Gold Lottery. Registrants for the 1832 lotteries had to be residents of Georgia since January 1, 1829. Qualifications for this lottery were the same as for the 1827 lottery, except that extra chances were also given to veterans of the Indian Wars of 1784–1797. The winners are published, with land lot maps, in James F. Smith, *The 1832 (Cherokee) Land Lottery* (1838; Reprint, Greenville, SC: Southern Historical Press, 1976).

1832 Gold Lottery

This land lottery was created to dispense the forty-acre lots of the gold region of the four sections of the original Cherokee County in today's northwest Georgia. Registration was within four months after the Governor's proclamation of February 20, 1832, and was held concurrently with the 1832 Cherokee Land Lottery. However, the smaller land lots resulted in many more draws. Even though the first drawing of the gold lottery was one day after the land lottery began in October 1832, the land lottery ended in mid-February 1833, and the gold lottery ended the first of May 1833. The 1832 Gold Lottery was open to adult males, heads of families, widows, and orphans who were residents of Georgia since January 1, 1829. The winners of the gold lottery are listed in Silas E. Lucas Jr., *The 1832 Gold Lottery of Georgia* (Greenville, SC: Southern Historical Press, 1976). Also see Mary B. Warren, *Alphabetical Index to Georgia's 1832 Gold Lottery*, (Danielsville, GA: Heritage Papers, 1981).

Contrary to some accounts, there was no 1838 lottery. Land lots won in the 1832 lotteries that were occupied by the Indians were withheld from the winners until the occupants left or were removed. The remaining Cherokees were forcibly removed in 1838. When writing a century later, this sudden release of land lots created a misunderstanding among historians, who believed that a lottery had been held in 1838.

1833 Land Lottery

Names of other land lottery winners are found in Robert S. Davis, *The 1833 Land Lottery of Georgia and Missing Names of Winners in the Georgia Land Lotteries* (Greenville, SC: Southern Historical Press, 1991). The 1833 Land Lottery was primarily a fractions lottery. It was held to dispense land lots of less than forty acres from within the land area of the 1832 Gold Lottery, using the losing tickets from the 1832 Land Lottery and 1832 Gold Lottery. Some additional lots not drawn in earlier lotteries were also included in the 1833 drawing.

Military Records

The Georgia Archives has nine volumes of indexed typescripts entitled "Georgia Military Affairs" covering 1775–1842, and six volumes of indexed transcripts on microfilm entitled "Georgia Military Records" for the period 1779–1902. These two series often duplicate each other, and "Georgia Military Records" is largely abstracted in the General Name File card catalog at the Georgia Archives. Also see National Archives microfilm M1745 *Claims for Georgia Militia Campaigns Against Indians on the Frontier, 1792–1827*. Military and civil commissions typed on the General Name File cards usually include all of the information found in the commission records, except for the militia district numbers. The Georgia Archives also has in Record Group 22 various unindexed collections of military records for the 1780s and later. Also see Gordon B. Smith, *History of the Georgia Militia, 1783–1861*, 4 vols. (Milledgeville, GA: Boyd Publishing, 2000) and Watson W. Jennison, *Cultivating Race: The Expansion of Slavery in Georgia, 1750-1860* (Chapel Hill: University of North Carolina Press, 2011).

National Archives Micropublication M233 *Registers of Enlistments in the U.S. Army, 1798–1914*, provides information on the enlistees in the Regular United States Army that usually includes county and state of birth, age, and physical description. This whole microfilm publication is included in the subscription database Ancestry.com as U.S. Army, Register of Enlistments, 1798–1914. These records include scouts in the Indian wars of the 1870s. All of the men in these records born in or enlisting from Virginia to 1815 are published in Stuart Lee Butler, *Virginia's Soldiers in the United States Army, 1800–1815* (Athens, GA: Iberian Pub. Co., 1986). Sometimes additional information can be found in the much less comprehensive National Archives microfilm M1856 *Discharge Certificates and Miscellaneous Records relating to the Discharge of Soldiers from the Regular Army, 1792–1815*. Georgians were prominently recruited in 1812–1815, 1846–1848, and 1855, see for example "Some Georgia Soldiers with Place of Birth (1855)," *Georgia Genealogical Society Quarterly* 44 (Summer 2008): 141–52.

For officers of the regular army see Francis B. Heitman, *Historical Register and Dictionary of the United States Army* (Washington, DC: Government Printing Office, 1904), which also includes lists of the officers of volunteers in the Mexican, Spanish American, and Philippine conflicts, as well as lists of battles and forts. For Navy and Marine officers see Edward W. Callahan, *List of Officers of the Navy of the United States and of the Marine Corps From 1775 to 1900* (New York: L. R.

Hamersly, 1901). Also see Lloyd D. Bockstruck, comp., *Naval Pensioners of the United States, 1800–1851* (Baltimore: Genealogical Publishing Company, 2002).

Indian Wars

For federal volunteers in Georgia's conflicts with the Indians, see:

> White, Virgil D. *Index to Volunteer Soldiers in Indian Wars and Disturbances, 1815–1858.* Waynesboro, TN: National Historical Publishing Company, 1994.
>
> ———. *Index to Indian Wars Pension Files, 1891–1926.* Waynesboro, TN: National Historical Publishing Company, 1987.
>
> ———. *Index to Old Wars Pension Files.* Waynesboro, TN: National Historical Publishing Company,1987. These service and pension records can be ordered from Military Records, National Archives and Records Administration, Washington, DC 20408.

War of 1812

The United States officially fought a war with Great Britain from June 18, 1812, to December 24, 1814. This conflict knew many names including, in Georgia, as "the late war with Great Britain and the Indians" but eventually it became the War of 1812. Except for British destruction of St. Marys, Georgia, and battles with certain groups of the Creek Indians, the war was not fought in Georgia; see Gordon B. Smith, *History of the Georgia Militia, 1783–1861,* 4 vols. (Savannah: privately printed, 2000). However, see Mary R. Bullard, *Black Liberation on Cumberland Island in 1815* (n.p.: n.p., 1983) for an account of the British occupation of Cumberland Island, GA, which discusses the slaves taken away to the Bahamas and is based on original records.

Sources that relate specifically to Georgia in the War of 1812 (1812–1814) include Judy Kratovil, *An Index to War of 1812 Service Records for Volunteer Soldiers From Georgia* (Atlanta: privately printed, 1986), which indexes service records of about 20,000 federal volunteer soldiers, roughly one-fifth of the adult male population in Georgia in 1812. This book is compiled from National Archives microcopy M602—*Index to Compiled Service Records of Volunteer Soldiers who Served During the War of 1812,* available at the National Archives at Atlanta and other libraries. Also see:

> Butler, Stuart L. "Genealogical Records of the War of 1812." *Prologue: The Quarterly of the National Archives* 23 (1991): 420–425.
>
> Davis, Robert S. *A Researcher's Library of Georgia.* 2 vols. Greenville, SC: Southern Historical Press, 1987, 1991.
>
> ———. *Georgia Black Book, Volume, II.* Greenville, SC: Southern Historical Press, 1987.
>
> Deeben, John P. and Claire Preschtel-Kluskens, "Leaving the Army during Mr. Madison's War: Certificates of Discharge for [the Regular Army] for the War of 1812," *Prologue: The Quarterly of the National Archives* 43 (3) (Fall 2011): http://www.archives.gov/publications/prologue/2011/fall/discharge-certs.html.
>
> Peterson, Clarence Stewart. *Known Military Dead During the War of 1812.* Baltimore: Clearfield, 1955.

The National Archives and Records Administration has many other records of the War of 1812-era including naval service records, claims for private property lost, and certificates of citizenship given to civilian sailors in a failed effort to save them from foreign impressments. For descriptions of such records see Stuart L. Butler, "Genealogical Records of the War of 1812," *Prologue: The Quarterly of the National Archives* 23 (1991): 420–425; John P. Deeben, "Maritime Proofs of Citizenship: The Essential Evidence Behind Seamen's Protection Certificates, 1792–1875," *National Genealogical Society Quarterly* 96 (June 2008): 139–148; Ruth Priest Dixon, "Genealogical Fallout From the War of 1812," *Prologue: The Quarterly of the National Archives* 24 (1992): 70–77; Trevor K. Plante, *Military Service Records at the National Archives* (Washington, DC: National Archives and Records Administration, 2007); *Guide to Genealogical Research at the National Archives* (Washington, DC: National Archives Trust, 1990); *Military Service Records: A Select Catalog of National Archives Microfilm Publications* (Washington, DC: National Archives Trust, 1985); and *Guide to Federal Records in the National Archives of the United States* (Washington, DC: National Archives and Records Administration, 1995). The National Archives and Records Administration has more information on the War of 1812 at its website: http://www.archives.gov/research/military/war-of-1812/index.html.

Many records of genealogical value were created after the war. An 1883 list of Georgia federal Civil War and War of 1812 pensioners has been published many times, including in *Georgia Genealogical Society Quarterly* 15 (1979): 169–200. A complete list is Virgil D. White, *Index to War of 1812 Pension Files* (Waynesboro, TN: National Historical Pub. Co., 1992). For some other post-war records, see "Some Georgia Widows and Orphans of the War of 1812," *Georgia Genealogical Society Quarterly* 31 (1995): 28–30; and "Some More Georgia Widows and Orphans of the War of 1812," *Georgia Genealogical Society Quarterly* 30 (1994): 120–121. Also see Clarence Stewart Peterson, *Known Military Dead During the War of 1812*. (Baltimore: Clearfield, 1955). For records of British aliens in the United States during the war, researchers should check see Kenneth Scott, *British Aliens in the United States During the War of 1812* (Baltimore: Genealogical Publishing Company, 1979). The National Society, United States Daughters of 1812, and the General Society of the War of 1812 have, respectively, published various lineage books that provide genealogies back to War of 1812 veterans.

Texas Rebellion from Mexico and the War with Mexico

Georgians served at the Alamo, Goliad, and San Jacinto during the Texas revolt from Mexico (1835–1836), see, for example, Robert S. Davis, "Goliad and the Georgia Battalion: Georgia Participation in the Texas Revolution," *Journal of Southwest Georgia History* 4 (1986): 25–55, for whom the lone star in the Texas flag has been dedicated. Rosters of the Georgia Battalion in the Texas revolt from Mexico (1835–1836) are published in *Central Georgia Genealogical Society Quarterly* 7 (1985): 64–69, 117. Also see "Georgians at San Jacinto," *Georgia Genealogical Society Quarterly* 22 (1986): 89–90; Daughters of the Republic of Texas, *Muster Rolls of the Texas Revolution* (Austin, TX: privately printed, 1986); and Gifford White, *They Also Served—Texas Service Records from Headright Certificates* (Nacogdoches, TX: Ericson Books, 1994). For records of Texas bounty land allotted to these men and their heirs, write to Texas State Land Office, General Land Office, 1700 N. Congress Avenue, Austin, TX 78701, and use Thomas Lloyd Miller, *Bounty and Donation Land Grants of Texas, 1835–1888* (Austin: University of Texas Press, 1967). For other sources on the revolt from Mexico, see Jean Carefoot, *Guide to Genealogical Resources in the Texas State Archives* (Austin: Texas State Library, 1984).

Several different sources document service in the War with Mexico, 1846–1848. A very incomplete roster of the Georgia volunteers is published in George White, *Historical Collections of Georgia,* 1855; (Reprint with index, Athens, GA: Heritage Papers, 1968), 115–120. Also see:

> *Alabama Volunteers in the Mexican War 1846–1848: A History and Annotated Roster.* Richardson, TX: The Descendants of Mexican War Veterans, 1996.
>
> "Birthplace of Some Georgia Soldiers, Mexican War, 1848." *Georgia Genealogical Society Quarterly* 37 (2001): 22–27.
>
> Brooks, Nathan C. *Index to a Complete History of the Mexican War.* Lakeland, FL: Alvie Davidson, 1996.
>
> *Index to the Dispatches and the Names of United States Soldiers who Fought in the Final Battles of the Mexican War.* Dallas, TX: Mew Publishing, 1991.
>
> "Officers of Georgia Volunteer Units in the Mexican War, 1846–1848." *Georgia Genealogical Society Quarterly* 32 (1996): 260–261.
>
> Peterson, George Stewart. *Known Military Dead During the Mexican War.* Baltimore: no publisher, 1957.
>
> "Some Georgia Soldiers in the Mexican War." *Georgia Genealogical Society Quarterly* 27 (1991): 104–106.
>
> "Some Sick Georgians in the Mexican War." *Georgia Genealogical Society Quarterly* 30 (1994): 97–104. Based on microfilm at the Georgia Archives in Drawer 309, Box 98.

Also see National Archives microfilm M616—*Index to Compiled Service Records of Volunteer Soldiers Who Served During the Mexican War* and National Archives information on its records on its website: http://www.archives.gov/research/alic/reference/military/mexican-war.html.

Nationwide lists of War with Mexico pensioners have been published twice. See:

> White, Virgil D. *Index to Mexican War Pension Files.* Waynesboro, TN: National Historical Publishing Company, 1989.
>
> Wolfe, Barbara Schull. *Index to Mexican War Pension Applications.* Indianapolis: Heritage House, 1985.

Federal Bounty and Pension Claims

Georgia sent thousands of volunteer soldiers to a number of federally sponsored military campaigns categorized as the Indian Wars (1783–1858), the War of 1812 (1812–1815), and the War with Mexico (1846–1848). The applications for bounty land warrants and for pensions, which often contain extensive personal information, such as date of death of a veteran, maiden name of widow, names of veteran's children, and service in the Georgia military, should be requested from Military Records, National Archives and Records Service, 700 Pennsylvania Ave. SW, Washington, DC 20408-0001. These records can be searched for free and copies obtained for a fee from the National Archives and Records Administration website: http://www.archives.gov/.

Originally, federal bounty land for veterans and heirs of veterans, including for the War of 1812 (1812–1815) could only be taken out in designated districts in Arkansas, Illinois, and Missouri.

See Katheren Christensen, *Arkansas Military Bounty Grants, War of 1812* (Hot Springs, AR: Arkansas Ancestors, 1971); James D. Walker, *War of 1812 Bounty Lands in Illinois* (Thomson, IL: Heritage House, 1977); Maxine Dunaway, *Missouri Military Land Warrants, War of 1812* (Springfield, IL: privately printed, 1985); and Walter Lowrie, *Early Settlers of Missouri* (Greenville, SC: Southern Historical Press, 2001). An act of 1842 allowed the claimants to receive their land in any federal land state, including Alabama, Arkansas, Florida, Louisiana, and Mississippi. (Georgia, Kentucky, and Tennessee are not federal land states; North Carolina Revolutionary War veterans or their heirs received bounty land in Tennessee.) Until 1852, veterans/heirs of veterans could not sell their bounty land claims but they could accept government land script in lieu of a grant and, starting in 1830, could sell that script to anyone. Acts of 1850 and 1855 offered bounty lands to veterans and widows of veterans of all conflicts from 1790 on, and the act of 1855 granted bounty lands on service of as little as fourteen days. In 1856, bounty lands were offered based upon Revolutionary War service. The last additional warrants for military bounty lands were issued in 1858, and lands on such warrants were no longer allowed to be located after 1863.

Other records of Georgians getting bounty land include, Robert S. Davis, *A Researcher's Library of Georgia*, 2 vols. (Greenville, SC: Southern Historical Press, 1987, 1991), 2: 257–64. An index to the bounty land warrants of the War of 1812 is in National Archives microcopy M848—*War of 1812 Military Bounty Land Warrants, 1815–1858*. War of 1812 bounty land claims are filed at the National Archives among the pension files, when the veteran and/or survivor had both. The other 300,000 to 450,000 bounty land claims, without regard to pensions, are filed alphabetically by name of the veteran at the National Archives in the "Unindexed Bounty Land Warrant Applications." For use of these records see E. Wade Hone, "Federal Military Bounty Lands," *Heritage Quest* 15 (May/June 1999): 9–16, and Kenneth Hawkins, *Research in the Land Entry Records of the General Land Office* (Washington, DC: National Archives, 1997), 10–15, and for historical background, see James W. Oberly, *Sixty Million Acres: American Veterans and the Public Lands Before the Civil War* (Kent, OH: Kent State University Press, 1990).

Sometimes the bounty land warrant number can be learned and the file obtained, if the person used the warrant to receive federal land in a federal land state such as Alabama, Florida, or Mississippi. Searches of federal land records for such land grants can be made by request to the National Archives and to the Bureau of Land Management, Eastern States Office, 7450 Boston Boulevard, Springfield, VA 22153. Indexes to federal land patent records are available on the internet through the Bureau of Land Management Eastern States website: http://www.glorecords.blm.gov. These land patent lists do not currently include canceled homestead grants and pre-1820 credit land grants, although those are included in the index to federal land entries for Alabama, Alaska, Arizona, Florida, Louisiana, Nevada, and Utah at the National Archives in Washington, DC. See Kenneth Hawkins, *Research in the Land Entry Records of the General Land Office* (Washington, DC: National Archives, 1997).

The National Archives and Records Administration is currently preparing a single public consolidated index to bounty land claims, and the Bureau of Land Management is adding the land patents for military service to its website. Several finding aids help in identifying federal pensions. Some of the Georgia pensions and bounty claims have been abstracted in Dorothy E. Payne, *Georgia Pensioners*, 2 vols. to date (McLean, VA: privately printed, 1985). Virgil D. White has published nationwide indexes to all federal pensions for American wars from the American Revolution to 1860, all of which are cited above. The following sources include some War of 1812 and War with Mexico veterans, as well as soldiers from the Revolution:

> National Archives microcopy M1746—*Georgia's Final Revolutionary War Pay Vouchers*, indexed in *Georgia Genealogical Magazine* 36 (2) (1996): 98–100. Includes more than for the American Revolution.
>
> National Archives microcopy T718—*Ledger of Payments, 1818–1872*. Available at the Georgia Archives.
>
> Scott, Craig R. *The "Lost" Pensions: Settled Accounts of the Act of 6 April 1838* (Lovettsville, VA: Willow Bend Books, 1996). Covers from the American Revolution through the War with Mexico of 1846–1848.

Poor School and Academy Lists

Georgia poor school records usually give each child's age and sometimes the names of parents. No bibliography currently exists of the collections of pre-1860 poor school children and academy lists that are extant in Georgia's county and state records. Some of these records are on microfilm at the Georgia Archives, cataloged in the Georgia Official Records Drawer under "Executive Department." The pre-1851 records of that particular collection are included in R. J. Taylor, Jr., Foundation, *Index to Poor School and Academy Records, 1826–1850* (Spartanburg, SC: The Reprint Company, 1980). A bibliography of this whole collection is in Robert S. Davis, *The Wilkes County Papers, 1773–1833* (Greenville, SC: Southern Historical Press, 1979), 333–338. County copies of other poor school records are found in the county records microfilm at the Georgia Archives.

Original Native American (Indian) Records

Researchers should be warned that many family stories of Indian heritage turn out to be (1) not documentable because Indians were listed as whites or blacks, (2) referring to black ancestors, or (3) referring to black and white ancestors remembered for Indian-like physical features. When a "grandmother" remembered in family lore as a "Cherokee Princess" can be documented, the ancestor almost invariably proves to be several generations farther back in the family tree than remembered and not to be Cherokee but a member of some now lost tribe of coastal North Carolina or Virginia. Native Americans were counted in the federal censuses of 1860, 1870, and 1880 only when they paid taxes, see James P. Collins, "Native Americans in the Census, 1860–1880," *Prologue: The Quarterly of the National Archives* 38 (2) (summer 2006): http://www.archives.gov/publications/prologue/2006/summer/indian-census.html and "Some Indians in the 1860 Census of Georgia," *Georgia Genealogical Society Quarterly* 21 (1985): 46. Interracial marriages are often remembered in family stories as Caucasian men marrying Native American or African American women but records show the opposite to have also frequently happened.

The records that do exist for southeastern Indians, however, can be a rich source of personal information not found elsewhere. Specifically for Cherokee Indian research, see Tony Mack McClure, *Cherokee Proud: A Guide for Tracing and Honoring Your Cherokee Ancestors* (Somerville, TN: Chunannee Books, 1996), and for the Creeks, see the last section of Billie Ford Snider, *Full Name Indexes—Eastern Creek Indians* (Pensacola, FL: Antique Compiling, 1993). Many libraries and archives have brochures on their respective Indian resources. *The Southeastern Native American Exchange* is a periodical devoted to Native American research in the Old South. Also see Laurie Beth Duffy, *Who's Looking for Whom in Native American Ancestry* (Bowie, MD: Heritage Books, 1997) and Ronald Chepesiuk and Arnold M. Shankman, *American Indian Archival Material: A Guide to Holdings in the Southeast* (Westport, CT: Greenwood, 1982). For African American relations with the Indians, see Angela Y. Walton-Raji, *Black Indian Genealogy Research: African American Ancestors among the Five Civilized Tribes* (Bowie, MD: Heritage Books, 1993).

Most Native American records are federal. The best guides to those sources are the following:

American Indians: A Select Catalog of National Archives Microfilm Publications. Washington, DC: National Archives, 1995.

Collins, James P. "Native Americans in the Antebellum U.S. Military." *Prologue: The Quarterly of the National Archives* 39 (4) (Winter 2007): http://www.archives.gov/publications/prologue/2007/winter/indians-military.html.

Hill, Edward E. *Guide to Records in the National Archives of the United States Relating to American Indians*. Washington, DC: National Archives, 1981.

Kirkham, E. Kay. *Our Native Americans and Their Records of Genealogical Value*. 2 vols. Logan, UT: Everton, 1984.

Smith, Jessie Carney. *Ethnic Genealogy*. Westport, CT: Greenwood Press, 1983.

The National Archives at Atlanta has an extensive collection of National Archives microfilms of southeastern Indian tribes, including the claims made by Creek orphans for damages from the Creek Removal of 1836. See its handout on Native American research.

For research into Native Americans specifically in Georgia, see:

Davis, Robert S. *A Guide to Native American (Indian) Research Sources at the Georgia Department of Archives and History*. Jasper, Georgia: privately printed, 1985.

Hemperley, Marion R. *Indian Heritage of Georgia*. privately printed, 1994.

"Supplement to Indian Guide." *Georgia Genealogical Society Quarterly* 25 (1989): 172–173.

The Davis work includes a list of Cherokee and Creek families declared white for legal purposes by the Georgia legislature. Of particular value at the Georgia Archives are the "Cherokee Indian Letters" and the "Creek Indian Letters," indexed typescripts of records relating to Indians and the whites living among them in Georgia. These typescripts are on microfilm and available on loan at Latter-day Saints Family History Centers and are supplemented by Mary B. Warren, *Whites Among the Cherokees* (Athens, GA: Heritage Papers, 1987). The Georgia Archives also has eleven volumes of transcripts of Creek Indian related records at the National Archives, entitled "Creek Letters, 1800–1849." Prepared by T. Joseph Peddy, these typescripts have no index. Also see the "Indian Affairs" volumes in *American State Papers*, Class 2, Volumes 1–2, available in all major libraries and Federal Depository Libraries and on the subscription website GenealogyBank.

Many early issues of the *Georgia Genealogical Society Quarterly* contain extensive information on Georgia's pre-removal Cherokee and Creek Indian families. Volume 8, nos. 2 and 3 (1972) includes the list from National Archives microcopy T275—*The Parsons & Abbott Census or Roll of the Creeks in 1832*, which has also been published by James L. Douthat as *1832 Creek Census* (Signal Mountain, TN: Mountain Press, 1994). Prepared by the late James M. Puckett, these issues are included in the *Quarterly's* twenty-year, every-name index. Many other articles, especially abstracts of Cherokee records, have since appeared in *Georgia Genealogical Society Quarterly, Northwest Georgia Historical and Genealogical Society Quarterly,* and *Georgia Genealogical Magazine*. For an early bibliography, see Robert S. Davis, A *Guide to Native American (Indian) Research Sources*, 16–18.

Bob Blankenship has published the names from the various censuses (rolls or enrollments) of the Cherokees in *Cherokee Roots* (2 vols., Cherokee, NC: privately printed, 1992). However, this work omits the Georgia and Tennessee families from the 1869 Swetland roll. See "Some Georgia Cherokees in 1869," *Northwest Georgia Historical and Genealogical Society Quarterly* 28, no. 3 (1996): 28–32. Also see:

- Baker, Jack D., and David Keith Hampton. *Old Cherokee Families: Notes of Dr. Emmet Starr*. 3 vols. Oklahoma City: Baker Publishing, 1988).

- Bell, George Morrison, Sr. *Genealogy of "Old & New Cherokee Indian Families."* Bartlesville, OK: privately printed, 1972.

- Crumpton, Barbara J., comp., *1884 Hester Roll of the Eastern Cherokee*. Duncan, OK: privately printed, 1986.

- Hampton, David Keith. *Cherokee Mixed-Bloods: Additions and Corrections to Family Genealogies of Dr. Emmett Starr*. 1 vol. to date. Lincoln, AR: ARC Press, 2005–.

- Siler, David W. *The Eastern Cherokees: A Census of the Cherokee Nation in North Carolina, Tennessee, Alabama, and Georgia in 1851*. Cottonport, LA: Polyanthus, 1972.

- Starr, Emmet. *History of the Cherokee Indians*. Muskogee, OK: Oklahoma Yesterday, 1984. Contains genealogies of many of the prominent Cherokee families.

The Georgia Archives has a number of special sources for Native American research. Some of the 1830s Cherokee Indian property evaluations from entries 217 to 251 of Record Group 75, Bureau of Indian Affairs, National Archives, Washington, DC, can be found on microfilm in Drawer 194, Box 2. The Georgia Archives also has surveyor notebooks, district plat maps, and plats of northwest Georgia land lots in the 1832 land lotteries occupied by Indians, although usually without the names of the specific Indians. Charles O. Walker and Don Shadburn have combined these sources with National Archives microcopy T496—*The Henderson Roll of Cherokees East of the Mississippi River (1835)* to create several books on individual Cherokee communities in North Georgia, including:

- Shadburn, Don L. *Cherokee Planters in Georgia, 1832–1838*. Cumming, GA: privately printed, 1990.

- ———. *Unhallowed Intrusion*. Cumming, GA: privately printed, 1995.

- ——— and Strange, John D., III. *Upon Our Ruins: a Study in Cherokee History and Genealogy*. Cumming, GA: Cottonpatch Press, 2012.

- Walker, Charles O. *Cherokee Footprints*. 3 vols. to date. Jasper, GA: privately printed, 1988.

- Wilms, Douglas C. *"Cherokee Indian Land Use in Georgia, 1800–1838."* Ph.D. dissertation, University of Georgia, 1973.

A number of records relating to Cherokee Indian claims from the War of 1812 through the 1840s survive. See, for example, "Cherokee 'Trail of Tears' Claims," *Georgia Genealogical Magazine* 36 (1996): 293–299. Many Cherokee claims are included in National Archives microcopy M574—*Special Files, 1807–1904, Bureau of Indian Affairs*. A copy of this microfilm is at the National Archives at Atlanta. The Georgia Historical Society has, in Collection 927, "Cherokee Indian Spoliations, 1835–1836." See "Some Cherokee Indian Spoliations, 1836–1837," *Northwest Georgia Historical and Genealogical Society Quarterly* 22, no. 3 (1990): 10–11 and Marybelle W. Chase, *1842 Cherokee Claims* series. For Creek Indian property claims, see *Creek Documents* (Signal Mountain, TN: Mountain Press, 1997).

Records of the earliest white involvements with the Indians survive largely in the British archives and libraries. Much of this material has not been microfilmed, indexed, or published. The materials in print include the following:

- Hicks, Theresa M. *South Carolina Indians, Indian Traders and Other Ethnic Connections*. Columbia, SC: Peppercorn Publications, 1997.

- Lewis, William L., and, James A. Lewis. *A Guide to Cherokee Documents in Foreign Archives*. Metuchen, NJ: Scarecrow Press, 1983.

- McDowell, William L. *Journals of the Commissioners of Indian Trade*. 3 vols. Columbia: South Carolina Department of Archives and History, 1955. A part of the Colonial Records of South Carolina Series.

Lists of white men living among the Cherokees in 1796–1797 appear in Dorothy Williams Potter, *Passports of Southeastern Pioneers, 1770–1823* (Baltimore: Genealogical Publishing Company, 1982), 328–329. Many white men living among the Indians are mentioned in the following:

- Abbott, Belle K. *The Cherokee Indians in Georgia*. University, AL: Confederate Publishing Company, 1980.

- Hawkins, Benjamin. *Letters, Journals, and Writings of Benjamin Hawkins*. 2 vols. Edited by C. L. Grant. Savannah, GA: Beehive Press, 1980.

- Stiggins, George. *Creek Indian History*. Edited by Virginia Pounds. Birmingham, AL.: Birmingham Public Library Press, 1989.

- Warren, Mary B. *Whites Among the Cherokees*. Athens, GA: Heritage Papers, 1987.

- Woodward, Thomas S. *Woodward's Reminiscences of the Creek, or Muscogee Indians*. Montgomery, AL.: Babrett and Wimbisu, 1859. Alvie L. Davidson has published an index to *Woodward's Reminiscences*.

Many of the white men, and their children, living among the Creeks, appear in *Index to the Records of Old Mobile Cathedral of the Immaculate Conception, 1704–1891* (Pascagoula, MS: Jackson County Genealogical Society, 1994). White men living among the Cherokees are listed and indexed in the 1830 federal censuses of Carroll, DeKalb, Hall, and (chiefly) Gwinnett Counties. An 1831 list of white "intruders" in the Creek Nation and an 1835 Cherokee voter list appear in Sharron S. Ashton, *Indians and Intruders,* 4 vols. to date (Norman, OK: Ashton Books, 1997).

The Georgia Archives has a large collection of records of the missionaries among the Creeks and Cherokees, prior to the Indian removal. Most of these records are described, and in some instances abstracted and indexed, in Paul Kutsche, *A Guide to Cherokee Documents in the Northeastern United States* (Metuchen, NJ: Scarecrow Press, 1986). For historical background on the Cherokee missionaries, see:

> Gardner, Robert G. *Cherokees and Baptists in Georgia.* Atlanta: Georgia Baptist Historical Society, 1989.
>
> McLoughlin, William G. *Cherokees and Missionaries, 1789–1839.* Signal Mountain, TN: Mountain Press, 1995.

Microfilm of records of the multi-denominational American Board of Commissioners of Foreign Missions (Brainard and New Echota Cherokee Missions) are in Drawer 70, Boxes 1–2, at the Georgia Archives; American Baptist Foreign Mission Society records are in microfilm Drawer 291, Boxes 21–26; and the Moravian Brethren records are in microfilm Drawer 104, Boxes 53–54 (Creek and Cherokee missions), while an incomplete translation of the Moravian Spring Place Cherokee Mission diaries, 1800–1836, are on the book shelf at E99. C5 M79. For the Brainard Mission, also see Joyce B. and Paul Gary Phillips, editors, *The Brainard Journal: A Mission to The Cherokees, 1817–1823* (Lincoln: University of North Carolina Press, 1998). For the Spring Place Mission for 1805–1823, see Rowena McClinton, *The Moravian Springplace Mission to the Cherokees,* 2 vols. (Lincoln: University of Nebraska Press, 2007) and Tiya Miles, *The House on Diamond Hill: A Cherokee Plantation Story* (Chapel Hill: University of North Carolina Press, 2010). The originals of the Moravian diaries are in the Moravian Archives in Winston-Salem, North Carolina. For death notices of Presbyterian missionaries among the Cherokees, see Brent Holcomb, *Marriage and Death Notices from the Charleston Observer, 1827–1845* (Greenville, SC: A Press, 1980). For the Creek mission diaries, also see Johann Christian Burckard, *Partners in the Lord's Work: The Diary of Two Moravian Missionaries in the Creek Indian Country, 1807–1813* (Atlanta: Georgia State College, 1969).

Genealogically rich claims filed in 1909 from more than 40,000 families, most of them in the southeastern United States and claiming Cherokee descent, are included in National Archives microcopy M1104—*Eastern Cherokee Applications of the United States Court of Claims, 1906–1909.* Known as the "Guion Miller" claims, they have two indexes published by Bob Blankenship in *Guion Miller Roll 'Plus'* (Cherokee, NC: Cherokee Roots, 1994) and a set of indexes by Jeff Bowen in *Cherokee Descendants,* 4 vols. (Signal Mountain, TN: Mountain Press, 1994–1997). Indexed abstracts of most of these claims have been published by Jerry Wright Jordan as *Cherokee by Blood,* 9 vols. to date (Bowie, MD: Heritage Books, 1987–1997). Other helpful works for using the Guion Miller claims include Billy Dubose Edington and Carol Anne Buswell, *Vital Information from the Guion Miller Roll* (Eastern Cherokee Court of Claims) 1906–1909 (Mill Creek, WA: Indian Scout Publications, 1998) and Jo Ann Curls Page, *Extract of the Rejected Applications of the Guion Miller Roll of the Eastern Cherokee,* 3 vols. (Westminster, MD: Heritage Books, 2003).

Similar applications by descendants of Oklahoma Cherokee, Chickasaw, Choctaw, Creek, and Seminole families for land in 1898–1914 are found in the records of the Dawes Commission in the National Archives at Fort Worth. Many of the applicants for these lands document Georgia ancestors; see Rachal Mills Lennon, *Tracing Ancestors Among the Five Civilized Tribes* (Baltimore: Genealogical Pub. Co., 2009).

Georgia Research

Chapter II: Research by Time Period

DAWES RECORDS WORK SHEET   **CHART NO.**_____

by Robert S. Davis, Jr., Family & Regional History Program, Wallace State College, P. O. Box 2000, Hanceville, AL 35077-2000

Consult the index on roll one of National Archives microfilm M1186 Enrollment Cards . . . Final Roll of the Five Civilized Tribes to copy names and the FINAL ROLL NUMBERS for individuals below. Then use those numbers to search National Archives Microfilm T529 Final Roll of the Five Civized Tribes. Use the information from that microfilm to fill out the spaces this chart and to obtain the CENSUS CARD or FIELD NO. for use in obtaining additional information from National Archiv microfilms M1301 Applications for Enrollment and M1186 Enrollment Cards.

CENSUS CARD OR FIELD NO: _____ DATE OF ENROLLMENT: _____
TRIBE:_____GROUP WITHIN TRIBE:_____
POST OFFICE:_____RESIDENCE:_____

1. NAME:_____ AGE:____ SEX:____ BLOOD:_____
YEAR ENROLLED:_____DISTRICT ENROLLED:_____DAWES ROLL NUMBER:_____
FATHER OF ABOVE:_____YEAR ENROLLED:____DISTRICT:_____
MOTHER OF ABOVE:_____YEAR ENROLLED:____DISTRICT:_____
NOTES : _____

2. NAME:_____ AGE:____ SEX:____ BLOOD:_____
YEAR ENROLLED:_____DISTRICT ENROLLED:_____DAWES ROLL NUMBER:_____
FATHER OF ABOVE:_____YEAR ENROLLED:____DISTRICT:_____
MOTHER OF ABOVE:_____YEAR ENROLLED:____DISTRICT:_____
NOTES : _____

3. NAME:_____ AGE:____ SEX:____ BLOOD:_____
YEAR ENROLLED:_____DISTRICT ENROLLED:_____DAWES ROLL NUMBER:_____
FATHER OF ABOVE:_____YEAR ENROLLED:____DISTRICT:_____
MOTHER OF ABOVE:_____YEAR ENROLLED:____DISTRICT:_____
NOTES : _____

CONTINUED ON REVERSE

4. NAME:_____ AGE:____ SEX:____ BLOOD:_____
YEAR ENROLLED:_____DISTRICT ENROLLED:_____DAWES ROLL NUMBER:_____
FATHER OF ABOVE:_____YEAR ENROLLED:____DISTRICT:_____
MOTHER OF ABOVE:_____YEAR ENROLLED:____DISTRICT:_____
NOTES : _____

5. NAME:_____ AGE:____ SEX:____ BLOOD:_____
YEAR ENROLLED:_____DISTRICT ENROLLED:_____DAWES ROLL NUMBER:_____
FATHER OF ABOVE:_____YEAR ENROLLED:____DISTRICT:_____
MOTHER OF ABOVE:_____YEAR ENROLLED:____DISTRICT:_____
NOTES : _____

6. NAME:_____ AGE:____ SEX:____ BLOOD:_____
YEAR ENROLLED:_____DISTRICT ENROLLED:_____DAWES ROLL NUMBER:_____
FATHER OF ABOVE:_____YEAR ENROLLED:____DISTRICT:_____
MOTHER OF ABOVE:_____YEAR ENROLLED:____DISTRICT:_____
NOTES : _____

7. NAME:_____ AGE:____ SEX:____ BLOOD:_____
YEAR ENROLLED:_____DISTRICT ENROLLED:_____DAWES ROLL NUMBER:_____
FATHER OF ABOVE:_____YEAR ENROLLED:____DISTRICT:_____
MOTHER OF ABOVE:_____YEAR ENROLLED:____DISTRICT:_____
NOTES : _____

4. NAME:_____ AGE:____ SEX:____ BLOOD:_____
YEAR ENROLLED:_____DISTRICT ENROLLED:_____DAWES ROLL NUMBER:_____
FATHER OF ABOVE:_____YEAR ENROLLED:____DISTRICT:_____
MOTHER OF ABOVE:_____YEAR ENROLLED:____DISTRICT:_____
NOTES : _____

FOR ADDITIONAL NAMES USE A SECOND CHART

Figure 6 – The Dawes Records Work Sheet is helpful in collecting information on members of the Five Civilized Tribes on Native American Indians.

Generally, only those applications that were accepted are indexed. However, the National Archives at Fort Worth now has a computerized index to doubtful and rejected Cherokee applications and is preparing a more comprehensive index to all of the Dawes records. It is partially available now on the National Archives website at http://www.archives.gov/research/native-americans/dawes/intro.html; also see *The Final Rolls of Citizens and Freedmen of the Five Civilized Tribes in Indian Territory* (1906; Reprint Baltimore: Genealogical Publishing Company, 2003) and *Index to the Final Rolls of Citizens and Freedmen of the Five Civilized Tribes in Indian Territory* (1906; Reprint, Baltimore: Genealogical Publishing Company, 2003). For the descendants of former slaves of the Cherokees, see Jo Ann Curls Page, *Index to the Cherokee Freedmen Enrollment Cards of the Dawes Commission, 1901–1906* (Bowie, MD: Heritage Books, 1996).

To search for an accepted application look in the alphabetical indexes on Reel 1 of the National Archives enrollment cards (M1186). These indexes provide the Dawes Roll numbers used in National Archives microcopy T529—*Final Roll of the Five Civilized Tribes, 1907–1914*. The rolls on that microfilm provide the "Census Card" or "Field Number" that is used to access the genealogically valuable applications for enrollment on National Archives microcopy M1301 and the cards used to cross-reference the applications on microcopy M1186.

Related sources include National Archives microcopy M1314—*Index to Letters Received by the Commission to the Five Civilized Tribes*. The accepted Cherokee claims are indexed by surname in Bob Blankenship, *Dawes Roll 'Plus'* (Cherokee, NC: Cherokee Roots, 1994). Also see James W. Tyner and Alice Timmons, *Our People and Where They Rest*, 8 vols. (Norman, OK: privately printed, 1969), which gives records of Cherokee cemeteries in Oklahoma. For historical background, see Kent Carter, *The Dawes Commission and the Allotment of the Five Civilized Tribes, 1893–1914* (Orem, UT: Ancestry.com, 1999). Many records relating to the Dawes Commission and the Indian tribes of Oklahoma can be found at the National Archives at Fort Worth, and others have been published.

Slave Sources

Slaves are often identified only as statistics in records (including in federal census records) or by given names only, as in county records such as estate proceedings, slave importer registers (1818–1849), bills of sale (often found in deed books), etc. Without some additional information to help identify the owners or even the individual slaves on the larger plantations, tracing a slave family is extremely difficult. By the early twentieth century, ownership of slaves was sometimes omitted in publications of abstracts of records such as in the version of the Ceded Lands journal (1773–1775) published and since reprinted from volume one of Grace G. Davidson, comp., *Early Records of Georgia Wilkes County* (1932). For the specifics of slave life, see Kenneth Stampp, *The Peculiar Institution: Slavery in the Ante-Bellum South* (New York: Vintage Books, 1956).

Manuscript repositories like the Georgia Archives will indicate in finding aids when information on slaves is available, but the chances of finding such data on a particular family are small. Although genealogically valuable information exists on many former slave families, the records at the National Archives and other repositories are frequently fragmentary, scattered among unrelated records, and without useful indexes. See for example, "Biographies of Some Former Georgia Slaves," *Georgia Genealogical Magazine* 37 (1997): 137–139. Similarly, identities of former owners of several freedmen (none from Georgia) appear in records of failed attempts to win pensions for former slaves. See "Some Former Slaves and Their Masters," *Heritage Quest* no. 69

(May–June 1997): 85–87. Also see "Some Georgia Slave Owners in 1850," and "Some Georgia Slave Owners in 1860," in *Georgia Genealogical Society Quarterly* 37 (1997): 116–127. For lists of the largest slave owners in each state see William Kauffman Scarborough, *Masters of the Big House Elite Slave Holders of the Mid-Nineteenth Century South* (Baton Rouge: Louisiana State University Press, 2003).

For slave record research and African American genealogy in general, several works are available. See:

    Blockson, Charles L. *Black Genealogy*. Baltimore: Black Classic Press, 1991.

    Dillard, J. L. *Black Names*. New York: Moulton, 1976.

    Smith, Jessie Carney. *Ethnic Genealogy*. Westport, CT: Greenwood, 1983.

Especially for slave genealogy, see:

    Austin, Allen D. *African Moslems in Antebellum America: A Sourcebook*. New York: Garland Publishing, 1984.

    Fears, Mary L. Jackson. *Slave Ancestral Research: It Is Something Else*. Bowie, MD: Heritage Books, 1995.

    Streets, David H. *Slave Genealogy: A Research Guide with Case Studies*. Bowie, MD: Heritage Books, 1986.

Several sources are specifically available on Georgia slaves. These include the 2,539 slave references and 1,368 seller/buyer references in the African-American Family History Association, *Slave Bills of Sale Project* (Atlanta: privately printed, 1986). Also see:

    "*African-American Newspapers: The Nineteenth Century,*" a database on CD-ROM available from Scholarly Resources of Wilmington, Delaware that is also found at many research institutions.

    Davis, Mrs. Terry H., Jr. "Georgia Index to Runaway Slave Advertisements: A Documentary History from the 1730s to 1790." *Georgia Genealogical Society Quarterly* 21 (1985): 66–74.

    McPherson, Robert. "Georgia Slave Trials." *American Journal of Legal History* 4 (1960): 257–284, 364–377, compiled from the Elbert County Inferior Court minutes, 1837–1849.

    Rawick, George P., editor. *The American Slave: A Composite Biography*. Westport, CT: Greenwood, 1972. The Georgia slave reminiscences are in volumes 12 and 13. A list of slaves interviewed for the series is in Howard E. Potts, *A Comprehensive Name Index for The American Slave* (Westport, CT: Greenwood, 1997). The Library of Congress has posted free access to the slave interviews on its website: http://memory.loc.gov/ammem/snhtml/. Some access is also available through the subscription site Ancestry.com.

    Singleton, Royce Gordon. "The Trial and Punishment of Slaves in Baldwin County, Georgia 1812–26." *Southern Humanities Review* 8, no. 1 (1974): 67–73.

Windley, Lathan A. *Runaway Slave Advertisements: A Documentary History From 1730s to 1790*. Westport, CT: Greenwood, 1983. Georgia is in Volume 4.

Records of Free Persons of Color

Georgia law required that each free person of color (African American, Native American, etc.) have a white guardian and be taxed in the county of residence. These laws were frequently ignored. Freed persons of color who complied with the law had such public records as guardian bonds, annual returns, etc., as if they were orphans. Starting in 1818, free persons of color had to be registered in the local inferior court each year, and the court had to publish in a local or state newspaper a list of the free persons of color with identifying information. The list was to be published by the first Monday in May of each year. See Thomas R. R. Cobb, *A Digest of the Statute Laws of the State of Georgia* (Athens, GA: Christy, Kelsea and Burke, 1851), 989–95. No bibliography of these lists has been compiled. A few county lists are on microfilm at the Georgia Archives. Some counties, such as Henry, did not keep separate registers of free persons of color but recorded registrations in the court minutes. Free persons of color were enumerated in the same population schedules as whites in the federal censuses. For a discussion of Georgia laws regarding free persons of color and slaves, see Ruth Scarborough, *The Opposition to Slavery in Georgia Prior to 1860* (Nashville, TN.: George Peabody College, 1933). Emancipations of slaves can be found in acts of the Georgia Legislature, estate records of masters, and county deed books. Sometimes emancipations were not recorded at all. Emancipations by dead masters were not always honored. Also see "Free African-American Families in Georgia in 1830," *Georgia Genealogical Society Quarterly* 37 (1997):128–136.

Gold and Other Mining Information

For persons residing in the Georgia gold fields in the 1830s, see Mary B. Warren, *Whites Among the Cherokees* (Athens, GA: Heritage Papers, 1987). The McGruder Collection of the Atlanta History Center includes dozens of North Georgia newspapers during the years of the Cherokee Removal and Georgia gold rush. For historical background, see:

Coulter, E. Merton. *Auraria: The Story of a Georgia Gold Mining Town*. Athens: University of Georgia Press, 1956.

Williams, David. *The Georgia Gold Rush*. Columbia: University of South Carolina Press, 1993.

The Georgia Bureau of Mines and Mineralogy published information on various Georgia mining operations over the years, including some data about the owners. For a bibliography of the publications, see J. Steven Storey, *Resource Index* (Atlanta: Georgia Department of Natural Resources, 1976), 29–33. For information on ordering the publications of the Georgia Geologic Survey, see its website at: http://ggsstore.dnr.state.ga.us/ or write to 19 M. L. King, Jr., Drive SW, Room 400, Maps and Publications, Atlanta, GA 30334. The Georgia Archives has the photographic archives of the Bureau, arranged by county, in Record Group 50-2-20.

Many records exist of persons in the California gold rush. Names of persons born in, or residents of, Georgia in the California gold fields in the 1850s appear in Carroll Hart and Betty Willis, "California Census of 1852," *Georgia Genealogical Society Quarterly* 4 (6) (1968) and 10 (2) (1974), which are included in the twenty-year every-name index to the *GGSQ*. This same 1852 state census of California and the 1850 and later federal census of California are included on Ancestry.com. Other sources, aside from the many websites devoted to the various mineral rushes, include the following:

>Allsworth, Mary Dean. *Gleanings From Alta, California: Marriages and Deaths Reported in the First Newspaper Published in California, 1846–1850*. Rancho Cordova, CA: Dean Publishing, 1980.

>Carr, Peter E. *San Francisco Passenger Departure Lists*. 5 vols,. San Luis Obispo, CA: TCI Genealogical Resources, 1991–1994.

>Dove, Lois A. *Wagon Trains, 1849–1865*. Sacramento, CA: L. A. Dove, 1989.

>Hawkins, C. W. *Index to the Argonauts of California*. Baton Rouge, LA: Polyanthos Press, 1986.

>Humphrey, Effingham P. "Gone West—Georgians to California." *Georgia Genealogical Magazine* 63 (1977): 102.

>Parker, J. Carlyle. *Gold Rush Days: Vital Statistics Copied From Early Newspapers of Stockton, California, 1850–1854*. Stockton, CA San Joaquin Genealogical Society, 1977.

>Parker, Nathan C. *Personal Name Index to the 1856 City Directories of California*. Detroit: Gale Research, 1980.

>Rasmussen, Louis J. *San Francisco Ship Passenger Lists [1850–1853]*. 4 vols. Colma, CA: San Francisco Historic Record and Genealogy Bulletin, 1965–1970.

>———. *California Wagon Train Lists [1849–1852]*. Colma, CA: San Francisco Historic Records, 1997.

For later arrivals in California, see Louis J. Rasmussen, *Railway Passenger Lists* [1870–1873] (Colma, CA: San Francisco Historic Records, 1966) and the California passenger lists, 1882–1957, on the subscription website Ancestry.com.

Records on Postmasters and Other Federal Employees

Published lists of federal employees from 1816 to 1825 frequently give state or country of birth. A set of these books, extending to 1959, is at the Alabama Department of Archives and History and other libraries. Places of birth of Georgia postmasters and other federal employees from these lists for 1816 and 1819, were published in *Georgia Genealogical Magazine* 83 (1982): 43–48, and for 1825, in *Georgia Genealogical Society Quarterly* 32 (1996): 168–172. Also see John P. Deeben, "The Official Register of the United States, 1816–1959," *Prologue: The Quarterly of the National Archives* 36 (4) (Spring 2004): http://www.archives.gov/publications/prologue/2004/winter/genealogy-official-register.html; Claire Prelchtel-Kluskens, "Documenting the Career of Federal Employees," *Prologue: The Quarterly of the National Archives* 26 (1994): 180–183; and *Genealogical and Biographical Research: A Catalog of National Archives Microfilm Publications* (Washington, DC: National Archives and Records Administration, 1983).

Records of the names of Georgia post offices and postmasters from 1789 to 1971 from National Archives microfilm are available on microfilm at the Georgia Archives in Drawer 21, Box 45, and Drawer 281, Boxes 26–33. For mail carriers see National Archives microfilms M2075 Index Records of Substitute Mail Clerks . . . 1899–1905, M2076 Index to Substitute Mail Carriers . . . 1885–1903, and M1846 Service Cards of Carriers Separated from the Postal Service, 1863–1899.

These films are available at the National Archives at Atlanta, 5780 Jonesboro Rd., Morrow, GA 30260.

The Early Republic, 1783–1811

Federal Census Records, 1790–1810

Georgia's federal census records are lost for 1790, 1800, and 1810. Contrary to popular myth, these records were not destroyed when the British burned Washington, DC, in 1814. One theory is that they were destroyed after their statistics had been compiled and sent to the national capital. Until 1830, census records were kept in federal district courts, and several searches of the records of the federal court of Georgia have failed to locate these lost records. A county copy of the 1800 census of Oglethorpe County survives and has been published. Some tax, land grant, land lottery, military, and other records serve as census substitutes. See for example, Marie DeLamar and Elizabeth Rothstein, *The Reconstructed 1790 Census of Georgia* (1976; Reprint with index, Baltimore: Genealogical Publishing Company, 1985). As forty-five percent of Georgia's population lived in Wilkes County in 1790, the various books of Wilkes County abstracts serve as particularly good census substitutes. The 1790–1810 federal censuses do survive for some other states that are important to Georgia family research, particularly North Carolina and South Carolina.

Headright and Bounty Grants, 1755–1909

Land in the eastern fifth of Georgia was initially granted to settlers through the headright land system; men were granted land based on the number of persons who were a part of their households or for their military service. These grants were known as headright grants or bounty grants. The rest of Georgia was granted through a system of land lotteries (see the previous section). For detailed information on the headright and bounty land grant legal processes, see:

Cadle, Farris. *Georgia Land Surveying History and Law*. Athens: University of Georgia Press, 1991.

Wood, Virginia Steele. "Georgia's Colonial and Public Land Records, 1732–1832." *National Genealogical Society Quarterly* 72 (1984): 113–131.

Georgia's Land Grants

These records are housed in the Georgia Archives. Access to them takes many forms. The Georgia Archives free website the Virtual Vault has access to the loose headright and bounty land grants, district plat books, and other records: http://cdm.sos.state.ga.us. An index to the land grants is in Silas Emmett Lucas Jr., editor, *Index to Headright and Bounty Grants of Georgia, 1755–1909* (Greenville, SC: Southern Historical Press, 1970).

The plats to these grants sometimes give valuable additional information, such as names of chain-carriers who may have been relatives (relationships, if any, are never explained in land grant records). See Nathan and Kaydee Mathews, *Abstracts of Georgia Land Plat Books A and B, 1779–1785* (Fayetteville, GA: privately printed, 1995). The Georgia Archives has an index to the plats in microfilm Drawer 286, Box 42. The inventory to the extensive files of loose headright and bounty land grant files at the Georgia Archives has been published in Robert S. Davis, editor, *The Early Settlers of Georgia: List of File Headings of Loose Headright and Bounty Land Grant Files* (Milledgeville, GA: Boyd Publishing, 1997).

Headright Grants

Tracts of land were given by the colony or state to heads of families, with maximum allowable acreage determined by the number of persons in the household, including slaves and servants. Seldom did anyone petition for the maximum acreage to which he or she could qualify.

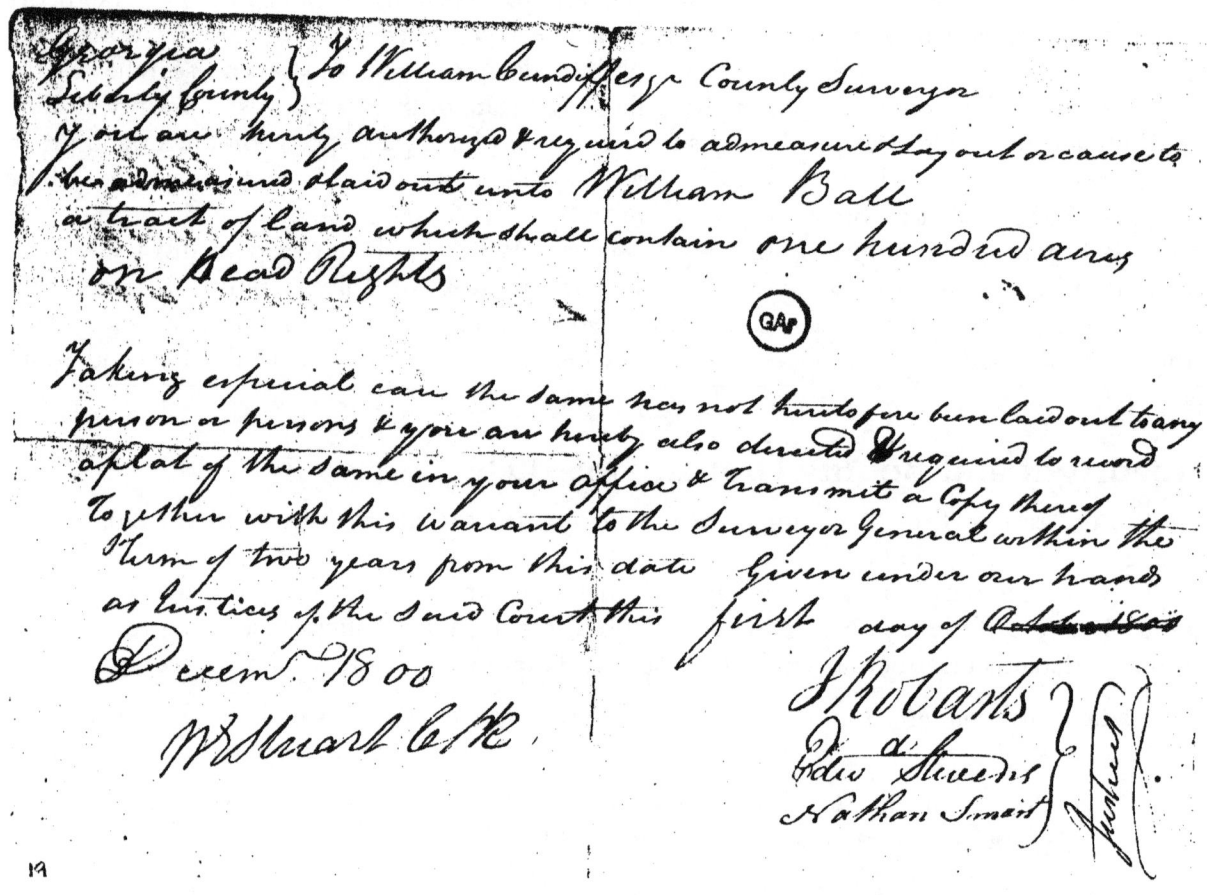

Figure 7 - **Warrant to the surveyor of Liberty County to issue a Headright land grant.**

Revolutionary War Bounty Grants

These grants were made by the state of Georgia to men who had served in the Georgia forces and to certain Georgia civilian residents of the state during the war. These grants are discussed in more detail in the next section.

Georgia also gave bounty land certificates to volunteers in the state's so-called "Oconee War" of 1787–1790 against the Creek Indians. No lands were ever granted on those certificates and, starting in 1808, the state of Georgia tried to buy back the certificates. A list of the soldiers in this campaign is published in *Georgia Genealogist* under "State Records—Bounty Land Warrants." A history of the Oconee War by Gordon B. Smith and a list of the certificates that were bought back are in Marion R. Hemperley, *Military Certificates of Georgia* (Atlanta: Georgia Secretary of

State, 1983). Personal information on fifteen of these soldiers is published in *Georgia Genealogical Magazine* Issue 32 (1969): 2217. Also see "Some Soldiers of the Oconee War," *Georgia Genealogical Society Quarterly* 26 (1990): 187–188. For a national list of state (but not federal) bounty land grants for Revolutionary War service see Lloyd DeWitt Bockstruck, *Revolutionary War Bounty Land Grants Awarded by State Governments* (Baltimore: Genealogical Publishing Company, 1996).

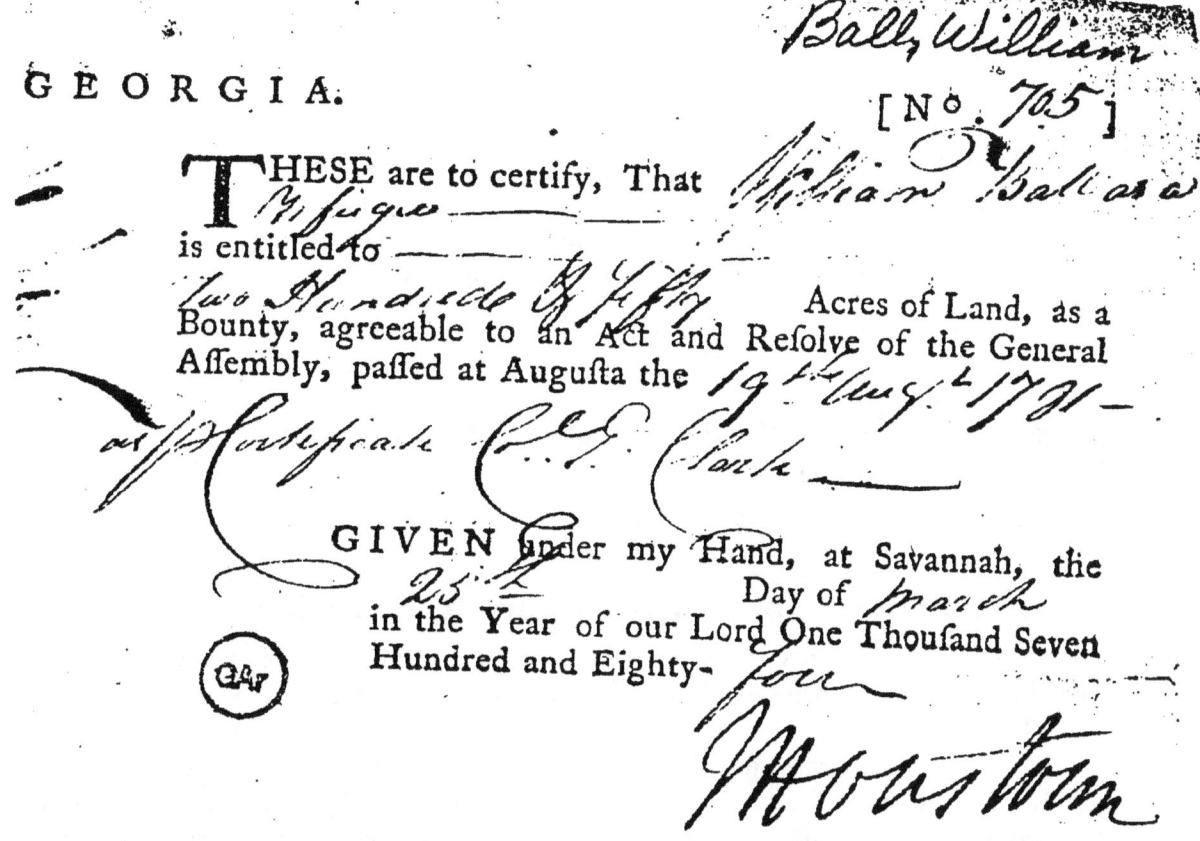

Figure 8 - Certificate to issue a bounty land grant of two hundred and fifty acres.

Land Court Warrants

Starting in 1783, land courts in headright counties dispensed warrants for lands in their respective counties based upon size of family or payment of fees. Sometimes the land court minutes give such genealogical data as the number of persons in each family or the earliest recorded date that a person appears in the county. When they survive, these records frequently can be found on the county records microfilm at the Georgia Archives.

Plat Books

Georgia's early county plat books sometimes contain descriptions of property not found anywhere else, including instances where neighboring plats are drawn to show how they adjoin. In the counties that were previously part of colonial Georgia, sometimes county copies of otherwise lost colonial Georgia plats can be found. Not all Georgia county plat books have been microfilmed (some pages of plat books were too big to be filmed), and some plats were recorded in the county deed books instead of separate plat books (including many of the otherwise lost colonial plats). Always check early county deed books for re-recorded and otherwise not recorded colonial deeds and plats. The official state copies of the plats for land grants, both recorded and original, are at the Georgia Archives.

Mary A. Abbe compiled and published a database index on CD-ROM, *Georgia Colonial and Headright Plat Index, 1735-1866* (Taylor Foundation and Georgia Archives, 2005). She has agreed to share her data with the public, and the data from her index appears on the website of the Georgia Archives at http://cdm.sos.state.ga.us/cdm4/platindex.php.

Grants of Town Lots

The Georgia Archives has records of the grants of town lots made by the commissioners of the cities of Brunswick, Columbus, Macon, and Milledgeville. For information on specific holdings see Marion R. Hemperley, *The Georgia Surveyor General* (Atlanta: Georgia Secretary of State, 1982).

The state grant records of town lots are on microfilm at the Georgia Archives as follows:

Brunswick, microfilm Drawer 286 Roll 40

Columbus, microfilm Drawer 54 Roll 32 and Drawer 286 Rolls 41 and 42

Macon, microfilm Drawer 286 Roll 41

Milledgeville, microfilm Drawer 70 Roll 37

Federal Bounty Grants for Revolutionary War Service

The United States also gave bounty lands to veterans of the American Revolution who served in the continental (not the state or militia) forces, although these grants were not made until many years after the Revolution and after most of the soldiers had sold their certificates to land speculators. For Georgia and the southeastern United States, most of this information is published in Volume 1 of Robert S. Davis, *A Researcher's Library of Georgia* (Greenville, SC: Southern Historical Press, 1987). None of the federal bounty lands were in Georgia, although some of the claimants were Georgia residents. Additional records of these grants can be found in the following:

"Abstracts of Bounty Land Book NN." *Georgia Genealogical Society Quarterly* 18 (1982): 194–200, which gives abstracts of claims for bounty by heirs of Continental soldiers. Microfilm of these records has been donated to the Georgia Archives.

Brown, Margie G. *Genealogical Abstracts [of] Revolutionary War Veterans [of Virginia] — Script Act 1852*. Oakton, VA: privately printed, 1990.

McMullin, Philip W. *Grassroots of America*. Salt Lake City: Gendex Corp., 1972, which is an index to the land and claims volumes of the *American State Papers*, a series of published early American records. The American State Papers through 1875 are also included on the Library of Congress free "American Memory website: http://memory.loc.gov/ammem/hlawquery.html

"Some Notes on Revolutionary War Claims." *Heritage Quest* no. 70 (July–August 1997): 27–29.

White, Virgil D. *Genealogical Abstracts of Revolutionary War Pension Files*. Waynesboro, TN: National Historical Pub. Co., 1990.

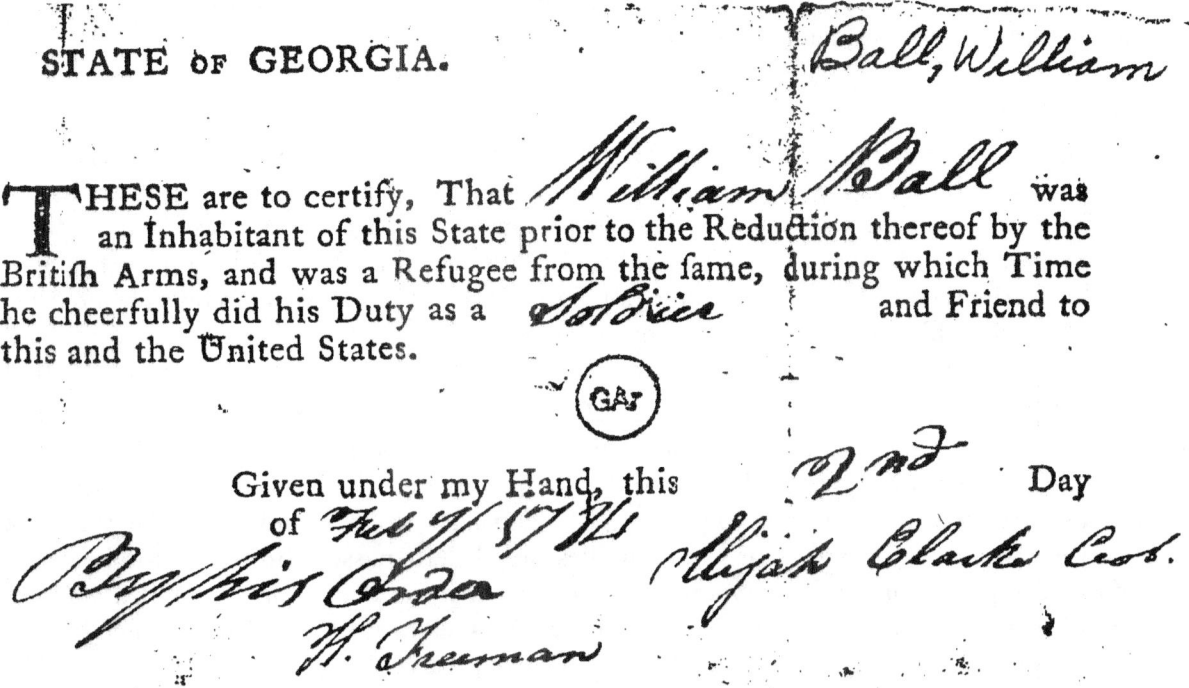

Figure 9 - This affidavit certified that William Ball did his duty as a soldier prior to 1784.

Indian Depredations Claims

Claims filed by persons or their heirs who had suffered property loss in Creek Indian raids in Georgia, 1770s–1820s, are included in eight books of indexed typescripts at the Georgia Archives called the "Indian Depredations." Although only a small number of people filed such claims, these records do contain a great deal of personal information and sometimes even proof of Revolutionary War service. Abstracts of these volumes are published in Donna B. Thaxton, *Georgia Indian Depredations Claims* (Americus, GA: privately printed, 1990). Not included in any of the above are the Indian claims listed in "Georgia Indian Depredations Claims, 1836–1837," *Muscogiana* 4 (1993): 53–58. For historical background, see Larry C. Skogen, *Indian Depredation Claims, 1796–1920* (Norman: University of Oklahoma Press, 1996).

Migration Records Including Passports by Georgia Governors

Bibliographies of many types of records for research in Georgia migration are in the following:

Davis, Robert S. *Research in Georgia*. Greenville, SC: Southern Historical Press, 1980, 206–207, 209–210.

Dorsey, James E. *Georgia Genealogy and Local History*. Spartanburg, SC: The Reprint Company, 1983, 15–16.

The Dorsey book also includes citations to unpublished tavern registers and other manuscript sources for documenting migration. Migration to and from Georgia can sometimes be documented through deeds and powers of attorney recorded in county deed books. Frequently, however, the powers of attorney are omitted in the indexes to these records. For biographical data on leaders on the southern frontier, see Dan L. Thrapp, *Encyclopedia of Frontier Biography*, 3 vols. (Signal Mountain, TN: Mountain Press, 1995).

Claims Filed by British Merchants

These claims for money owed to British Merchants before the American Revolution can document migration to and through Georgia before and after the war. For most of the claims relevant to Georgia, check the past issues of *The North Carolina Genealogical Society Journal* and *The Virginia Genealogist*. At least some of this material is also abstracted in Peter Coldham, *American Migrations* (Baltimore: Genealogical Publishing Company, 1999). The Georgia Archives has received a donation of microfilm of the original claims.

Passports

The United States government and some state governments issued "passports" or letters of good conduct to persons traveling through Indian lands on lawful business. Often the bearers of these passports were pioneers moving through Indian lands to new homes in the west. The passports are useful for proving that some families only briefly passed through Georgia and did not settle there. Passports for the Southern states are abstracted in Dorothy Williams Potter, *Passports of Southeastern Pioneers, 1770–1823* (Baltimore, MD: Gateway Press, 1982), which includes the sources used in the earlier Mary G. Bryan [Louise F. Hays], *Passports Issued by Georgia Governors, 1785–1820*, 2 vols., (Washington, DC: National Genealogical Society, 1959–1964). Additional records of a few of these passports can be found in "File II Names" at the Georgia Archives.

Georgians in Other States

Useful for documenting Georgians in what became Alabama, Mississippi, and other states is the *American State Papers*, the land and claims volumes which have a combined index in Philip W. McMullin, *Grassroots of America* (Salt Lake City: Gendex Corp., 1972); this series, through 1875, is also included in the Library of Congress free website "American Memory;" the series known as the *Territorial Papers of the United States*; the books on the records of the Mississippi Territory by Ben and Jean Strickland; and the Alabama land office records published by Marilyn Barefield, Marilyn Hahn, Margaret Cowart and Marilyn Davis Hahn, comp., *Old Cahaba Land Office Records & Military Warrants 1817–1853*, rev. ed. (Birmingham: Southern University Press, 1986). Records of many of the first American settlers of the Mississippi Territory and the Southwest, before 1820, appear in the earliest county records of the western counties of Georgia in those years, especially Baldwin, Pulaski, and Twiggs Counties. Many of these records have been abstracted and published.

Georgians in French and Spanish Territories

Several sources exist for information on Georgians who resided in what became the states of Alabama, Arkansas, Florida, Louisiana, and Mississippi before those areas passed to the United States. For northern Florida see the Index to the East Florida Collection of the University of Florida: http://www.uflib.ufl.edu/EastFlorida/search_by.asp and the West Florida History Center of the University of Florida: http://libguides.uwf.edu/universityarchives. Also see:

Georgia Research
Chapter II: Research by Time Period

Beers, Henry Putney. *French and Spanish Records of Louisiana: A Bibliographical Guide.* Baton Rouge: Louisiana State University Press, 1989, 183–236.

Mills, Elizabeth S. "Spanish Records: Locating Anglo and Latin Ancestry in the Colonial Southeast." *National Genealogical Society Quarterly* 73 (1985): 243–261.

Servies, James Albert. "A Bibliography of West Florida." Microfiche 011 at the Georgia Archives. The P. K. Yonge Library of the University of Florida has extensive holdings on British East Florida.

Thompson, Shirley Joiner. *The People of East Florida During the Revolutionary War/War of 1812 Period.* Waynesville, GA: privately printed, 1982.

Books of indexes or abstracts to such records include, among others:

Feldman, Lawrence H. *Anglo-Americans in Spanish Archives.* Baltimore: Genealogical Publishing Company, 1991.

Hays, Louise F. "Georgia, East Florida, West Florida and Yazoo Land Sales, 1764–1850." Unpublished typescript. Atlanta: Georgia Department of Archives and History, 1941.

Index to the Records of Old Mobile Cathedral of the Immaculate Conception, 1704–1891. Pascagoula, MS: Jackson County Genealogical Society, 1994.

McBee, Mary Wilson. *The Natchez Court Records, 1767–1805.* Baltimore: Genealogical Publishing Company, 1979.

Rowland, Dunbar, and A. G. Sanders. *Mississippi Provincial Archives: French Dominion* [1729–1763]. 5 vols. Baton Rouge: Louisiana State University Press, 1927.

The Microfilm Library of the Georgia Archives also has binders containing early records of St. Augustine and East Florida, including the Anglo-American settlers there, as in "Roman Catholic Records, St. Augustine Parish, Florida: White Baptisms 1784–1838." Also see Alex D. Williams, "Some East Florida Records That Show . . . Camden-Glynn County Families" on microfilm at the Georgia Archives in Drawer 21, Box 36, and Drawer 32, Box 30. Also included on the microfilm from Drawer 32, Box 30, are the censuses of Spanish East Florida for 1813 and 1814 in Spanish.

Slave Importation

From 1818 to 1849, persons importing slaves into Georgia from other states were required to register those slaves in Georgia's county superior courts. These records are found in the county records microfilm of the Georgia Archives. The records for Camden, Columbia, and Jackson Counties sometimes give the residence of the importers, although most of these men are merely listed as residents of Georgia.

Typescripts of Early Government Records

The Georgia Archives has various indexed typescripts of state executive, house, and senate records of Georgia, 1783–1893. Most of this material covers 1783 to 1800. Although the chances of finding information on any particular person in these records is remote, the fact that these indexed volumes can be quickly checked makes using them worthwhile, particularly when researching someone of prominence. The *Southeastern Genealogical Exchange* has published some of these typescripts for the period 1799–1800.

Fleeing Felons

Proclamations issued by Georgia governors for the arrest of fleeing felons are abstracted to 1900 in Robert S. Davis, *The Georgia Black Book* (Greenville, SC: Southern Historical Press, 1982). Aside from giving a reason for why certain persons left Georgia suddenly, these proclamations also give names and dates of death of murder victims of these fleeing felons. Similar information for captured murderers can be found in indictments in superior court minute books; also see A. J. Wright, *Criminal Activity in the Deep South, 1700–1930: An Annotated Bibliography* (Westport, CT: Greenwood Press, 1989) and Thomas M. McDade, *The Annals of Murder: A Bibliography of Books and Pamphlets on American Murders from Colonial Time to 1900* (Norman, OK: University of Oklahoma Press, 1991) as well as http://www.blacksheepancestors.com.

The printed indexes to Georgia newspapers and the abstracts from Georgia newspapers prepared by Tad Evans and his associates (cited elsewhere) frequently access information on murder and on vigilantism, even in newspapers far from the events being reported. A unique, related source for this time period is Jimmy E. Anderson, *Deaths, Murders, and Lynchings Abstracted from Lumpkin County, Georgia, Newspapers, Volume 1, 1873–1900* (Dahlonega, GA: privately printed, 1998.)

Military Rosters and Commissions

Rosters often provide proof of a person serving or enlisting in a certain place on a certain date. For federal volunteers see:

> Clark, Murtie June. *American Militia in the Frontier Wars, 1790–1796.* Baltimore, MD: Genealogical Publishing Company, 1990.
>
> Kratovil, Judy Swaim. *Georgia Governor's Journals 1789–1798 County, State and Militia Officers.* Fernandina Beach, FL: Wolfe Publishing, 2000.
>
> "Pay Claims for Georgia Militia, 1792–1827." *Georgia Genealogical Magazine* 36, no. 1 (1997): 22–35.
>
> White, Virgil D. *Index to Volunteer Soldiers, 1784–1811.* Waynesboro, TN: The National Historical Pub. Co., 1987.

Federal Direct Tax Records

Lists of defaulters from the federal tax of 1798, published in 1812, are in Robert S. Davis, *Georgia Black Book, Volume II* (Greenville, SC: Southern Historical Press, 1987), 65–100. No records survive that define the boundaries of the 1798 federal tax districts. A good explanation of these records is Judith Green Watson, "A Discovery: 1798 Federal Direct Tax Records for Conneticut," *Prologue: The Quarterly of the National Archives* 39 (1) (Spring 2007): http://www.archives.gov/publications/prologue/2007/spring/tax-lists.html.

Yazoo Land Fraud Records

The state of Georgia did little more than claim the lands that today are the states of Alabama and Mississippi. In 1794–1795, however, a bribed Georgia legislature and governor sold the claim to those lands to companies of land speculators. Petitions opposing this sale, signed by hundreds of Georgians, were published in the *Georgia Genealogical Magazine* in 1992–1993. Names of purchasers in the Yazoo lands appear in the following:

> Babcock, Elisha. *Georgia Speculation Unveiled.* 2 vols. Hartford, CT: privately printed, 1997–1998.
>
> Clark, Helen. *The Yazoo Land Fraud.* Louisville, GA: Jefferson County Historical Society, 2009.
>
> Hays, Louise F. "Georgia, East Florida, West Florida and Yazoo Land Sales, 1764–1850." Unpublished typescript. Atlanta: Georgia Department of Archives and History, 1941.
>
> *Sundry Papers, in Relation to Claims, Commonly Called the Yazoo Claims, December 18, 1809.* Washington, DC: A. and G. Way, 1809.

For historical background see C. Peter Magrath, *Yazoo: Law and Politics in the New Republic* (Providence, RI: Brown University Press, 1966).

The American Revolution, 1776–1782

Most Georgians did not voluntarily serve in the military of either side during the American Revolution, and many were sympathetic to, if not openly active in, the British cause. Georgia had the highest percentage of Loyalists (Tories) of any colony that rebelled. The severe fighting devastated the entire state, as it existed at that time, and drove many persons into fleeing to other provinces. At the end of the war, many persons left Georgia either as expelled Loyalists or voluntarily to remain under the British government. For the military history of the conflict, with biographical information on thousands of Georgians, see Gordon B. Smith, *Morningstars of Liberty: The Revolutionary War in Georgia, 1775–1783,* 2 vols. to date (Milledgeville, GA: Boyd Publishing, 2006, 2011).

Basic Sources

The most commonly used resources in documenting an ancestor's activities in Revolutionary War Georgia are as follows:

> Candler, Allen D. *The Revolutionary Records of the State of Georgia.* 3 vols. Atlanta: Franklin-Turner, 1906. This set has a composite index at the Georgia Archives, the University of Georgia Libraries, and the Georgia Historical Society Library.
>
> Davis, Robert S. *Georgia Citizens and Soldiers of the American Revolution.* Greenville, SC: Southern Historical Press, 1979. For other sources see Davis, *Georgia Citizens and Soldiers,* 311.

Warren, Mary B. *Georgia Governor and Council Journals.* 9 vols. to date. Athens, GA: Heritage Papers, 1991–. Vols. 5–9 cover 1774–1782, years during the American Revolution.

Warren, Mary B. *Revolutionary War Memoirs and Muster Rolls.* Athens, GA: Heritage Papers, 1994.

The National Archives at Atlanta has a number of nationwide microfilms of the Revolutionary War records. These holdings include microcopies M246—*Revolutionary War Rolls, 1775–1783*; and microcopies M257 and M847—*War Department Miscellaneous Collection of Revolutionary War Records.*

The Georgia Archives has the Georgia reels of these series and, from the North Carolina Archives, the pay records of the North Carolina soldiers and citizens of the American Revolution. Similar records have been published for several states, such as:

Gwathmey, John H. *Historical Register of Virginians in the Revolution: Soldiers, Sailors, Marines, 1775–1783.* 1938. Reprint, Baltimore: Genealogical Publishing Company, 1987.

Moss, Bobby Gilmer. *Roster of South Carolina Patriots in the American Revolution.* Baltimore: Genealogical Publishing Company, 1983.

North Carolina, Daughters of the American Revolution. *Roster of Soldiers from North Carolina in the American Revolution.* 1932. Reprint, Baltimore: Genealogical Publishing Company, 1972.

State and Continental Accounts

The Revolutionary War state and continental accounts are abstracted in Volume 1 of Caroline Price Wilson, *Annals of Georgia* (1928; Reprint, Greenville, SC: Southern Historical Press, 1969). In connection with the accounts in the Wilson book, also see:

"Georgians with U.S. Accounts, 1783–1784." *Georgia Genealogical Society Quarterly* 32 (1996): 252–54.

U.S. Pay Department, *Pierce's Register* (Baltimore: Genealogical Pub. Co., 1987). Payments in the register to Georgia Continental soldiers are certificate numbers 92777 to 92900.

Land Grants During The Revolution

No land grants are known to have been issued in Georgia during the Revolution (the bounty grants were made after the war). However, a book of receipts for headright grants in Georgia for 1775 and 1778 has been published in Robert S. Davis, *A Researcher's Library of Georgia,* 2 vols. (Greenville, SC: Southern Historical Press, 1987), 1:69–94.

Bounty Land Certificates

In addition to the bounty lands that the federal government gave to Continental soldiers (see the previous section), the state of Georgia gave bounty grants to men who served in Georgia's military forces (including many soldiers recruited from North Carolina, South Carolina, and Virginia) and to certain Georgia civilians and rebel refugees. The military certificates are in the Georgia Archives and have been published in Marion R. Hemperley, *Military Certificates of Georgia* (Atlanta:

Secretary of State, 1983). The bounty land register books have been published by Mary B. Warren and Nicole M. O'Kelley in *Georgia's Revolutionary Bounty Land Records, 1783–1785* (Athens, GA: Heritage Papers, 1992). A list of the bounty land grants issued by the various state governments is in Lloyd D. Bockstruck, *Revolutionary War Bounty Land Grants* (Baltimore: Genealogical Publishing Company, 1996).

Citizens receiving bounty land grants for not having aided the British and Indians between August 20, 1781, and July, 1782, have largely not been published, although they are in the alphabetically arranged loose headright and bounty grant papers at the Georgia Archives. It is interesting to note that these citizens' certificates outnumber the military certificates, including those given to soldiers recruited from outside of Georgia, by 2,923 to 1,458. The inventory to these papers have been digitized and added to the Georgia Archives website at http://find.sos.state.ga.us/archon/?p=collections/controlcard&id=330. Also, bounty land and headright plat images are available on the Virtual Vault at http://cdm.sos.state.ga.us:2011/cdm/landingpage/collection/looseplats.

For more information on Georgia's bounty certificates and grants, see Alex M. Hitz, "Georgia's Bounty Land Grants," *Georgia Historical Quarterly* 38 (1954): 337–348. Researchers should be warned that several "authentic" or "official" lists of Georgia Revolutionary War bounty grants were published in the early decades of the twentieth-century with no documentation. Some of these lists include any land grant of the same size as a bounty grant, ignoring that most of the soldiers sold their bounty certificates, and therefore, the grants were often taken out by other persons. Some grants happen to be the same size as bounty allotments only by coincidence. The Georgia Archives has several bound volumes of grants where someone, mistakenly, wrote "bounty" on the grants in the early 1900s. Such lists can be found, for example, in the following:

> Knight, Lucian Lamar. *Georgia's Roster of the Revolution*. Atlanta: privately printed, 1920. This volume by Knight also includes some Revolutionary War service bounty certificates that were subsequently lost.
>
> Smith, George Gillman. *The Story of Georgia and the Georgia People*. 2nd ed. Macon, GA: Burke, 1902.

Revolutionary War Pension Claims

These records can provide evidence of migration, information on military service, names of relatives, and other information that is often not available from any other source. Sometimes even personal information on witnesses is included. The subscription website HeritageQuest includes a few pages from each pension, and detailed indexing is being conducted on the full pensions for the subscription website Fold3. The Georgia Archives has microfilm of a few pages from each of the claims by Georgia veterans. The National Archives at Atlanta and many libraries have National Archives microcopy M804, microfilm of all of the pages of all of the claims for all of the United States that survived and reached the federal government. Pension records can be searched and, for a fee, copies made by writing to National Archives and Records Administration, Washington, DC 20408. When ordering copies of a pension file, specifically insist upon getting copies of all of the documents in the file. Also see "A Beginners Guide to Revolutionary War Pension Claims," *Heritage Quest* no. 44 (1993): 14–15.

Georgia Research
Chapter II: Research by Time Period

Federal pension claim files are listed, and partially abstracted, in Virgil D. White, *Genealogical Abstracts of Revolutionary War Pension Files* (Waynesboro, TN: National Historical Pub. Co., 1992). They are also indexed by claimant in The National Genealogical Society's *Index to Revolutionary War Pension Applicants in the National Archives* (Washington, DC: privately printed, 1976). Many Revolutionary War pension applications for Georgia service have been transcribed on the free website Southern Campaigns of the American Revolution: http://revwarapps.org/

Other pension records are more obscure and less helpful. The records of the few Revolutionary War pension claims paid by the State of Georgia are included in Robert S. Davis, *Citizens and Soldiers of the American Revolution* (Greenville, SC: Southern Historical Press, 1979) and in Lloyd D. Bockstruck, *Revolutionary War Pensions awarded by State Governments, 1775–1874, the General and Federal Governments prior to 1814* (Baltimore: Genealogical Publishing Company, 2011). Documentation of some early federal pensions for which no pension papers survive appears in *The American State Papers*, which is indexed in Philip W. McMullin, *Grassroots of America* (Salt Lake City: Gendex Corp., 1972) and abstracted for Georgia and the Carolinas in Robert S. Davis, *A Researcher's Library of Georgia*, 2 vols. (Greenville, SC: Southern Historical Press, 1981), 1: 95-112. The National Archives and Records Administration, 700 Pennsylvania Ave. NW, Washington, DC 20408-0001 has many records of early federal Revolutionary War pensions in Record Groups 15 Records of the Veterans Administration and Record Group 217 Records of the Accounting Officers of the Treasury Department. Most of these records have not been microfilmed. Lists of federal pensioners have been compiled and reprinted by the Genealogical Publishing Company in the following volumes:

A Census of Pensioners . . . 1840 (1965).

Index to U.S. Invalid Pension Records, 1801–1815 (1991).

Pensioners of the Revolutionary War—Struck Off the Roll (1998).

Rejected or Suspended Applications for Revolutionary War Pensions (1969).

Revolutionary Pensions of 1818 (1959).

The Pension Lists of 1792–1795 (1992).

The Pension List of 1820 (1991).

The Pension Roll of 1835 (1968).

Also see Claire Prechtel-Kluskens, "Follow the Money: Tracking Revolutionary War Army Pension Payments," *Prologue: The Quarterly of the National Archives* 40 (4) (Winter 2008): http://www.archives.gov/publications/prologue/2008/winter/follow-money.html.

Many people brought petitions before Congress requesting pensions. These petitions survive today in the Legislative Research Center, National Archives and Records Administration, Washington, DC, 20408, and are indexed in *Digested Summary and Alphabetical List of Private Claims* [1789–1851] (Baltimore: Genealogical Publishing Company, 1970) and U. S. House of Representatives, Resolutions, Laws, and Ordinances Relating to. . . Officers and Soldiers of the Revolution (1838; Reprint, Baltimore : Genealogical Publishing Company, 1998). Some pension depositions are found in Georgia county superior court minute books, some of which copies never reached the pension office in Washington. No statewide compilation of such records has been made for Georgia. Also see "When a Revolutionary War Pensioner's Pension File Cannot Be Found," *National Genealogical Society Quarterly* 77 (1989): 129–132.

Final payment records sometimes give information on Revolutionary War pensions, even when the pension files have not survived, and can also provide information on when and where a pensioner died. A list of such records from National Archives microcopy M1746—*Georgia's Final Revolutionary War Pay Vouchers*, is indexed in *Georgia Genealogical Magazine* 36 (2) (1996): 98–100. Other records of final payments are found in National Archives microcopy T718—*Ledgers of Payments, 1818–1872* (available at the Georgia Archives) and in Craig Scott, *The "Lost" Pensions: Settled Accounts of the Act of 6 April 1838* (Lovettsville, MD: Willow Bend Books, 1996). Also see "Death Dates of Revolutionary War Pensioners in the South," *Georgia Genealogical Society Quarterly* 16 (1980): 239–244.

DAR Records

The National Society of the Daughters of the American Revolution (NSDAR) has compiled extensive files of records of descent from Revolutionary War soldiers. The DAR website has many valuable resources for research including an updated edition of its compilation of information on Native American and African American Patriots: http://www.dar.org/. The most current Patriot Index is available on this same website and is open to the public. Beyond its local publications and typescripts of records at archives and libraries, its major nationwide publications include the following:

> *DAR Patriot Index, Centennial Edition.* 3 vols. Washington, DC, 1990.
>
> *Genealogical Guide Master Index of Genealogy in the Daughters of the American Revolution Magazine. Volumes 1–84 (1892–1950), with Supplement Volumes 85–89, 1950–1955, Combined Edition.* Baltimore: Genealogical Publishing Company, 1994.
>
> *Index of the Rolls of Honor (Ancestor's Index) in the Lineage Books of the N.S.D.A.R.* Reprinted as 4 vols. in 2. Baltimore: Genealogical Publishing Company, 1988. First published 1916–1940 by the NSDAR.

Also see:

> Arnold, H. Ross, and Clifton Burnham. *Georgia Revolutionary War Soldiers' Graves.* Athens, GA: Georgia Sons of the American Revolution, 1993.
>
> Carter, Mary. *Georgia Revolutionary War Soldiers, Patriots, and Families.* 2 vols. Albany, GA: Georgia Pioneers, 1977.
>
> McCall, Mrs. Howard H. *Roster of Revolutionary Soldiers in Georgia.* 3 vols. Baltimore: Genealogical Pub. Co., 1968.
>
> Sons of the American Revolution: A list of its lineage files and a list of patriot graves are digitized and available on CD-ROM.

Some publications include undocumented lists of men alleged to have fought at the Battle of Kettle Creek in Wilkes County, Georgia, on February 14, 1779. Frequently these lists include hundreds of names in addition to the 140 Georgians actually in the battle. See Robert S. Davis, *Georgians in the Revolution* (Greenville, SC: Southern Historical Press, 1986): 33, and "Change and

Remembrance: How Promoting the Kettle Creek Battlefield went from the Means to Becoming the End in Itself," *Journal of the Georgia Association of Historians* 24 (2003): 61–79.

Loyalist Records

Persons claiming loyalty to the British cause during the American Revolution often filed claims with the British government for compensation for property lost as a result of their loyalty. These claims often contain a great deal of personal history on the claimants and information on colonial Georgians mentioned incidentally in the claims. The original records are in the National Archives of the United Kingdom, Ruskin Avenue, Kew, Richmond, Surrey TW9 4DU, England, and for the Georgians, most, but not all, of the records are on microfilm at the Georgia Archives in Drawer 286, Boxes 51–75 and Drawer 287, Boxes 1–5. These claims are sometimes badly organized and individually difficult to locate. For background on the Georgia claims, see Robert G. Mitchell, "The Losses and Compensations of Georgia Loyalists," *Georgia Historical Quarterly* 68 (1984): 233–243.

Biographical information on each person who filed such a claim is included in Gregory Palmer, *Biographical Sketches of Loyalists of the American Revolution* (Westport, CT: Meckler Publishing, 1984). The claims are abstracted in Peter Wilson Coldham, *American Migrations* (Baltimore: Genealogical Pub. Co., 1999) and *American Loyalist Claims,* Special Publication No. 45 (Washington, DC: National Genealogical Society, 1980). The most complete list of only the Georgia Loyalist claims is in *Georgia Genealogical Society Quarterly* 7 (1971): 93–100. The Georgia Archives microfilm reel numbers cited in that article are often incorrect.

Other Loyalist source material also exists. Records of the confiscation of Loyalist property by the state of Georgia are indexed in R. J. Taylor, Jr., Foundation, *An Index to Georgia Colonial Conveyances and Confiscated Lands Records, 1750–1804* (Spartanburg, SC: The Reprint Co., 1981). Loyalist military records are included in:

> Clark, Murtie June. *Loyalists in the Southern Campaign of the Revolutionary War.* 3 vols. Baltimore: Genealogical Publishing Company, 1981.

> Davis, Robert S. *Georgia Citizens and Soldiers of the American Revolution.* Greenville, SC: Southern Historical Press, 1979.

Accounts of monies paid to Georgians by the British army for supplies and services during the Revolution is on microfilm at the Georgia Archives in Drawer 286, Box 15, from Audit Office Papers 3/119, British Public Record Office (now at the National Archives of the United Kingdom at Kew).

Many persons left Georgia during or after the American Revolution to escape the war or American rule. Some records of these people include:

> "A Return of Refugees With Their Negroes, Who Came to the Province of East Florida in Consequence of the Evacuation of the Province of Georgia," which was published in *Georgia Genealogist* under "State Records—Tory Refugees." The photostats of records in the British Public Record Office that were used in this article are in MS 328—*Revolution: Refugees and Loyalists* in the Hargrett Rare Book and Manuscript Library at the University of Georgia.

Feldman, Lawrence H. *The Last Days of British Saint Augustine, 1784–1785: A Spanish Census of East Florida.* Baltimore: Clearfield, 1998.

Hays, Louise F. "Georgia, East Florida, West Florida and Yazoo Land Sales, 1764–1850." Unpublished typescript. Atlanta: Georgia Department of Archives and History, 1941.

Hodges, Graham Russell. *The Black Loyalist Directory: African-Americans in Exile After the American Revolution.* New York: Garland Publishing, 1996, for African American Loyalists.

Lang, Beatrice. "The 1783 Spanish Census of East Florida," serialized in *Georgia Genealogical Magazine*, beginning with Volume 39 (1971), and which gives a census of East Florida including many Loyalists. Related censuses for 1784 (mislabeled 1793) in English and for 1813 and 1814 in Spanish are on microfilm at the Georgia Archives in Drawer 32, Box 30.

"Loyalists From Georgia Who Settled in Jamaica." *Georgia Genealogical Society Quarterly* 17 (1981): 119–120.

Mowart, Charles Loch. *East Florida as a British Province, 1763–1784.* Gainesville, FL: University of Florida Press, 1964.

Parrish, Lydia Austin. "Records of Some Southern Loyalists." *Georgia Genealogical Society Quarterly* 8 (1972): 272–273, which lists the Loyalists in Ms. Parrish's unpublished work on southern Loyalists who moved to the Caribbean. Her manuscript is on microfilm at the Georgia Archives in Drawer 12, Box 1.

Peters, Thelma Peterson. "The American Loyalists and the Plantation Period in the Bahama Islands," which is on microfilm in Drawer 190, Box 76 at the Georgia Archives.

Peterson, Jean. *The Loyalist Guide: Nova Scotia Loyalists and Their Descendants.* Halifax, Nova Scotia: Public Archives of Nova Scotia, 1983, for Loyalists who went to Canada.

Siebert, Wilbur Henry. *Loyalists in East Florida.* 2 vols. Deland, FL: Florida Historical Association, 1929.

Thompson, Shirley Joiner. *The People of East Florida During the Revolutionary War/War of 1812 Period.* Waynesville, GA: privately printed, 1982.

Troxler, Georgia Carole Watterson. "Migration of Carolina and Georgia Loyalists to Nova Scotia and New Brunswick," in *Georgia Genealogist* under "Military Records—Loyalists." Ph.D. dissertation, University of North Carolina, 1974, which lists biographical sketches of Georgians. The Georgia Archives has a copy of this dissertation in microfilm Drawer 283, Box 1.

Miscellaneous Records

The Georgia Archives has microfilm of the guide, index, and originals of the Sheftall Family Papers of the American Jewish Historical Society of Waltham, Massachusetts, in Drawer 216, Box 1. These papers contain 2,500 references to Georgians and Georgia places of the Revolutionary War era. The original records, and other documents including thousands more names of Georgians during the American Revolution, in the Papers of Mordecai Sheftall (1735–1797) have been digitized and indexed with free access on the website of the Center for Jewish History in New York: http://findingaids.cjh.org/?pID=1358081. See Carolyn W. Cunningham, ed. *Sheftall Diaries (1733–1808): Georgia's First Jewish Colonists* (n.p., 2011).

The Georgia Archives also has a copy of the every-name index to persons and places in the Georgia Governors Papers of the Telamon Cuyler Collection, 1756–1786, in the Hargrett Rare Book and Manuscript Library at the University of Georgia. The names from all of the above indexes are also reproduced in volume 2 of Robert S. Davis, *A Researcher's Library of Georgia*, 2 vols., (Greenville, SC: Southern Historical Press, 1992).

John P. Butler, *Index to the Papers of the Continental Congress, 1774–1789* 5 vols. (Washington, DC: Government Printing Office, 1980) is an every-name index to National Archives microcopies M247 and M332. The index and microfilm of these papers, containing considerable personal information, are at the National Archives at Atlanta.

Also see "New Research Materials on the American Revolution in Georgia," *Georgia Historical Quarterly* 65 (1981): 316–22 and *A Guide to Pre-Federal Records in the National Archives* (Washington, DC: National Archives, 1989). For seamen held in British jails during the Revolution, see Marion and Jacob Kaminkow, *Mariners of the Revolution* (Baltimore: Magna Carta, 1967).

The website of the LAMAR Institute has, for public access, archaeological surveys and historical reports on several Revolutionary War sites in Georgia: http://www.thelamarinstitute.org/. The reports include, to date, documented information on Revolutionary War sites in Chatham and Effingham Counties as well as the specific sites Ebenezer, Kettle Creek, Spring Hill (Savannah), and Sunbury.

The Colonial Period, 1733–1775 and 1779–1782

Georgia began at Savannah on February 12, 1733, as the thirteenth and last British colony created on the American mainland. The province was initially governed by a non-profit board of trustees in England who attempted to control all aspects of the settlers' lives and to obtain as much financial support for the colony from the British government as possible. After the Trustees surrendered the province to the Crown in 1752, Georgia became a royal colony with all of the usual functions and records of a British possession. An invasion by the British army and navy in December 1778 restored the colonial civil government to Georgia during the years 1779–1782.

The best single source for information on colonial Georgians is the published and unpublished volumes of Allen D. Candler, *The Colonial Records of the State of Georgia*, which (with indexes) are both hardbound and on microfilm at the Georgia Archives. These volumes can also be found in hardcover at the Georgia Historical Society and the Hargrett Rare Book and Manuscript Library at the University of Georgia. For all but Volume 20, the indexes are bound separately.

Between the Georgia Archives and the Hargrett Rare Book and Manuscript Library of the University of Georgia, the state of Georgia has the most extensive collections of copies of its colonial records in foreign archives of any state. Almost none of this material has indexes, however, and some of it at the Georgia Archives remains unprocessed. Most of the material of obvious genealogical value has been published in sources cited below and in back issues of the *Georgia*

Genealogical Society Quarterly. Most of the records of the beginnings of the colony of Georgia from Sir John Perceval, known as Sir John Percival Papers or Earl of Egmont Papers, 1732–1745, containing information on thousands of the first Georgia colonists, have been transcribed, digitized, and indexed from the holdings of the Hargrett Library: http://fax.libs.uga.edu/egmont/.

For historical background on this period, see:

    Coleman, Kenneth. *Colonial Georgia—A History*. Millwood, NY: KTO, 1976.

    Davis, Harold E. *The Fledgling Province: A Social and Cultural History of Colonial Georgia, 1733–1776*. Chapel Hill: University of North Carolina Press, 1976.

The First Georgians

Most of the settlers sent from Europe to Georgia by the Trustees died soon after arrival or fled Georgia for more established and less restrictive British provinces. Information on the first Georgians can be found in the following:

    Baine, Rodney M. "New Perspectives on Debtors in Colonial Georgia." *Georgia Historical Quarterly* 77 (1993): 1–19, which gives historical background on the initial settlement of colonial Georgia.

    Bockstruck, Lloyd Dewitt. *Denizations and Naturalizations in the British Colonies in America, 1607–1775*. Baltimore: Genealogical Publishing Company, 2005.

    Coulter, E. Merton, and Albert B. Saye. *A List of the Early Settlers of Georgia*. 1949. Reprint, Athens: University of Georgia Press, 1967, which is a roster of the settlers sponsored by the Georgia Trustees. The 1967 edition also includes a list of the settlers sent to Georgia on the *Ann*, the first ship to arrive in Georgia. Supplements to this volume include "Georgia's First Settlers: Revised, Corrected, Annotated, and Cross-Referenced." *Georgia Genealogical Society Quarterly* 19 (1983): 111–131; and Thomas B. Jones Jr., *Passengers of the Ann and Their Descendants; Georgia's Original Families* (Albany, GA: privately printed, 1985).

    Temple, Sarah B. Gober, and Kenneth Coleman. *Georgia Journeys*. Athens: University of Georgia Press, 1965, which is a book on the lives of Georgia's first settlers.

Colonial Georgia Censuses

Some national publications erroneously identify certain letters in the British Public Record Office as colonial Georgia censuses. The only known colonial Georgia censuses are published as "Settlers In and Around Savannah [1738]," *Georgia Genealogical Society Quarterly* 26 (1990): 2–6; "A 1738 Census of Frederica, Georgia," *Georgia Genealogical Society Quarterly* 25 (1989): 150–155; "A Census of Darien, Georgia, 1741," *Georgia Genealogical Society Quarterly*. 24 (1988): 212–224; and "The 1743 Census of Georgia and Its Critic," *Georgia Genealogical Society Quarterly* 21 (1985): 2–15. Also see Jeannette Holland Austin, *Emigrants from Great Britain to the Georgia Colony* (Riverdale, GA: privately printed, 1970), which also includes many American-born Georgians.

Georgia Research
Chapter II: Research by Time Period

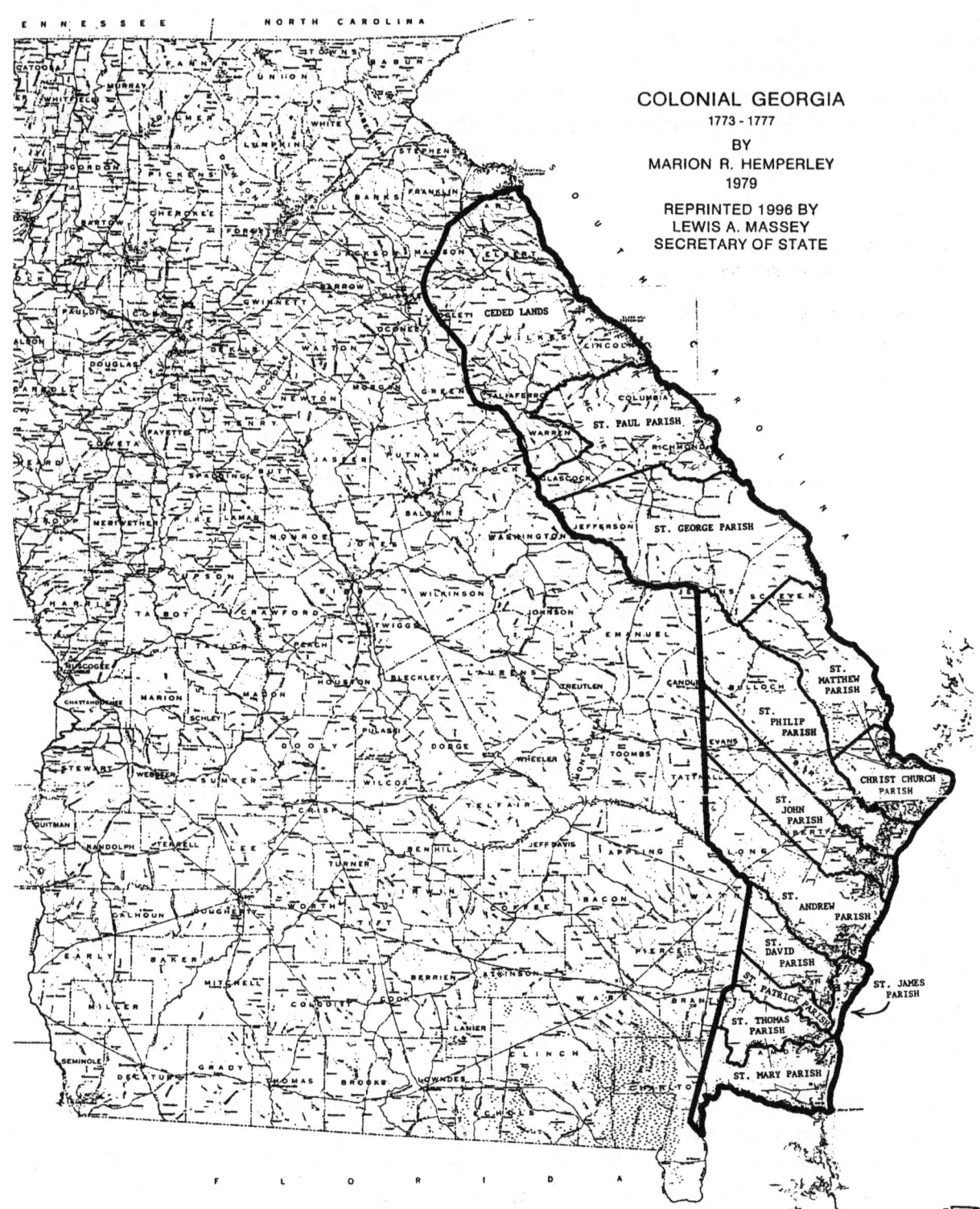

Map 6 - Parishes of Georgia between the years of 1773 and 1777.

Land Grants

The conditional land grants made by the Georgia Trustees, 1733–1739, are listed in "Georgia's First Land Grants, 1733–1739," *Georgia Genealogical Magazine* 95 (1985): 35–40, based upon a list from the British Public Record Office and on microfilm in Drawer 21, Box 47, at the Georgia Archives. Other lists can be found in George White, *Historical Collections of Georgia* (New York: Pudney and Russell, 1855), 35–40 and George Gillman Smith, *The Story of Georgia and the Georgia People,* 2nd ed. (Macon, GA: privately printed, 1902), 557–560. The original sources for these lists are not known. For a list of the original town lot owners of Savannah, see "The First Savannahians, 1733–1755," *Georgia Genealogical Society Quarterly* 29 (1993): 84–86.

Land Grants, 1752–1775

For a description of how land was granted when Georgia was a royal colony, see Farris Cadle, *Georgia Land Surveying History and Law* (Athens: University of Georgia Press, 1991). The land grant records include:

Trustee Grants that Became Royal Grants

Records of registrations of trustee grants as royal grants, sometimes containing personal information, are published in Pat Bryant, *Entry of Claims for Georgia Landholders,* 1733–1755 (Atlanta: Georgia Secretary of State, 1975), based upon manuscript Volume M/U3 at the Georgia Archives. Also see Frances Beckemeyer, *Abstracts of Georgia Colonial Conveyance Book C-1, 1750–1761* (Spartanburg, SC: The Reprint Co., 1975).

Royal Land Grants and Colonial Plats

Georgia's state copies of royal land grants and surviving colonial plats are abstracted, by parish, in the incomplete nine volumes of Pat Bryant and Marion Hemperley, *English Crown Grants in Georgia* (Atlanta: Georgia Secretary of State, 1972–1976). Note: St. James Parish is included in the volume by Pat Bryant, *English Crown Grants for Islands in Georgia, 1755–1775* (Atlanta: Georgia Secretary of State, 1972). Also see *An Index to English Crown Grants in Georgia* (Atlanta: R. J. Taylor, Jr., Foundation, 1989). All of Georgia's colonial land grants survive except for the contents of Book N, the last land grant book, although copies of only one-fourth of the colonial plats still exist. These land grant records are at the Georgia Archives. Information on the lost grants and plats is found in sources cited below. A few private copies of plat maps survive in the holdings of the National Archives. See *Pre-Federal Maps in the National Archives: An Annotated List* (Washington, DC: National Archives: 1971) and Robert S. Davis, *A Researcher's Library of Georgia,* 2 vols. (Greenville, SC: Southern Historical Press, 1987, 1991), 1: 19–28, 2: 169–171. For British colonial military bounty lands see Lloyd DeWitt Bockstruck, *Bounty and Donation Land Grants in British Colonial America* (Baltimore: Genealogical Publishing Company, 2007).

Petitions for Colonial Headright Grants

The genealogically–valuable petitions for colonial headright grants are abstracted in Mary B. Warren and Jack Moreland Jones, *Georgia Governor and Council Journals,* 9 vols. to date (Athens, GA: Heritage Papers, 1991–). The petitions also are abstracted in Candler, *The Colonial Records of Georgia* except, for those for 1773; see "Lost 1773 Petitions for Land," *Georgia Genealogical Society Quarterly* 36 (2000): 32–37.

Memorials for Quit Rents

The most complete list of Georgia's royal land grants is believed to be the memorials for quit rents. This record has been published by Mary B. Warren as *Georgia Land Owners Memorials, 1758–1776* (Athens, GA: Heritage Papers, 1988). For historical background, see Beverly W. Bond, Jr., *The Quit-Rent System in the American Colonies* (Gloucester, MA: Peter Smith, 1965), 350–354.

Military Records

Accounts of monies paid to Georgians for supplies and services during the War of Jenkins' Ear, 1738–1741, are on microfilm at the University of Georgia Libraries in FILM Georgia E303 C55, and at the Georgia Archives in Drawer 286, Box 15. A roster of General Oglethorpe's regiment, including the names of several men who remained in Georgia, and rosters of Georgia rangers in the 1750s and 1760s, are published in Murtie June Clark, *Colonial Soldiers of the South* (Baltimore: Genealogical Publishing Company, 1983), 968–992. Rosters, frequently with biographical sketches, of General Oglethorpe's rangers are included in Daniel T. Elliott, *Argyle: Historical Archaeological Study of a Colonial Georgia Fort* (Athens, GA: LAMAR Institute, 1997); available for free on the website of the LAMAR Institute: http://www.thelamarinstitute.org/ along with reports on Argyle, Bethany, Ebenezer, Fort St. Andrew, Sansavilla Bluff, and Vernonburg. Rosters of the Ceded Lands rangers are in Robert S. Davis, *The Wilkes County Papers, 1773–1833* (Greenville, SC: Southern Historical Press, 1979), 38–43. For historical background on the military in the colonial period, see Larry E. Ivers, *British Drums on the Southern Frontier: The Military Colonization of Georgia, 1733–1749* (Chapel Hill: University of North Carolina Press, 1974); James M. Johnson, *Militiamen, Rangers, and Redcoats: The Military in Georgia, 1754–1776* (Macon, GA: Mercer University Press, 1992); and James Biser Whisker, *The American Colonial Militia*, 5 vols. (Lewiston, NY: Edwin Millen, 1997). In the latter, the South is included in Volume 5.

Colonial Georgia Books of Record, 1754–1782

Prior to 1778, all local government functioned through the courthouse of colonial Savannah County in Savannah, Georgia. The records that survive today at the Georgia Archives have largely been published or indexed:

Estate Records

Colonial Georgia estate records, loose and bound, are indexed in R. J. Taylor, Jr., Foundation, *Index to Probate Records of Colonial Georgia, 1733–1778* (Spartanburg, SC: The Reprint Co., 1983). Some other loose Georgia colonial estate records are in manuscript archives across the county such as the J. P. Morgan Library and the Historical Society of Pennsylvania. Sometimes such records can be located by Internet searches that include manuscript departments of individual libraries.

Wills

The colonial Georgia wills are abstracted in Mary Givens Bryan, *Abstracts of Colonial Wills of the State of Georgia, 1733–1777* (1962; Reprint with index, Spartanburg, SC: The Reprint Company, 1981) and Mabel F. LaFar and Caroline P. Wilson, *Abstracts of Wills of Chatham County, Georgia, 1773–1817* (Washington, DC: National Genealogical Society, 1936). The latter includes "Colonial Will Book B," long thought to have been lost, but now correctly identified as Chatham County Will Book B. Also see "Corrections on Some Colonial Georgia Wills," *Georgia Genealogical Society Quarterly* 27 (1991): 116 and the corrected copy of the LaFar and Wilson book in the Georgia Historical Society Library.

Conveyances

The colonial conveyance (deed) books—but not the mortgage and deed of gift books—are indexed in R. J. Taylor, Jr., Foundation, *An Index to Georgia Colonial Conveyances and Confiscated Estates Land Records, 1750–1804* (Spartanburg, SC: The Reprint Co., 1981). Page numbers in this index refer to the first page upon which the individual deed is recorded and not necessarily to the page or pages where the name appears. Many land records of different types are abstracted in William H. Dumont, *Colonial Georgia Genealogical Data, 1748–1783,* Special Publications Number 36 (Washington, DC: National Genealogical Society, 1976). For a bibliography of publications of Georgia's colonial land records, see Robert S. Davis, *Research in Georgia* (Greenville, SC: Southern Historical Press, 1980), 169–172.

Miscellaneous

Additional colonial records include the following:

Deeds of Gift, Bonds, Marriage Settlements, and Miscellaneous.

> The marriage settlements from these records and other miscellaneous personal information from these books is abstracted in William H. Dumont, *Colonial Georgia Genealogical Data 1748–1783* (Washington, DC: National Genealogical Society, 1971), as are the names from the marks and brands books.

Microfilm Collection at the Georgia Archives:

> 1751–1775. Unbound records. Record Group 49-1-20; Drawer 230, Box 23.
>
> 1755–1762. Book J. Record Group 49-1-9; Drawer 40, Box 34. The contents of this book have been abstracted in George F. Walker, *Abstracts of Colonial Book J, 1755–1762* (Atlanta: R. J. Taylor, Jr., Foundation, 1977).
>
> 1762–1765. Book O (indexed). Record Group 49-1-9; Drawer 40, Box 34.
>
> 1765–1772. Book R (indexed). Record Group 49-1-9; Drawer 40, Box 34.
>
> 1772–1774. Book Y-1 (indexed). Record Group 49-1-9; Drawer 40, Box 35.
>
> 1774–1777. Book Y-2 (indexed). Record Group 49-1-9; Drawer 40, Box 35.
>
> 1777–1787. Book HH (indexed). Record Group 49-1-9; Drawer 40, Box 37.
>
> 1779–1780. Book JJ (not indexed). Record Group 49-1-9; Drawer 40, Box 37.
>
> 1780–1781. Book KK-1 (not indexed). Record Group 49-1-9; Drawer 40, Box 37.
>
> 1781–1782. Book KK-2 (not indexed). Record Group 49-1-9; Drawer 40, Box 37.
>
> 1783–1792. Book CCC (not indexed). Record Group 49-1-9; Drawer 40, Box 38.
>
> 1792–1813. Book DDD (not indexed). Record Group 49-1-9; Drawer 40, Box 38.

Marks and Brands.

    1755–1778. Book K or Y3. Record Group 49-1-12; Drawer 40, Box 42.

Mortgages. (no index)

    1755–1763. Book E. Record Group 49-1-4; Drawer 40, Box 26; rough index at Georgia Archives

    1762–1765. Book P. Record Group 49-1-4; Drawer 40, Box 26.

    1765–1770. Book Q. Record Group 49-1-4; Drawer 40, Box 27.

    1770–1775. Book W. Record Group 49-1-4; Drawer 40, Box 27.

    1776–1778. Book EE. Record Group 49-1-4; Drawer 40, Box 28; rough index at Georgia Archives.

The Salzburgers

A number of sources are available for research on these central European Protestants who settled in what is today Effingham, Screven, and Chatham Counties. Daniel T. Elliott has done several archaeological and historical reports on the Bethany and Ebenezer that are available for free from the LAMAR Institute's website: http://www.thelamarinstitute.org/. Also see:

    Gnann, Pearl. Georgia *Salzburger and Allied Families*. rev. ed. Greenville, SC: Southern Historical Press, 1993.

    Jones, George Fenwick. *The Salzburger Saga*. Athens: University of Georgia Press, 1983, 145–191, which includes a list of the Salzburgers with personal information, although the list is not included in the index. Dr. Jones has also published several volumes of translations of Salzburger records and other works including:

    ———. *The Germans of Colonial Georgia, 1733–1783*. Baltimore: Genealogical Publishing Compnay, 1986.

    ———. *Ebenezer Record Book, 1754–1781*. Baltimore: Genealogical Publishing Compnay, 1991, which is translated from German.

    Works Progress Administration (WPA). "The Beginning of Salzburger Settlement in Georgia," which is a two-volume typescript on microfilm at the Georgia Archives in Drawer 55, Box 63. Volume 2 contains considerable information on individual Salzburgers.

The Georgia Salzburger Society, 2980 Ebenezer Road, Georgia Highway 275, Rincon, GA 31326, website http://www.georgiasalzburgers.com/ is an active organization of Salzburger descendants.

Other Groups in Colonial Georgia

Many different groups settled in colonial Georgia, within their own special communities. Some of these groups left records:

Congregationalists

For information on the Congregationalist community at Midway in present-day Liberty County, see James Stacy, *History and Published Records of the Midway Congregational Church* (1894; Reprint, Spartanburg, SC: The Reprint Company, 1979). Also see John M. Sheftall, *Sunbury on the Midway* (1977; Reprint, Norcross, GA: National Society Daughters of American Colonists, 1995).

Queensborough

The history and land records of the Queensborough Scots-Irish township in what is now Jefferson and surrounding counties are in Loris D. Cofer, *Queensborough or the Irish Town and Its Citizens* (Louisville, GA: privately printed, 1977).

Quakers

Records of the Quakers and non-Quakers of Georgia's Wrightsborough settlement in what is now McDuffie and surrounding counties are published in Robert S. Davis, comp., *Quaker Records in Georgia* (Augusta, GA: Augusta Genealogical Society, 1991).

Moravians

The Moravians in Georgia are included in Adelaide L. Fries, *The Moravians in Georgia, 1735–1740* (1905; Reprint, Baltimore: Genealogical Publishing Compnay, 1967).

Bethesda

Colonial Georgia's famous orphanage Bethesda is discussed in Edward J. Cashin, *Beloved Bethesda* (Macon, GA: Mercer University Press, 2000); and Boyd Stanley Schlenther, "To Convert the Poor People in America: The Bethesda Orphanage and the Thwarted Zeal of the Countess of Huntingdon," *Georgia Historical Quarterly* 78 (1994): 225–256. The earliest list of the orphans appears in George White, *Historical Collections of Georgia* (New York: Putney and Russell, 1955), 332–335. For a partial list for 1785 to 1858 see *Minutes of the Union Society . . . From 1750 to 1858* (Savannah, GA: John M. Cooper, 1860), reprinted in "Some Early Orphans of Georgia, 1741–1746," *Georgia Genealogical Magazine* 36 (1996): 22–27.

Scottish Highlanders

James Oglethorpe brought a regiment of Scottish Highlanders to Georgia as troops in Georgia's struggle with Spanish Florida. See Anthony W. Parker, *Scottish Highlanders in Colonial Georgia* (Athens: University of Georgia Press, 1996). They settled in Darien and have many descendants in Georgia today. A roster of these men is published in Murtie June Clark, *Colonial Soldiers of the South* (Baltimore: Genealogical Pub. Co., 1983).

Passenger Lists

The few surviving colonial Georgia passenger lists are included in P. William Filby and Mary R. Meyer, *Passenger and Immigration Lists Index,* 3 vols. (Detroit: Gale Pub.Co., 1981, and annual supplements, 1981–).

Marriage Records

The few surviving colonial Georgia marriage records are compiled in *Georgia Genealogist* under "State Records—Marriages."

Cemeteries

Many colonial cemetery records are published in *Some Early Epitaphs in Georgia, Georgia Society of the Colonial Dames of America* (Durham, NC: Georgia Society of Colonial Dames of America, 1924).

Newspapers

Georgia's newspapers began in Savannah with the *Georgia Gazette* in 1763. An every-name index to the surviving issues of this newspaper, and Savannah newspapers in general, 1763–1845, is available at the Georgia Archives, other major Georgia libraries, and on loan through Latter-day Saints Family History Centers. Also see Elizabeth Evans Kilbourne, *Savannah, Georgia, Newspaper Clippings (Georgia Gazette)*, 1763–1806, 5 vols. (Savannah, GA: Tad Evans, 1999–2003) and Genealogical Committee, *Early Deaths in Savannah, 1763–1803: Obituaries and Legal Notices* (Savannah, GA: Georgia Historical Society, 1993).

Most of the surviving issues of the newspaper the *Georgia Gazette*, 1763–1774, and the *Royal Georgia Gazette*, 1779–1782, both Savannah newspapers, have been scanned onto the subscription websites GenealogyBank and (for big research libraries) Historic American Newspapers from microfilm of the Library of Congress. This microfilm is available at the Georgia Archives, Georgia Historical Society Library, and the University of Georgia. Colonial newspaper print presents special difficulties when optical character recognition (OCR) is used to digitize them.

The Woodruff Library of Emory University has free public access to two British newspaper databases, the Burney Collection for the 17th and 18th centuries and British Newspapers for the 19th century. Emory also allows public access to databases for early British periodicals. British Newspaper Archives can be searched for free at http://www.britishnewspaperarchive.co.uk/, but one has to subscribe to read and copy the actual pages.

Miscellaneous

The Margaret Davis Cate Collection contains extensive files on coastal Georgia families, but particularly for the colonial period. The originals of this collection are at the Georgia Historical Society in Savannah, although also on microfilm at the Georgia Archives and other libraries. A catalog/index is in Mary Linda Leslie, *Margaret Davis Cate Collection* (St. Simons, GA: Fort Frederica Association, 1976).

The claims by persons loyal to the British cause during the American Revolution, mentioned in the previous section, name thousands of colonial Georgians in various records included as evidence in the claims. See, for example, "A Census of Sunbury Before the Revolution," *Georgia Genealogical Society Quarterly* 32 (1996): 111–114. No index to persons incidentally mentioned in the claims currently exists.

Similarly, no index exists to the thousands of colonial Georgians mentioned in the business records of the Telfair Company. These records are located at the Georgia Historical Society in Savannah; in Special Collections of the William R. Perkins Library, Duke University; and on microfilm at the Georgia Archives in Drawer 281, Boxes 66–67. In addition there is no index for the George Galphin store account books at the Georgia Historical Society.

Finally, for more information on colonial Georgia, see:

"Some Residents of Augusta, 1774–1783." *Georgia Genealogical Magazine* 36, no. 4 (1996): 300–305.

"The Colonial Georgia Account Book of John Glen, 1769–1804." *Georgia Genealogical Society Quarterly* 29 (1993): 74–83.

"Some Colonial Georgia Signatures." *Georgia Genealogical Magazine* 36, no. 1 (1996): 8–10.

Georgia Research
Chapter II: Research by Time Period

Researcher Notes

CHAPTER III
COUNTIES, COUNTY RECORDS, AND LOCAL HISTORY SOURCES

Local Government Records

Most original Georgia county records remain in the individual county courthouses across the state; however, some counties have lost records in courthouse fires and by other means. It should be noted that some records were re-recorded from private copies after the county records were lost, and sometimes records of families in "burned out" counties can be found in adjoining counties and even in counties in adjoining states. For a general listing of Georgia's county records, in addition to this chapter, see Robert S. Davis, *Research in Georgia* (Greenville, SC: Southern Historical Press, 1980): 83–145.

The Georgia Archives has microfilm of the most genealogically significant recorded and bound pre-1900 county records and some original county records. For information on records not microfilmed, see:

"Georgia County Records That Have Not Been Microfilmed." *Georgia Genealogical Society Quarterly* 23 (Summer 1987): 93.

"Some County Records in Georgia Missed by Previous Microfilming Projects." *Georgia Genealogical Society Quarterly* 22 (Fall 1986): 164–65.

Basic types of Georgia records include:

Probate Court or Ordinary's Records

Georgia estate records, including those for orphans, free persons of color before 1865, deceased persons, and mental incompetents, are maintained in this office. Marriage licenses and, in most counties, birth and death records from 1919–1927 can also be found here. In some counties the county health departments keep vital records. The Georgia State Vital Records Office also maintains birth and death records beginning in 1919. In Georgia, birth records are available only to the individual named on the certificate and to his or her parents. Georgia Death Records from 1919–1930 are available online in the Georgia Archives Virtual Vault (www.GeorgiaArchives.org). Before 1868, the ordinary was part of the inferior court where the records were often grouped for ordinary, court, and county purposes.

Following is more specific information on various kinds of Georgia probate court records:

Marriages
Georgia began requiring the recording of marriage licenses with an act of December 6, 1805. The following Georgia counties have marriage records (bonds, licenses, registers, or marriage

books) that predate 1805, and the earliest marriage date is in parentheses: Bulloch (1795), Columbia (1787), Effingham (1791), Elbert (1804), Greene (1786), Glynn (1800), Jefferson (1803), Liberty (1784), Oglethorpe (1794), Richmond (1785), Warren (1794), and Wilkes (1792).

Even after 1805 many couples, ministers, and officials were negligent in having marriage licenses recorded. Georgia law required marriage licenses to be issued in the bride's county of residence and returned there for recording. Most Georgia counties have indexes to marriage records, although frequently the indexes are incomplete, and usually they list only the names of grooms.

Scanned images from microfilm of marriage records for most Georgia counties through about 1900 are available in the Georgia Archives Virtual Vault. See: http://www.GeorgiaArchives.org.

Additional information about early Georgia marriage records can be found in the guide, *Documenting Marriages in Georgia, Colonial Period Through 1900* by the Georgia Archives, (Atlanta: Georgia Secretary of State, 1996). It is also available on the Georgia Archives website under the "What Do We Have" area.

A comprehensive guide to Georgia marriage records is: Georgia Genealogical Society, *A Resource Guide to Georgia Marriage Records* (Atlanta: privately printed, 2006).

Although only the Warren books below have any documentation, among the published sources for Georgia marriages records are:

> Dodd, Jordan R., ed. *Georgia Marriages Early to 1800*. Bountiful, UT: Precision Indexing Publishers, 1990.
>
> Ingmire, Frances T. *Colonial Georgia Marriage Records From 1760–1810* . St. Louis, MO: privately printed, 1985.
>
> Ingmire, Frances T. *Georgia Marriage Records*. Frances Ingmire published early marriage records for most Georgia counties. Each county is arranged alphabetically by groom and contains an index to the brides. The Georgia Archives bound these into a nine volume set titled *Georgia Marriage Records*.
>
> ———. *Georgia Marriages 1801 to 1825*. Orem, UT: Liahona Research, 1993.
>
> Liahona Research. *Georgia Marriages, 1826–1850*. Bountiful, UT: Heritage Quest, 1999.
>
> Warren, Mary B. "State Records: Marriages" in the *Georgia Genealogist*. List of marriage licenses to 1810.
>
> Warren, Mary B. *Georgia Marriages, 1811 Through 1820*. Athens, GA: Heritage Papers, 1988.

Four volumes of Georgia marriages, arranged by county, have been published under various titles by Joseph Maddox and Mary Carter, but without the sources given and with marriage records that came from sources other than county records.

Estates

Not all persons who died in Georgia left wills or even estate records. Many people had little or no property, and some gave away their estates before they died. Sometimes the heirs did not bother with the paperwork. Many estate records are incomplete. In a few counties such as Baldwin and Lincoln, general indexes to estate records were compiled, but for most counties a researcher must check the individual volumes of the estate records for an index. The researcher should be aware that the individual estate record volumes are sometimes indexed by the name of the administrator rather than the decedent. Unbound or loose estate case files for many counties have been microfilmed and are available at the Georgia Archives. For additional background information on estate records, see Carole Shammas, et al., *Inheritance in America from Colonial Times to the Present* (New Brunswick, NJ: Rutgers Press, 1997).

Some statewide indexes to Georgia estate records exist. A published index of Georgia wills before the Civil War is in Ted O. Brooke, *In the Name of God Amen: Georgia Wills, 1733–1860* (Marietta, GA: privately printed, 1976). Mr. Brooke is preparing a revision of that volume and a second volume to list wills from 1861 through 1900. For lists of many surviving early Georgia estate records, see Jeannette H. Austin, *Georgia Intestate Records* (Baltimore: Genealogical Publishing Company, 1986) and *Index to Georgia Wills* (same publisher, 1985). This latter work is incomplete and not all references given are to wills. The inclusive dates of records included in these two volumes are not given.

Superior Court Records

Records of property transactions, divorces, minutes, tax records, and civil and criminal court actions are kept in this office. Below is specific information on these types of records:

Property Records

Local Georgia property records can include mortgages, deeds, deeds of gift, powers of attorney, depositions, marriage contracts, and even wills and emancipations, recorded in what are usually titled "deed books." In most Georgia counties the individual volumes are indexed, and there is a cumulative index to grantors (direct) and grantees (indirect or reverse) to all of the volumes. However, these indexes usually are only to the deeds and not the other documents recorded in the deed books. Frequently, when property is sold for taxes or debt, the sheriff rather than the owner is indexed as the grantor. Some land lottery counties have deed indexes that are arranged by land lot numbers and list all of the deeds relating to each lot. Many deeds were never recorded or were recorded many years after being signed. For background on land records, see E. Wade Hone, *Land and Property Research in the United States* (Salt Lake City: Ancestry, 1997).

Deeds and other property records should be recorded in the county where the property lay at the time the document was recorded, not necessarily the county where the owner resided or the county where the land lay at the time that the deed was signed. Some deeds were recorded years—as much as fifty years or more—after being signed. For example, if a family of orphans in Burke County won a land lot in Cherokee County in the 1832 land lottery and sold the land lot, the deed would not normally have been recorded in Burke County. It would be found recorded in Cherokee County or whatever county the land was in when the deed was recorded. However, sometimes it could be found recorded in the purchaser's or seller's county. This situation provides some hope to researchers whose families lived in counties like Burke County where the early deed records were destroyed.

Published Georgia deed resources are listed under the individual counties in this chapter. Many deed abstracts are published in periodicals and may be located by using the *Periodical Resource In-*

dex (PERSI), which is available online through HeritageQuest. No other comprehensive finding aid exists for published Georgia deed records.

Modern deeds may be searched through the Georgia Superior Court Clerk's Association at http://www.gsccca.org, a pay site.

Divorces

Georgia began allowing divorces in 1793. The petitions for divorce were always filed in the superior court of the county where the couple resided. Until 1833, after two assenting jury trials in the superior court, couples were also required to obtain the consent of the Georgia Legislature to obtain a divorce. Some couples still obtained divorces through the Legislature as late as 1847, and many married women obtained the right to their own property through legislative act until that right was granted universally in 1868. Divorce records in Acts of the Georgia Legislature from 1793–1868 are abstracted in Robert S. Davis, *Georgia Black Book, Volume II* (Greenville, SC: Southern Historical Press, 1987), 9–30.

Court Case Records

Court case records for divorces and other actions are difficult to use. The minute books are often not indexed and, in any event, usually give the barest details on a case. However, in an indictment for murder, the date of death of the victim is usually given in the minute books. Except for depositions from witnesses unable to appear in court, recorded testimony from court cases did not usually exist until the 1880s, and then only for capital cases (cases where death existed as a potential punishment). The court case files, when they survive in local courthouses, are often unorganized and unavailable for use by the public from lack of storage space.

Beginning in 1846, court cases could be appealed to the Georgia Supreme Court. These files are at the Georgia Archives. The Archives has an in-house finding aid to the pre-1917 Georgia Supreme Court Case Files. See Supreme Court of Georgia on page 12.

Tax Records

Georgia tax records can provide, depending upon the year, such information as residence, potential residence, original grantee, absence suggesting death or removal, number of males liable for militia duty (the poll tax), neighbors, and much more. Tax records make good substitutes and supplements for census records. This is especially true for 1790 when some forty per cent of the state's population lived in Wilkes County, where the tax records survive for that period. See Frank Parker Hudson, *Wilkes County, Georgia, Tax Records, 1785–1805*, 2 volumes (Atlanta: privately printed, 1996). Georgia tax records, starting in 1851, include the number of men in each household eligible for militia duty and the number of free persons of color. In 1854, they indicate the number of school-age children in each household and starting in 1906, names and service of Confederate veterans.

Until an act of December 23, 1840, Georgians could pay their taxes in any county. This 1840 law was, however, ignored for many years as individual Georgians continued to pay taxes in any county where they owned property, usually the county with the cheapest rates. Consequently, tax records through 1840 can be valuable for identifying counties where a person possibly was living or would live later in Georgia. Names on tax defaulters' lists may suggest sudden migration to other counties or even states.

The Georgia Archives has a large collection of early Georgia tax digests on microfilm and a complete set of original tax digests for each county starting about 1872, many of which have not been microfilmed. The list of tax digests available at the Georgia Archives may be accessed through the "Finding Aids @ Georgia Archives" link on the Georgia Archives website (http://www.GeorgiaArchives.org). A list of tax digests on microfilm at the Georgia Archives is in Robert S. Davis, *Research in Georgia* (Greenville, SC: Southern Historical Press, 1980), 173–81. This book also includes an explanation of tax laws and digests. Published tax records can be found in some county histories and periodicals. The latter may be located by use of the *Periodical Source Index* (PERSI). Also see James E. Dorsey, *Georgia Genealogy and Local History: Bibliography* (Spartanburg, SC: Southern Historical Press, 1983). Unfortunately, no single bibliography of Georgia tax digests exists, so it is often difficult to identify extant digests and to locate published records. The major publications of Georgia tax records include:

> Accelerated Indexing Systems International. *Early American Series: Georgia*, which contains a cumulative index to the tax digests of Camden (1809), Chatham (1793, 1806), Franklin (1800–1811, 1818, 1819), Glynn (1790), Hancock (1812), Lincoln (1818), Montgomery (1797, 1798, 1805, 1806), Oglethorpe (1800), Pulaski (1818), and Warren (1794, 1805) Counties.
>
> Blair, Ruth. *Some Early Tax Digests of Georgia.* 1926; reprint edition with index added. Greenville, SC: Southern Historical Press, 1971, which includes transcripts of tax records for Camden (1794, 1809), Chatham (1806), Glynn (1790, 1794), Hancock (1812), Lincoln (1818), Montgomery (1797, 1798, 1805, 1806), Pulaski (1818), Richmond (1818), Warren (1794, 1805, 1818), and Wilkes (1792, 1793, 1794) Counties.
>
> R. J. Taylor, Jr., Foundation. *An Index to Georgia Tax Digests,* which has five volumes of indexes to tax digests of Baldwin (1810, 1815), Burke (1798), Chatham (1793, 1798, 1816), Clarke (1802, 1805, 1809, 1815), Columbia (1806), Elbert (1801, 1814), Franklin (1800, 1805), Greene (1789, 1797, 1801, 1805, 1809, 1815), Hancock (1794, 1796, 1804), Jackson (1799, 1801, 1804, 1810, 1817), Jefferson (1799, 1802, 1805, 1810, 1816), Jones (1811, 1816), Liberty (1800, 1806, 1809, 1814–1815), Lincoln (1801, 1805, 1810, 1815), Madison (1817), Montgomery (1811), Morgan (1810, 1817), Oglethorpe (1798, 1800, 1805, 1810, 1815), Pulaski (1810, 1816), Putnam (1815), Richmond (1795, 1797, 1800, 1809, 1816), Tattnall (1802, 1805, 1810, 1817), Warren (1798, 1801, 1817), and Wilkes (1791, 1801, 1805, 1809, 1816) Counties.

Many other early Georgia tax digests also survive; see for example, "First Families of Baldwin, Morgan, and Putnam Counties, 1807," *Georgia Genealogical Society Quarterly* 30 (1994): 105–10.

Some individual county tax digests have been published and are cited later in this chapter.

Other County Records

Many other kinds of records can be found in the courthouses of Georgia and in the microfilm collection of the Georgia Archives, including lists of poor school children, registrations of persons for land lotteries, state and school censuses, and much more. These records might be found in any office or room in a courthouse. Early tax records, for example, may be found in the probate court or the superior court but almost never in the tax commissioner's office. The Georgia Archives has state copies of some county records in its miscellaneous collections of loose government records concerning individuals, counties, and subjects, known as "File II Counties" and "File II Counties Oversize."

Records of illegitimate children, child apprenticeships, and sometimes adoptions frequently appear in minutes and other probate court records. Also see the name changes approved by the Georgia Legislature, 1800–1856, in Robert S. Davis, *Georgia Black Book, Volume II* (Greenville, SC: Southern Historical Press, 1987), 31–62; and Lloyd DeWitt Bockstruck, "Name Changes in Georgia by Legislative Act, 1802–1854," *Georgia Genealogical Society Quarterly* 36 (Winter 2000): 218–235 and 37 (Spring 2001): 2–37.

County Data and Special Sources

The Georgia Archives has microfilm of the most genealogically significant bound pre-1900 county records, except where noted. Should anyone know of any such records that the Georgia Archives does not have on microfilm, please contact Robert S. Davis, c/o the Georgia Genealogical Society.

Researchers should be aware that Georgia has instances of a city and county having the same name, which can cause confusion. For example, the city of Forsyth, Georgia, is in Georgia's Monroe County and not in Georgia's Forsyth County. Similarly, Monroe County should not be confused with the city of Monroe. These identical names of thirty-two Georgia cities and counties occur for Appling, Baldwin, Bartow, Cobb, Colquitt, Crawford, Dawson, Decatur, Douglas, Evans, Forsyth, Franklin, Gordon, Haralson, Jackson, Jasper, Jefferson, Lumpkin, Macon, Madison, Mitchell, Monroe, Morgan, Newton, Oconee, Oglethorpe, Pulaski, Quitman, Screven, Towns, Washington, and White.

Researchers should also be aware that, although only Georgia counties are included in the summaries listed below, many Georgia families appear in records of nearby counties in adjoining states. For example, many early Wilkes County, Georgia, families appear in contemporary records of the then adjoining Edgefield County/District, South Carolina. Similarly, families may appear simultaneously in Muscogee County, Georgia, and adjoining Russell County, Alabama. Sometimes this situation appears regionally, as when families of coastal McIntosh County, Georgia, and Beaufort County/District, South Carolina, also appear in the local records of Georgia's port of Savannah in Chatham County.

The capsule summaries of Georgia's counties, beginning after the included maps, give the following information:

1. Name of county

    Included are names of counties that have been abolished and Georgia's colonial parishes, from which Georgia's first counties were created.

2. Map number of county

Use to find the location of the county on the present-day Georgia map located in this chapter.

3. County seat and ZIP code

    Use for writing county officials about records.

    Letters to the superior court should be addressed to the Clerk of Superior Court at the county courthouse at the city and ZIP code indicated.

    Letters to the probate court should be addressed to the Clerk of Probate Court at the county courthouse at the city and ZIP code indicated.

    A complete list of county officials may be found in the *Official Directory of U.S. Congressmen, State and County Officers*, which may be accessed online from: http://www.sos.georgia.gov/elections.

4. Date of creation of the county and source of the lands making up the county

5. First year and type of land distribution in the area of each county

    The year Georgia began issuing land grants to settlers is approximately the same year the area was initially settled, although in most instances the present county was created from other counties long after the first grants were issued.

    Georgia dispensed headright, bounty, and trustee grants from 1733 to 1909 in the eastern part of the state, and the central and western areas of Georgia were granted in a series of land lotteries from 1805 to 1833.

    For more information on the land lottery grants in Georgia, see "Land Lotteries, 1805–1833" on page 95.

6. Superior court

    The year is given when extant records begin. This may not be same as date of county formation due to fire, flood, theft, etc.

    Records include deeds, divorces, court minutes, etc.

7. Probate court

    The year is given when extant records begin.

    Records include marriages, estates, court minutes, and birth and death records.

8. Tax digests

    The year is given when extant records begin.

9. Obscure types of records

    Apprenticeship indentures

    Free persons of color registers

    Homestead and pony homestead records

    Land court minutes

Georgia Research
Chapter III: Counties, County Records, and Local History Sources

Plat books

Poor school records

This information is listed by county in "Some of What You Have Been Missing in Georgia County Records," (*Georgia Genealogical Society Quarterly* 28 (1992): 146–162). Consult the microfilm library card catalog for complete holdings of the Georgia Archives. The microfilm catalog of county records at the Georgia Archives is available online in the Archives Virtual Vault (http://www.GeorgiaArchives.org).

10. Libraries and Records Repositories

    Only major libraries in Georgia with significant genealogical collections are included. However, almost every local library in Georgia has genealogical holdings, if only a collection of local family histories. Hours at the archives and libraries listed below vary. Always call or write ahead before planning a visit. Many libraries and records repositories are listed on the GGS website (http://www.gagensociety.org) under "Research Tools" if more information is needed. Also a google search for the county library is helpful.

11. Citations to all published compilations of only the record types below are listed

    Cemetery records

    Newspaper indexes or abstracts

    Marriage records (only if published after the 2006 marriage guide)

    Land records (deeds or tax lists)

    Estate records

    Court records

    Local Histories

    Where no citation is given for a record type, no published compilation exists for that kind of record for that county. Although there are other books such as county histories, record abstracts, marriage records, etc., which partly containing these types of records, they are not cited here, and researchers should look elsewhere for them.

Publications listed in the comprehensive guide to published Georgia marriage records that was produced by the Georgia Genealogical Society are not listed. See *A Resource Guide to Georgia Marriage Records*, 2006. Published marriage resources for the counties of Atkinson, Berrien, Dawson and Ware Counties are listed below as they were published after this guide was compiled.

Chapter IV contains listings of genealogical periodicals concerning particular areas.

Georgia Research
Chapter III: Counties, County Records, and Local History Sources

Map 7 - Georgia counties in 2012.

Georgia Research
Chapter III: Counties, County Records, and Local History Sources

Map 8 - Seats of government for each of Georgia's 159 counties.

Georgia Research
Chapter III: Counties, County Records, and Local History Sources

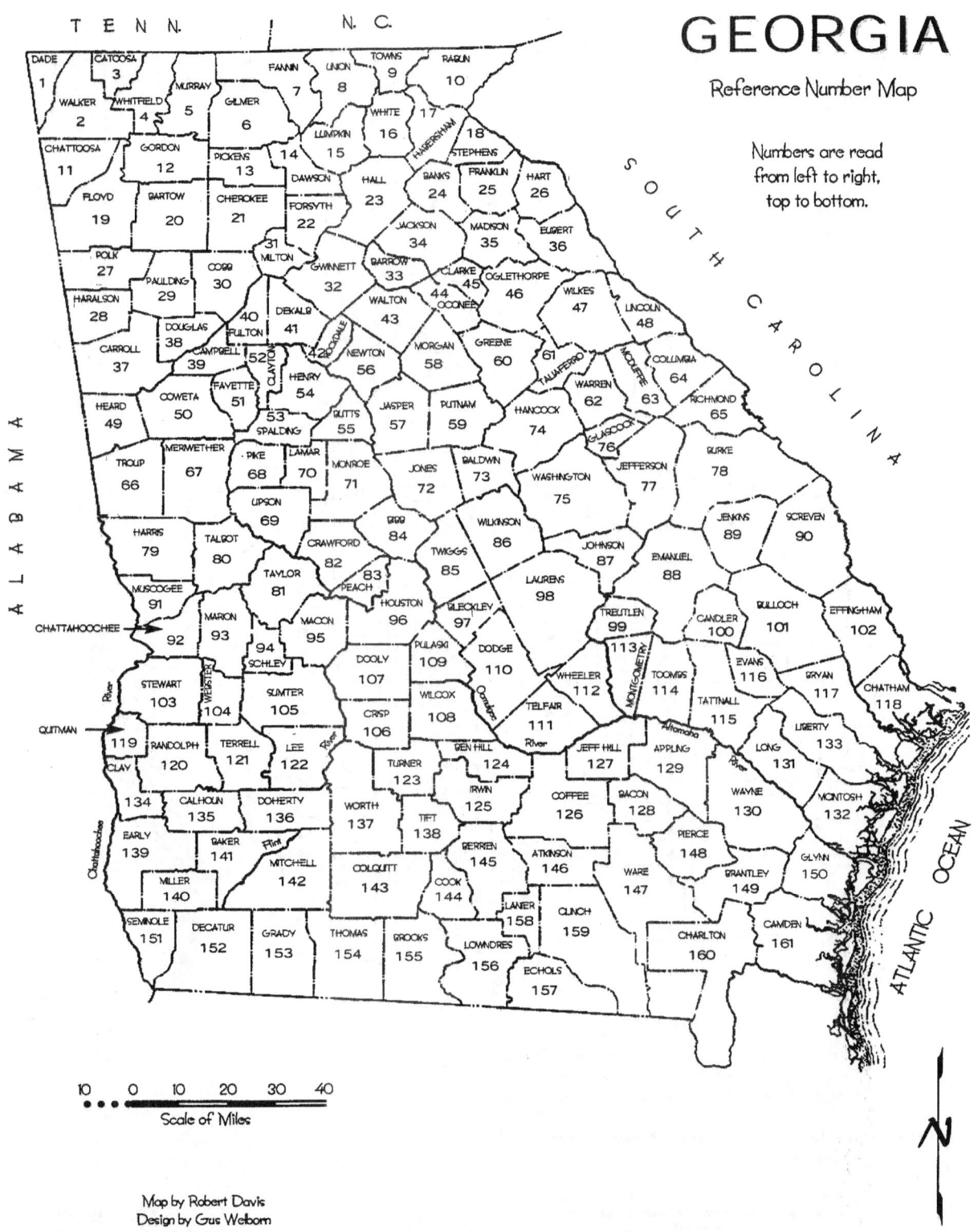

Map 9 - Use reference numbers found with county listings in this chapter to locate the county on Georgia Counties and Colonial Parishes.

Georgia Research
Chapter III: Counties, County Records, and Local History Sources

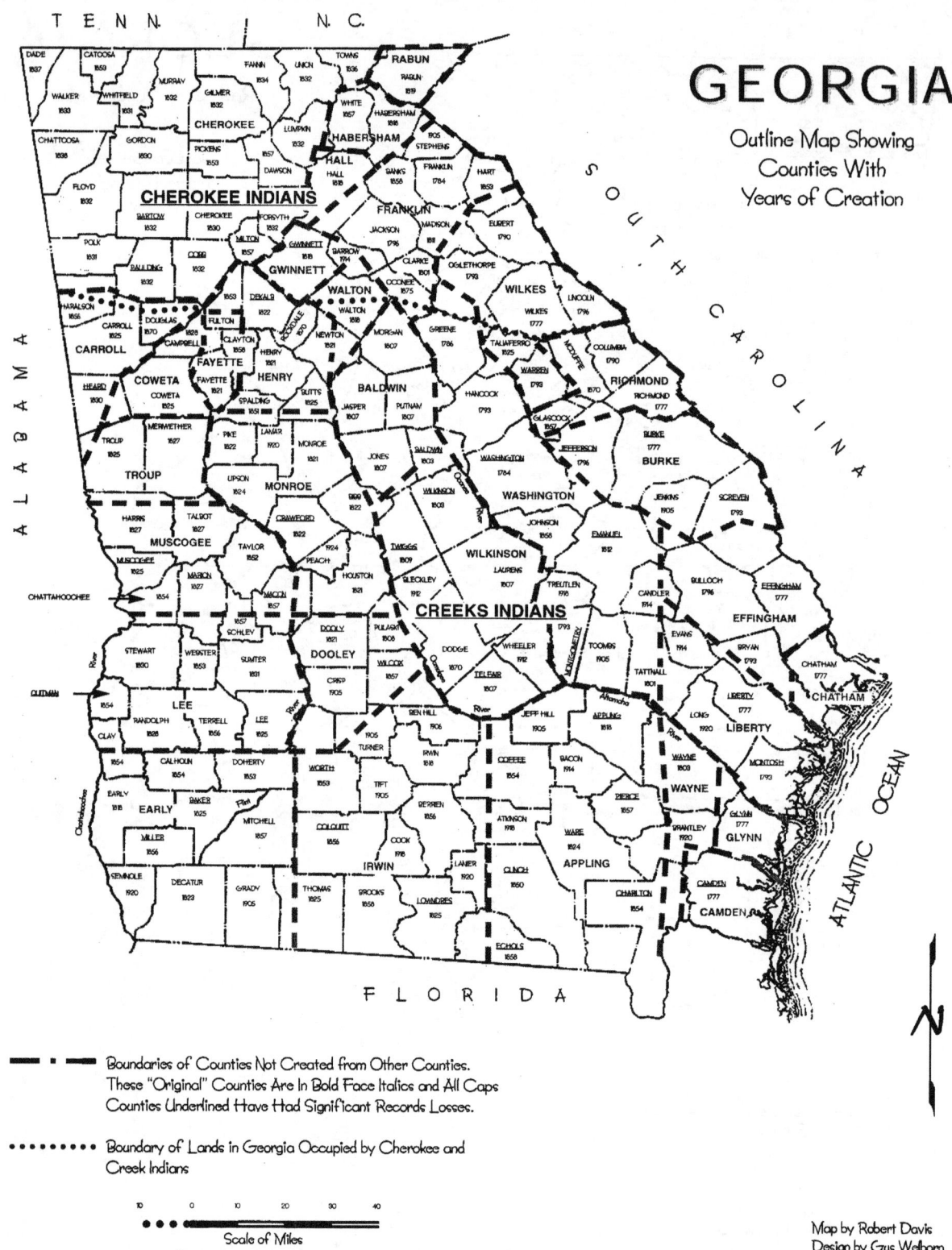

Map 10 - Year of creation of each Georgia county.

Georgia Colonial Parishes

The following colonial Georgia Parishes were created in 1758 and 1765 as a means of subdividing the colony for purposes of locating land, collecting taxes, regulating the militia, holding elections, etc. Parishes never functioned as local governments; all local government functions for Georgia were handled at the colonial capital of Savannah. The state constitution of 1777 used these parish boundaries to create Georgia's first eight counties.

CHRIST CHURCH PARISH. Created in 1758; boundaries used to create Chatham County.

ST. ANDREW PARISH. Created in 1758; boundaries used to create Liberty County.

ST. DAVID PARISH. Created in 1765; boundaries used to create Glynn County.

ST. GEORGE PARISH. Created in 1758; boundaries used to create Burke County.

ST. JAMES PARISH. Created in 1758; boundaries used to create Liberty County.

ST. JOHN PARISH. Created in 1758; boundaries used to create Liberty County.

ST. MARY PARISH. Created in 1765; boundaries used to create Camden County.

ST. MATHEW PARISH. Created in 1758; boundaries used to create Effingham County.

ST. PATRICK PARISH. Created in 1765; boundaries used to create Glynn County.

ST. PAUL PARISH. Created in 1758; boundaries used to create Richmond and Wilkes Counties.

ST. PHILIP PARISH. Created in 1758; boundaries used to create Effingham and Chatham Counties.

ST. THOMAS PARISH. Created in 1765; boundaries used to create Camden County.

Georgia Counties

APPLING COUNTY. Map #129.

County seat is Baxley, 31513.

Created December 15, 1818, from Indian lands ceded in 1814 and 1818.

Land was first distributed in the 1820 Land Lottery.

Superior court records begin in 1828.

Probate court records begin in 1857.

Tax digests begin in 1870; 1851 also available.

Major published records

　Cemetery

　　Maneely, Margaret and Edward. *Marked Graves of Appling County, Georgia.* Olney, MD: privately printed, 1984.

　　Shaw, Aurora C. *Some Appling County, Georgia, Cemeteries.* Jacksonville, FL: privately printed, 1973.

ATKINSON COUNTY. Map #146.

County seat is Pearson, 31642.

Created November 5, 1918, from Coffee and Clinch Counties.

Land was first distributed in the 1820 Land Lottery.

All records begin in 1919.

The Georgia Archives has no records on microfilm of this post-1900 county, although original tax digests beginning in 1920 are available.

Major published records

　Newspaper

　　Register, Zoie Cribb. *Pearson, Georgia, Newspaper Clippings, Volume I, 1917–1925.* Homerville, GA: Huxford Genealogical Society, 2010.

　Marriage

　　Register, Zoie Cribb, *Marriages of Atkinson County, Georgia 1919-1950.* Homerville, GA: Huxford Genealogical Society, 2010.

BACON COUNTY. Map #128.

County seat is Alma, 31510.

Created November 3, 1914, from Appling, Pierce, and Ware Counties.

Land was first distributed in the 1820 Land Lottery.

All records begin in 1915.

The Georgia Archives has no records on microfilm of this post-1900 county, although original tax digests beginning in 1915 are available.

Major published records

> Cemetery
>
>> Baker, Bonnie Taylor. *The History of Alma and Bacon County, Georgia*, Volume I. Alma, GA: privately printed, 1984, 83–115, 173–188.
>>
>> Medders, Mr. and Mrs. Jimmy. *Marked Graves of Bacon County, Georgia as of December 1969*. No place: Historical Society of Alma-Bacon County, Georgia, 1981.
>
> Local History
>
>> Baker, Bonnie Taylor. *The History of Alma and Bacon County, Georgia*, Volume I. Alma, GA: privately printed, 1984.

BAKER COUNTY. Map #141.

County seat is Newton, 31770.

Created December 12, 1825, from Early County.

Land was first distributed in the 1820 Land Lottery.

Superior court records begin circa 1866.

Probate court records begin in 1874.

Tax digests begin in 1874; 1845 also available.

Major published records

> Cemetery
>
>> Baker County Historical Society. *Cemeteries of Baker County, Georgia*. Newton, GA: privately printed, 1990.

BALDWIN COUNTY. Map #73.

County seat is Milledgeville, 31061.

Created May 11, 1803, from Indian lands ceded in 1802 and 1805 and from Hancock County. Part of Baldwin County east of the Oconee River was part of Hancock from 1793 until 1807, and thus settlers were there long before the 1805 Land Lottery opened Baldwin for settlement.

Land was first distributed in 1784 as headrights.

Superior court records begin in 1861.

Probate court records begin in 1807.

In addition to records on microfilm, the Georgia Archives also has unbound original inferior court case files and an index to delayed birth certificates, 1807–1948, in Record Group 105.

Tax digests begin in 1807.

Major published records

Cemetery

Nancy Hart Chapter, Daughters of the American Revolution. *Tombstone Records of Baldwin County, Georgia, Exclusive of Milledgeville.* Milledgeville, GA: Georgia Society, DAR, Volume 431, 1939.

Dawson, Elizabeth L., Louise M. Horne, and Anne M. King. *One Hundred Three Lost or Found Cemeteries of Baldwin County, Georgia, 1814–1999.* Milledgeville, GA: Mary Vinson Memorial Library, 1999.

Harrington, Hugh T. and Susan J. Harrington. *The Dead Book, Burials in the City Cemetery, Milledgeville, Georgia, 1869–1904.* Milledgeville, GA: Boyd Publishing Company, 1998.

Harrington, Susan J., et al. *Historic Memory Hill Cemetery, Milledgeville, Georgia, 1804–1997.* Milledgeville, GA: Boyd Publishing Company, 1998.

Tunnell, G. H., and L. H. Andrews. *Index to Graves in Milledgeville [Ga.];City Cemetery [and] Tombstone Records of Baldwin County, Ga., Exclusive of Milledgeville.* Danielsville, GA: Heritage Papers, 1974.

Newspaper

A subject index to the *Milledgeville Southern Recorder* for 1820–1874 is at the library of Georgia College and State University in Milledgeville and is on microfiche at the Georgia Archives. Mrs. LeMaster, listed below, compiled her index from a different set of these newspapers.

Anonymous. Scrapbook containing miscellaneous obituaries of people from Milledgeville and surrounding area, 1860–1890, oversized bound copy in the Georgia Archives.

Dasher, Wayne and Judy. *Milledgeville, Ga., Newspapers 1808–1810.* Nashville, GA: privately printed, 2000.

Evans, Tad. *Baldwin County, Georgia, Newspaper Clippings (Union Recorder), (1830–1887).* 12 vols. Savannah, GA: privately printed, 1994–1997.

———. *Milledgeville, Georgia, Newspaper Clippings (Southern Recorder), (1820–1872).* 12 vols. Savannah, GA: privately printed, 1995–1997. Volume XII of this series also includes "Miscellaneous Papers, 1825–1841."

Hartz, Fred R., et al. *Genealogical Abstracts From the Georgia Journal (Milledgeville) Newspaper, 1809–1840.* 5 vols. Vidalia and Savannah, GA: 1990–1995.

LeMaster, Elizabeth Tidd. *Abstracts of Georgia Marriage Notices from the Southern Recorder 1830–1855.* Garden Grove, CA: privately printed, 1968.

LeMaster, Mrs. Vernon L. *Abstracts of Georgia Death Notices from the Southern Recorder 1830–1855.* Orange, CA: privately printed, 1971.

Land

Ingmire, Frances Terry. *Baldwin County, Georgia, 1813 Tax List*. Signal Mountain, TN: Mountain Press, 1980.

Court Records

Baldwin County (GA). *Records of Baldwin County, Georgia*. Milledgeville, GA: Boyd Pub. Co, 1997.

Ingmire, Frances Terry. *Baldwin County, Georgia Will Book A: Abstracts, 1807–1832*. St. Louis, MO: F. T. Ingmire, 1985.

McNair, Glenn. *The Trials of Slaves in Baldwin County, Georgia, 1812–1838*. Savannah, GA: Georgia Historical Society, 1998.

Wynd, Frances. *Baldwin County, Georgia, Wills, Marriages, Lottery Registrants*. N.p.: privately published,1965.

Local History

Bonner, James C. *Millegeville, Georgia's Antebellum Capital*. Athens: University of Georgia Press, 1978.

Cook, Anna Marie Green. *History of Baldwin County, Georgia*. 1925. Reprint, Salem, MA: Higginson Book Co., 1997.

BANKS COUNTY. Map #24.

County seat is Homer, 30547.

Created December 11, 1858, from Habersham and Franklin Counties.

Land was first distributed in 1784 as headrights.

Superior court records begin in 1859.

Probate court records begin in 1859.

Tax digests begin circa 1874.

In addition to records on microfilm, the Georgia Archives also has unbound original Banks County wills, 1853–1946, in Record Group 106.

Major published records

Cemetery

Chambers, Richard J. *Cemeteries and Deaths in Banks County, Georgia*. Toccoa, GA: Commercial Printing Company, 2000.

Hebron Historical Society. *Hebron Presbyterian Church Cemetery, Banks County, Georgia*. Watkinsville, GA: privately printed, ca. 2006.

Mize, Jessie Julia. *The History of Banks County, Georgia 1858–1976*. Homer, GA: Banks County Chamber of Commerce, 1977: 276–409.

Local History

Mize, Jessie Julia. *The History of Banks County, Georgia 1858–1976*. Homer, GA: Banks County Chamber of Commerce, 1977.

BARROW COUNTY. Map #33.

County seat is Winder, 30680.

Created November 3, 1914, from Gwinnett, Walton, and Jackson Counties.

Land was first distributed in 1784 as headrights.

All records begin in 1915.

The Georgia Archives has no records on microfilm of this post-1900 county, although original tax digests beginning in 1915 are available.

Major published records

Cemetery

East Georgia Genealogical Society. *Barrow County, Georgia Cemeteries*. Winder, GA: privately printed, 2000.

Local History

Ingram, Culpepper Fred. *Beadland to Barrow: A History of Barrow County, Georgia from the Earliest Days to the Present*. Atlanta: Cherokee Publishing Company, 1978.

BARTOW COUNTY. Map #20.

County seat is Cartersville, 30120.

Created as Cass County on December 3, 1832, from original Cherokee County. The name was changed from Cass County to Bartow County on December 6, 1861.

Land was first distributed in the 1832 Land and/or Gold Lotteries.

Superior court records begin circa 1837.

Probate court records begin in 1853, although some earlier records exist.

Tax digests begin in 1871.

In addition to records on microfilm, the Georgia Archives has unbound original superior court case files, 1868–1903, and marriages from 1866–1927 in Record Group 108 (also on microfilm in Drawer 301, Boxes 67–95).

Major published records

Cemetery

Etowah Valley Historical Society. *Bartow County, Georgia Formerly Cass, Cemeteries Volume I*. Alpharetta, GA: W. H. Wolfe Associates, 1993.

Land

Belew, Imogene Basham, and Jodeen Blazer Brown. *Old Cass County (Now Bartow), Georgia Deeds, 1837–1838, 1845–1850*. Alpharetta, GA: W. H. Wolfe Associates, 1993.

Local History

Cunyus, Lucy J. *History of Bartow County, Formerly Cass*. Easley, SC: Southern Historical Press, 1976. Reprint of 1933 edition.

BEN HILL COUNTY. Map #124.

County seat is Fitzgerald, 31750.

Created November 6, 1906, from Irwin and Wilcox Counties.

Land was first distributed in the 1820 Land Lottery.

All records begin in 1906.

The Georgia Archives has no records on microfilm of this post-1900 county, although original tax digests beginning in 1907 are available.

Major published records

Cemetery

Dove, Barbara O'Neil. *Gone But Not Forgotten, Volume I, Cemeteries of Ben Hill County, Georgia*. N. p.: privately printed, 1983.

BERRIEN COUNTY. Map #145.

County seat is Nashville, 31639.

Created February 25, 1856, from Lowndes, Irwin, and Coffee Counties.

Land was first distributed in the 1820 Land Lottery.

Superior court records begin in 1856.

Probate court records begin in 1856.

Tax digests begin in 1872; 1867 also available.

Major published records

Cemetery

Griffin, Myrtie Lou, and R. A. Stallings. *Twenty Cemeteries of Berrien County, Georgia*. Homerville, GA: Huxford Genealogical Society, n.d.

Hancock, Sue, and Johnny Hancock. *Cemeteries of Berrien County, Georgia*. Rebecca, GA: privately printed, 2002.

Newspaper

Dasher, Wayne & Judy. *Clippings From the Nashville Herald*. 12 vols. Nashville, GA: privately printed, 2004–2009.

Marriage

Paulk, Jessie H. *Berrien County, Georgia Marriage Records Index 1856 to 1949*. Homerville, GA: Huxford Genealogical Society, 2008.

BIBB COUNTY. Map #84.

County seat is Macon, 31202.

Created December 9, 1822, from Jones, Monroe, Houston, and Twiggs Counties.

Land was first distributed in the 1807 and 1821 Land Lotteries.

Superior court records begin in 1823.

Probate court records begin in 1823.

Tax digests begin in 1871; 1835, 1836, and 1845 also available.

Major library resource is the Washington Memorial Library, 1180 Washington Ave., Macon, GA 31201. See Washington Memorial Library section on page 22.

Major published records

Cemetery

Gregorie, Charles C., Jr. "Bibb County Cemeteries." Typescript in Washington Memorial Library, Macon, GA, 1970.

Hallman, Lawrence Edward. *Rose Hill Cemetery Bibb County, Georgia, 1840–1871*. N.p., 1996.

Thomas, Jack G., and Katherine Moore Thomas. *Confederate Burials: Rose Hill Cemetery Macon, Georgia*. Macon, GA: Jack G. Thomas, 2003.

Willingham, Jean S., and Berthenia C. Smith. *Bibb County, Georgia Early Wills and Cemetery Records*. Macon, GA: privately printed, 1961: 22–53.

Newspaper

Evans, Tad. *Macon, Georgia, Newspaper Clippings (Messenger)*. (1823–1869). 9 vols. Savannah, Georgia: privately printed, 1997–2001.

Evans, Tad. *Macon, Georgia Newspaper Clippings (Weekly Telegraph)*. 1826–1895. 14 vols. Savannah, GA: privately printed, 2001–2010.

Farmer, Michal Martin, et al. *The Macon (Georgia) Telegraph 1826–1832*. Danielsville, GA: Heritage Papers, 1991.

Georgia Society, Daughters of the American Revolution. *Abstracts of Legal Notices in Central Georgia 1860–1862 (Macon Daily Telegraph)*. Ft. Valley, GA: privately printed, Volume 209, 1976–77.

Georgia Society, Daughters of the American Revolution. *Abstracts of Legal Notices in Central Georgia, 1863–1865 (Macon Daily Telegraph)*. No place: privately printed, Volume 215, 1977–78.

Georgia Society, Daughters of the American Revolution. *Abstracts of Legal Notices in Central Georgia, 1865–1882 (Macon Daily Telegraph)*. Jeffersonville, GA: privately printed, Volume 224, 1978–79.

Georgia Society, Daughters of the American Revolution. *Abstracts of Legal Notices of Some Middle Georgia Counties from the Journal and Messenger and the Macon Telegraph and Messenger, 1883–1885*. No place: privately printed, Volume 269, 1983–84.

"Middle Georgia Obituaries 1907–1995 in the Macon Telegraph and News," on CD-ROM in the Washington Memorial Library in Macon, Georgia. The Washington Memorial Library also has typescript indexes by Jean and Walter Ard to obituaries of early Macon newspapers for 1870–1910 and they have microfilm of all Macon newspapers for locating the actual obituaries.

Middle Georgia Regional Library (Macon, Ga.). *An Index to the Macon Telegraph & News: 1921–1991*. Macon, GA: Washington Memorial Library, 1991.

Rocker, Willard R. *Marriages and Obituaries from the Macon Messenger, 1823–1869*. Easley, SC: Southern Historical Press, 1988.

Warren, Mary Bondurant, and William Brett Hill. *The Macon (GA) Telegraph, 1833–1839*. 2 vols. Athens, GA: Heritage Papers, 1993.

Washington Memorial Library, and Middle Georgia Regional Library. *An Index to the Obituaries 1932–1987*. Macon, GA: Genealogical & Historical Room, Washington Memorial Library, Middle Georgia Regional Library, 1988.

Estate

Georgia Society, Daughters of the American Revolution. *Bibb County, Georgia Will Book B 1840–1872*, Volume 357. Macon, GA: privately printed, 1968.

Willingham, Jean Saunders. *Abstract, Bibb County, Georgia, Will Book B, 1840–1872*. Macon, GA: Mary Hammond Washington Chapter, Georgia Society, DAR, 1967.

Willingham, Jean S., and Berthenia C. Smith. *Bibb County, Georgia Early Wills and Cemetery Records [Will Book A]*. Macon, GA: privately printed, 1961: 22–53.

Local History

Barfield, James E. *Historic Macon: An Illustrated History*. San Antonio, TX: Historical Publishing Network, 2007.

Butler, John C. *Historical Record of Macon and Central Georgia…* Macon, GA: J. W. Burke Co., 1958. Reprint of 1879 edition.

Young, Ida, et. al. *History of Macon, Georgia*. Macon, GA: Marshall and Brooks, 1950.

BLECKLEY COUNTY. Map #97.

County seat is Cochran, 31014.

Created October 2, 1912, from Pulaski County.

Land was first distributed in the 1807 Land Lottery.

All records begin in 1913.

The Georgia Archives has no records on microfilm of this post-1900 county, although original tax digests beginning in 1913 are available.

Major published records

   Cemetery

   Bleckley County Elementary School. *Cemetery Survey of Bleckley County, Georgia.* N. p.: privately printed, 1977.

BOURBON COUNTY.

Created on February 7, 1785, and was abolished on February 1, 1788. Bourbon County was to have been on the Mississippi River when Georgia extended that far west, but it never functioned as a county.

BRANTLEY COUNTY. Map #149.

County seat is Nahunta, 31553.

Created November 2, 1920, from Charlton, Pierce, and Wayne Counties.

Land was first distributed in 1733 by the Trustees and formally granted beginning in 1755 and in the 1807 and 1820 Land Lotteries.

All records begin in 1921.

The Georgia Archives has no records on microfilm of this post-1900 county, although original tax digests beginning in 1921 are available.

Major published records

   Cemetery

   Durbin, Larry. *Brantley County, Georgia, Cemeteries.* Miscellaneous Publication Number 5. Jacksonville, FL: Southern Genealogist's Exchange Society, 1993.

   Stokes, Mrs. Alvin. *Brantley County Cemeteries.* Homerville, GA: Huxford Genealogical Society, 1983.

   Brantley County Historical and Preservation Society. *Cemeteries & More: Genealogy Reference, Brantley County, Georgia.* Nahunta, GA: privately printed, 2002.

BROOKS COUNTY. Map #155.

County seat is Quitman, 31643.

Created December 11, 1858, from Lowndes and Thomas Counties.

Land was first distributed in the 1820 Land Lottery.

Superior Court records begin in 1859.

Probate Court records begin in 1859.

Tax digests begin in 1866.

Georgia Research
Chapter III: Counties, County Records, and Local History Sources

Major published records

    Cemetery

        Kilpatrick, Elizabeth P. *Rural Cemeteries in Brooks County, Georgia.* N.p.: Brooks County Historical Society, 1983. Unpublished Brooks County cemetery records are available as of 1989 at the Brooks County Public Library and in the Brooks County probate court in Quitman, Georgia. Some of these records have been typed and photocopied and are available in the Georgia Archives cemetery (vertical) files and elsewhere.

        Logan, Jean and Alene Kitchens. *A Survey of Brooks County Cemeteries.* Quitman, GA: Brooks County Historical Society, 1999.

    Newspaper

        Brooks County Historical Society. *Early Brooks County Newspaper Extractions.* Quitman, GA: privately printed, 1992.

        Evans, Tad. *Brooks County, Georgia, Newspaper Clippings, Volume I (1866–1889).* Savannah, GA: privately printed, 1995.

        Huxford, Folks. *Excerpts from the Quitman Reporter, 1847–1877.* Homerville, GA: privately printed, 1947.

    Local History

        Brooks County Historical Society. *Brooks County: Echoes of Its People,* Quitman, GA: privately printed, 1993.

        Brooks County Historical Society. *Brooks County: Echoes of Its People, Vol. II,* Quitman, GA: privately printed, 2000.

        Huxford, Folks. *The History of Brooks County, Georgia, 1853-1948.* 1949. Reprint, Spartanburg, SC: The Reprint Co., 1978.

        White, George. *Brooks County, Georgia Biographies.* Signal Mountain, TN, Mountain Press, 2002.

BRYAN COUNTY. Map #117.

County seat is Pembroke, 31321.

Created December 19, 1793, from Chatham County, and took a large area from Effingham County in 1794.

Land was first distributed in 1733 by the Trustees and formally granted beginning in 1755.

Superior court records begin circa 1794.

Probate court records begin circa 1794.

Tax digests begin in 1871; 1861 also available.

Major published records

    Cemetery

        Davis, Charles H. *Bryan County, Ga. Cemeteries.* Darien, GA: Sea Griffin Pub, 1999.

Court

Wilson, Caroline Price. *Abstracts of Court Records of Bryan County, Georgia.* N.p.: 1929.

Local History

Sullivan, Buddy. *From Beautiful Zion to Red Bird Creek: A History of Bryan County, Georgia; Including Chronicles of the Old Canoochee-Ogeechee River Country.* Darien, GA: McIntosh County Board of Commissioners, 2000.

BULLOCH COUNTY. Map #101.

County seat is Statesboro, 30458.

Created February 8, 1796, from Bryan and Screven Counties.

Land was first distributed in 1733 by the Trustees and formally granted beginning in 1755.

Superior court records begin in 1796.

Probate court records begin in 1796.

Tax digests begin in 1874; 1854, 1866, and 1868 also available.

In addition to the records on microfilm, the Georgia Archives has Bulloch County original superior court case files in Record Group 116. The Telamon Cuyler Collection of the Hargrett Rare Book and Manuscript Library of the University of Georgia has two boxes of loose original Bulloch County records.

Major library resource is the Statesboro Regional Library, 124 S. Main Street, Statesboro, GA 30458. The telephone number is 912-764-1341.

Major published records

Cemetery

Bulloch County Regional Library. *Eastside Cemetery Records, Volume I, and Bulloch County Cemetery Records, Volumes I–VII.* N.p.: Georgia Society, DAR, various dates.

Newspaper

Bulloch County Regional Library. *Births, Marriages and Deaths from Bulloch County, Georgia, Newspapers 1889–1949, Volumes I–XII.* N.p.: Georgia Society, DAR, various dates.

Miscellaneous

Register, Alvaretta Kenan. *Bulloch County, Georgia Genealogical Source Material.* Swainsboro, GA: Magnolia Press, 1985. Mrs. Register's files are in the Bulloch County public library in Statesboro.

BURKE COUNTY. Map #78.

County seat is Waynesboro, 30830.

Created February 5, 1777, with the boundaries of colonial St. George Parish.

Land was first distributed in 1733 by the Trustees and formally granted beginning in 1755.

Superior and probate court records begin in 1856, although some earlier records exist.

Tax digests begin in 1855; 1798 also available.

Major published records

> Cemetery
>
>> Braswell, James A., Sr., and Marjorie Abbott. *Cemetery Records of Burke County, Georgia, August 1997*. Augusta, GA: privately printed, 1997. This book is a supplement to the work by Lillian Powell below.
>>
>> Powell, Lillian. *Grave Markers in Burke County, Georgia*. Waynesboro, GA: Chalker Publishing Company, 1974.
>
> Newspaper
>
>> Dorsey, James E. *Herndon and Lawtonville, A Collection of Newspaper Sources, 1883–1900*. Swainsboro, GA: Emanuel County Junior College, 1980.
>>
>> Knight, Jo Goodson. *Burke County Folks 1851-1900: The Events in Their Lives As Published in Early Newspapers Covering Burke and Neighboring Counties in Georgia*. Baltimore: Gateway Press, 2004.
>>
>> Knight, Jo Goodson. *Burke County Folks: The Events in Their Lives As Published in The True Citizen*. 1882-1930. 4 vols. Waynesboro, GA: J.G. Knight, 1998–2001[?].
>
> Land
>
>> Crumpton, Daniel Nathan. *Burke County, Georgia Land Records: Boundaries As of 1777*. Warrenton, GA: privately printed, 2009.

BUTTS COUNTY. Map #55.

County seat is Jackson, 30233.

Created December 24, 1825, from Henry and Monroe Counties.

Land was first distributed in the 1821 Land Lottery.

Superior court records begin in 1826.

Probate court records begin in 1826.

Tax digests begin circa 1878; 1831 and 1871 also available.

In addition to the records on microfilm, the Georgia Archives has the original index to loose superior court case files in Record Group 118.

Major published records

> Cemetery
>
>> Butts County Genealogical Society. *Butts County, Georgia Cemeteries*. Fernandina Beach, FL: Wolfe Publishing, 2000.
>>
>> Roberts, Joy. *Miscellaneous Cemetery Records of Spalding, Pike, Lamar, Butts and Henry Counties*. Milner, GA: Roberts, 1977.

Newspapers

Moss, Oliver. *Butts County Georgia Obituary Index 1900–1999*. Fernandina Beach, FL: Wolfe Pub, 2001.

Land

"Butts County Taxables, 1828," *Georgia Genealogical Magazine* No. 97 (1985): 177-83.

Marriage

Murray, Nicholas Russell, Dixie A. Murray, and Dorothy Murray. *Early Butts County, Georgia, Marriage Records, 1826–1899: Computer Indexed Marriage Records*. Salt Lake City: Hunting for Bears, 2010.

Local History

Hageness, MariLee Beatty. *Officials of Butts County, Georgia, 1826–1869*. Anniston, AL: MLH Research, 1999.

Maddox, Joseph T. *Some Mid-1800 People: Butts County, Georgia*. N.p.: privately printed, 1980.

McMichael, Lois. *History of Butts County Georgia, 1825–1976: Revised Edition*. Easley, SC: Southern Historical Press, 1988.

CALHOUN COUNTY. Map #135.

County seat is Morgan, 31766.

Created February 20, 1854, from Baker and Early Counties.

Land was first distributed in the 1820 Land Lottery.

Superior Court records begin in 1854.

Probate Court records begin in 1854.

Tax digests begin circa 1872; although some earlier records exist.

Major published records

Cemetery

Calhoun County Historical Society. *Against Oblivion: History of Calhoun County, Georgia*. Alpharetta, GA: W. H. Wolfe Associates, 1994: 501–580.

Southwest Georgia Genealogical Society, Inc. *Cemeteries of Calhoun County, Georgia*. Albany, GA: Southwest Georgia Genealogical Society, 1990.

Local History

Calhoun County Historical Society. *Against Oblivion: History of Calhoun County, Georgia*. Alpharetta, GA: W. H. Wolfe Associates, 1994: 501–580.

CAMDEN COUNTY. Map #161.

County seat is Woodbine, 31569.

Georgia Research
Chapter III: Counties, County Records, and Local History Sources

Created February 5, 1777, with boundaries that included colonial St. Thomas and St. Mary parishes.

Land was first distributed in 1733 by the Trustees and formally granted beginning in 1755.

Superior court records begin circa 1790, although some earlier records exist.

Probate court records begin in 1794.

Tax digests begin in 1819; 1794 and 1809 also available.

Major library resource is the Bryan Lang Library, 311 Camden Ave., Woodbine, GA 31569. The telephone number is 912-576-5841. Specializes in Camden and Charlton counties as well as the Georgia-East Florida borderlands.

Major published records

Cemetery

Durbin, Larry. *Camden County, Georgia, Cemeteries.* Jacksonville, FL: Southern Genealogist's Exchange Society, Inc., 1993.

Reddick, Marguerite, *Camden's Challenge: A History of Camden County, Georgia.* Alpharetta, GA: W. H. Wolfe Associates, 1976: 511–590.

Land

"The Camden County, Georgia, Land Grant Map." *Georgia Genealogical Society Quarterly* 27 (1991): 88-96. The original of this map is in the Camden County File II, Georgia Archives, Morrow.

Court

Hageness, MariLee Beatty. *Abstract of Court Minutes, 1794–1852, Camden County, Georgia.* Anniston, AL: MLH Research, 2001.

Huxford, Folks. *Camden County, Georgia Court House Records.* Homerville, GA: Huxford Genealogical Society, 1983[?].

Local History

Reddick, Marguerite, et. al. *Camden's Challenge: A History of Camden County, Georgia.* Woodbine, GA: Camden County Historical Commission, 1994.

CAMPBELL COUNTY. Map #39.

Created December 20, 1828, from Coweta, Carroll, DeKalb, and Fayette Counties.

Land was first distributed in the 1821 and 1827 Land Lotteries.

Tax digests begin in 1855.

Campbell County was abolished on January 1, 1932, when it became what is now the southern portion of Fulton County. The Campbell County records are now maintained by Fulton County in Atlanta, Georgia 30303. Some Campbell County records have been deposited at the Atlanta History Center.

Major published records

Cemetery

Cornell, Nancy Jones. *Campbell County, Georgia, Cemeteries, Volume I*. Riverdale, GA: Inkwell Publications, 1985.

Many Campbell County cemetery records are available in the *Franklin Garrett's Necrology* at the Atlanta History Center, Atlanta, Georgia. Franklin Garrett surveyed area cemeteries in the 1930s and 1940s. See http://Garrett.AtlantaHistoryCenter.com/.

Newspaper

Cornell, Nancy Jones. *Campbell County, Georgia Newspapers, 1871–1898*. Riverdale, GA: Inkwell Publications, 1984.

Land

Redmond, LaGroon, and Sylvia Watkins. *Campbell County, Georgia, Superior Court Deeds and Mortgages Grantee-Grantor Index, 1829–1931*. Roswell, GA: W. H. Wolfe Associates, 1994.

Westmoreland, Joan Turbyfield. *Old Campbell County, Georgia Land Records, 1828–1854, Deed Books A, C, D, and E*. Roswell, GA: W. H. Wolfe Associates, 1993.

Estate

Cornell, Nancy Jones. *Campbell County, Georgia Wills (1829–1931)*. N.p.: privately printed, 1988.

Hageness, MariLee Beatty. *Abstracts of Will Book B, 1863–1908, Campbell County, Georgia*. [Anniston, AL]: privately printed, 1995.

———. *Abstract of Will Book A, 1855–1862, Campbell County, Georgia*. N.p.: privately printed, 1995.

LeMaster, Mrs. Vernon L. *Abstracts of Wills of Campbell County, Georgia, 1825–1900*. Decatur, GA: privately printed, 1949.

CANDLER COUNTY. Map #100.

County seat is Metter, 30439.

Created November 3, 1914, from Bulloch, Emanuel, and Tattnall Counties.

Land was first distributed in 1733 by the Trustees and formally granted beginning in 1755.

All records begin in 1915.

The Georgia Archives has no records on microfilm of this post-1900 county, although original tax digests beginning in 1915 are available.

Major published records

Cemetery

Candler County Historical Society. *Cemeteries of Candler County, Georgia*. Metter, GA: Candler County Historical Society, 2003.

Coleman, Moses M., and Emilie K. Hartz. *Cemeteries of Candler & Evans Counties, Georgia.* Vidalia, GA: Coleman Ferrotype, 2003.

CARROLL COUNTY. Map #37.

County seat is Carrollton, 30117.

Created June 9, 1825, from Indian land ceded in 1826 and 1827.

Land was first distributed in the 1827 Land Lottery.

Superior court records begin in 1827.

Probate court records begin in 1827.

Tax digests begin in 1841; 1832 also available.

Major library resource is the West Georgia Regional Library, Neva Lomason Memorial Library, 710 Rome St., Carrollton, GA 30117. The telephone number is 770-836-6711.

Major published records

Cemetery

Parsons, Betty Jo. *Carroll County Georgia Cemeteries. Land Districts 2, 3, 4, 5, and 6 (Eastern Section) Volume 2.* Saline, MI: McNaughton & Gunn, 2006.

———. *Carroll County Georgia Cemeteries. Land Districts 7, 8, 9, 10, and 11 (Western Section) Volume 1.* Saline, MI: McNaughton & Gunn, 2005.

Newspaper

Williams, Arden, et. al. *Carroll County Times Index, 1872–1879.* Carrollton, GA: State University of West Georgia, 2002.

Land

Word, Mary Florence Arthur. *Carroll County, Georgia, Abstract of Deed Book A & B, 1827–1836; C & D, 1836–1843; E–G, 1843–1855.* 3 vols. Cullman, AL: The Gregath Publishing Company. 1992–1996.

Local History

Bonner, James C. *Georgia's Last Frontier: The Development of Carroll County.* Athens: University of Georgia Press, 1971.

CASS COUNTY.

Created December 3, 1832, from original Cherokee County and renamed Bartow County on December 6, 1861. See Bartow County.

CATOOSA COUNTY. Map #3.

County seat is Ringgold, 30736.

Created December 5, 1853, from Walker and Whitfield Counties.

Land was first distributed in the 1832 Land Lottery.

Superior court records begin in 1854.

Probate court records begin in 1854.

Tax digests begin circa 1872; although some earlier lists exist.

Major published records

> Cemetery
>
> Catoosa County Historical Society. *Catoosa County, Georgia: Cemeteries and Genealogy.* Fernandino Beach, FL: Wolfe Publishing Company, 1998.

CHARLTON COUNTY. Map #160.

County seat is Folkston, 31537.

Created February 18, 1854, from Camden and Ware Counties.

Land was first distributed in 1733 by the Trustees and formally granted beginning in 1755 and in the 1805 and 1820 Land Lotteries.

Superior court records begin in 1879.

Probate court records begin in 1854.

Tax digests begin in 1871; 1855 also available.

Major published records

> Cemetery
>
> Barnes, Elgin J. R., and Dorothy Mobley Barnes. *Cemeteries of Charlton County, Georgia.* Macclenny, FL: Baker County Historical Society, [199-].
>
> Local History
>
> McQueen, Alexander Stephens. *History of Charlton County.* Spartanburg, SC: Reprint Co., 1978.

CHATHAM COUNTY. Map #118.

County seat is Savannah, 31402.

Created February 5, 1777, with the boundaries of colonial Christ Church Parish.

Land was first distributed in 1733 by the Trustees and formally granted beginning in 1755.

Superior court records begin in 1785, although some earlier records exist.

Probate court records begin in 1777.

Tax digests begin in 1798; 1793 also available.

In addition to the records on microfilm, the Georgia Archives has unbound original marriage licenses, 1866–1877 and 1924, in Record Group 125. The Georgia Archives has the Travis Index on microfilm, Drawer 18, Roll 20, that abstracts principally but not exclusively Chatham County area marriage settlements, deeds of gift, and other genealogically valuable records from the Chatham County deeds. It is also on microfilm at the Georgia Historical Society Library. The Georgia Archives also has the Myrick Index to Savannah area marriages and deaths, 1733-1837, on microfilm in Drawer 91, Roll 60.

The Schreck Abstracts are detailed compilations of records on Chatham County property going back to the founding of Georgia . The Chatham County Records Room (Clerk of Court) has a computerized index to these abstracts and the Georgia Historical Society has the original work by Victor G. Schreck (MS1906). The latter also has vertical files and compilations on Chatham County plantations put together by the Works Projects Administration in the 1930s. The Georgia Historical Society and the Chatham County Records Room (Clerk of Court) also have the indexes to early Chatham County Superior Court case files, ca. 1782 to ca. 1911, and have the files divided between them.

Major library resource is the Chatham-Effingham-Liberty Regional Library, 2002 Bull St., Savannah, GA 31401. The telephone number is 912- 652-3697. The library has some typescript, photocopy, and manuscript materials available nowhere else. Also see Georgia Historical Society on page 19. Many Savannah area records of value to researchers are found in the Research Library and Municipal Archives of the City of Savannah, City Hall Room 103, Bay Street at Bull, POB 1027, Savannah, GA 31402. The telephone number is 912-651-6412.

Major published records

Cemetery

Bonaventure Historical Society. *Bonaventure Cemetery, Savannah, Georgia Index Sections A–H.* Savannah, GA: privately printed, 2000.

Catholic Church. *Savannah's Catholic Cemetery, Chatham County, Georgia. Volume I, The Old Section.* Savannah, GA: Savannah Catholic Cemetery Preservation Society, 2005.

Catholic Church. *Savannah's Catholic Cemetery, Chatham County, Georgia. Volume II, Magnolia and Palmetto Sections.* Savannah, GA: Savannah Catholic Cemetery Preservation Society, 2008.

Catholic Church. *Savannah's Catholic Cemetery, Chatham County, Georgia. Volume III, The Dogwood, Holy Cross and Gartland Sections.* Savannah, GA: Savannah Catholic Cemetery Preservation Society, 2010.

Genealogical Committee of Georgia Historical Society. *Laurel Grove Cemetery, Savannah Georgia, Volume I, 1852–1861.* Savannah, GA: privately printed, 1993. These are sexton records from 1852 to 1861.

Piechocinski, Elizabeth Carpenter. *The Old Burying Ground: Colonial Park Cemetery, Savannah, Georgia, 1750–1853.* Savannah, GA: Oglethorpe Press, 1999.

Newspaper

An index for Savannah newspapers, 1763–1845, and a newspaper digest beginning in 1850 exist for the Savannah newspapers. Up to the 1820s, the index includes every name but is limited to only those of the Savannah area in later years. A complete set of this index is at the University of Georgia Libraries in Athens and at the Georgia Archives in Atlanta. A set of these volumes is divided between the Georgia Historical Society and the Savannah Public Library. See Meredith B. Colket Jr., "Indexes to

Savannah, Georgia Newspapers," *National Genealogical Society Quarterly* 69 (1981): 181–183. Until 1786, Savannah had Georgia's only newspaper and, for many years afterward, the Savannah press carried news from across the state. However, these indexes were compiled in the 1930s and were without the benefit of many early Savannah newspapers discovered since then. The subscription website GenealogyBank includes many early Savannah newspapers that have been microfilmed by the Library of Congress.

Genealogical Committee, Georgia Historical Society. *Early Deaths in Savannah, Georgia 1763–1803, Obituaries and Legal Notices.* Savannah, Georgia: privately printed, 1993.

Kilbourne, Elizabeth Evans. *Savannah, Georgia, Newspaper Clippings (Georgia Gazette)*, 5 vols, 1763–1806. Savannah, Georgia: privately printed, 1999–2003.

Kilbourne, Elizabeth Evans. *Savannah, Georgia Newspaper Clippings (Columbian Museum) Vol. I 1796–1808; Vol. II 1798–1802; Vol. III 1803–1814.* Savannah, GA: privately printed, 2005–2011.

Land

Stanley, E.A., Mrs., and Mrs. Thomas C. Johnson. *Chatham County, Georgia Tax-digest for the Year 1798.* Reprint from *The Georgia Genealogical Magazine*, 1968 (July and August). An alphabetical listing from the original tax digest at the Georgia Historical Society in Savannah.

Estate

General Index to Wills, Estates, Administrations, Etc., in Chatham County, Georgia. N.p.: WPA, 1937; Typescript estate index. Inclusive dates of this index are not stated, but appear to include from 1773 to 1937. A copy of this work is at the Georgia Archives in Morrow.

LeFar, Mabel Freeman, and Caroline Price Wilson. *Abstracts of Wills, Chatham County, Georgia, 1773–1817.* Washington, DC: National Genealogical Society, 1963.

Wills, Chatham County, Georgia, 1817–1826, Book F. N.p.: WPA, 1937. Typescript at the Georgia Archives.

Miscellaneous

The Genealogical Committee, Georgia Historical Society, *Register of Deaths in Savannah, Georgia.* 1803–1853 6 vols. Savannah, GA: privately printed, 1983–1989.

CHATTAHOOCHEE COUNTY. Map #92.

County seat is Cusseta, 31805.

Created February 13, 1854, from Muscogee and Marion Counties.

Land was first distributed in the 1827 Land Lottery.

All records begin in 1854.

In addition to the records on microfilm, the Georgia Archives has unbound original miscellaneous Chattahoochee County records, 1848 through circa 1918 in Record Group 126.

Major published records

   Cemetery

      Thomas, Ken. *Georgia Genealogical Society Quarterly* 12 (Fall 1976): 116–131. Fifty-one numbered cemeteries located on the Fort Benning military property in Chattahoochee and Muscogee Counties are in this quarterly.

   Local History

      Rogers, Norma Kate. *History of Chattahoochee County, Georgia*. 1933. Reprint Greenville, SC: Southern Historical Press, 1997, with an every-name index, making this reprint the only useful volume.

CHATTOOGA COUNTY. Map #11.

County seat is Summerville, 30747.

Created December 28, 1838, from Floyd and Walker Counties.

Land was first distributed in the 1832 Land Lottery.

Superior court records begin in 1839.

Probate court records begin in 1839.

Tax digests begin in 1871.

Major published records

   Local History

      Baker, Robert S. *Chattooga, the Story of a County and Its People*. Roswell, GA: W.H. Wolfe Associates, 1988.

      Chattooga County Heritage Book Committee and County Heritage, Inc. *The Heritage of Chattooga County, Georgia 1838-2006*. Waynesville, NC: County Heritage, Inc., 2006.

CHEROKEE COUNTY. Map #21.

County seat is Canton, 30114.

Land was first distributed in the 1832 Land and/or Gold Lotteries.

Superior court records begin in 1833.

Probate court records begin in 1833.

Tax digests begin in 1871; 1849 also available.

   Major published records

   Cemetery

      Morris, Shirley. *Cemeteries of Cherokee County, Georgia*. Fernandina Beach, FL: Wolfe Publishing, 1997.

Land

Taylor, Wyndell O., and Bernice O. Taylor. *Cherokee County Georgia Land Records, including Deed Books A–G, 1833–1846*. 7 vols. Powder Springs, GA: Bot's Books, 1992–1996.

Estate

Carver, John. *Abstracts of Cherokee County, Georgia, Wills and Bonds, 1847–1921*. Jasper, GA: Woodward-Geiger.com, 2005.

Newspaper

Carver, John. *Annotated Obituaries from the Cherokee Advance, Canton, Georgia, 1880 – 1938*. Jasper, GA: Woodward-Geiger.com, 2003.

Miscellaneous

Hageness, MariLee Beatty. *1834 State Census, Cherokee County, Georgia*. Anniston, AL: privately printed, 1995.

———. *Voters, 1832, Cherokee County, Georgia*. Anniston, AL: privately printed, 1995.

Local History

Martin, Lloyd G. *The History of Cherokee County*. Atlanta: Walter W. Brown Pub. Co., 1932.

By an act of 19 December 1829, which was ruled unconstitutional by the United States Supreme Court in 1832, the state of Georgia extended the northern and northwestern boundaries of Carroll, Gwinnett, Habersham, Hall, and Rabun Counties to cover all of the Cherokee Indian nation. Whites living among the Cherokees in these "extended" areas are included in the 1830 federal census for these counties. See William Thorndale and William Dollarhide, *Map Guide to the U. S. Federal Censuses 1790–1920* (1987), 83. An act of 21 December 1830 created an original Cherokee County from the same land and subdivided it into four sections and various numbered districts and lots for distribution in the 1832 and 1833 land lotteries. This original Cherokee County was abolished and several new counties, including the current Cherokee County, were created by an act of 3 December 1832.

CLARKE COUNTY. Map #45.

County seat is Athens, 30601.

Created on December 1, 1801, from Jackson County, originally Franklin County, and on December 1, 1802, the upper two militia districts of Greene County were added.

Land was first distributed in 1784 as headrights, while still in Jackson or Franklin County; only about 48 plats were granted in Clarke County.

All records begin in 1802 or 1803.

In addition to the records on microfilm, the Georgia Archives has unbound original marriage records, 1803–1823; inferior court case files, 1800–1895; and estate records, 1801–1923, in Record Group 129. Those loose county records of Clarke County are indexed on line at the web site of the Clarke County Probate Court: http://www.athensclarkecounty.com/index.aspx?NID=1156.

Georgia Research
Chapter III: Counties, County Records, and Local History Sources

Major library resource is the Athens-Clarke County Public Library, 2025 Baxter St., Athens, GA 30606. The telephone number is 706-613-3650. The Heritage Room has extensive collections on the eastern area of Georgia, North and South Carolina and Virginia. The library also has microfilm of Clarke County newspapers and county records, Sanborn Fire Insurance maps, and more. For more thorough coverage of the features of this library, see the *Georgia Genealogical Society Quarterly*, Vol. 37 Number 2 (Summer 2001) 84–89.

Major published records

Cemetery

Athens Historical Society, Inc. *Athens-Clarke County, Georgia Cemeteries*. Athens, GA: privately printed, 1999.

Marshall, Charlotte Thomas. *Oconee Hill Cemetery of Athens, Georgia, Volume 1*. Athens, GA: Athens Historical Society, 2009.

Newspaper

Kilbourne, Elizabeth Evans. *Athens, Georgia, Newspaper Clippings (Southern Banner)*. 1814–1851. 7 vols. Savannah, GA: privately printed, 2000–2007.

Poss, Faye Stone. *Clarke County (Athens) Georgia Newspaper Abstracts, 1808–1829*. 2 vols. Snellville, GA: privately printed, 1998–1999.

Poss, Faye Stone. *The Southern Watchman, Athens, Georgia: Civil War Home Front Coverage, 1861–1865*. Snellville, GA: privately printed, 2008.

Taylor, Prudence. *Index to Deaths, Marriages and Other Articles of Genealogical Interest Found in the Athens Banner for the Year 1913, for the Years 1904–1912 including the January 1909–March 1912 Supplement, for the Period of April 1914–September 1945*, 3 vols. One copy in the Athens Regional Library in Athens.

Many newspapers are available in the historic newspaper collection and searchable by any term on the website http://athnewspapers.galileo.usg.edu/athnewspapers/search.

Land

Parr, Larry W. *Clarke County, Georgia Tax Digests: 1802–1810*. Atlanta: Callaway Publishing, 2003

Abbe, Mary Hoit *Clarke County, Georgia Tax Digests, 1811–1820, 1821–1830, 1847–1850*. 3 vols. Athens, GA: Clarke-Oconee Genealogy Society, 2004–2006.

Estate

The website of the Clarke-Oconee Genealogy Society has an index to the estate records called *Mixed Records and Returns* and an index to *Will Books A–E*. This index is also available at the Georgia Archives.

Miscellaneous

Davis, Robert S. *Records of Clarke County, Georgia, 1801–1892, in the Georgia Department of Archives and History*. Greenville, SC: Southern Historical Press, 1993.

CLAY COUNTY. Map #134.

County seat is Fort Gaines, 31751.

Created February 16, 1854, from Early and Randolph Counties.

Land was first distributed in the 1820 and 1827 Land Lotteries.

Superior court records begin in 1854.

Probate court records begin in 1854.

Tax digests begin in 1871; 1855, 1857, and 1864 also available.

Major published records

    Cemetery

    Dr. Andrew Turnbull Chapter, Daughters of the American Colonists. *The History of Clay County*. Clay County, GA: privately printed, 1976: 44–136.

    Local History

    Dr. Andrew Turnbull Chapter, Daughters of the American Colonists. *The History of Clay County*. Clay County, GA: privately printed, 1976.

    Greene, E. A *History of Fort Gaines and Clay County, Georgia*. N.p., 1976.

    King, P. C. *Ft. Gaines and Environs*. Auburn, AL: Warren Enterprises, 1976.

CLAYTON COUNTY. Map #52.

County seat is Jonesboro, 30236.

Created November 30, 1858, from Fayette and Henry Counties.

Land was first distributed in the 1821 Land Lottery.

Superior court records begin in 1859.

Probate court records begin in 1859.

Tax digests begin in 1861.

Major published records

    Cemetery

    Ancestors Unlimited, Inc. *All Known Cemeteries of Clayton County, Georgia*. 2nd ed.. Riverdale, GA: Ancestors Unlimited Inc., 1986.

    Estate

    Curry, Doris F. *Record of Wills, Book A, Clayton County, Georgia* [1859–1919]. Riverdale, GA: privately printed, n.d., ca. 1982.

    ———. *Record of Wills, Book B, Clayton County, Georgia* [1921–1940]. Riverdale, GA: privately printed, n.d., ca. 1985.

Local History

Kilgore, Alice Copeland, et. al. *A History of Clayton County, Georgia, 1821–1983*. College Park, GA: Ancestors Unlimited, 1983.

Kemp, Kathryn W. *Historic Clayton County: The Sesquicentennial History*. San Antonio, TX: Historical Pub. Network, 2009.

CLINCH COUNTY. Map #159.

County seat is Homerville, 31634. Original County seat was Polk.

Created February 14, 1850, from Ware and Lowndes Counties.

Land was first distributed in the 1820 Land Lottery.

Superior court records begin in 1867.

Probate court records begin in 1867.

Tax digests begin in 1868.

Major published records

Cemetery

McClaine, Joseph W. *Cemeteries of Clinch County, Georgia*. Homerville, GA: Joseph W. McClaine, 2003.

Local History

Bennett, Kenneth W. *A Chronicle of Clinch County Georgia*. Waycross, GA: Brantley Print Co., 1991.

Huxford, Folks. *History of Clinch County, Georgia*. 1916 Reprint N.p.: Huxford Genealogical Society, 1992. Digital copy available online Library of Congress, GoogleBooks, and Ancestry.com.

COBB COUNTY. Map #30.

County seat is Marietta, 30060.

Created December 3, 1832, from original Cherokee County.

Land was first distributed in the 1832 Land and/or Gold Lotteries.

Superior and probate court records begin in 1865, although some earlier records exist.

Tax digests begin in 1873; 1848, 1849, and 1851 also available.

In addition to the records on microfilm, the Georgia Archives has unbound original Cobb County estate records in Record Group 133.

Major library resource is the Cobb County Public Library, the Georgia Room, 266 Roswell St., Marietta, GA 30060-2004. The telephone number is 770-528-2320. For more thorough coverage of the features of this library, see the *Georgia Genealogical Society Quarterly*, Vol. 35 No. 4 (Winter 1999) 245–51.

Major published records

Cemetery

Cobb County Genealogical Society. *Cobb County, Georgia Cemeteries, Volume II*. Marietta, GA: privately printed, 1991.

Cobb County Genealogical Society. *Cobb County, Georgia Cemeteries, Volume III*. Marietta National Cemetery. Marietta, GA: privately printed, 1994.

Northeast Cobb Genealogical Society. *Cobb County Cemeteries, Volume I*. Marietta, GA: privately printed, 1984.

Smith, Harold, and Betty Smith. *Smyrna Memorial Cemetery, Founded 1838: Map and History*, Smyrna, GA: Smyrna Historical & Genealogical Society, 1989.

Temple, Sarah. *The First Hundred Years, A Short History of Cobb County, in Georgia*. Atlanta: Walter W. Brown Publishing Company, 1935: 586–860.

Land

Lister, Betty White. *Cobb County, Georgia, Deed Book A, Volumes I and II*. Marietta, GA: privately printed, 1988–1989.

Estate

Georgia Society, Daughters of the American Revolution. *Will Book 2-A, Cobb County, Georgia, 1865–1900*. Volume 526. N.p.: privately printed, 1995–96.

Local History

Temple, Sarah. *The First Hundred Years, A Short History of Cobb County, in Georgia*. Atlanta: Walter W. Brown Publishing Company, 1935.

COFFEE COUNTY. Map #126.

County seat is Douglas, 31533.

Created February 9, 1854, from Clinch, Ware, Telfair, and Irwin Counties.

Land was first distributed in the 1820 Land Lottery.

Superior court records begin circa 1854.

Probate court records begin circa 1854.

Tax digests begin in 1869.

Major published records

Cemetery

Paulk, Jessie H., and Delma Wilson Paulk. *Survey of Coffee County, Georgia Cemeteries*. Salem, FL: Paulk Genealogy & Research, 2004.

Satilla Regional Library. *Coffee County, Georgia, Cemeteries, 1837–1978*. Douglas, GA: The Library, 1980.

Local History

Ward, Warren P. *Ward's History of Coffee County*. 1930. Reprinted, Spartanburg, SC: The Reprint Co., 1978.

COLQUITT COUNTY. Map #143.

County seat is Moultrie, 31768.

Created February 25, 1856, from Thomas and Lowndes Counties.

Land was first distributed in the 1820 Land Lottery.

Superior court records begin in 1881.

Probate court records begin circa 1903.

Tax digests begin in 1869; 1857 also available.

Major library resource is the Ellen Payne Odom Genealogy Library, 204 5th St, SW, Moultrie, GA 31768. The telephone number is 229-985-6540. Website: http://www.mccls.org/odom_gen.htm. This library is part of the Moultrie Colquitt Library and is a major repository for archives of various family associations, most of them Scottish-American families, as well as records for southwest Georgia.

Major published records

Cemetery

Ellen Payne Odom Genealogy Library. *Colquitt County Cemeteries*. Moultrie, GA: Ellen Payne Odom Genealogy Library, 2012. Ring binder typescript collection of Colquitt County cemetery records.

Hickey, Paul D. *Some Colquitt County Cemeteries*. Norman Park, GA: privately printed, 1996–1997.

Newspaper

Southwest Georgia Genealogical Society. *Obituaries, the Moultrie Observer, 1983–1991*, 3 vols. Albany, GA: privately printed, 1992.

COLUMBIA COUNTY. Map #64.

County seat is Appling, 30802.

Created December 10, 1790, from Richmond County.

Land was first distributed in 1733 by the Trustees and formally granted beginning in 1755.

Superior court records begin in 1791.

Probate court records begin in 1791.

Tax digests begin in 1805.

In addition to the records on microfilm, the Georgia Archives has Columbia County original estate records, 1789–1931, and marriage records, 1787–1935, in Record Group 136.

Major published records

Cemetery

Braswell, Marjorie. *Cemetery Records of Columbia County, Georgia.* Augusta, GA: privately printed, 1998.

Butler, David Alan. *Columbia County Gray: Burial Locations for Confederate Soldiers in Columbia County, Georgia (Including McDuffie County).* Martinez, GA: Rough and Ready Publishing, 2007.

Estate

Century of Columbia County, Georgia, Wills, 1790–1890. Albany, GA: Georgia Pioneers, n.d.

Court

Columbia County, Georgia, Early Court Records. Albany, GA: Georgia Pioneers Publications, n.d.

Local History

Smith, Gerald J. *To Seek a Newer World: A History of Columbia County, Georgia.* Murfreesboro, TN: Southern Heritage Press, 2001

COOK COUNTY. Map #144.

County seat is Adel, 31620.

Created November 5, 1918, from Berrien County.

Land was first distributed in the 1820 Land Lottery.

The Georgia Archives has no records on microfilm of this post-1900 county, although original tax digests beginning in 1919 are available.

Major published records

Cemetery

Ensley, Dillard D. *A Survey of Cemeteries, Cook County, Georgia.* Knoxville, TN: Tennessee Valley Publishing, 2000.

Local History

Parrish, June J. *History of Cook County and its Municipalities.* Adel, GA: Adel News Pub. Co., 1968.

COWETA COUNTY. Map #50.

County seat is Newnan, 30263.

Created June 9, 1825, from Indian lands ceded in 1826 and 1827.

Land was first distributed in the 1827 Land Lottery.

Superior court and probate court records begin in 1827.

Tax digests begin in 1845.

Major library resource is the Coweta County Historical & Genealogical Research Library, 5 West Broad St., Grantville, GA. Mailing address: Coweta County Genealogical Society, P.O. Box

1014, Newnan, GA, 30264. Website: http://www.ccgsinc.org. Email: info@ccgsinc.org. The library is home to 3000 books and publications. It has the original surviving historical newspapers from Newnan and Coweta County, as well as microfilm of the papers. The society also houses many original Courthouse ledger books, mortgage books, land index books, etc. It has the annual Georgia Congressional Books dating back to 1848. It has self-published Coweta County Georgia Censuses beginning with the 1827 Georgia Land Lottery continuing through the 1920 Census. The library has at least one book or publication from each county in Georgia, as well as at least one book or publication from each of the 50 states. It also has about 150 Family History books and manuscripts.

Major published records

Cemetery

Coweta County Genealogical Society. *Coweta County, Georgia, Cemeteries*. Roswell, GA: W. H. Wolfe Associates, 1986.

Newspaper

Georgia Society, Daughters of the American Revolution. *Coweta County Obituaries 1974–1975 (Newnan Times-Herald)*. Volume 188. Atlanta: privately printed, 1976.

Land

Storey, Artie May Jones. *1890 Tax Digest of Coweta County, Georgia, A Partial 1890 Census Substitute*. Newnan, GA: Coweta County Genealogical Society, 1992.

Estates

Coweta County Genealogical Society. *Coweta County, Georgia, Distribution of Estates: From Probate Court Office*. Newnan, GA: privately printed, 2001.

Coweta County Genealogical Society. *Distribution of Estates Book 1 1844–1892*. Newnan, GA: privately printed, n.d.

Coweta County Genealogical Society. *Early Wills, Coweta County, Georgia, 1827–1910*. Newnan, GA: privately printed, 2001

Coweta County Genealogical Society. *Letters of Guardianship, Book B, Coweta County, Georgia*. Newnan, GA: privately printed, 2001.

Hageness, MariLee Beatty. *Abstract of Will Book A, 1827–1847, Coweta County, Georgia*. Anniston, AL: MLH Research, 1999.

———. *Letters of Guardianship, Book A, 1856–1879, Coweta County, Georgia*. Anniston, AL: privately printed, 1995.

Miscellaneous

Gossett, Joyce Hill. *Coweta County, Georgia Muster Roll, C.S.A*. 1981.

Hageness, MariLee Beatty. *Members, New Hope Baptist Church, Coweta County, Georgia*. Anniston, AL: privately printed, 1995.

Hageness, MariLee Beatty. *Poor School Students, 1853, Coweta County, Georgia.* Anniston, AL: privately printed, 1995.

———. *Students, Newnan Academy, 1850, Coweta County, Georgia.* Anniston, AL: privately printed, 1995.

———. *Students, Longstreet Institute, 1849, 1850, Coweta County, Georgia.* AL: privately printed, 1995.

Local History

Anderson, W. U. *A History of Coweta County from 1825 to 1880.* Newnan, GA: Newnan-Coweta Historical Society, 1977.

Coweta County Genealogical Society. *A Decade of Georgia Information, 1851–1861: Abstracts of Genealogical and Historical Interest from Selected Acts of the Georgia General Assembly.* Newnan, GA: Coweta County Genealogical Society, 1990.

Jones, Mary Gibson, and Lily Elizabeth Reynolds. *Coweta County Chronicles for One Hundred Years, With an Account of the Indians from Whom the Land Was Acquired, and Some Historical Papers Relating to Its Acquisition by Georgia, with Lineage Pages.* Atlanta: Stein Print. Co., 1928.

Newnan-Coweta Historical Society. *A History of Coweta County, Georgia.* Roswell, GA: W. H. Wolfe Associates, 1988.

Newnan-Coweta Historical Society. *Index to W.U. Anderson's History of Coweta, County (Georgia).* Newnan, GA: Newnan-Coweta Historical Society, 1981.

Wolak, Edward W., and Helen T. Wolack. *Vanished Communities of Coweta County: Originally Compiled for a Talk Given to the Coweta County Genealogical Society and the Newnan-Coweta Historical Society, November 15, 1984.* Moreland, GA: 1999.

CRAWFORD COUNTY. Map #82.

County seat is Knoxville, 31050.

Created December 9, 1822, from Houston County.

Land was first distributed in the 1821 Land Lottery.

Superior court records begin in 1830.

Probate court records begin in 1830, although some earlier records exist.

Tax digests begin circa 1840.

In addition to the records on microfilm, the Georgia Archives has original unbound estate records, 1822–1900, and marriages, 1814–1930, in Record Group 139.

Major published records

Cemetery

George, Elizabeth Howell. *Tombstone Inscriptions, Peach & Crawford County, Georgia.* Fort Valley, GA: Governor Treutlen Chapter, Daughters of the American Revolution, 1976.

Georgia Research
Chapter III: Counties, County Records, and Local History Sources

Newspaper

Evans, Tad. *Georgia Newspaper Clippings Crawford County Extracts 1824–1904*. Savannah, GA: privately printed, 2004.

Estate

Henry, William R. *Miscellaneous Estate Records of Crawford County, Georgia*. 3 vols. Warner Robins, GA: Central Georgia Genealogical Society, 1988, 1989.

Wilder, Sunnie, and William R. Henry. *Wills of Crawford County, Georgia (1835–1948)*. Warner Robins, GA: Central Georgia Genealogical Society, 1989.

Court

Henry, William R. *Inferior Court Records for Crawford County, Georgia*. Warner Robins, GA: Central Georgia Genealogical Society, 1989.

Local History

Crawford County Historical Society (Knoxville, GA). *Crawford County, Georgia Families on the Fall Line*. Fernandina Beach, FL: Wolfe Publishing, 2006.

CRISP COUNTY. Map #106.

County seat is Cordele, 31015.

Created August 17, 1905, from Dooly County.

Land was first distributed in the 1821 Land Lottery.

Superior court records begin in 1905.

Probate court records begin in 1905.

Tax digests begin in 1906.

The Georgia Archives has no records on microfilm of this post-1900 county, although original tax digests beginning in 1906 are available.

Major published records

Newspaper

Southwest Georgia Genealogical Society. *Obituaries From the Cordele Dispatch 1989–1991*. Albany, GA: privately printed, 1992.

Local History

Cordele-Crisp Co. Historical Society. *Crisp Co.'s History in Pictures and Stories*. Atlanta: W. H. Wolfe Assoc., 1978.

DADE COUNTY. Map #1.

County seat is Trenton, 30752.

Created December 25, 1837, from Walker County.

Land was first distributed in the 1832 Land and/or Gold Lotteries.

Superior court records begin in 1854, although some earlier records exist.

Probate court records begin in 1853.

Tax digests begin in 1874; 1864 and 1871 also available.

Major published records

    Cemetery

        Leavitt, Pamela Clark Whitson. *Cemetery Survey of Dade County, Georgia*. Atlanta: Fort Peachtree Chapter, National Society, DAR, no date, surveyed 1992–1993. This book also appears as Volume 517 of the Georgia Society, D. A. R., Genealogical Records series.

DAWSON COUNTY. Map #14.

County seat is Dawsonville, 30534.

Created December 3, 1857, from Lumpkin and Gilmer Counties.

Land was first distributed in the 1832 Land and/or Gold Lotteries.

Superior court records begin in 1858.

Probate court records begin in 1857.

Tax digests begin in 1872.

Major published records

    Cemetery

        Dawson County Historical and Genealogical Society. *Cemeteries of Dawson County, Georgia*. Dawsonville, GA: privately printed, 2002.

        Whitmire, Rhonda Ivey, Eva Lance Jenson, and Sue B. Cates. *Memories in Stone, Cemetery Records of Dawson County Georgia and Related History*. N.p.: Georgia Gold Researchers, 1992.

    Newspaper

        Carver, John. *Abstracts of Obituaries in Dawson County, Georgia Newspapers, 1879–1952*. Canton, GA: J. Carver, 2010.

    Marriage

        Jones, Patricia K. *Marriages of Dawson County, Georgia Books A-D (1858-1950)*. Oakwood, GA: privately printed, 2008.

    Local History

        Dawson County Georgia Bicentennial Committee. *A Bicentennial Look at Dawson County: Its Churches, Its Government, Its People*. Dawsonville, GA: privately printed, 1976.

DECATUR COUNTY. Map #152.

County seat is Bainbridge, 31717.

Created December 8, 1823, from Early County.

Land was first distributed in the 1820 Land Lottery.

All records begin in 1824.

In addition to the records on microfilm, the Georgia Archives has original marriage records, 1846–1921, in Record Group 143. Another source is by Eustus Howard Hayes, *Some Decatur County, Georgia, and Neighboring Counties Genealogical References*, which consists of tombstone inscriptions for Decatur, Grady, and Early Counties available in the Georgia Archives microfilm library, Drawer 91, Roll 61.

Major library resource is the Southwest Georgia Regional Library, 301 South Monroe St., Bainbridge, GA 39819. The telephone number is 229-248-2665.

Major published records:

Cemetery

Unpublished cemetery records, which were collected by Eustus Howard Hayes and Louise (Harper) Lee, may be found in the Southwest Georgia Regional Library, genealogy section, filed by index number. These are primarily Decatur County tombstone inscriptions found listed in Appendix B (pages 431–433) of Decatur County Historical Society, *Decatur County Georgia Past and Present 1823–1991* (Roswell, GA: W. H. Wolfe Associates, 1991).

Newspapers

Evans, Tad. *Decatur/Early Counties, Georgia, Newspaper Clippings*. 2 vols. 1863–1885. Savannah, GA: privately printed, 1998–99.

DEKALB COUNTY. Map #41.

County seat is Decatur, 30030.

Created December 9, 1822, from Fayette, Gwinnett, and Henry Counties.

Land was first distributed in the 1821 Land Lottery.

Superior court deed records begin in 1842. Superior court minutes begin in 1836.

Probate court records begin in 1842, although a small number of marriages and court minutes date from 1840. Years support records begin in 1874.

Inferior court minutes begin in 1823, which contain records of county business (county officers, public works, road crews, etc.).

Tax digests begin in 1873; partial surviving tax digests from 1846 and 1847; complete pre-Civil War tax digests survive for 1848, 1849, 1850, and 1855.

In addition to the records on microfilm, the Georgia Archives has original DeKalb County miscellaneous records (mostly naturalizations), 1845–1950, in Record Group 144. The register of free people of color starting in 1851 is at the DeKalb History Center. Registers of physicians, embalmers, and pharmacists begin in 1881. The county probate court has some early plat books and homestead records not available on microfilm. The first county directory, from 1939, is available at the DeKalb History Center and the Georgia Archives. The DeKalb History Center maintains multiple database indexes of county records at http://research.dekalbhistory.org/online_databases.asp.

Major library resource is the DeKalb County Public Library, Decatur Branch, 215 Sycamore St., Decatur, GA 30030. The telephone number is (404) 370-8450. For more thorough coverage of the features of this library, see the *Georgia Genealogical Society Quarterly*, Vol. 34 No. 3 (Fall 1998) 168–172. Also, the DeKalb History Center, 101 East Court Square, Decatur, GA 30030. Website: http://www.dekalbhistory.org. The center maintains a museum and archive dedicated to preserving the county's history. Also, Emory University Libraries, Robert W. Woodruff Library, Emory University, 540 Asbury Circle, Atlanta, GA30322-2870. The telephone number is 404-727-6873. Website: http://marbl.library.emory.edu/ Open seven days a week when the university is in session. Includes a manuscript department of historical Georgia private papers (closed on Sundays); a U.S. Government Documents Center; and microfilm of the Lyman C. Draper Collection relating to the frontier South.

Major published records

Cemetery

Many DeKalb County records are available in the *Franklin Garrett's Necrology* at the Atlanta History Center, Atlanta, GA. Mr. Garrett surveyed primarily Atlanta area cemeteries in the 1930s and 1940s.

Brooke, Ted. *Cemetery Records of Tucker, Georgia, and Environs (DeKalb and Gwinnett Counties)*. Cumming, GA: privately printed, 2012. Contains many DeKalb County grave marker records.

Land

The DeKalb History Center's website includes a "Land Records Database" with most land transactions dating from 1842 to 1900.

Estate

Austin, Jeannette Holland. *DeKalb County, Georgia, Probate Records*. Westminster, MD: Willow Bend Books, 2001.

Local History

Barre, Laura, and Ken Barre. *The History of Doraville, Georgia*. Roswell, GA: Wolfe Pub., 1995.

Clarke, Caroline McKinney. *The Story of Decatur, 1823–1899*. Decatur, GA: DeKalb Historical Society, 1973.

DeKalb Historical Society. *Vanishing DeKalb: A Pictorial History*. Decatur, GA: privately printed, 1985.

Garrett, Franklin M., and Harold H. Martin. *Atlanta and Environs*. 3 vols. New York: Lewis Historical Pub. Co, 1954, 1987.

Mason, Herman "Skip," Jr. *African-American Life in DeKalb County, 1823–1970*. Charleston, SC: Arcadia, 1998.

Price, Vivian. *The History of DeKalb County, Georgia, 1822–1900*. Fernandina Beach, FL: W. H. Wolfe, 1997.

Spruill, Ethel W., and Elizabeth L. Davis. *The Story of Dunwoody, 1821–2001*. Fernandina Beach, FL: Wolfe Pub., 2002.

DODGE COUNTY. Map #110.

County seat is Eastman, 31023.

Created October 26, 1870, from Pulaski, Telfair, and Montgomery Counties.

Land was first distributed in the 1807 Land Lottery.

All records begin in 1871.

Major published records

  Cemetery

   Daughters of the American Revolution. *Cemetery Records, Dodge County, Georgia, Vol. 1,2,3*. [Georgia]: Colonel William Few Chapter, NSDAR, 1977(Vol. 341), 1987 (Vol. 342), 1990 (Vol. 491).

   Daughters of the American Revolution. *Cemetery Records, Dodge County, Georgia*. [Georgia]: Colonel William Few Chapter, NSDAR, 1985 (Vol. 282).

   Saunders, Chester, and Martha M. Saunders. *Cemeteries of Dodge County, Georgia, 1827–1989*. Utica, KY: McDowell Publications, 1995.

  Newspaper

   Evans, Tad. *Dodge County Newspaper Clippings (1873–2011)*, 22 vols. Savannah, GA: privately printed, 1991–2009.

   ———. *The News From Milan, Rhine and Old Telfair Volume I 1807–1919*. Savannah, GA: privately printed, 2007.

DOOLY COUNTY. Map #107.

County seat is Vienna, 31902.

Created May 25, 1821, from Indian lands ceded in 1821.

Land was first distributed in the 1821 Land Lottery.

Superior court records begin in 1847.

Probate court records begin in 1847, although some earlier records exist.

Tax digests begin in 1872; 1851 also available.

Major published records

  Cemetery

   Powell, Nora, and Watts Powell. *Historical and Genealogical Collections of Dooly County, Georgia*. Volume 2. Vienna, GA: privately printed, 1974: 240–380.

Newspaper

Evans, Tad, *Georgia Newspaper Clippings Dooly County Extracts 1822–1907*. 2 vols. Savannah, GA: privately printed, 2003.

Local History

Powell, Nora, and Watts Powell. *Historical and Genealogical Collections of Dooly County, Georgia*. 3 vols. Vienna, GA: privately printed, 1973–present.

DOUGHERTY COUNTY. Map #136.

County seat is Albany, 31701.

Created December 15, 1853, from Baker County.

Land was first distributed in the 1820 Land Lottery

Superior court records begin in 1854.

Probate court records begin in 1854.

Tax digests begin in 1873; 1854 also available.

Major published records

Cemetery

Southwest Georgia Genealogical Society. *Dougherty County, Georgia, Cemeteries, Book I*. Albany, GA: privately printed, 1984.

———. *Dougherty County, Georgia Cemeteries Book Two*. (Riverside and Crown Hill). Albany, GA: privately printed, 1990.

Newspaper

Evans, Tad. *Albany, Georgia, Newspaper Clippings, 1845–1874*. 3 vols. Savannah, GA: privately printed, 1996–97.

Georgia Society, Daughters of the American Revolution. *1983 and 1984 Obituary Notices, The Albany Herald*. Volume 487. Albany, GA: privately printed, 1990.

———. *1985 Obituary Notices, The Albany Herald*. Volume 486. Albany, GA: privately printed, 1988–89.

———. *1986–1988 Obituary Notices, The Albany Herald. Volume 488*. Albany, GA: privately printed, 1990.

The Southwest Georgia Genealogical Society. *Albany, Georgia Obituaries, 1938–1991*. 5 vols. Albany, GA: privately printed, 1991–1992. Volumes I–IV, covering 1938–1982, have a consolidated index in a separate volume, although each volume has an index.

DOUGLAS COUNTY. Map #38.

County seat is Douglasville, 30134.

Created October 17, 1870, from Campbell and Carroll Counties.

Land was first distributed in the 1827 Land Lottery.

Superior court records begin in 1871.

Probate court records begin in 1871.

Tax digests begin circa 1871.

Major published records

    Cemetery

    Davis, Fannie Mae. *Douglas County, Georgia; From Indian Trail to Interstate 20*. Roswell, GA: W. H. Wolfe Associates, 1987: 578–628.

    Local History

    Baggett, Joe. *Douglas County, Georgia Who Was Who*. Douglasville, GA : privately published, 1981.

    Whatley, Robert L. *Honestly I Love You Douglas County*. Lithia Springs, GA : Lithia Springs Press, 1983.

EARLY COUNTY. Map #139.

County seat is Blakely, 31723.

Created December 15, 1818, from Indian land ceded in 1814.

Land was first distributed in the 1820 Land Lottery.

Superior court records begin in 1821.

Probate court records begin in 1821.

Tax digests begin in 1872; 1820, 1840, 1842, and 1850 also available.

Major published records

    Cemetery

    Early County Historical Society. *Collections of Early County Historical Society*. Blakely, GA: privately printed, 1971: Volume I, 189–235.

    Georgia Society, DAR. *Early County, Georgia Tomb Index*. DAR Genealogical Records Collections, [typescript], vol. 394. 1960.

    Preservation Restoration Committee of the Blakely-Early Bicentennial Commission. *Early County, Georgia, Tomb Index of the Black Citizens of the County*. N.p.: privately printed, 1976.

    Whitehead, Mary G. *Collections of Early County Historical Society*. Blakely, GA: Early County Historical Society, 1980: Volume II, 341–358.

    Newspaper

    Evans, Tad. *Decatur/Early Counties, Georgia, Newspaper Clippings*. 2 vols, 1863–1885. Savannah, GA: privately printed, 1998–99.

Local History

    Early County Historical Society. *Collections of Early County Historical Society*. 2 vols. Blakely, Georgia: privately printed, 1971, 1980.

ECHOLS COUNTY. Map #157.

County seat is Statenville, 31648.

Created December 13, 1858, from Lowndes and Clinch Counties.

Land was first distributed in the 1820 Land Lottery.

Superior court records begin in 1897.

Probate court records begin in 1898, although some earlier records exist.

Tax digests begin in 1873; 1867 also available.

Major published records

    Cemetery

    Echols County Historical Society (Statenville, Ga.). *Cemeteries of Echols County, Georgia*. Nashville, GA: Wayne and Judy Dasher, 2004.

EFFINGHAM COUNTY. Map #102.

County seat is Springfield, 31329.

Created February 5, 1777, with boundaries that included colonial St. Philip and St. Mathew Parishes.

Land was first distributed in 1733 by the Trustees and formally granted beginning in 1755.

Superior court records begin circa 1786.

Probate court records begin circa 1791.

Tax digests begin in 1855.

Major published records

    Cemetery

    Historic Effingham Society. *Effingham County Cemeteries*. Thomasville, GA: Craigmiles and Associates, 1995.

    Miscellaneous

    Lucas, S. Emmett. *Records of Effingham County, Georgia*. Easley, SC: Southern Historical Press, 1976.

ELBERT COUNTY. Map #36.

County seat is Elberton, 30635.

Created December 10, 1790, from Wilkes County.

Land was first distributed in 1773 as headrights.

Superior court records begin in 1791.

Probate court records begin in 1791.

Tax digests begin in 1873; 1815, 1849, 1851, and 1860 also available.

Major published records

> Cemetery
>
>> Butler, Larry Raymond, and Janice Butler Turner. *Elbert County Cemeteries 2002: Vol. 1*. N.p.: privately printed, 2002.
>>
>> Elbert County Historical Society. *Early Cemeteries and Gravestones, Elbert County, Georgia, 1798–1919*. Elberton, GA: privately printed, 1984.
>
> Newspaper
>
>> McRee, Fred W., Jr. *Elbert County, Georgia Deaths 1873–1918*. Dahlonega, GA: privately printed, 2009.
>
> Land
>
>> Farmer, Michal Martin. *Elbert County, Georgia Deed Books A–J, 1791–1806, K–R, 1806–1819, S–W, 1820–1835*. 3 vols. Dallas, TX: Farmer Genealogy Company, 1997.
>
> Estate
>
>> McRee, Fred W., Jr. *Elbert County, Georgia Abstracts of Wills 1791–1919*. Dahlonega, GA: privately printed, 2011.

EMANUEL COUNTY. Map #88.

County seat is Swainsboro, 30401.

Created December 10, 1812, from Bulloch and Montgomery Counties.

Land was first distributed in 1784 as headrights.

Superior court records begin in 1830, although some earlier records exist.

Probate court records begin circa 1817.

Tax digests begin in 1874; 1841 and 1851 also available.

Major published records

> Cemetery
>
>> Coleman, Moses M., Jr. *Cemeteries of Emanuel County, Georgia*. Vidalia, GA: Vesco, Inc., 1998.
>>
>> Dorsey, James E., and John K. Derden. *Gone But Not Forgotten: A Tombstone Registry of Emanuel County, Georgia*. Rev. ed. Swainsboro, GA: Magnolia Press, 1983.
>>
>> Ridgill, John Michael. *Confederate Graves of Emanuel County, Georgia*. N.p., 2009.
>
> Newspaper
>
>> Dorsey, James E. *Emanuel County Legal Notices, Pre-1860 Notices Appearing in Selected Georgia Newspapers*. N.p.: Emanuel Historic Preservation Society, 1978.

Evans, Tad. *Georgia Newspaper Clippings, Emanuel County Extracts*. 1815-1889. Savannah, GA: Tad Evans, 1999.

An Index to Swainsboro, Georgia Newspapers 1901–1910. Swainsboro, GA: no publisher, 1980.

Miscellaneous

Hageness, MariLee Beatty. *Register of Marks and Brands, 1841–1899, Emanuel County, Georgia*. N.p., 1995.

Local History

Dorsey, James E. *Collections of the Emanuel Historic Preservation Society*. Swainsboro, GA: The Emanuel Historic Preservation Society, 1981.

———. *Footprints Along the Hoopee: A History of Emanuel County*. 2 vols. Gainesville, GA: Magnolia Press, 1990, 2012.

Emanuel County Historic Preservation Society. *Emanuel County, Georgia*. Images of America Series. Charleston, SC: Arcadia, 1998.

Rogers, William Curan. *Memories of Emanuel, 1776–1976*. Swainsboro, GA: Swainsboro Forest Blade Publishing, 1976.

EVANS COUNTY. Map #116.

County seat is Claxton, 30417.

Created November 3, 1914, from Bulloch and Tattnall Counties.

Land was first distributed in 1784 as headrights.

All records begin in 1915.

The Georgia Archives has no records on microfilm of this post-1900 county, although original tax digests beginning in 1915 are available.

Major published records

Cemetery

Coleman, Moses M., and Emilie K. Hartz. *Cemeteries of Candler & Evans Counties, Georgia*. Vidalia, GA: Coleman Ferrotype, 2003.

Hodges, Lucile. *A History of Our Locale, Mainly Evans County, Georgia*. Claxton, GA: privately printed, 1965: 253–322.

Local History

Evans County Historical Society. *A History of Evans County: "A Small Warm Place Around the Heart."* Claxton, GA: Evans County Historical Society, 2000.

Hodges, Lucile. *A History of Our Locale, Mainly Evans County, Georgia*. Claxton, GA: privately printed, 1965.

FANNIN COUNTY. Map #7.

County seat is Blue Ridge, 30513.

Created January 21, 1854, from Gilmer and Union Counties.

Land was first distributed in the 1832 Land Lottery.

Superior court records begin in 1854.

Probate court records begin in 1865, although some earlier records exist. There is a "miscellaneous" volume of estate records beginning in 1854 that is on microfilm at Georgia Archives. It contains wills and other items. Marriages also begin in 1854.

Tax digests begin in 1874; 1863 and 1866 also available.

Major published records

    Cemetery

    Casada, Helen W. *Fannin County Georgia Cemeteries*. 5 vols. Charleston, TN: privately printed, n.d..

    Dyer, Dale, and Ethelene D. Jones. *Fannin County, Georgia Cemeteries*. Blue Ridge, GA: Fannin County Heritage Foundation, 2003.

    Newspaper

    Casada, Helen W. *Fannin County, Georgia and Copper Basin GA/TN Area Obituaries, 1930–1998*. Charleston, TN: privately printed, 1998[?].

    Jones, Viola H. *Blue Ridge and Vicinity Weddings and Obituaries from the Blue Ridge Summit Post 1893–1968*. 2 vols. Louisville, TN: privately printed, 1999.

    Poteet-Pitts, Jennie Vee. *Obituaries from the "Fannin County Times" Fannin County, Georgia and Surrounding Area, 1931–1964*. Atlanta: privately printed, 1985.

    Local History

    Jones, Ethelene D., and Dale Dyer. *Facets of Fannin: a History of Fannin County Georgia*. Dallas: Curtis Media Corp., 1989.

FAYETTE COUNTY. Map #51.

County seat is Fayetteville, 30214.

Created May 15, 1821, from Indian lands ceded in 1821.

Land was first distributed in the 1821 Land Lottery.

All records begin in 1823.

Major published records

    Cemetery

    Fayette County Historical Society. *Cemetery Records, Fayette County, Georgia: Covers Engraved Gravestones 1824–2000, Various Sites Included with Just Field Stones*. Fayetteville, GA: privately printed, 2005.

    Wells, Joel Dixon, and Donald R. Schultz. *All Known Cemeteries in Fayette County, Georgia: A Genealogically Oriented Survey*. Hampton, GA: J.D. Wells, 1980.

Land

First Tax Digests [of] Fayette County, Georgia, 1823–1834. Jonesboro, GA: Ancestors Unlimited, 1988.

Estate

Austin, Jeannette Holland. *Fayette County, Georgia Probate Records, 1824–1871*. Roswell, GA: W. H. Wolfe Associates, 1995.

———. *Fayette County, Georgia Probate Records: Annual Returns, Inventories, Sales, Bonds 1845–1897, Volume II*. Westminster, MD: Willow Bend Books, 2000.

Wells, Joel Dixon. *Fayette County, Georgia Will Book A, 1828–1897*. Hampton, GA: Armchair Publications, 1981.

Local History

Cary, Carolyn C. *Historic Fayette County: An Illustrated History*. San Antonio, TX: Historical Pub. Network, 2009.

Fayette County Historical Society. *History of Fayette County, 1821-1971* Fayetteville, GA: privately printed, 1977.

FLOYD COUNTY. Map #19.

County seat is Rome, 30161.

Created December 3, 1832, from original Cherokee County.

Land was first distributed in the 1832 Land and/or Gold Lotteries.

Superior court records begin circa 1840, although some earlier records exist.

Probate court records begin circa 1837, although some earlier records exist.

Tax digests begin in 1872; 1852 also available.

Major library resource is the Carnegie Library, 607 Broad St., Rome, GA 30161, the headquarters for the Northwest Georgia Historical and Genealogical Society. Also, the Rome-Floyd County Public Library, 205 Riverside Parkway, Rome, GA 30161. The telephone number is 706-236-4601. For more thorough coverage of the features of this library, see the *Georgia Genealogical Society Quarterly*, Vol. 34 No. 4 (Winter 1998) 245–248.

Major published records

Cemetery

Northwest Georgia Historical and Genealogical Society. *Floyd County, Georgia, Cemeteries, Volume I*. Rome, GA: privately printed, 1985.

———. *Floyd County, Georgia, Cemeteries, Volume II*. Rome, GA: privately printed, 1989.

Miscellaneous

Mrs. Shirley F. Kinney of Rome has published ten volumes of miscellaneous Floyd County records.

FORSYTH COUNTY. Map #22.

County seat is Cumming, 30040.

Created December 3, 1832, from original Cherokee County.

Land was first distributed in the 1832 Land and/or Gold Lotteries.

Superior court records begin in 1833.

Probate court records begin in 1833.

Tax digests begin in 1874; 1853 also available.

In addition to the records on microfilm, the Georgia Archives has original marriage records, 1834–1910, in Record Group 158.

Major published records

    Cemetery

    Parrish, Donna, et al. *Cemeteries of Forsyth County, Georgia.* Cumming, GA: privately printed, 1981.

    Salter, John. *Forsyth County, Georgia, Cemeteries.* Cumming, GA: GA Ancestors Press, 2011.

    Newspaper

    Brooke, Ted O. *Stray Obituaries & Death Notices From Forsyth County (GA) Newspapers 1881–1960.* Typescript in Forsyth and Hall County libraries.

    Local History

    Don Shadburn of Cumming has written seven volumes in his Pioneer-Cherokee Heritage series: Volume 1, *Pioneer History of Forsyth County, Georgia*; Volume 2, *Cherokee Planters in Georgia, 1832–1838*; Volume 3, *Unhallowed Intrusion: A History of Cherokee Families in Forsyth County, Georgia*; Volume 4, *Crimson and Sabres: A Confederate Record of Forsyth County, Georgia*; Volume 5, *Blood Kin: Pioneer Chronicles of Upper Georgia*, Volume 6, *The Cotton Patch Chornicles: Reflections on Cherokee Heritage, People, Places, and the Events in Forsyth County, Georgia*, and Volume 7, *Upon Our Ruins: A Study in Cherokee History and Genealogy*.

    Bagley, Garland C. *History of Forsyth County, Georgia.* Easley, SC: Southern Historical Press, 1985.

    ———. *History of Forsyth County, Georgia, Volume II.* Milledgeville, GA: Boyd Pub. Co., 1990.

FRANKLIN COUNTY. Map #25.

County seat is Carnesville, 30521.

Created February 25, 1784, from land ceded by the Indians in 1783.

Land was first distributed in 1784 as headrights.

Superior court records begin in 1785.

Probate court records begin in 1785.

Georgia Research
Chapter III: Counties, County Records, and Local History Sources

Tax digests begin in 1798.

In addition to the records on microfilm, the Georgia Archives has almost all the original Franklin County records to circa 1900, including unbound records that have not been microfilmed and some county record books that have been compiled in indexed typescripts, all in Record Group 159.

Major published records

Cemetery

Franklin County Historical Society. *History of Franklin County, Georgia.* Roswell, GA: W. H. Wolfe Associates, 1986: 561–748.

Newspaper

Reddish, Melinda, Compiler and Editor. *Franklin County, GA, Obituaries and Death Notices, 1878–1910*, FCO Publications, ca. 2001.

Land

Acker, Martha Walters. *Deeds of Franklin County, Georgia, 1784–1826.* Greenville, SC: Southern Historical Press, 1976.

———. *Franklin County, Georgia Tax Digests, 1798–1839.* 4 vols. Birmingham, AL: privately printed, 1980–87.

———. *Index to Deeds of Franklin County, Georgia, 1784–1860.* Birmingham, AL: privately printed, 1979.

The Georgia Archives has 10 bound volumes of WPA typescripts for deeds 1786–1797, Deed Book Y (general index to old deeds), and miscellaneous deeds 1789–1831.

Estate

Aker, Martha Walter. *Franklin County, Georgia, Court of Ordinary Records, 1787–1849.* Birmingham, AL: privately printed, 1989.

Hageness, MariLee Beatty. *Abstracts of Will Book A, 15 March 1824–6 July 1849, Franklin County, Georgia.* N.p.: MLH Research, 1997.

———. *Abstract of Wills and Inventories, Ordinary Court, 15 May 1786–6 Sep 1813, Franklin County, Georgia.* N.p.: MLH Research, 1997.

———. *Index to Wills 1848–1933, Franklin County, Georgia.* N.p.: MLH Research, 1997.

———. *Loose Estate Records, 1786–1916, Franklin County, Georgia: Court of Ordinary.* N.p.: MLH Research, 1995.

Court

Seven bound volumes of WPA typescripts for Court of Ordinary minutes, 1786–1849, are in the Georgia Archives.

FULTON COUNTY. Map #40.

County seat is Atlanta, 30303.

Created December 20, 1853, from DeKalb County.

Land was first distributed in the 1821 Land Lottery.

All records of the Probate and Superior courts begin in 1854. Deed books B, F, and H were stolen in the 1880s and never recovered.

Most tax digests are available, beginning in 1854.

Years support books beginning in 1866 are available at the Fulton County Probate Court. Criminal court record books can be found in the criminal division of the Superior Court. County plat books are available in the Superior Court deed record room. Historical records of the City of Atlanta and other cities annexed by Atlanta are available at the Atlanta History Center.

On January 1, 1932, Milton County was abolished and merged with Fulton County on the north, and Campbell County was abolished and merged with Fulton County on the south. Fulton County maintains the records of Campbell and Milton Counties.

Major library resources include the Atlanta-Fulton Public Library, 1 Margaret Mitchell Square, Atlanta, GA 30303. The telephone number is 404-730-1897. Website: http://afplweb.com/special-collections-m. The library's "Genealogy and Georgia Historical Collections" section has a Georgia biographies index and index to biographies of prominent black Americans. Its book collection has many rare volumes including Virginia and other states. The library also has six vertical file drawers of "Miscellany" for which there is an inventory available in a ring binder at the librarian's desk. For more thorough coverage of the features of this library, see the *Georgia Genealogical Society Quarterly*, Vol. 36 Number 3 (Fall 2000) 181–186. Also, the Auburn Avenue Research Library on African-American Culture and History, 101 Auburn Ave., NE, Atlanta, GA 30303. The telephone number is 404-730-4001. Website: http://www.afpls.org/aarl This library is part of the Atlanta-Fulton Public Library System. It is dedicated to the research and study of African-American culture, particularly in the Southeast. It has a large reference collection, a special collection of rare books and materials, and archives for unpublished papers and documents. Also, the Atlanta History Center, 130 West Paces Ferry Rd., Atlanta, GA 30305. The telephone number is 404-814-4000. Website: http://www.atlantahistorycenter.com. The Atlanta History Center has library, historical quarterly, newsletter, and manuscript collections. The Center has many original city of Atlanta, Campbell County, Fulton County, and Milton County records. The library also features a working model of the *Franklin Garrett's Necrology*, which is an indexed collection of his compilations of pre-1930 metropolitan Atlanta obituaries, cemetery surveys, census, estate records, etc. Also, the Old Campbell Historical Society, 45 North East Broad St., Fairburn, GA 30213. They house books, maps, funeral home records, original obituaries, family and subject files, and various other loose papers not available elsewhere.

Major published records (See also "Major published records" for Campbell and Milton counties in this chapter.)

Cemetery

Anglin, Phillip B. *Dunwoody, Georgia Historic Cemeteries: Silent Storytellers*. Dunwoody, GA: Dunwoody Preservation Trust, 2004.

———. *Milton County, Georgia Cemeteries: Present Day Northern Fulton County.* Baltimore: Gateway Press, 2002.

Franklin Garrett's Necrology at the Atlanta History Center, Atlanta, Georgia, includes tombstone inscriptions and other information from white cemeteries surveyed by Franklin Garrett primarily in the 1930s and 1940s (website: http://Garrett.AtlantaHistoryCenter.com/). Some published information on cemeteries in the north Fulton County area may be found in Hitt work listed below.

Georgia Society, DAR. *Record of Burials, Oakland Cemetery, City of Atlanta, Georgia 1851–1951.* 3 vols. DAR Genealogical Records Collections, [typescript], vols. 401, 402, 403, 1952.

Hitt, Michael D., and Chuck Brown. *In Memory of: Cemetery Records of Roswell, Georgia.* Roswell, GA: privately printed, 1994.

Westfall, Penny. *Georgia Cemeteries.* Bowie, MD: Heritage Press, 1999.

Newspaper

Atlanta newspaper obituaries for 1837–1932 are included in the *Franklin Garrett's Necrology*, specifically including 1857–1932 for both the *Atlanta Constitution* and the *Atlanta Journal*.

Austin, Jeannette Holland. *Atlanta Constitution, 1868–1884, 1887, 1890.* Riverdale, GA: privately printed, n.d.

———. *Georgia Obituaries, 1905–1910.* Riverdale, GA: privately printed, ca. 1989, contains obituaries 1905–1910 from the *Atlanta Georgian* and the *Atlanta Constitution*. Also reprinted by Willow Bend Books, 1997.

A large collection of scanned, searchable Atlanta newspapers are available through the Digital Library of Georgia (http://atlnewspapers.galileo.usg.edu).

Local History

Garrett, Franklin M., and Harold H. Martin. *Atlanta and Environs.* 3 vols. New York: Lewis Historical Pub. Co, 1954, 1987.

GILMER COUNTY. Map #6.

County seat is Ellijay, 30540.

Created December 3, 1832, from original Cherokee County.

Land was first distributed in the 1832 Land Lottery.

Superior court records begin in 1833.

Probate court records begin in 1835, although some earlier records exist.

Tax digests begin in 1864; 1855 also available.

In addition to the records on microfilm, the Georgia Archives has original unbound superior court case files, 1847–1943; estate records, 1835–1940; marriages, 1835–1943; pensions, 1866–1922; and apprenticeships, 1840–1915, in Record Group 161.

Major published records

    Miscellaneous

    Davis, Robert S. *Early Families and Records of Gilmer County, Georgia, 1834 – 1943*. Gainesville, GA: Magnolia Press, 2010.

    Parker, Ernest. *Days Gone By: Early Gilmer County Georgia*. Ellijay, GA: Gilmer County Genealogical Society, 1999.

    Local History

    Stanley, Lawrence L. *A Little History of Gilmer County*. Ellijay, GA: privately printed, 1975.

GLASCOCK COUNTY. Map #76.

County seat is Gibson, 30810.

Created December 19, 1857, from Warren County.

Land was first distributed in the 1750s as headrights.

All records begin in 1858.

Major published records

    Cemetery

    Crumpton, Nathaniel David. *Cemeteries & Genealogy, Warren County, Georgia, and Immediate Vicinity, 1792–1987*. Roswell, GA: W. H. Wolfe Associates, 1987: 70–101.

GLYNN COUNTY. Map #150.

County seat is Brunswick, 31520.

Created February 5, 1777, with boundaries that included colonial St. David and St. Patrick Parishes.

Land was first distributed in 1733 by the Trustees and formally granted beginning in 1755.

Superior court records begin in 1787.

Probate court records begin in 1815, although some earlier records exist.

Tax digests begin in 1874; 1792–1794 also available.

Major published records

    Cemetery

    There is no countywide cemetery publication for Glynn County; see the following citation to one large cemetery in Glynn County.

    Vicent, Ruth N. Cassidy, and Sara Rogers Cassidy. *Palmetto Cemetery, Ross Road, Brunswick, Glynn County, Georgia*. Knoxville, TN: Tennessee Valley Pub, 2000.

    Local History

    Cate, Margaret Davis. *Our Todays and Yesterdays; A Story of Brunswick and the Coastal Islands*. Spartanburg, SC: Reprint Co, 1972.

GORDON COUNTY. Map #12.

County seat is Calhoun, 30701.

Created February 13, 1850, from Floyd and Cass (now Bartow) Counties.

Land was first distributed in the 1832 Land Lottery.

Superior court records begin in 1850.

Probate court records begin in 1856, although some earlier records exist.

Tax digests begin in 1851.

In addition to the records on microfilm, the Georgia Archives has original unbound superior court case files, 1869–circa 1920 and estate records, 1864 to circa 1920, in Record Group 164.

Major published records

    Cemetery

        The Gordon County Historical Society. *1976 Bicentennial History of Gordon County, Georgia.* Calhoun, GA: privately printed, 1976: 239–256.

        Henderson, Sue, et al. *Gordon County, Georgia Cemetery Records.* Calhoun, GA: Gordon County Historical Society, 1988.

        Pitts, Lulie. *History of Gordon County, Georgia.* Calhoun, GA: privately printed, 1933: 279–306.

    Newspaper

        Kilbourne, Elizabeth Evans. *Gordon County, Georgia, Newspaper Clippings, 1870–1890.* 4 vols. Savannah, GA: privately printed, 1997–98.

    Land

        Gladney, Mrs. Robert Hoyt. *Gordon County, Georgia, Deed Books A & B, Abstracts, 1834–1854.* Calhoun, GA: privately printed, 1988.

    Estate

        Georgia Society, Daughters of the American Revolution. *Will Book A, 1852–1894, Gordon County, Georgia.* Volume 260. Adairsville, GA: privately printed, 1982.

        ———. *Will Book B, 1894–1912, Gordon County, Georgia,* Volume 271. Adairsville, GA: privately printed, 1984.

    Court

        Gladney, Mrs. Robert Hoyt. *Gordon County, Georgia, Superior Court Minute Book A, 1850–1854.* Calhoun, GA: privately printed, 1986.

    Local History

        Pitts, Lulie. *History of Gordon County, Georgia.* Calhoun, GA: Press of the Calhoun Times, 1934.

Reeve, Jewell B. *Stories of Gordon County and Calhoun, Georgia*. Easley, SC: Southern Historical Press, 1979.

GRADY COUNTY. Map #153.

County seat is Cairo, 31728.

Created August 17, 1905, from Decatur and Thomas Counties.

Land was first distributed in the 1820 Land Lottery.

All records begin in 1906.

The Georgia Archives has no records on microfilm of this post-1900 county, although original tax digests beginning in 1906 are available.

Major published records

    Cemetery

    Grady County Historical Society. *Cemeteries of Grady County, Georgia: A Compilation of Cemetery Surveys*. Cairo, GA: Grady County Historical Society, 2006.

    Varick, Florida, and Phyllis R. Smith. *Grady County, Georgia, Tomb Index*. 2nd ed. Tallahassee, FL: privately printed, 1980.

    Local History

    Waldorf, Gwendolyn Brock. *The Genesis of Grady County, Georgia*. Tallahassee, FL: Sentry Press, 2006.

GREENE COUNTY. Map #60.

County seat is Greensboro, 30642.

Created February 3, 1786, from Washington County.

Land was first distributed in 1784 as headrights.

Superior court records begin in 1786.

Probate court records begin in 1786.

Tax digests begin in 1788.

In addition to the records on microfilm, some of which were filmed at Duke University, the Georgia Archives has unbound original inferior and superior court case files, 1809–1907, and miscellaneous records, 1830s–circa 1900, in Record Group 166. The Georgia Archives has many unbound original records on microfilm: guardianship records, 1790–1943, in Drawer 305, Boxes 42 to 45; wills, 1798–1914, in Drawer 305, Boxes 46 to 50; estate records, 1790–1940, in Drawer 305, Boxes 50 to 117; and Drawer 307, Boxes 1 to 96.

Major published records

    Cemetery

    Armor, E. H. *The Cemeteries of Greene County, Georgia*. Athens, GA: Agee Publishers, Inc., 1987.

Newspaper

Evans, Tad. *Greene County, Georgia, Newspaper Clippings*. 1852–1886. 2 vols. Savannah, GA: privately printed, 1997, 1999.

McRee, Fred W., Jr. *Greene County, Georgia Deaths 1860–1918*. Dahlonega, GA: privately printed, 2010.

Land

Abbe, Mary Hoit and Elaine Collier Neal, *Greene County Georgia Tax Digests Pre-1800*. Athens, GA: privately printed, 2009.

Turner, Freda R. *Greene County, Georgia Land Records Deeds 1785–1810*. Fernandina Beach, FL: Wolfe Publishing, 1997.

———. *Greene County, Georgia Land Records, Deeds 1810–1815 Volume II*. Milledgeville, GA: Boyd Publ. Co., 2005.

———. *Greene County, Georgia Land Records, Deeds 1816–1826 Volume III*. Milledgeville, GA: Boyd Publ. Co., 2006.

———. *Greene County, Georgia Land Records, Deeds 1824–1851 Volume IV*. Milledgeville, GA: Boyd Publ. Co., 2006.

Estate

Turner, Freda R. *Greene County, Georgia, Wills 1786–1877*. Fernandina Beach, FL: Wolfe Publishing, 1998.

GWINNETT COUNTY. Map #32.

County seat is Lawrenceville, 30245.

Created December 15, 1818, from Indian lands ceded in 1817 and 1818.

Land was first distributed in the 1820 Land Lottery.

Superior court records begin in 1871.

Probate court records begin in 1856, although some earlier records exist.

Tax digests begin in 1872; 1860, 1861, 1864, and 1866 also available.

Major published records

Cemetery

McCabe, Alice Smythe. *Gwinnett County, Georgia, Deaths 1818–1989*. Lawrenceville, GA: Gwinnett Historical Society, 1991.

Newspaper

Parr, Larry W. *Gwinnett County Records As Recorded in Athens, Georgia Newspapers, 1827–1849*. Atlanta: Callaway Pub, 1986.

Land

Manning, Terry Edward Pyatt. *Gwinnett County, Georgia 1890 Tax Digest with Land Lots, Substitute for Lost 1890 Federal Census*. Lawrenceville, GA: Gwinnett Historical Society, Inc., 2002. Includes abstract of the 1890 tax digest with background information and land lot maps.

Court

McCabe, Alice Smythe. *Gwinnett County, Georgia, Inferior Court, Minutes for Ordinary Purposes, 1819–1861*. Lawrenceville, GA: Gwinnett Historical Society, 1987.

Local History

Flanigan, James C. *History of Gwinnett County, Georgia*. 2 vols. Hapeville, GA: Printed by Tyler & Co, 1943.

Redd, Bryan L., Arla Bateman Redd, and James C. Flanigan. *Index of History of Gwinnett County, Georgia by Judge James C. Flanigan*. Decatur, GA: privately printed, 2001.

Stewart, William C. *Gone to Georgia: Jackson and Gwinnett Counties and their Neighbors in the Western Migration*. 1965. Reprinted, Washington, DC: National Genealogical Society, 1979.

Worthy, Marvin Nash. *History of Gwinnett County Georgia: 1818–1993*. Lawrenceville, GA: Board of Commissioners of Gwinnett County, 1994.

HABERSHAM COUNTY. Map #17.

County seat is Clarkesville, 30523.

Created December 15, 1818, from Indian lands ceded in 1817 and 1818.

Land was first distributed in the 1820 Land Lottery.

Superior court records begin in 1819.

Probate court records begin in 1819.

Tax digests begin in 1872; 1850 also available.

Major library resource is the Clarkesville/Habersham County Library, 178 East Green St., Clarkesville, GA 30523. The telephone number is 706-754-4413. For more thorough coverage of the features of this library, see the *Georgia Genealogical Society Quarterly*, Vol. 35 No. 1 (Spring 1999) 32–34.

Major published records

Cemetery

Northeast Georgia Regional Library. *Habersham and White Counties Cemeteries*. Roswell, GA: W. H. Wolfe Associates, 1986: 1–114.

Miscellaneous

Kimzey, Herbert B., and Nancy Kimzey Dempsey. *Early Genealogical and Historical Records: Habersham County, Georgia*. [Athens, GA]: privately printed, 1988.

HALL COUNTY. Map #23.

County seat is Gainesville, 30501.

Created December 15, 1818, from Indian lands ceded in 1817 and 1818, with lands taken from Franklin and Jackson Counties.

Land was first distributed in 1784 as headrights and in the 1820 Land Lottery.

Superior court records begin in 1819.

Probate court records begin in 1819.

Tax digests begin in 1873; 1848 and 1852–1854 also available.

Major library resource is the Hall County Library, 127 North Main St., NW, Gainesville, GA 30501. The telephone number is 770-532-3311. Has genealogical and historical files on Hall County compiled by Sybil McRay and her notes on persons in the 1820 census of Hall County. It also has some original Hall County records. For more thorough coverage of the features of this library, see the *Georgia Genealogical Society Quarterly*, 36: 1 (spring 2000) 25–31.

Major published records

Cemetery

McRay, Sybil W. *Tombstone Inscriptions of Hall County, Georgia*. Gainesville, GA: privately printed, 1971. Ms. McRay has also published many of the early county records. Her files are in the Chestatee Regional Library in Gainesville.

White, Louise W. *Index of The Tombstones of Hall County, by Sybil McRay: Index*. Gainesville, GA: 1971. This is a separate full name index to the above book..

Newspapers

Dorsey, James Edward. *Hall County, Georgia: Abstract of Newspaper Sources for the Period 1818–1864*. Gainesville, GA: Magnolia Press, 2009.

———. *Hall County, Georgia: Abstract of Newspaper Sources for the Period 1865–1889*. Gainesville, GA:: Magnolia Press, 2008.

Jones, Patricia K. *Annotated Abstracts of Extant Gainesville, Georgia Newspapers, 1861–1910: Unfortunate Events and Items of Genealogical Interest*. Oakwood, GA.: privately printed, 2012.

Land

McDonald, Robert H., and Barbara E. McDonald. *Wills and Deeds of Hall County, Georgia, Court of Ordinary: Will Book A, 1837–1867 & 1868–1890, Will Book A-1, 1890–1907*. Fernandina Beach, FL: Wolfe Pub, 2002.

Estate

Jones, Patricia K. *Twelve Months Support for Widows and Orphans of Hall County, Georgia, Book A*. Oakwood, GA: privately printed, 2009.

McDonald, Robert H. and Barbara E. *Wills and Deeds of Hall County Georgia; Court of Ordinary Will Book A 1837–1867 & 1868–1890; Will Book A-1 1890–1907*. Fernandina Beach, FL: Wolfe Publishing, 2002.

McRay, Sybil Wood. *Book "A" Wills, 1837–1867, and Wills Recorded in Minute Book, Misc. "A" 1819–1837, Hall County, Georgia*. Gainesville, GA: privately printed ,1968.

———. *Misc.-D, 12 Months Support-Inventory and Appraisement, 1850–1868, Hall County, Georgia: (with Some Added Genealogical Data)*. Gainesville, GA: privately printed, 1969.

Local History

Davis, Robert S. *The Families of Hall County, 1817–1849*. Gainesville, GA: Magnolia Press, 1991.

Dorsey, James E. *The History of Hall County*. 2 vols. Gainesville, GA: Magnolia Press, 1991, 2009.

Hutchens, Linda Rucker, and Ella J. Wilmont Smith. *Hall County, Georgia*. Charleston, SC: Arcadia, 2004.

Jones, Patricia K. *Confederate Veterans of Hall County, Georgia*. Oakwood, GA: privately printed, 2003.

A Pictorial History of Gainesville & Hall County, Georgia. Marceline, MO: D-Books Publishing, Inc, 2007.

Norton, William L. *Historic Gainesville & Hall County: An Illustrated History*. San Antonio, TX: Historical Pub. Network, 2001.

HANCOCK COUNTY. Map #74.

County seat is Sparta, 31087.

Created December 17, 1793, from Washington and Greene Counties.

Land was first distributed in 1784 as headrights.

All records begin in 1794.

In addition to the records on microfilm, the Georgia Archives has unbound original inferior and superior court case files, 1794–1900; petitions for dower, 1821–1880; and freedmen marriages, circa 1866, in Record Group 170. Many of the early tax digests are in the office of the clerk of court and have never been microfilmed.

Major published records

Cemetery

Friends of Hancock County Cemeteries. *Cemeteries of Hancock County, Georgia*. Milledgeville, GA: Friends of Cemeteries of Middle Georgia, 2004.

Newspaper

Evans, Tad. *Georgia Newspaper Clippings, Hancock County Extracts Volume I 1809–1844 & Volume II 1845–1890*. Savannah, GA: privately printed, 2000.

Poss, Faye Stone. *Hancock County, Georgia Early Newspaper Abstracts "Farmer's Gazette" 1803–1804, 1806–1807*. Snellville, GA: privately printed, 2001.

———. *Hancock County, Georgia Supplement to Early Newspaper Abstracts Farmer's Gazette 1803–1806*. Snellville, GA: privately printed, 2002.

Land

Georgia Society, Daughters of the American Revolution. *Hancock County, Georgia Tax Returns, 1795*. Volume 414. Milledgeville, GA: privately printed, 1940–42.

Georgia Society, Daughters of the American Revolution. *Hancock Co., Georgia Tax Returns, 1802*. Volume 415. Milledgeville, GA: privately printed, 1940–42.

Georgia Society, Daughters of the American Revolution. *Hancock Co., Georgia Tax Returns, 1813*. Volume 416. Milledgeville, GA: privately printed, 1940–42.

Marsh, Helen, Tim Marsh, and Edward E. Van Schaick Jr., editors. *Land Deed Genealogy of Hancock County, Georgia, [Deed Books A–E, 1794–1802]*. Greenville, SC: Southern Historical Press, 1997.

Court

Brantley, J. Kenneth. *Hancock County Georgia Court of Ordinary Minutes, 1799–1863*. 3 vols. Powder Springs, GA: Brantley Association of America, 1999–2000.

———. *Hancock County Georgia Inferior Court Minutes (for county purposes), 1809–1833*. Powder Springs, GA: Brantley Association of America, 2000.

HARALSON COUNTY. Map #28.

County seat is Buchanan, 30113.

Created January 26, 1856, from Polk and Carroll Counties.

Land was first distributed in the 1827 Land Lottery and 1832 Land and/or Gold Lotteries.

Superior court records begin in 1856.

Probate court records begin in 1856.

Tax digests begin in 1866.

Major published records

Cemetery

Haralson County Historical Society. *Haralson County, Georgia, Cemeteries*. Baltimore: Gateway Press, 2004.

HARRIS COUNTY. Map #79.

County seat is Hamilton, 31811.

Created December 14, 1827, from Troup and Muscogee Counties.

Land was first distributed in the 1827 Land Lottery.

Superior court records begin in 1828.

Probate court records begin in 1828.

Tax digests begin in 1841; 1831 and 1836 also available.

Major published records

    Cemetery

    Barfield, Louise Calhoun. *History of Harris County, Georgia, 1827–1961*. 1961. Reprint Atlanta: W. H. Wolfe Associates, 1978: 319–704, selected.

    Newspaper

    Evans, Tad. *Georgia Newspaper Clippings, Harris County Extracts, 1828–1888*. Savannah, GA: privately printed, 2005.

    Local History

    Barfield, Louise Calhoun. *History of Harris County, Georgia, 1827–1961*. 1961. Reprint Atlanta: W. H. Wolfe Associates, 1978.

    Hammett, Frances Pauline. *Comprehensive topical index, all names and places in the compiled History of Harris County, Georgia, 1827–1961*. Columbus, GA: Cherith Creek Designs, 1991.

    Harris County, Georgia, and Her People. LaGrange, GA: Family Tree, Jan. 1985–Winter 1987. This was a periodical about the county; very good material.

HART COUNTY. Map #26.

County seat is Hartwell, 30643.

Created December 7, 1853, from Franklin and Elbert Counties.

Land was first distributed in 1773 as headrights.

Superior court records begin in 1854.

Probate court records begin in 1854.

Tax digests begin in 1872; 1867 also available.

Major published records

    Cemetery

    Kaufhold, Shirley, editor. *Cemeteries of Hart County, Georgia*. N.p.: Savannah River Valley Genealogical Society, 1989.

    Newspaper

    Georgia Society, Daughters of the American Revolution. *Birth, Marriage and Death Notices from old Copies of the Hartwell Sun 1881–1896*. Volume I, Book 421. N.p.: privately printed, 1943.

    Georgia Society, Daughters of the American Revolution. *Birth, Marriage and Death Notices from old Copies of the Hartwell Sun 1897–1903*. Volume II Book 423. N.p.: privately printed, 1943.

Savannah River Valley Genealogical Society, *Obituaries Abstracted From The Hartwell Sun 1877–1902*. Fernandina Beach, FL: Wolfe Publishing, 2003.

Savannah River Valley Genealogical Society. *Obituaries Abstracted from the Hartwell Sun, 1903 – 1922: Hartwell, Hart County, Georgia*. Hartwell, GA: privately printed, 2007.

Local History

Baker, John William. *History of Hart County*. N.p., 1933.

Kaufhold, Shirley, and Tony Bryant. *The Hart of Georgia: A History of Hart County*. Alpharetta, GA: W. H. Wolfe Associates, 1992. Includes indexes to various minute, will, and deed books.

HEARD COUNTY. Map #49.

County seat is Franklin, 30217.

Created December 22, 1830, from Troup, Coweta, and Carroll Counties.

Land was first distributed in the 1827 Land Lottery.

Superior court records begin in 1894.

Probate court records begin in 1894.

Tax digests begin in 1871.

Major published records

    Cemetery

    Eller, Lynda S. *Heard County, Georgia, Cemeteries*. Lanett, AL: privately printed, 1977.

HENRY COUNTY. Map #54.

County seat is McDonough, 30253.

Created May 15, 1821, from Indian lands ceded in 1821.

Land was first distributed in the 1821 Land Lottery.

Superior court records begin in 1822.

Probate court records begin in 1822.

Tax digests begin in 1852; 1831, 1832, and 1837 also available.

Major published records

    Cemetery

    Ranier, Vessie Thrasher. *Henry County, Georgia, Cemeteries; Family Graveyards*. Stockbridge, GA: privately printed, 1980.

    ———. *Henry County, Georgia, Cemeteries; McDonough, Eastlawn, Stockbridge*. McDonough, GA: privately printed, 1981.

    ———. *Henry County, Georgia, Churchyard Cemeteries*. Stockbridge, GA: privately printed, 1980.

Newspaper

Bowen, Rhoda Apperson. *Henry County, Georgia Obituaries, 1879–1899, 1900–1907, 1908–1929*. 3 vols. Roswell, GA: W. H. Wolfe Associates, 1993–1995.

Bowen, Rhoda Anne, and Freda R. Turner. *Georgia Confederate Soldier Obituaries; Henry, Newton and Rockdale Counties, 1879–1943*. Alpharetta, GA: W. H. Wolfe Associates, 1992.

Turner, Freda R. *Henry County, Georgia Obituaries*. [McDonough, GA]: privately printed, 2000.

Land

Turner, Freda Reid. *Henry County, Georgia Land Records*. 3 vols. Roswell, Georgia: W. H. Wolfe Associates, 1991, 1993. 1821–1828, Deed Books A and B (Volume I); 1824–1838, Deed Books C, D, F, G, and H (Volume II); 1839–1851 Deed Books J, K, L, and M (Volume III).

Local History

Rainer, Robert A., and Vessie Thrasher Rainer. *Index to Henry County, Georgia: The Mother of Counties*. McDonough, GA: R.A. Rainer, 1988.

Rainer, Vessie Thrasher. *Henry County, Georgia: Landmark Houses*. McDonough, GA: R.A. Rainer Jr, 1986.

———. *Henry County, Georgia: The Mother of Counties*. McDonough, GA: Robert A. Rainer Jr, 1988.

Rocky Creek Social Club (Hampton, Ga.). *History of Henry County, [Georgia], May 1821–1921*. Hampton, GA: privately printed, 1988.

HOUSTON COUNTY. Map #96.

County seat is Perry, 31069.

Created May 15, 1821, from Indian lands ceded in 1821.

Land was first distributed in the 1821 Land Lottery. (Georgia also created a Houston County in what is presently Muscle Shoals, Alabama, on February 20, 1784. It never functioned as a county and was abolished August 14, 1786.)

Superior court records begin in 1822.

Probate court records begin in 1822.

Tax digests begin in 1829.

Major published records

Cemetery

Howell, Addie Paramore. *Cemeteries and Obituaries of Houston County, Georgia*. Macon, GA: privately printed, 1982: 1–129, 288–290.

Mills, William A. *Houston County, Georgia, Evergreen Cemetery Tombstone Transcripts 1827–1997*. Perry, GA: privately printed, 1996.

Newspaper

Evans, Tad. *Houston County, Georgia, Newspaper Clippings.* 2 vols. Savannah, GA: privately printed, 2002, 2005. Volume I, 1870–1883, Volume II, 1884–1891.

———. *Georgia Newspaper Clippings, Houston County Extracts.* 1821-1907. 2 vols. Savannah, GA: privately printed, 2005.

Howell, Addie Paramore. *Cemeteries and Obituaries of Houston County, Georgia.* Macon, GA: privately printed, 1982: 130–284.

Land

Campbell, Davine V., and William R. Henry. *Land Records of Houston County, Georgia.* 5 vols. Warner Robins, GA: Central Georgia Genealogical Society, 1991–1994. Volume 1, 1822–1829, Deed Books A, B, C; Volume 2, 1829–1831, Deed Book D; Volume 3, 1831–1834, Deed Book E; Volume 4, 1834–1836, Deed Book F; Volume 5, 1836–1840, Deed Book G

Estate

Hageness, MariLee Beatty. *Wills, Houston County, Georgia: Will Book A, 1827–1855; Will Book B, 1855–1896, Will Book C, 1896–.* N.p.: Privately published, 1995.

Henry, William R. *Miscellaneous Estate Records of Houston County, Georgia, Volume I.* Warner Robins, GA: Central Georgia Genealogical Society, 1988.

———. *Wills and Inferior Court Minutes of Houston County, Georgia.* Warner Robins, GA: Central Georgia Genealogical Society, 1987.

Court

Mills, William A. *Houston County, Georgia Administrators & Guardians Bond Abstracts 1852–1870.* Perry, GA: privately printed, 1998.

———. *Houston County, Georgia Administrators & Guardians Bond Abstracts 1871–1900.* Perry, GA: privately printed, 1999.

Local History

Central Georgia Genealogical Society. *First Hundred and Ten Years of Houston County, Georgia, 1822–1932.* Chelsea, MI: privately printed, 1983.

Hickson, Bobbe Smith. *A Land So Dedicated: Houston County, Georgia.* Perry, GA: Houston County Library Board, 1976.

Houston County Historical Book Committee. *The Heritage of Houston County, Georgia.* Waynesville, NC: County Heritage, Inc., 2001.

IRWIN COUNTY. Map #125.

County seat is Ocilla, 31774.

Created December 15, 1818, from Indian lands ceded in 1814 and 1818.

Land was first distributed in the 1820 Land Lottery.

Superior court records begin in 1820.

Probate court records begin in 1820.

Tax digests begin in 1830.

Major published records

    Cemetery

        Paulk, Jessie H., and Delma Wilson Paulk. *Survey of Irwin County, Georgia, Cemeteries*. Thomasville, GA: Craigmiles Historical Publications, 1993.

    Newspaper

        Evans, Tad. *Georgia Newspaper Clippings Irwin County Extracts, 1820–1899*. Savannah, GA: privately printed, 2000.

    Land

        Wells, Catherine Fussell. *Irwin County, Georgia Deed Books 1 & 3 1820–1847*. Valdosta, GA: Wells-Gen Search, 2001.

        ———. *Irwin County, Georgia Deed Books 4 & 6 1848–1858, 1860–1873*. Valdosta, GA: Wells-Gen Search, 2001.

        ———. *Irwin County, Georgia Deed Book 5 1855–1865*. Valdosta, GA: Wells-Gen Search, 2001.

JACKSON COUNTY. Map #34.

County seat is Jefferson, 30549.

Created February 11, 1796, from Franklin County.

Land was first distributed in 1784 as headrights.

Superior court records begin in 1796.

Probate court records begin in 1796.

Tax digests begin in 1797.

Original unbound superior court case files are in Special Collections of the Hargrett Library at the University of Georgia.

Major published records

    Cemetery

        Austin, Jeannette Holland, and Dorothy Holland Herring. *Jackson County, Georgia, Tombstones*. Westminster, MD: Willow Bend Books, 2001.

        Mathis, James A., and Betty Ann Waddell. *Jackson County, Georgia, Cemetery Records*. Danielsville, GA: Heritage Papers, 1980.

        Sailors, Don. *Cemetery Database of Jackson County, Georgia*. Jefferson County, GA: privately printed, 2003. http://www.adsd.com/jackson/.

Newspaper

Poss, Faye Stone. *Jackson County, Georgia, Newspaper Clippings, The Forest News, June 1875 to January 1881*. Snellville, GA: privately printed, 2005.

———. *Jackson County, Georgia Newspaper Clippings, Jackson Herald, February 1881 to December 1882*. Snellville, GA: privately printed, 2007.

———. *Jackson County, Georgia, Newspaper Clippings, The Jackson Herald, 1883–1885, Volume II*. Snellville, GA: privately printed, 2010.

Land

Poss, Faye Stone. *Jackson County, Georgia, Deed Abstracts, Books A–D, 1796–1808*. Fernandina Beach, FL: Wolfe Publishing, 1998.

———. *Jackson County, Georgia, Deed Abstracts, Book E–G 1808–1822*. Snellville, GA: privately printed, 2000.

Savadge, Belinda E. *1797–1802 Tax Digest, Jackson County, Georgia, Vol. I*. Jefferson, GA: Genealogy Bin, 2000.

Court

Dunn, Teresa Wilson, and Vivian Phillips Walls. *Jackson County, Georgia, Superior Court Records, 1796–1803*. Roswell, GA: W. H. Wolfe Associates, 1994.

Poss, Faye S. *Jackson County, Georgia Early Court Records, 1796–1831*. Alpharetta, GA: W. H. Wolfe Associates, 1994.

———. *Jackson County, Georgia Will Abstracts, Books A & B, 1803–1888*. Fernandina Beach, FL: Wolfe Publishing, 1995.

JASPER COUNTY. Map #57.

County seat is Monticello, 31064.

Created as Randolph County on December 10, 1807, from Baldwin County.

Jasper County was originally named Randolph County, but the name was changed to Jasper County on December 10, 1812. The present Randolph County, Georgia, was created in 1828.

Land was first distributed in the 1807 Land Lottery.

Superior court records begin in 1808.

Probate court records begin in 1808.

Tax digests begin in 1871; 1866 and 1868 also available.

In addition to the records on microfilm, the Georgia Archives has unbound original records in Record Group 179.

Major published records

Cemetery

Lancaster, Mrs. Edgar M. *Jasper County, Georgia, Cemetery and Bible Records.* Shady Dale, GA: privately printed, 1969: 1–153.

Newspaper

Evans, Tad. *Georgia Newspaper Clippings, Jasper County Extracts.* 1812-1887. 2 vols. Savannah, GA: privately printed, 1999.

Land

Bruno, John I. *Jasper County, Georgia, Deed Books 1 & 2, 1807–1810.* Fernandina Beach, FL: Wolfe Publishing, 1999.

———. *Jasper County, Georgia, Deed Books 3 & 4, 1810–1811.* Mansfield, GA: privately printed, 1999.

Miscellaneous

Davis, Robert S. *Records of Jasper County, Georgia, from the Georgia Department of Archives and History.* Greenville, SC: Southern Historical Press, 1990.

Local History

Carnes, Marcia Hayes, John P. Harvey, and Irene Roberts Malone. *History of Jasper County, Georgia.* Roswell, GA: W. H. Wolfe Associates, 1984.

JEFF DAVIS COUNTY. Map #127.

County seat is Hazelhurst, 31539.

Created August 18, 1905, from Appling and Coffee Counties.

Land was first distributed in the 1820 Land Lottery.

All records begin in 1906.

The Georgia Archives has no records on microfilm of this post-1900 county, although original tax digests beginning in 1906 are available.

Major published records

Cemetery

Satilla Regional Library. *Jeff Davis County, Georgia, Cemeteries.* Douglas, GA: privately printed, 1987.

JEFFERSON COUNTY. Map #77.

County seat is Louisville, 30434.

Created February 20, 1796, from Burke and Warren Counties.

Land was first distributed in the 1750s as headrights.

Superior court records begin in 1865, although some earlier records exist.

Probate court records begin circa 1796.

Tax digests begin in 1796.

In addition to the records on microfilm, the Georgia Archives has the unbound original records in Record Group 181. Many early tax records are indexed.

Major published records

Cemetery

Andrus, Sara Margaret Stone. *Jefferson County, Georgia, Cemetery Records.* Augusta, GA: John Franklin Wren Chapter, DAR, 1969.

Records from part of the county's cemeteries have been published by the Wrens High School in *Jefferson County, Georgia, Tombstone Inscriptions: A Beginning.* Wrens, GA: privately printed, 1980.

Lewis, Leroy. *Cemeteries of Jefferson County, Georgia, 1794–2000.* Louisville, GA: privately printed, 2002.

Newspaper

Poss, Faye Stone. *Early Jefferson County, Georgia Newspaper Abstracts, 1799–1811.* Snellville, GA: privately printed, 2011.

Land

Crumpton, Daniel Nathan. *Burke County, Georgia Land Records: Boundaries As of 1777.* Warrenton, GA: privately printed, 2009.

———. *Jefferson County, Georgia, and Some Surrounding Areas: Land Records, Volume One, Mid 1700s–Mid 1800s.* Warrenton, GA: privately printed, 2003.

———. *Jefferson County, Georgia, and Some Surrounding Areas Including Camp Gordon, Georgia: Land Records, Volume Two, Mid 1800s–1900s.* Warrenton, GA: privately printed, 2004.

Hageness, MariLee Beatty. *Index to 1812 Tax Digest, Jefferson County, Georgia.* Anniston, AL: MLH Research, 2001.

Court

Hageness, MariLee Beatty. *Abstracts of Wills 1777–1874 Jefferson County, Georgia.* Anniston, AL: MLH Research, 2002.

JENKINS COUNTY. Map #89.

County seat is Millen, 30442.

Created August 17, 1905, from Bulloch, Burke, Emanuel, and Screven Counties.

Land was first distributed in the 1750s as headrights.

All records begin in 1906.

The Georgia Archives has no records on microfilm of this post-1900 county, although original tax digests beginning in 1906 are available.

Major published records

Cemetery

Bulloch County Regional Library. *Jenkins County, Georgia Cemeteries*. 4 vols. Statesboro, GA: privately printed, 1996–97. These also appear in Volumes 530, 531, 540, and 541 of the Georgia Society, Daughters of the American Revolution, Genealogical Records Collection.

Newspaper

Dorsey, James E. *Herndon and Lawtonville: A Collection of Newspaper Sources, 1883–1900*. Swainsboro, GA: Emanuel County Junior College, 1980.

JOHNSON COUNTY. Map #87.

County seat is Wrightsville, 31096.

Created December 11, 1858, from Washington, Emanuel, and Laurens Counties.

Land was first distributed in 1784 as headrights.

Superior court and probate court records begin in 1859.

Tax digests begin in 1872; 1864 and 1866 also available.

Major published records

Cemetery

Meadows, Mattie Lee Hoover. *Searching for our Ancestors Among the Gravestones: A Cemetery Record of Johnson County, Georgia*. N.p.: Johnson County Historical Society, 1980.

Local History

Johnson County Historical Society. *A History of Johnson County Churches*. Swainsboro, GA: Magnolia Press, 1986.

JONES COUNTY. Map #72.

County seat is Gray, 31032.

Created December 10, 1807, from Baldwin County.

Land was first distributed in the 1807 Land Lottery.

Superior court and probate court records begin in 1808.

Tax digests begin in 1811.

Original unbound Jones County records are in the Telamon Cuyler Collection, Hargrett Rare Book and Manuscript Library, University of Georgia Libraries.

Major published records

Cemetery

Abbott, Frank M. *Cemetery Records*. Macon, GA: privately printed, 1977.

———. *More Cemeteries, Obituaries and Wills*. Volume 10 N.p.: privately printed, n.d.

Colvin, Earl, Beth Colvin, and Susan J. Harrington. *Fields of Stone: The Cemeteries of Jones County, Georgia.* Milledgeville, GA: Friends of Cemeteries of Middle Georgia, 2004.

Newspaper

Evans, Tad. *Georgia Newspaper Clippings, Jones County Extracts.* 1810-1883. 2 vols. Savannah, GA: privately printed, 2001.

Land

Georgia Society, Daughters of the American Revolution. *Tax Digest, Jones County, Georgia, 1811; Index to Digests 1811, 1813, 1814, 1818, 1819.* Volume 429. N.p.: privately printed, 1942.

Estate

Hageness, MariLee Beatty. *Index to Will Books A–D, Jones County, Georgia.* N.p.: Privately published, 1995.

Court

Hageness, MariLee Beatty. *Index, Ordinary Minutes, 1808–1814, Jones County, Georgia.* N.p.: Privately published, 1995

Local History

Abbott, Frank M. *History of the People of Jones County, Georgia.* Volume 4. Macon, GA: National Printing Co., 1977.

Williams, Carolyn White. *History of Jones County, Georgia, for One Hundred Years, Specifically 1807–1907.* Macon, GA: J. W. Burke Company, 1957. Separate index; reprint with index included 2003.

KINCHAFOONEE COUNTY.

Created December 16, 1853, from Stewart County.

The name was changed to Webster County on February 21, 1856. See Webster County.

LAMAR COUNTY. Map #70.

County seat is Barnesville, 30204.

Created November 2, 1920, from Monroe and Pike Counties.

Land was first distributed in the 1821 Land Lottery.

All records begin in 1921.

The Georgia Archives has no records on microfilm of this post-1900 county, although original tax digests beginning in 1921 are available.

Major published records

Cemetery

Torbert, Robert E. *Lamar County, Georgia, Cemetery Records.* Florence, AL: privately printed, 1987.

LANIER COUNTY. Map #158.

County seat is Lakeland, 31615.

Created November 2, 1920, from Berrien, Lowndes, and Clinch Counties.

Land was first distributed in the 1820 Land Lottery.

Superior court records begin in 1921.

Probate court records begin in 1920.

Tax digests begin in 1921.

The Georgia Archives has no records on microfilm of this post-1900 county, although original tax digests beginning in 1922 are available.

Major published records

Cemetery

Hancock, Sue, and Johnny Hancock. *Eleven Cemeteries of Lanier County*. Rebecca, GA: privately printed, 2006.

LAURENS COUNTY. Map #98.

County seat is Dublin, 31021.

Created December 10, 1807, from Wilkinson County.

Land was first distributed in the 1805 and the 1807 Land Lotteries.

Superior court records begin in 1808.

Probate court records begin in 1808.

Tax digests begin in 1857; 1841, 1850, and 1851 also available.

Major published records

Cemetery

Adams, June Selph. *Northview Cemetery, Dublin, Laurens County, Georgia, 1902–1992*. Dublin, GA: privately printed, 1993.

Laurens County Historical Society. *Laurens County, Georgia, Cemeteries*. 2 vols. Dublin, GA: privately printed, 1999.

Newspaper

Georgia Society, Daughters of the American Revolution. *Marriages and Deaths from Dublin Newspapers, 1878–1912*. 9 vols. N.p.: privately printed, 1999.

Evans, Tad. *Georgia Newspaper Clippings, Laurens County Extracts, 1810–1892*. Savannah, GA: privately printed, 1998.

———. *Laurens County, Georgia, Newspaper Clippings*. 1878-1911. 3 vols. Savannah, GA: privately printed, 2002 & 2011.

Dorsey, James E. *Laurens County, Georgia, 1873–1883: A Collection of Newspaper Sources.* Swainsboro, GA: privately printed, 1981.

Court

Thomas, Allen. *Laurens County, Georgia, Legal Records, 1807–1832.* Roswell, GA: W. H. Wolfe Associates, 1991.

———. *Laurens County, Georgia, Legal Records Superior Court, 1833–1857.* Roswell, GA: Wolfe Associates, 1993.

Local History

Hart, Bertha Sheppard. *The Official History of Laurens County, Georgia, 1807–1941.* Atlanta: Cherokee Publishing, 1972.

LEE COUNTY. Map #122.

County seat is Leesburg, 31763.

Created June 9, 1825, from Indian lands ceded in 1825 and 1826.

Land was first distributed in the 1827 Land Lottery.

Superior court and probate court records begin in 1858, although some earlier records exist.

Tax digests begin in 1871; 1852 also available.

Major published records

Cemetery

Lee County Historical Society. *Lee County, Georgia, A History.* Atlanta: W. H. Wolfe Associates, 1983: 600–659.

Local History

Lee County Historical Society. *Lee County, Georgia, A History.* Atlanta: W. H. Wolfe Associates, 1983.

LIBERTY COUNTY. Map #133.

County seat is Hinesville, 31313.

Created February 5, 1777, with boundaries that included parts of colonial St. John, St. Andrew, and St. James Parishes.

Land was first distributed in 1733 by the Trustees and formally granted beginning in 1755.

Superior court records begin in 1784, although some earlier records exist.

Probate court records begin in 1789, although some earlier records exist.

Tax digests begin in 1806; 1800 and 1801 also available.

Major published records

Cemetery

Groover, Robert Long. *Sweet Land of Liberty, A History of Liberty County, Georgia*. Roswell, GA: W. H. Wolfe Associates, 1987: 192–202.

Estate

Hageness, MariLee Beatty. *Testator's [sic] 1786–1848, Liberty County, Georgia: Will Book A, Will Book B*. Anniston, AL: MLH Research, 1998.

Daughters of the American Revolution. *Abstracts of Wills of Liberty County, Georgia, 1772–1887*. Savannah, GA: DAR, 1954.

Miscellaneous

Wilson, Caroline Price. *Annals of Georgia*. 3 vols. N.p.: Braid, 1933.

Local History

Groover, Robert Long. *Sweet Land of Liberty, A History of Liberty County, Georgia*. Roswell, GA: W. H. Wolfe Associates, 1987.

LINCOLN COUNTY. Map #48.

County seat is Lincolnton, 30817.

Created February 20, 1796, from Wilkes County.

Land was first distributed in 1773 as headrights.

Superior court records begin in 1796.

Probate court records begin in 1796.

Tax digests begin in 1799.

Major published records

Cemetery

Bunch, Betty Sue Dunaway, and Larry Raymond Butler. *Lincoln County Cemeteries*. Lincolnton, GA: privately printed, 2000.

Sheahan, John J. Jr. *Military Markers and Data: Cemeteries Located in Lincoln County, Georgia*. N.p.: Privately published, 1995.

Land

Wells, Judith Crow. *Petition for Homestead, 1868–1879, Lincoln County, Georgia*. Lincolnton, GA: privately published, 2003.

Estate

Hageness, MariLee Beatty. *Wills, 1796–1857, Lincoln County, Georgia*. Anniston, AL: Privately published, 1994.

———. *Estate Administrators, 1796–1899, Lincoln County, Georgia*. Anniston, AL: Privately published, 1994.

Smith, Sarah Quinn. *Early Georgia Wills Lincoln County*. N.p.: privately printed, 1960.

Court

Hageness, MariLee Beatty. *Guardians and Trustees, 1796–1899, Lincoln County, Georgia*. Anniston, AL: Privately published, 1994.

Wells, Joel Dixon. *Lincoln County, Georgia: Guardianship Bonds, 1800–1895*. Hampton GA: Armchair Publications, n.d.

Local History

Davis, Robert S. and James E. Dorsey. *Lincoln County Genealogy and History*. Swainsboro, GA: Magnolia Press, 1987.

Perryman, Clinton J. *History of Lincoln County, Georgia*. 1933. Reprint Milledgeville, GA: Boyd Publishing Company, 1999.

LONG COUNTY. Map #131.

County seat is Ludowici, 31316.

Created November 2, 1920, from Liberty County.

Land was first distributed in 1733 by the Trustees and formally granted beginning in 1755.

All records begin in 1920.

The Georgia Archives has no records on microfilm of this post-1900 county, although original tax digests beginning in 1921 are available.

Major published records

Cemetery

Garrison, Cecil C. *Annotated Inscriptions of Long County, Georgia*. Newark, NJ: privately printed, 1968.

LOWNDES COUNTY. Map #156.

County seat is Valdosta, 31601.

Created December 23, 1825, from Irwin County.

Land was first distributed in the 1820 Land Lottery.

Superior court records begin in 1859.

Probate court records begin in 1870, although some earlier records exist.

Tax digests begin in 1834; 1830 also available.

Lowndes County deeds are not available on microfilm at the Georgia Archives, although other Superior Court records are.

Major published records

Cemetery

Adams, Charles W. *Survey of Lowndes County, Georgia, Cemeteries, 1825–1987.* Valdosta, GA: Colson Printing, 1988.

Clifton, Geraldine McLeod, and Dorothy Peterson Neisen. *Church and Family Cemeteries in Lowndes County, Georgia, 1825–2005.* Baltimore: Gateway Press, 2005.

Genealogy Unlimited Society. *Addendum to Survey of Lowndes County, Georgia, Cemeteries, 1825–1987.* Valdosta, GA: privately printed, 1993.

Newspaper

Newspaper sources include an alphabetical index on computer of all death notices, marriages and divorces reported in the *Valdosta Daily Times*, 1868 through 1945 and from 1983 to 1990, located at the South Georgia Regional Library.

Dasher, Wayne, and Judy Dasher. *Wiregrass Obituaries and Death Notices.* 6 vols. Nashville, GA: privately printed, 1998–2001. This includes obituaries from the *South Georgia Times*, 1868–1869, and *The Valdosta Times*, 1875–1899.

Estate

Corbett, Charles R., et al. *Lowndes County, Georgia, Probate Records, 1847–1852.* Tallahassee, FL: privately printed, 1998. This is a transcription of the only probate book to survive the destruction of Lowndes County records in 1869.

Local History

Shelton, Jane T. *Pines and Pioneers: A History of Lowndes County, Georgia, 1825-1900.* Atlanta: Cherokee Publishing Co., 1976.

LUMPKIN COUNTY. Map #15.

County seat is Dahlonega, 30533.

Created December 3, 1832, from original Cherokee County.

Land was first distributed in the 1832 Land and/or Gold Lotteries.

Superior court records begin in 1833.

Probate court records begin in 1833.

Tax digests begin in 1871; 1836 and 1866 also available.

In addition to the records on microfilm, the Georgia Archives also has unbound original records in Record Group 193, including marriage records, 1828–1910, pension rolls, 1912-1921, and miscellaneous, 1830s-1886.

Major library resource is the Lumpkin County Public Library, 342 Courthouse Hill, Dahlonega, GA 30555. The telephone number is 706-864-3668. Has several large research collections relating to local families and also to Georgia's first gold rush, including the files of local historian Madeline Anthony. The Kenan Research Center of the Atlanta History Center has the McGruder Collection that includes many one-of-a-kind early Lumpkin County and other North Georgia newspapers.

Major published records

    Cemetery

    Brooke, Ted O., and John Carver. *Lumpkin County, Georgia Cemeteries*. Cumming, GA: privately printed, 2005.

    Newspaper

    Anderson, Jimmy E. *Deaths, Murders, and Lynchings Abstracted From Lumpkin County, Georgia, Newspapers, Volume 1 1873–1900*. Fernandina Beach, FL: Wolfe Publishing, 1998.

    Anonymous. *Dahlonega Nuggets Obituaries Index, 1930 – 2008*. N.p.: 2009.

    Estate

    Wright, Buster W. *Abstracts of Book A Wills, Guardians, Administrations, Lumpkin County, Georgia, 1833–1852*. N.p.: privately printed, no date.

    Local History

    Amerson, Anne Dismukes. *I Remember Dahlonega: Memories of Growing up in Lumpkin County*. 4 vols. Alpharetta, GA: Legacy Communications,1990–.

    Cain, Andrew W. *History of Lumpkin County for the First Hundred Years 1832–1932*. Atlanta: Stein Printing, 1932.

    Coulter, E. Merton. *Auraria: the Story of a Georgia Gold Mining Town*. Athens: University of Georgia, 1956.

    Lumpkin County Heritage Book Committee. *Heritage of Lumpkin County, Georgia 1832–1996*. Waynesville, NC: Walsworth Publishing, 1996.

MACON COUNTY. Map #95.

County seat is Oglethorpe, 31068.

Created December 14, 1837, from Houston and Marion Counties.

Land was first distributed in the 1821 and 1827 Land Lotteries.

Superior court records begin in 1857.

Probate court records begin in 1857.

Tax digests begin in 1871; 1838 and 1852 also available.

Major published records

    Cemetery

    Hay, Guelda L., Millie C. Stewart, and Davine V. Campbell. *Cemeteries of Macon County, Georgia*. Warner Robins, GA: Central Georgia Genealogical Society, 1995.

    Hays, Louise Frederick. *History of Macon County, Georgia*. Reprint, Spartanburg, SC: The Reprint Company, 1979: 466–481.

Newspaper

Evans, Tad *Georgia Newspaper Clippings Macon County Extracts 1837–1902*. Savannah, GA: privately printed, 2008.

Land

Campbell, Davine V., and William R. Henry. *Land Records of Macon County, Georgia, 1857–1863, Deed Book A*. Warner Robins, GA: Central Georgia Genealogical Society, 1994.

Campbell, Davine V. *1838 Tax Digest for Macon County, Georgia*. Warner Robins, GA: Central Georgia Genealogical Society, 1993.

———. *1852 Tax Digest for Macon County, Georgia*. Warner Robins, GA: Central Georgia Genealogical Society, 1989.

Local History

Hays, Louise Frederick. *History of Macon County, Georgia*. Reprint, Spartanburg, SC: The Reprint Company, 1979.

MADISON COUNTY. Map #35.

County seat is Danielsville, 30633.

Created December 5, 1811, from Oglethorpe, Clarke, Franklin, Jackson, and Elbert Counties.

Land was first distributed in 1773 as headrights.

Superior court records begin in 1812.

Probate court records begin in 1812.

Tax digests begin in 1820; 1813 and 1817 also available.

Major published records

Cemetery

Madison County Heritage Foundation. *Madison County Cemetery Book*. Danielsville, GA: The Foundation, 1986.

Newspaper

McRee, Fred W., Jr. *Madison County, Georgia Deaths 1854–1925*. Dahlonega, GA: privately printed, 2011.

Estate

Sanders, Amy Warren. *Madison County, Georgia, Probate Records, 1812–circa 1870*. Athens, GA: Heritage Papers, 1994.

Local History

Tabor, Paul. *The History of Madison County, Georgia*. N.p., 1974.

Georgia Research
Chapter III: Counties, County Records, and Local History Sources

MARION COUNTY. Map #93.

County seat is Buena Vista, 31803.

Created December 14, 1827, from Lee and Muscogee Counties.

Land was first distributed in the 1827 Land Lottery.

Superior court records begin in 1846.

Probate court records begin in 1842, although some earlier records exist.

Tax digests begin in 1848.

Major published records

> Cemetery
>
> Jernigan, Jeanne Wells. *Marion County Cemeteries.* N.p., 1980.
>
> Daughters of the American Revolution. *Marion County, Georgia Cemeteries.* N.p.: DAR., Roanoke Chapter, 1998.
>
> Newspaper
>
> Evans, Tad. *Georgia Newspaper Clippings Marion County Extracts, 1830–1906.* Savannah, GA: privately printed, 2009.
>
> Local History
>
> Cobb, Rena S. *A History of Marion County, Georgia, Motherland of Many.* Fernandina Beach, FL: Wolfe Publishing, 1997.
>
> Powell, Nettie. *History of Marion County.* Columbus, GA: Historical Publishing Co., 1931.

MCDUFFIE COUNTY. Map #63.

County seat is Thomson, 30824.

Created October 18, 1870, from Warren and Columbia Counties.

Land was first distributed in the 1750s as headrights.

All records begin in 1871.

Major published records

> Cemetery
>
> Baker, Pearl. *'Neath Georgia Sod: Cemetery Inscriptions.* Albany, GA: Georgia Pioneers Publications, 1980.
>
> Butler, David Alan. *Columbia County Gray: Burial Locations for Confederate Soldiers in Columbia County, Georgia (Including McDuffie County).* Martinez, GA: Rough and Ready Publishing, 2007.
>
> Crumpton, Daniel Nathan. *Cemeteries and Genealogy, Warren County, Georgia, and Immediate Vicinity, 1792–1987.* Roswell, GA: W. H. Wolfe Associates, 1987: 114–134.

McCommons, Mrs. W. C., and Miss Clara Stovall. *History of McDuffie County, Georgia, 1870–1933*. Tignall, GA: Boyd Publishing Company, 1988: 229–241.

Newspaper

McRee, Fred Warren. *McDuffie County, Georgia Deaths, 1872–1935*. Dahlonega, GA: Fred W. McRee Jr., 2008.

Court

McRee, Fred W., Jr. *McDuffie County, Georgia Ordinary Court Records 1872–1927*. Dahlonega, GA: privately published, 2009.

Local History

Baker, Pearl. *A Handbook of History, McDuffie County, Georgia 1870–1970*. Thomson, GA: Progress-News Publishing Co., 1971.

———. *The Story of Wrightsboro, 1768–1964*. Thomson, GA: Wrightsboro Foundation, 1965.

McCommons, Mrs. W. C., and Miss Clara Stovall. *History of McDuffie County, Georgia, 1870–1933*. Tignall, GA: Boyd Publishing Company, 1988.

Taylor, A. J. *A History of Dearing, McDuffie County, Georgia From 1850 to 1904*. Dearing, GA: Robert Printup, 1929.

MCINTOSH COUNTY. Map #132.

County seat is Darien, 31305.

Created December 19, 1793, from Liberty County.

Land was first distributed in 1733 by the Trustees and formally granted beginning in 1755.

Superior court records begin in 1873.

Probate court records begin in 1873.

Tax digests begin in 1871; 1825, 1837, and 1862 also available.

In addition to the records on microfilm, the Georgia Archives has unbound original superior court case files, 1875–1925; estate records, circa 1862–1920; and oyster leases, circa 1850s–circa 1900, in Record Group 198.

Major published records

Cemetery

Gladstone, Mattie R. *Cemeteries of McIntosh County, Georgia*. Darien, GA: Lower Altamaha Historical Society, 2000.

White, Evelyn K. H. *McIntosh County Georgia Cemetery Records*. Darien, GA: privately printed, 1958.

Newspaper

Evans, Tad. *Darien, Georgia, Newspaper Clippings.* 1818-1903. 3 vols. Savannah, GA: privately printed, 2001–2002. Volume I 1818–1878, Volume II 1879–1890, Volume III 1891–1903.

Land

Davis, Ann R. *McIntosh County Georgia Deed Book A: Notes for Genealogy & Research.* Darien, GA: Sea Griffin Pub, 2003.

Local History

Sullivan, Buddy. *Early Days on the Georgia Tidewater: The Story of McIntosh County & Sapelo : Being a Documented Narrative Account, with Particular Attention to the County's Waterway and Maritime Heritage; Plantation Culture and Uses of the Land in the 19th Century; and a Detailed Analysis of the History of Sapelo Island.* Darien, GA: McIntosh County Board of Commissioners, 1990.

———. *Early Days on the Georgia Tidewater: The Story of McIntosh County & Sapelo : Supplemental Appendixes.* Darien, GA: McIntosh County Board of Commissioners, 1991.

MERIWETHER COUNTY. Map #67.

County seat is Greenville, 30222.

Created December 14, 1827, from Troup County.

Land was first distributed in the 1827 Land Lottery.

Superior court and probate court records begin in 1828.

Tax digests begin in 1872; 1863 also available.

Major published records

Cemetery

Turner, Priscilla. *Meriwether County, Georgia, Cemeteries.* Spartanburg, SC: The Reprint Company, 1993.

Newspaper

Evans, Tad, *Georgia Newspaper Clippings Meriwether County Extracts, 1828–1889.* Savannah, GA: privately printed, 2009.

Isanhour, Clare. *Pioneers of Meriwether County, Georgia, as Reported in the Meriwether Vindicator.* Smyrna, GA: privately printed, 1991.

Local History

Davidson, William H. *Brooks of Honey and Butter; Plantations and People of Meriwether County, Georgia.* 2 vols. Alexander City, AL: Outlook Publishing Co., 1971.

Pinkston, Regina P. *Historical Account of Meriwether County 1827–1974.* Greenville, GA: Gresham Printing Co., 1974.

Threadgill, Anne, ed. *The Heritage of Meriwether County Georgia 1827–2004*. Marceline, MO: Walsworth Publishing Co., 2004.

MILLER COUNTY. Map #140.

County seat is Colquitt, 31737.

Created February 26, 1856, from Baker and Early Counties.

Land was first distributed in the 1820 Land Lottery.

Superior court records begin in 1873.

Probate court records begin in 1871.

Tax digests begin in 1871.

Major published records

Cemetery

Colquitt Garden Club. *The Cemetery Survey of Miller County, Georgia, 1824–1981*. Colquitt, GA: The Club, 1982.

Local History

Davis, Nellie C. *The History of Miller County, Georgia*. Colquitt, GA: Citizens Bank, 1980.

MILTON COUNTY. Map # 31.

Created December 18, 1857, from Cherokee, Cobb, and Forsyth Counties.

Land was first distributed in the 1832 Land and/or Gold Lotteries.

Superior court records begin in 1867, although some earlier records exist.

Probate court records begin in 1858.

Tax digests begin in 1870; 1866 and 1868 also available.

Milton County was abolished on January 1, 1932, when it became what is now the northern portion of Fulton County. The Milton County records are now maintained by Fulton County in Atlanta, Georgia 30303. Some original Milton County records are deposited in the Atlanta History Center.

Major published records

Cemetery

Many Milton County cemetery records are available in the *Franklin Garrett's Necrology* at the Atlanta History Center, Atlanta, Georgia. Franklin Garrett surveyed white cemeteries around Atlanta primarily in the 1930s and 1940s.

Anglin, Phillip B. *Milton County, Georgia Cemeteries: Present Day Northern Fulton County*. Baltimore: Gateway Press, 2002.

MITCHELL COUNTY. Map #142.

County seat is Camilla, 31730.

Created December 21, 1857, from Baker County.

Land was first distributed in the 1820 Land Lottery.

Superior court records begin in 1858.

Probate court records begin in 1858.

Tax digests begin in 1872.

Major published records

> Cemetery
>
> Spence, Margaret, and Anna M. Fleming. *History of Mitchell County*. N.p., ca. 1976: 44–51.
>
> Newspaper
>
> Wells, Catherine Fussell. *Marriage and Divorce Notices from the Camilla Enterprise, Camilla, Mitchell County, Georgia January 1904 – December 1909 Volume I*. Valdosta, GA: Wells Gen-Search, 2003.
>
> Wells, Catherine Fussell. *Marriage and Divorce Notices from the Camilla Enterprise, Camilla, Mitchell County, Georgia January 1910 – December 1913 Volume II*. Valdosta, GA: Wells Gen-Search, 2003.
>
> Wells, Catherine Fussell. *Obituaries & Death Notices from the Camilla Enterprise, Camilla, Mitchell County, Georgia January 1904 – December 1909*. Valdosta, GA: Wells Gen-Search, 2003.
>
> Wells, Catherine Fussell. *Obituaries & Death Notices from the Camilla Enterprise, Camilla, Mitchell County, Georgia January 1910 – December 1913 Volume II*. Valdosta, GA: Wells Gen-Search, 2003.
>
> Local History
>
> Spence, Margaret, and Anna M. Fleming. *History of Mitchell County*. N.p., 1976.

MONROE COUNTY. Map #71.

County seat is Forsyth, 31029.

Created May 15, 1821, from Indian lands ceded in 1821.

Land was first distributed in the 1821 Land Lottery.

Superior court records begin in 1826, although some earlier records exist.

Probate court records begin in 1824.

Tax digests begin in 1841; 1828 and 1834 also available.

In addition to the records on microfilm, the Georgia Archives has unbound original marriages, 1839–1900, in Record Group 202.

Major published records

Cemetery

Monroe County Historical Society. *Cemeteries in Monroe County, Georgia, and Vicinity.* Forsyth, GA: privately printed, 1997. This edition replaces and supplements Monroe County cemetery records published in: *Monroe County, Georgia, A History.* Forsyth, GA: Monroe County Historical Society, 1979.

Newspaper

Evans, Tad. *Georgia Newspaper Clippings Monroe County Extracts.* 1821-1906. 2 vols. Savannah, GA: privately printed, 2004. Volume I 1821–1837 & Volume II 1838–1906.

Local History

Monroe County Historical Society. *Monroe County, Georgia, A History.* Forsyth, GA: Monroe County Historical Society, 1979.

MONTGOMERY COUNTY. Map #113.

County seat is Mt. Vernon, 30445.

Created December 19, 1793, from Washington County.

Land was first distributed in 1784 as headrights.

Superior court records begin circa 1794.

Probate court records begin in 1809, although some earlier records exist.

Tax digests begin in 1805; 1797 and 1798 also available.

In addition to the records on microfilm, the Georgia Archives has unbound original Montgomery County miscellaneous records, 1790–1860, in Record Group 203.

Major published records

Cemetery

Coleman, Moses M., Jr., and Lavon Stone Palmer. *Graves of Montgomery, Treutlen, and Wheeler.* Vidalia, GA: Coleman Ferrotype, n.d. ca. 1994: 9–180.

Dorsey, James E., and John K. Derden. *Montgomery County, Georgia: A Sourcebook of Genealogy and History.* Swainsboro, GA: Magnolia Press, 1983: 225–270.

Newspaper

Dorsey, James E. *Montgomery County: A Collection of Newspaper Sources, 1873–1885.* Swainsboro, GA: Emanuel County Junior College, 1980.

Evans, Tad. *Montgomery County, Georgia, Newspaper Clippings, Volumes I, II, 1886–1919.* Savannah, GA: privately printed, 1993.

———. *Georgia Newspaper Clippings Montgomery County Extracts, 1811–1892.* Savannah, GA: privately printed, 1998.

Land

Dwyer, Clifford S. *Tax Digest 1893, Montgomery County, Georgia.* Pensacola, FL: C.S. Dwyer, 1966.

Court

Dwyer, Clifford S. *Montgomery County, Georgia, Jury Lists: 1791, 1795, 1804.* N.p.: Montgomery County Records Preservation Committee, 1986.

Fennell, Debra. *Minutes of the Inferior Court of Montgomery County, Georgia: Ordinary Purposes, 1809–1818, 1821–1837.* Mt. Vernon, GA: Debra Fennell, 1996.

Fennell, Debra. *Montgomery County, Georgia, Inferior Court Minutes, 1809–1849.* N.p.: Debra Fennell, c1999.

Local History

Davis, Robert Scott. *A History of Montgomery County, Georgia, to 1918.* Roswell, GA: W. H. Wolfe Associates, 1992.

MORGAN COUNTY. Map #58.

County seat is Madison, 30650.

Created December 10, 1807, from Baldwin County.

Land was first distributed in the 1805 and 1807 Land Lotteries.

All records begin in 1808.

In addition to the records on microfilm, the Georgia Archives has unbound original superior court case files, 1800s; newspapers, 1880–1908; and miscellaneous records, 1850–1920, in Record Group 204.

Major published records

Newspaper

Harris, Bonnie P. "Patsy". *Early Morgan County, Georgia, Newspapers, 1842–1861.* Buckhead, GA: privately printed, 2000.

———. *Early Morgan County, Georgia Newspapers, the 1870's Volume 1.* Buckhead, GA: privately printed, 2002.

———. *Early Morgan County, Georgia Newspapers, the 1870's Volume 2.* Buckhead, GA: privately printed, 2003.

Land

Auburg, Ann H. *Morgan County, Georgia, Superior Court Records, Abstracts of Deeds, Books A–C (1808–1812).* Midland, TX: privately printed, 1999.

Farmer, Michal Martin. *Morgan County, Georgia Deed Books A-G, 1808-1820.* Dallas, TX: M.M. Farmer, 2002.

Court

Auburg, Ann H. *Morgan County, Georgia, Superior Court Records, Abstracts of Deeds, Books A–C (1808–1812)*. Midland, TX: privately printed, 1999.

Farmer, Michal Martin. *Morgan County, Georgia Inferior Court for Ordinary Purposes, 1808–1834 and Will Books A & B, 1808–1820*. Dallas, TX: privately printed, 2003.

Local History

Hicky, Louise M. *Rambles Through Morgan County*. Madison, GA: Morgan County Historical Society, 1971.

MURRAY COUNTY. Map #5.

County seat is Chatsworth, 30705.

Created December 3, 1832, from original Cherokee County.

Land was first distributed in the 1832 Land Lottery.

Superior court records begin in 1833.

Probate court records begin in 1834.

Tax digests begin in 1868.

Major library resource is the Crown Gardens and Archives, 715 Chattanooga Ave., Dalton, GA 30722. The telephone number is (706) 278-0217. Operated by the Whitfield-Murray Historical Society.

Major published records

Cemetery

Whitfield-Murray Historical Society. *Cemeteries of Murray County, Georgia*. No place: privately printed, 1978.

Nicholson, Kaye. *Cemeteries of Murray County*. Printed by the Hall County (Georgia) Library from a website that is no longer accessible at the given address. It probably moved to http://freepages.genealogy.rootsweb.ancestry.com/~kaye/MCem.htm.

Local History

Murray County History Committee, Comp. *Murray County Heritage*. Roswell, GA: W H Wolfe Assoc., 1987.

MUSCOGEE COUNTY. Map #91.

County seat is Columbus, 31902.

Created June 9, 1825, from Indian land ceded in 1826.

Land was first distributed in the 1827 Land Lottery.

Superior court records begin in 1837.

Probate court records begin in 1838.

Tax digests begin in 1869; 1838, 1845, 1847, and 1867 also available.

Major library resource is the Columbus Public Library, 3000 Macon Road, Columbus, GA 31906. The telephone number is 706-243-2669.

Major published records

Cemetery

Thomas, Ken. *Georgia Genealogical Society Quarterly* 12 (Fall 1976): 116–131. Some are included in the 51 numbered cemeteries located on the Fort Benning military property in Chattahoochee and Muscogee Counties.

Autry, Dolores. *Historic Linwood Cemetery of Columbus, Muscogee Co., Georgia.* Updated and edited by Lea Lewis Dowd and Carol Johnson. On first two volumes, third volume removes Carol Johnson and adds names of Kimberly Martz. 3 vols.

Newspaper

Kilbourne, Elizabeth Evans. *Columbus, Georgia, Newspaper Clippings (Columbus Enquirer) 1832–1861.* 10 vols. Savannah, GA: Tad Evans, 1997–2010.

———. *Columbus, Georgia, Newspaper Clippings (Weekly Sun).* 1859-1862. 2 vols. Savannah, GA: Tad Evans, 2011.

Wright, Buster W. *Abstracts of Deaths Reported in the Columbus (Georgia) Enquirer 1832–1852.* Columbus, GA: privately printed, 1980.

———. *Abstracts of Marriages Reported in the Columbus (Georgia) Enquirer 1832–1852.* Columbus, GA: privately printed, 1980.

———. *Burials and Deaths Reported in the Columbus (Georgia) Enquirer 1832–1872.* Columbus, GA: privately printed, 1984.

Estate

Wright, Buster W. *Abstracts of Will Book A, Muscogee County, Georgia, 1838–1862.* N.p.: privately printed, n.d.

Local History

Martin, John H. *Columbus, Georgia, From Its Selection as a "Trading Town"… [to] 1865. 2 vols. printed as one.* Columbus, GA: Thomas Gilbert, 1874 and 1875. Reprinted as one, Easley, SC: Georgia Genealogical Reprints, 1972. Index published separately by Alvie Davidson in 1988. Note the book contains newspaper abstracts, marriages from the courthouse, and other local information, in a year-by-year format.

Telfair, Nancy. *A History of Columbus, Georgia, 1828–1928.* Columbus, GA: Historical Publishing Co., 1929.

Whitehead, Margaret Lacey and Barbara Bogart. *City of Progress: A History of Columbus, Georgia.* Columbus, GA: Columbus Office Supply Co., 1978.

Worsley Etta Blanchard. *Columbus on the Chattahoochee.* Columbus, GA: Columbus Office Supply Co., 1951.

NEWTON COUNTY. Map #56.

County seat is Covington, 30209.

Created December 24, 1821, from Jasper, Walton, and Henry Counties.

Land was first distributed in the 1820 and 1821 Land Lotteries.

Superior court records begin in 1822.

Probate court records begin in 1822.

Tax digests begin in 1873; 1848, 1849, and 1851 also available.

Major published records

    Cemetery

    Dixon, S. A., and M. J. Dixon. *Newton County, Georgia, Cemeteries*. 3 vols. Covington, GA: privately printed, 1968–78.

    Newspaper

    Austin, Jeannette Holland. *Newton County, Georgia Newspapers, 1868–1904: The Georgia Enterprise and Covington Star*. Riverdale, GA: J. H. Austin, 1991.

    Bowen, Rhoda Anne, and Freda R. Turner. *Georgia Confederate Soldier Obituaries: Henry, Newton, and Rockdale Counties, 1879–1943*. Alpharetta, Georgia: W. H. Wolfe Associates, 1992.

    Genealogical Enterprises. *The Georgia Enterprise and Covington Star, 1865–1904*. Morrow, GA: Genealogical Enterprises, 1969.

    Estate

    Bruno, John I. *Newton County, Georgia, Estate Records, 1822–1900*. 2 vols. Conyers, GA: privately printed, 1996.

    Court

    Bruno, John I. *Newton County, Georgia, Minutes of the Inferior Court for Ordinary Purposes, 1822–1838*. 3 vols. Mansfield, GA: privately printed, 1997–1999.

    Local History

    Bowen, Chris. *Inventory of Records Available to Public Researchers in the Newton County Court House, Covington, Georgia*. Covington, GA: Sergeant Newton Chapter, Georgia Society, DAR, 1973.

    Bruno, John I. *Newton County, Georgia Records*. Conyers, GA: privately printed, 1993.

    Hall, John, and Jodee Stallo. *Our Yesterdays: A Pictorial History of Newton County, Georgia*. Marceline, MO: D-Books Pub, 2002.

    Newton County Historical Society. *History of Newton County, Georgia*. Covington, GA: privately printed, 1988.

OCONEE COUNTY. Map #44.

County seat is Watkinsville, 30677.

Created February 25, 1875, from Clarke County.

Land was first distributed in 1784 as headrights.

All records begin in 1875.

In addition to the records on microfilm, the Georgia Archives has superior court case files, 1873–1914, in Record Group 208.

Major published records

Cemetery

Clarke-Oconee Genealogical Society. *Cemetery Inscriptions of Oconee County, Georgia.* Athens, GA: Iberian Publishing Co., 1994.

A copy of *Cemetery Markers in Oconee County*, known to be by Ernest Elder Jr., (Dahlonega, GA: n.p., n.d., ca. 1980–1990) is in the Oconee County Library, Watkinsville, GA.

Estate

McRee, Fred Warren. *Oconee County, Georgia, Abstracts of Wills, 1875–1966.* Dahlonega, GA: privately printed, 2002.

Court

McRee, Fred Warren. *Oconee County, Georgia, Superior and Ordinary Court Records, 1875–1912.* Dahlonega, GA: privately printed, 2008.

Local History

Sommer, Margaret F. *The History of Oconee County, Georgia.* Dallas, TX: Curtis Media, 1993.

OGLETHORPE COUNTY. Map #46.

County seat is Lexington, 30648.

Created December 19, 1793, from Wilkes County.

Land was first distributed in 1773 as headrights.

Superior court records begin in 1794.

Probate court records begin in 1794.

Tax digests begin in 1794.

In addition to records on microfilm, the Georgia Archives has unbound original records in Record Group 209. The Georgia Archives also has unbound original records on microfilm: Estate records, 1790–1962, in Drawer 306, Boxes 109 to 125 and in Drawer 307, Boxes 1 to 40; marriages, 1863–1942, in Drawer 306, Boxes 98 to 108; miscellaneous records, 1796–1925, in Drawer 307, Boxes 40 to 73.

Major published records

Cemetery

Historic Oglethorpe County, Inc. *Cemeteries of Oglethorpe County, Georgia, Fourth Edition.* Lexington, GA: Historic Oglethorpe County, Inc., 2009.

Newspaper

Kilbourne, Elizabeth Evans. *Oglethorpe County, Georgia, Newspaper Clippings.* 1874-1880 3 vols. Savannah, GA: privately printed, 2012.

McRee, Fred W. *Oglethorpe County, Georgia Deaths 1875–1938.* Dahlonega, GA: privately printed, 2006.

———— *Oglethorpe County, Georgia Deaths 1939–1967.* Dahlonega, GA: privately printed, 2007.

———— *Oglethorpe County, Georgia Newspaper Abstracts, The Oglethorpe Echo, 1874–1881.* Dahlonega, GA: privately printed, 2006.

———— *Oglethorpe County, Georgia Newspaper Abstracts, The Oglethorpe Echo, 1882–1888.* Dahlonega, GA: privately printed, 2007.

———— *Oglethorpe County, Georgia Newspaper Abstracts, The Oglethorpe Echo, 1889–1894.* Dahlonega, GA: privately printed, 2009.

———— *Oglethorpe County, Georgia Newspaper Abstracts, The Oglethorpe Echo, 1895–1899.* Dahlonega, GA: privately printed, 2010.

Land

Farmer, Michal Martin. *Oglethorpe County Georgia Deed Books A–E, 1794–1809.* Dallas, TX: Farmer Genealogy Company, 1999.

————. *Oglethorpe County, Georgia Deed Books F–J, 1809–1820.* Dallas, TX: privately printed, 2000.

Georgia Society, Daughters of the American Revolution. *Tax List, Oglethorpe County, Georgia, 1795–1799.* Volume 451. N.p.: privately printed, 1956.

Maddox, Joseph T. *1796 Tax List, Oglethorpe County, Georgia with Statistical Information Added.* Irwinton, GA: privately printed, 1980.

Estate

LeMaster, Mrs. Vernon L. *Abstracts of Wills of Oglethorpe County, Georgia, 1793–1834.* Decatur, GA: privately printed, 1956.

McRee, Fred W. *Oglethorpe County, Georgia Abstracts of Wills 1794–1903.* Dahlonega, GA: privately printed, 2002.

Smith, Mrs. Sarah Quinn. *Oglethorpe County* [wills, etc.]. Washington, GA: privately printed, 1962.

Court

McRee, Fred W. *Oglethorpe County, Georgia Inferior and Ordinary Court Records, 1794–1920.* 3 vols. Lexington, GA: Historic Oglethorpe County, 2003-2006.

Local History

Smith, Florrie Carter. *The History of Oglethorpe County, Georgia*. Milledgeville, GA: Boyd Pub. Co., 2005. Reprint of 1970 edition.

——— *Supplement to the History of Oglethorpe County, Georgia*. Washington, GA: Wilkes Pub. Co., 1972.

PAULDING COUNTY. Map #29.

County seat is Dallas, 30132.

Created December 3, 1832, from original Cherokee County.

Land was first distributed in the 1832 Land and/or Gold Lotteries.

Superior county records begin circa 1848.

Probate court records begin in 1866, although some earlier records exist.

Tax digests begin in 1866.

Major published records

Cemetery

Paulding County Historical Society, edited by LaGroon Redmond. *Cemeteries of Paulding County, Georgia*. Roswell, GA: W. H. Wolfe Associates, 1995.

PEACH COUNTY. Map # 83.

County seat is Fort Valley, 31030.

Created November 4, 1924, from Houston and Macon Counties.

Land was first distributed in the 1821 Land Lottery.

All records begin in 1925.

The Georgia Archives has no records on microfilm of this post-1900 county, although original tax digests beginning in 1925 are available.

Major published records

Cemetery

George, Elizabeth Howell. *Tombstone Inscriptions, Peach & Crawford County, Georgia*. Fort Valley, GA: Governor Treutlen Chapter, DAR, 1976.

Flournoy, Harriett H. *Tombstone Inscriptions, Oaklawn Cemetery, Fort Valley, Georgia*. Fort Valley, GA: Governor Treutlen Chapter, [DAR], 1975.

PICKENS COUNTY. Map #13.

County seat is Jasper, 30143.

Created December 5, 1853, from Cherokee and Gilmer Counties.

Land was first distributed in the 1832 Land Lottery.

Superior court records begin in 1854.

Probate court records begin in 1854.

Tax digests begin in 1871; 1867 also available.

The Pickens County Public Library has microfilm of the county's loose original records that are available nowhere else.

Major published records

    Cemetery

    Brooke, Ted O., and Linda A. Woodward Geiger. *Pickens County, Georgia Cemeteries*. Jasper, GA: Woodward-Geiger.com, 2009.

    Teague, Gene E., and Miranda E. Reece. *Cemeteries of Pickens County, Georgia*. Roswell, GA: W. H. Wolfe Associates, 1995.

    Newspaper

    Carver, John. *Births, Marriages, and Deaths in Pickens County, Georgia, Newspapers, 1884 – 1936*. Canton, GA: privately printed, 2007.

    Local History

    Tate, Lucius Eugene. *History of Pickens County*. 1935. Reprint, Spartanburg, SC: Reprint Co., 1978.

PIERCE COUNTY. Map #148.

County seat is Blackshear, 31516.

Created December 18, 1857, from Ware and Appling Counties.

Land was first distributed in the 1820 Land Lottery.

Superior court records begin in 1871.

Probate court records begin in 1871.

Tax digests begin in 1868; 1864 also available.

Major published records

    Cemetery

    Broome, Dean. *History of Pierce County, Georgia, Volume I*. Blackshear, GA: privately printed, 1973: 481–557.

    Walker, Randall M., Jr. *Marked Graves in Pierce County, Georgia*. Jesup, GA: privately printed, 1975.

    Local History

    Broome, Dean. *History of Pierce County, Georgia, Volume I*. Blackshear, GA: privately printed, 1973.

PIKE COUNTY. Map #68.

County seat is Zebulon, 30295.

Created December 9, 1822, from Monroe County.

Land was first distributed in the 1821 Land Lottery.

Superior court records begin in 1823.

Probate court records begin in 1823.

Tax digests begin in 1825.

Major published records

> Cemetery
>
> Morgan, Jack, et. al. *Pike County, Georgia Cemetery Records*. 1972. Reprint, n.p.: privately printed, 1991.
>
> Newspaper
>
> Cunningham, Lynn. *Pike County, Georgia Newspaper Clippings From the Pike County Journal, 1888–1898*. Williamson, GA: privately printed, 2008.
>
> Cunningham, Lynn. *Newspaper Clippings From the Pike County Journal, 1899–1909*. Williamson, GA: privately printed, 2008.
>
> Estate
>
> Gossett, Joyce Hill. *Pike County Wills, 1826–1854*. East Point, GA: privately printed, n.d. ca. 1981.
>
> Local History
>
> Coppedge, James Frederick. *Pike County, Georgia*. 1822. Reprint, [Marlow?], GA: ca. 1968.
>
> Historical Committee. *Sesquicentennial 1822-1972, Pike County, Georgia*. Zebulon, GA: privately printed, 1972.
>
> Rogers, Rev. Richard Wade, *History of Pike County from 1822 to 1922*. Zebulon, GA: privately printed, ca. 1922.
>
> Mitchell, Lizzie R., *History of Pike County, Georgia 1822–1932*. 1948. Reprint Spartanburg, SC: The Reprint Company, Publishers, 1980.

POLK COUNTY. Map #27.

County seat is Cedartown, 30125.

Created December 20, 1851, from Paulding and Floyd Counties.

Land was first distributed in the 1832 Land and/or Gold Lotteries.

Superior court records begin in 1852.

Probate court records begin in 1854, although some earlier records exist.

Tax digests begin in 1874; 1870 also available.

Major published records

   Cemetery

      Ayers, Ralph, and Jane Ayers. *Polk County, Georgia, Cemeteries in the Corners of Forever.* 2 vols. Cedartown, GA: privately printed, 1986.

      Polk County Cemetery Preservation Committee. *Polk County, Georgia Cemetery Survey Book: Volume One [South East Section].* Cedartown, GA: Privately printed, 2007.

PULASKI COUNTY. Map #109.

County seat is Hawkinsville, 31036.

Created December 13, 1808, from Laurens County.

Land was first distributed in the 1807 and 1821 Land Lotteries.

All records begin in 1809.

In addition to the records on microfilm, the Georgia Archives have unbound marriage records, 1810–1867, in Record Group 216.

Major published records

   Cemetery

      Evans, Elliot L., Sr. *Cemeteries of Pulaski County Georgia.* Hawkinsville, GA: Privately published, 1996–1997.

   Newspaper

      Evans, Tad. *Pulaski County, Georgia, Newspaper Clippings.* 1867–1917. 8 vols. Savannah, GA: privately printed, 2000–2010.

      Evans, Tad. *Georgia Newspaper Clippings Pulaski County Extracts 1810–1891.* Savannah, GA: privately printed, 1998.

      Nobles, Robert K. *Marriages, Deaths and Etc. from Hawkinsville (Georgia) Dispatch, 1870–1888.* Utica, KY: McDowell Publications, 1991.

   Estate

      Myrick, Victor R. *Wills of Pulaski County, Georgia: Will Books, 1810–1906.* Warner Robins, GA: Central Georgia Genealogical Society, 1994.

   Court

      Barrow, Lee G. *Early Court Records of Pulaski County, Georgia, 1809–1825.* Greenville, SC: Southern Historical Press, 1994.

PUTNAM COUNTY. Map #59.

County seat is Eatonton, 31024.

Created December 10, 1807, from Baldwin County.

Land was first distributed in the 1805 and 1807 Land Lotteries.

Superior court records begin in 1808.

Probate court records begin in 1808.

Tax digests begin in 1812.

In addition to the records on microfilm, the Georgia Archives has some unbound miscellaneous Putnam County records, 1800–1932, in Record Group 217.

Major published records

Cemetery

Lancaster, Mrs. Edgar M. "Putnam County, Georgia, Cemeteries." An original typescript of cemetery records, from the files of Edgar M. Lancaster, 1974, is at the Washington Memorial Library, Macon, GA.

Newspaper

Evans, Tad, *Georgia Newspaper Clippings Putnam County Extracts Volume I 1809–1834 & Volume II 1835–1889*. Savannah, GA: privately printed, 1998.

Estate

Hull, Edward F. *Early Records of Putnam County, Georgia, 1807–1860*. Ashland, AL: privately printed, n.d. The second chapter of this book has Putnam County will abstracts for 1808–1861.

QUITMAN COUNTY. Map #119.

County seat is Georgetown, 31754.

Created December 10, 1858, from Randolph and Stewart Counties.

Land was first distributed in the 1827 Land Lottery.

Superior court records begin in 1879.

Probate court records begin in 1875, although some earlier records exist.

Tax digests begin in 1871.

Major published records

Cemetery

Shepard, Jacquelyn M. *Cemeteries and Churches of Quitman County, Georgia*. N.p.: privately printed, n.d., ca. 1987.

RABUN COUNTY. Map #10.

County seat is Clayton, 30525.

Created December 21, 1819, from Indian lands ceded in 1817 and 1819.

Land was first distributed in the 1820 Land Lottery.

Superior court records begin in 1821. Superior Court minutes begin in 1829, while there are some docket volumes from about 1823.

Probate court records begin in 1822. Marriage records begin in 1820.

Tax digests begin in 1869; 1836, 1861, and 1862 also available.

In addition to the records on microfilm, the Georgia Archives has unbound Rabun County marriage records, 1896–1920, in Record Group 219.

Major published records

    Newspaper

    Watson, Dawn. *Rabun County, Georgia, Newspapers, 1894–1899*. Rabun Gap, GA: privately printed, 2012.

    Estate

    Coleman, John Thomas. *Ordinary Court Records, 1822–1850, Rabun County, Georgia*. Marietta, GA: Heritage Center, 1988.

    Court

    Koyle, Susan Lewis. *Genealogy Extracted from Forest Service Court Cases in Rabun County, Georgia*. Bowie, MD: Heritage Books, 2001.

    Local History

    Ritchie, Andrew Jackson. *Sketches of Rabun County History*. N.p.: privately printed, 1948[?].

RANDOLPH COUNTY. Map #120.

County seat is Cuthbert, 31740.

Created December 20, 1828, from Lee County.

Land was first distributed in the 1827 Land Lottery.

Superior court records begin in 1841, although some earlier records exist.

Probate court records begin in 1845, although some earlier records exist.

Tax digests begin in 1873; 1848 and 1849 also available.

Georgia created an earlier Randolph County on December 10, 1807, which was renamed Jasper County on December 10, 1812.

Major published records

    Cemetery

    Southwest Georgia Genealogical Society. *Cemeteries of Randolph County, Georgia*. Albany, GA: privately printed, 1993.

    Court

    Shepard, Jacquelyn. *Minutes of the Ordinary Court of Randolph County, Georgia*. N.p.: privately printed, 1991.

RICHMOND COUNTY. Map #65.

County seat is Augusta, 30903.

Created February 5, 1777, with the same boundaries as colonial St. Paul Parish.

Land was first distributed in 1733 by the Trustees and formally granted beginning in 1755.

Superior court records begin in 1788, although some earlier records exist.

Probate court records begin circa 1786.

Tax digests begin in 1807; 1789, 1794–1798, and 1800 also available.

The Augusta Genealogical Society and the Georgia Historical Society have separate collections of loose original Richmond County records.

Major library resource is the Augusta Genealogical Society Library, 1109 Broad St., Augusta, GA. The telephone number is 706-722-4073.

Major published records

> Cemetery
>
> > Augusta Genealogical Society. *Irish Nativities in Magnolia Cemetery Augusta Georgia*. Augusta, GA: Augusta Genealogical Society, 1991.
> >
> > Reese, Morton Lamar. *Cemetery Records, Mainly From Richmond County, Georgia*. 3 vols. Augusta, GA: privately printed, 1984.
>
> Newspaper
>
> > Walker, Alice O. *Personal Name Index to the Augusta Chronicle*. 4 vols: 1786–1799, 1800–1810, 1811–1820, 1821–1830. Augusta, GA: Augusta-Richmond County Public Library, 1987, 1988, 1991, 1993.
> >
> > The Augusta Public Library has a newspaper digest of Augusta newspapers for 1861–1872 that is also on microfilm at the University of Georgia and the Georgia Archives.
>
> Land
>
> > Crumpton, Daniel Nathan. *Richmond County, Georgia Land Records: Boundaries As of 1777*. Warrenton, GA: privately printed, 2007.
>
> Estate
>
> > Davidson, Grace G. *Historical Collections of Georgia Chapters of the Daughters of the American Revolution*. Volume II, 1926. Richmond County estate records of the 1770s and 1780s not on microfilm at the Georgia Archives have been abstracted in this book. The original records are in the Richmond County Probate Court.
>
> Miscellaneous
>
> > Rowland, Arthur Ray. *Boarding Houses Furnished Rooms, and Hotels. . . 1841-2000*. Augusta, GA: Augusta Genealogical Society, 2007.
> >
> > ———. *Business Directory of Augusta , Georgia , 1841-1901*. Augusta, GA: Augusta Genealogical Society, 2005.

———. *China and Immigrants to Augusta and Richmond County, Georgia from the United States Census Record 1870, 1880, 1900, 1910, 1920, 1930*. Augusta, GA: Augusta Genealogical Society, 2006.

———. *Classified Business Directory, 1901-1930*. Augusta, GA: Augusta Genealogical Society, 2007.

———. *Color: Black or Mulatto in Richmond County, Georgia Free persons of Color Listed in the 1850 and 1860 Federal Census Records*. North Augusta, SC: RR Books, 2006.

———. *Index to Marriage Licenses of Richmond County, Georgia for Book AA-Book GG Probate Court 1903-1917*. Augusta, GA: Augusta Genealogical Society, 2008.

———. *Women in Business in Augusta, Georgia Richmond County 1841-1901*. Augusta, GA: Augusta Genealogical Society, 2006.

Walker, Alice O., comp. *Register of Signatures of Depositors in the Augusta, Georgia, Branch of the Freedman's Savings and Trust Company* [1870-1871, includes African American and Irish depositors]. Augusta, GA: Augusta-Richmond County Public Library, 1998.

White, LeeAnn. *The Civil War as a Crisis in Gender: Augusta, Georgia, 1861-1890*. Athens: University of Georgia Press, 1995.

Local History

Cashin, Edward J. *The Story of Augusta*. Augusta, GA: Richmond County Board of Education, 1980.

Dutcher, Salem, and Charles C. Jones. *Memorial History of Augusta, Georgia*. 1890. Reprint, Spartanburg, SC: The Reprint Co., 1966.

ROCKDALE COUNTY. Map #42.

County seat is Conyers, 30207.

Created October 18, 1870, from Newton and Henry Counties.

Land was first distributed in the 1821 Land Lottery.

All records begin in 1871.

Major published records

Newspaper

Bowen, Rhoda Anne, and Freda R. Turner. *Georgia Confederate Soldier Obituaries: Henry, Newton and Rockdale Counties, 1879–1943*. Alpharetta, GA: W. H. Wolfe Associates, 1992.

Local History

Barksdale, Margaret G., E. L. Cowan, and Frances A. King. *A History of Rockdale County*. Conyers, GA: T. H. P., 1978.

Rockdale County Heritage Book Committee. *The Heritage of Rockdale County, Georgia*. Waynesville, NC: Don Mills, Inc, 1996.

SCHLEY COUNTY. Map #94.

County seat is Ellaville, 31806.

Created December 22, 1857, from Marion and Sumter Counties.

Land was first distributed in the 1827 Land Lottery.

Superior court records begin in 1858.

Probate court records begin in 1858.

Tax digests begin in 1873; 1858, 1866, and 1879 also available.

Major published records

> Cemetery
>
>> Schley County Preservation Society. *History of Schley County, Georgia.* Roswell, GA: W. H. Wolfe Associates, 1982: 522–578.
>
> Local History
>
>> Schley County Preservation Society. *History of Schley County, Georgia.* Roswell, GA: W. H. Wolfe Associates, 1982.

SCREVEN COUNTY. Map #90.

County seat is Sylvania, 30467.

Created December 14, 1793, from Burke and Effingham Counties.

Land was first distributed in 1733 by the Trustees and formally granted beginning in 1755.

Superior court records begin circa 1794.

Probate court records begin in 1811.

Tax digests begin in 1873; 1852 and 1864 also available.

Major published records

> Cemetery
>
>> Brier Creek Chapter, Daughters of the American Revolution. *Cemetery Records of Screven County, Georgia. Volume 1.* Sylvania, GA: Partridge Pond Press, 1981.
>>
>> Youmans, W. M. *Footprints . . . On the Sands of Time: Epitaphs of Tombstones in Old Family Cemeteries in Screven County, Georgia.* Sylvania, GA: Partridge Pond Press, 1979.
>
> Local History
>
>> Hollingsworth, Dixon. *The History of Screven County, Georgia.* Dallas, TX: Curtis Media Corps, 1989.

SEMINOLE COUNTY. Map #151.

County seat is Donalsonville, 31745.

Created November 2, 1920, from Decatur and Early Counties.

Land was first distributed in the 1820 Land Lottery.

All records begin in 1921.

The Georgia Archives has no records on microfilm of this post-1900 county, although original tax digests beginning in 1921 are available.

Major published records

Cemetery

Seminole County Historical Society. *Cornerstone of Georgia Seminole County, 1920–1991*. Roswell, GA: W. H. Wolfe Associates, 1991: 513–545.

Local History

Seminole County Historical Society. *Cornerstone of Georgia Seminole County, 1920–1991*. Roswell, GA: W. H. Wolfe Associates, 1991.

SPALDING COUNTY. Map #53.

County seat is Griffin, 30223.

Created December 20, 1851, from Pike, Fayette, and Henry Counties.

Land was first distributed in the 1821 Land Lottery.

All records begin in 1852.

Major published records

Cemetery

Griffin Historical and Preservation Society. *Cemeteries of Spalding County, Georgia*. N.p.: privately printed, 1986.

Newspaper

Hartz, Fred R., and Emilie K. Hartz. *Marriage and Death Notices from the Griffin (Georgia) Weekly News and the Griffin Weekly News and Sun, 1882–1896*. LaGrange, GA: Family Tree, 1987.

Estate

Griffin, Mary. *Abstracts of Will Book A (1852–1880), Spalding County, Georgia*. Griffin, GA: Griffin Historical and Preservation Society, 1983.

STEPHENS COUNTY. Map #18.

County seat is Toccoa, 30577.

Created August 18, 1905, from Franklin and Habersham Counties.

Land was first distributed in 1784 as headrights and in the 1820 Land Lottery.

All records begin in 1906.

The Georgia Archives has no records on microfilm of this post-1900 county, although original tax digests beginning in 1907 are available.

Major published records

> Cemetery
>
> > Stephens County Genealogical Society. *Cemetery Inscriptions of Stephens County, Georgia.* Toccoa, GA: privately printed, 2003.
> >
> > Trogdon, Kathryn C. *The History of Stephens County, Georgia.* Toccoa, GA: Toccoa Woman's Club, Inc., 1973: 459–506.
>
> Local History
>
> > Trogdon, Kathryn C. *The History of Stephens County, Georgia.* Toccoa, GA: Toccoa Woman's Club, Inc., 1973.

STEWART COUNTY. Map #103.

County seat is Lumpkin, 31815.

Created December 23, 1830, from Randolph County.

Land was first distributed in the 1827 Land Lottery.

Superior court records begin in 1831.

Probate court records begin in 1831.

Tax digests begin in 1853; 1841 also available.

In addition to the records on microfilm, the Georgia Archives has original unbound estate records, 1829–1899, and marriage records, 1828–1895, in Record Group 228.

Major published records

> Cemetery
>
> > Dixon, Sara Robertson. *History of Stewart County, Georgia, Volume II.* Waycross, GA: privately printed, 1975: 328–448.
> >
> > Terrill, Helen Eliza. *History of Stewart County, Georgia, Volume I.* Columbus, GA: privately printed, 1958: 178–203.
>
> Newspaper
>
> > Evans, Tad, *Georgia Newspaper Clippings Stewart County Extracts 1831–1889.* Savannah, GA: privately printed, 2008.
>
> Local History
>
> > Dixon, Sara Robertson. *History of Stewart County, Georgia, Volume II.* Waycross, GA: privately printed, 1975.
> >
> > Terrill, Helen Eliza. *History of Stewart County, Georgia, Volume I.* Columbus, GA: privately printed, 1958.

SUMTER COUNTY. Map #105.

County seat is Americus, 31709.

Created December 26, 1831, from Lee County.

Land was first distributed in the 1827 Land Lottery.

Superior court records begin in 1832.

Probate court records begin in 1832.

Tax digests begin in 1872; 1844, 1853, and 1864 also available.

Major library resource is the Lake Blackshear Regional Library, 307 East Lamar St., Americus, GA 31709. The telephone number is 229-924-8091. Serves Sumter, Crisp, Dooly, and Schley Counties of southwest Georgia.

Major published records

    Cemetery

    Cox, Jack F. *Cemeteries of Sumter County, Georgia*. Americus, GA: Jack & Earline Cox, 2004.

    Harvey, Mr. and Mrs. W. D. *Sumter County, Georgia, Cemetery Records*. Americus, GA: privately printed, 1972.

    Newspaper

    Evans, Tad, *Georgia Newspaper Clippings Sumter County Extracts 1832–1907*. Savannah, GA: privately printed, 2005.

    Southwest Georgia Genealogical Society. *Obituaries, Americus, Georgia, 1968–1988*. 4 vols. Albany, GA: privately printed, 1991.

    Estate

    Cox, Jack & Earline B. *Wills of Sumter County, Georgia 1836-2006*. Americus, GA: privately printed, 2006.

TALBOT COUNTY. Map #80.

County seat is Talbotton, 31827.

Created December 14, 1827, from Muscogee County.

Land was first distributed in the 1827 Land Lottery.

Superior court records begin in 1828.

Probate court records begin in 1828.

Tax digests begin in 1872; 1852 and 1856 also available.

Major published records

    Cemetery

    Torbert, Robert Ellington. *Talbot County, Georgia, Cemetery Records*. N.p.: privately printed, 1987.

    Georgia Society, DAR. *Talbot County, Georgia Cemeteries*. DAR Genealogical Records Collections, [typescript], vol. 463, 1946–1947.

Newspaper

Evans, Tad. *Georgia Newspaper Clippings Talbot County Extracts 1828–1906*. Savannah, GA: privately printed, 2008).

Local History

Davidson, William H. *A Rockaway in Talbot: Travels in an Old Georgia County*. 4 vols. West Point, GA: W.H. Davidson, 1983–1990.

Jordan, Robert H. *There Was a Land: A Story of Talbot County, Georgia and Its People*. Columbus, GA: Columbus Office Supply Co., 1971.

TALIAFERRO COUNTY. Map #61.

County seat is Crawfordville, 30631.

Created December 24, 1825, from Wilkes, Warren, Hancock, Greene, and Oglethorpe Counties.

Land was first distributed in 1773 as headrights.

All records begin in 1826.

Major published records

Cemetery

Crumpton, Daniel Nathan. *Cemeteries and Genealogy Warren County, Georgia, and Immediate Vicinity, 1792–1987*. Roswell, GA: W. H. Wolfe Associates, 1987: 1–67.

Jones, Wiley B. *Rest In Peace: A Cemetery Census of Taliaferro County, Georgia*. Washington, GA: Wilkes Publishing Company, 1984.

Jones, Wiley B. *The Crawfordville Baptist Church Cemetery*. Washington, GA: Georgia Baptist Association Press, c1981.

Martin, Mikki Johnson. *Carter's Grove Baptist Church Cemetery*. N.p.: privately printed, 1998.

Newspaper

McRee, Fred W., Jr. *Taliaferro County, Georgia, Deaths, 1877–1921*. Dahlonega, GA: privately printed, 2010.

Estate

Lunceford, Alvin Mell, Jr. *Early Records of Taliaferro County, Georgia*. Crawfordville, GA: privately printed, 1956.

Court

Hageness, MariLee Beatty. *Index to Ordinary Minutes, 1826–1831, Taliaferro County, Georgia*. Anniston, AL: MLH Research, 1995.

Miscellaneous

Lunceford, Alvin Mell. *Taliaferro County, Georgia: Records and Notes*. Spartanburg, SC: Reprint Co., 1988.

TATTNALL COUNTY. Map #115.

County seat is Reidsville, 30453.

Created December 5, 1801, from Montgomery County.

Land was first distributed in 1784 as headrights.

Superior court records begin in 1802.

Probate court records begin circa 1805.

Tax digests begin in 1802.

Major published records

    Cemetery

        Cawley, Henry Hughes. "Tattnall County, Georgia, Cemetery Records." Salt Lake City: Digitized by the Genealogical Society of Utah, 2006.

        Coleman, Moses M. Jr., and Emilie K. Hartz. *Cemeteries of Tattnall County, Georgia.* Vidalia, GA: Vesco, Inc., 2001.

        Folsom, Judith Kicklighter. *Beards Creek Church Cemetery Records, Tattnall County, Georgia.* Dumfries, VA: privately printed, 1993.

    Newspaper

        Evans, Tad. *Georgia Newspaper Clippings, Tattnall County Extracts, 1812–1891.* Savannah, GA: privately printed, 1998.

        Rabun, John P. *Stories from the Tattnall Journal, 1905–1950.* Reidsville, GA: Journal Print, ca. 2008.

    Estate

        Murray, Sabrina J. *Tattnall County, Georgia, Loose Papers.* 2 vols. Homerville, GA: Huxford Genealogical Society, 2005–2008.

    Court

        Thompson, Gordon Anthony. *Tattnall County, Georgia, Superior Court Records, 1805–1832.* Baltimore: Gateway Press, 2005.

        Thompson, Gordon Anthony. *The Tattnall County Inferior Court Records 1805–1832: Including the 1819 Land Lottery Winners Drawers & Districts.* Metter, GA: Gordon Anthony Thompson Publishing, 2003.

    Local History

        Rabun, John P., Jr. *A History of Tattnall County, 1801–1865.* N.p.: privately printed, 1994.

        Wildes, Charles Edward. *Once Upon a Time in Tattnall County, Georgia.* Claxton, GA: privately printed, 1990.

TAYLOR COUNTY. Map #81.

County seat is Butler, 31006.

Created January 15, 1852, from Talbot, Macon, and Marion Counties.

Land was first distributed in the 1827 Land Lottery.

All records begin in 1852.

Major published records

> Cemetery
>
> > Hay, Guelda L., and Millie C. Stewart. *Cemeteries of Taylor County, Georgia.* Warner Robins, GA: Central Georgia Genealogical Society, Inc., 1990.
> >
> > McGuffin, Essie Jones Childs. *A Guide to Taylor County Cemeteries and Vital Records Provided by Tombstone Inscriptions.* N.p.: privately printed, no date.
>
> Newspaper
>
> > Windham, Marilyn Neisler. *Marriages, Deaths, and Etc. from the Butler (Georgia) Herald 1876–1910.* 2 vols. Warner Robins, GA: Central Georgia Genealogical Society, 1995, 1998.
>
> Local History
>
> > Childs, Essie Jones. *They Tarried in Taylor…* Warner Robins, GA: Central Georgia Genealogical Society, 1992.

TELFAIR COUNTY. Map #111.

County seat is McRae, 31055.

Created December 10, 1807, from Wilkinson County.

Land was first distributed in the 1807 Land Lottery.

Superior court records begin in 1809.

Probate court records begin in 1845, although some earlier records exist.

Tax digests begin in 1870; 1853, 1854, 1856, and 1867 also available.

Major published records

> Cemetery
>
> > Coleman, Moses M., Jr., and Emilie K. Hartz. *Cemeteries of Telfair County, Georgia.* Vidalia, GA: Vesco, Inc., 1999.
> >
> > Pioneer Historical Society. *The History of Telfair County, Georgia.* Dallas, TX: Curtis Media Corporation, n.d., ca. 1987: 146–170.
>
> Newspaper
>
> > Evans, Tad. *Georgia Newspaper Clippings Telfair County Extracts 1810–1892.* Savannah, GA: privately printed, 1998.
> >
> > ———. *The News From Chauncey Volume I 1869–1916.* Savannah, GA: privately printed, 2005.

———. *The News From Milan, Rhine and Old Telfair Volume I 1807–1919*. Savannah, GA: privately printed, 2007.

Land

Wells, Catherine Fussell. *Telfair County, Georgia, Deed Book A, 1807–1813 [and] Deed Book H, 1830–1838*. Valdosta, GA: Wells Gen-Search, 2000.

———. *Telfair County, Georgia, Deed Books D, E, F & P*. Valdosta, GA: Wells Gen-Search, 2000.

———. *Telfair County, Georgia, Deed Books K & L, 1843–1850*. Valdosta, GA: Wells Gen-Search, 2000.

———. *Telfair County, Georgia: Deed Book N, 1854–1860*. Valdosta, GA: Wells Gen-Search, 2000.

Court

Wells, Catherine Fussell. *Telfair County, Georgia Superior Court Minutes 1810–1837*. Valdosta, GA: Wells Gen-Search, 2000.

Local History

Pioneer Historical Society. *The History of Telfair County, Georgia*. Dallas, TX: Curtis Media Corporation, n.d., ca. 1987.

TERRELL COUNTY. Map #121.

County seat is Dawson, 31742.

Created February 16, 1856, from Lee and Randolph Counties.

Land was first distributed in the 1827 Land Lottery.

All records begin in 1856.

Major published records

Cemetery

Melton, Ella Christie, and Augusta Griggs Raines. *History of Terrell County, Georgia*. Roswell, GA: W. H. Wolfe Associates, 1980: 318–337.

Newspaper

Kilbourne, Elizabeth Evans. *Terrell County, Georgia, Newspaper Clippings, 1866–1889*. 5 vols. Savannah, GA: Tad Evans, 1996–1998.

Local History

Melton, Ella Christie, and Augusta Griggs Raines. *History of Terrell County, Georgia*. Roswell, GA: W. H. Wolfe Associates, 1980.

THOMAS COUNTY. Map #154.

County seat is Thomasville, 31792.

Created December 23, 1825, from Decatur and Irwin Counties.

Land was first distributed in the 1820 Land Lottery.

Superior court records begin in 1826.

Probate court records begin in 1826.

Tax digests begin in 1870; 1854 also available.

Major published records

> Cemetery
>
> Craigmiles, Joe E., III. *Thomas County, Georgia, Cemeteries.* Thomasville, GA: Craigmiles Publishing, 1990.
>
> Newspaper
>
> Dasher, Wayne & Judy. *In the Shadow of the Pines; Thomas County, Georgia Newspapers.* 10 vols. Nashville, GA: privately printed, 2001–2003.
>
> Evans, Tad. *Georgia Newspaper Clippings Thomas County Extracts 1826–1907.* Savannah, GA: privately printed, 2005.
>
> ———. *Thomas County, Georgia, Newspaper Clippings, 1857–1888.* 3 vols. Savannah, GA: privately printed, 1995–1996.
>
> Local History
>
> Rogers, William Warren. *Ante-Bellum Thomas County (1825–1861).* Tallahassee: Florida State University, 1963
>
> ———. *Thomas County during the Civil War.* Tallahassee: Florida State University, 1964
>
> ———. *Thomas County, Georgia (1865–1900).* Tallahassee: Florida State University, 1973

TIFT COUNTY. Map #138.

County seat is Tifton, 31794.

Created August 17, 1905, from Berrien, Irwin, and Worth Counties.

Land was first distributed in the 1820 Land Lottery.

All records begin in 1905.

The Georgia Archives has no records on microfilm of this post-1900 county, although original tax digests beginning in 1906 are available.

Major published records

> Cemetery
>
> Chandler, Barry. *Cemeteries of Tift County, Georgia.* Tifton, GA: privately printed, 1999.

TOOMBS COUNTY. Map #114.

County seat is Lyons, 30436.

Created August 18, 1905, from Emanuel, Montgomery, and Tattnall Counties.

Land was first distributed in 1784 as headrights.

Superior court records begin in 1906.

Probate court records begin in 1905.

Tax digests begin in 1906.

The Georgia Archives has no records on microfilm of this post-1900 county, although original tax digests beginning in 1906 are available.

Major library resource is the John E. Ladson, Jr., Library, 119 Church St., Vidalia, GA 30474. The telephone number is (912) 537-8186. Extensive book and microfilm library on several states.

Major published records

    Cemetery

    Burnham, Hank. *Cemetery Records of Tattnall and Toombs Counties, Georgia.* (1988 typescript in the Washington Memorial Library, Macon, GA).

    Coleman, Moses M., Jr. *Cemeteries of Toombs County, Georgia.* 2nd. ed. Vidalia, GA: Coleman Ferrotype, 2000.

    Newspaper

    Hartz, Fred R. and Emilie K. Hartz. *Death Notices from the Vidalia Advance Newspaper, 1921–1930, Vidalia, Georgia (Toombs County).* Vidalia GA: privately printed, 1985.

    Local History

    Teasley, Amos Milton. "The History of Toombs County." Master's Thesis, University of Georgia, 1940.

TOWNS COUNTY. Map #9.

County seat is Hiawassee, 30546.

Created March 6, 1856, from Union and Rabun Counties.

Land was first distributed in the 1820 and 1832 Land Lotteries.

Superior court records begin in 1856.

Probate court records begin in 1856.

Tax digests begin in 1869.

Major published records

    Cemetery

    Brooke, Ted O. *Towns County, Georgia, Cemeteries.* Fernandina Beach, FL: Wolfe Publishing, 1996.

Local History

Taylor, Jerry A. *Hearthstones of Home: Foundations of Towns County, Georgia.* Young Harris, GA: J.A. Taylor, 1983.

TREUTLEN COUNTY. Map #99.

County seat is Soperton, 30457.

Created November 5, 1918, from Emanuel and Montgomery Counties.

Land was first distributed in 1784 as headrights.

All records begin in 1919.

The Georgia Archives has no records on microfilm of this post-1900 county, although original tax digests beginning in 1919 are available.

Major published records

Cemetery

Coleman, Moses M., and Lavon Stone Palmer. *Graves of Montgomery, Treutlen, and Wheeler.* Vidalia, GA: Coleman Ferrotype, no date, circa 1994: 181–337.

Stephens, J. Clayton. *Treutlen County Necrology (Or, Marked Graves in Treutlen County, Georgia).* Soperton, GA: privately printed, 1977.

Stephens, J. Clayton. *Supplement I to Marked Graves in Treutlen County, Georgia.* N.p.: privately printed, 1982.

Stephens, J. Clayton. *A Survey of Black Cemeteries in Treutlen County, Georgia.* Soperton, GA: privately printed, 1983.

Truitt, Paul and Montell. *Registry of Graves in Treutlen County, Georgia.* Stuart, FL: privately printed, 1998.

Truitt, Paul and Montell. *Registry of Graves in Treutlen County, Georgia, 2002.* Stuart, FL: Paul and Montell Truitt, 2002.

Miscellaneous

Braddy, Larry R. *Treutlen County, Images of America Series.* Mount Pleasant, SC: Arcadia Publishing, 2008.

TROUP COUNTY. Map #66.

County seat is LaGrange, 30240.

Created June 9, 1825, from Indian lands ceded in 1825 and 1827.

Land was first distributed in the 1827 Land Lottery.

Superior court records begin in 1827.

Probate court records begin in 1828.

Tax digests begin in 1861; 1850 and 1851 also available.

Major library resource is the Troup County Archives, 136 Main St., LaGrange, GA 30241. The telephone number is 706-884-1828. For more thorough coverage of the features of this library, see the *Georgia Genealogical Society Quarterly*, Vol. 36 No. 4 (Winter 2000) 237–240.

Major published records

Cemetery

Johnson, Forest Clark, II. *Memories In Marble: Hill View and Hill View Annex Cemeteries, LaGrange, Georgia.* LaGrange, GA: Jackson Printing and Graphics, 1992.

McClendon, Dorothy, Lillie Lambert, and Danny Knight. *Family, Church, and Community Cemeteries of Troup County, Georgia.* LaGrange, GA: Family Tree, 1990.

Newspaper

Evans, Tad. *Georgia Newspaper Clippings, Troup County Extracts, 1826–1888.* Savannah, GA: privately printed, 2005.

Estate

Allen, Randall A., and Danny Knight. *Estate Records of Troup County, Georgia, 1827–1850.* LaGrange, GA: Troup County Historical Society Archives, 1987.

Local History

Davidson, William H. *Pine Log and Greek Revival; Houses and People of Three Counties in Georgia and Alabama.* Alexander City, AL: Outlook Publishing Co., 1964.

Johnson, Forrest Clark. *Histories of LaGrange and Troup County, Georgia. Volumes I and III.* LaGrange, GA: Family Tree, 1987.

Smith, Clifford L. *History of Troup County.* Atlanta: Foote & Davies Co.,1935.

Troup County, Georgia and her people. LaGrange, GA: Family Tree Publications, 1981–1988. This periodical contains valuable county records.

TURNER COUNTY. Map #123.

County seat is Ashburn, 31714.

Created August 18, 1905, from Dooly, Irwin, Wilcox, and Worth Counties.

Land was first distributed in the 1820 and 1821 Land Lotteries.

The Georgia Archives has no records on microfilm of this post-1900 county, although original tax digests beginning in 1907 are available.

Major published records

Cemetery

Paulk, Jessie H., and Delma Wilson Paulk. *Survey of Turner County, Georgia, Cemeteries.* Thomasville, GA: Craigmiles Historical Publications, 1993.

TWIGGS COUNTY. Map #85.

County seat is Jeffersonville, 31044.

Created December 14, 1809, from Wilkinson County.

Land was first distributed in the 1807 Land Lottery.

Superior court records begin in 1901.

Probate court records begin in 1901.

Tax digests begin in 1870; 1818, 1826, 1830, 1833, 1853, and 1863 also available.

Major published records

> Cemetery
>
> Faulk, J. L. O'Neal, and Billy W. Jones. *History of Twiggs County, Georgia*. Columbus, GA: privately printed, 1960): 292–324.
>
> Newspaper
>
> Evans, Tad. *Georgia Newspaper Clippings Twiggs County Extracts Volume I 1810–1837 & Volume II 1838–1907*. Savannah, GA: privately printed, 2004, 2005.
>
> Land
>
> Georgia Society, Daughters of the American Revolution. *Tax Digests of Twiggs County 1818, 1826, 1830, 1833, 1853*. N.p.: privately printed, Volume 475, 1958.
>
> Miscellaneous
>
> Clark, Bess Vaughn. *Twiggs County, Georgia, Abstracts*. Macon, GA: privately printed, 1987. (Many Twiggs County records are included in this publication.)
>
> ———. *Twiggs County, Georgia, Records: A Reconstructed Heritage*. Fernandina Beach, FL: Wolfe Publishing, 1999.
>
> Local History
>
> Faulk, J. L. O'Neal, and Billy W. Jones. *History of Twiggs County, Georgia*. Columbus, GA: privately printed, 1960).

UNION COUNTY. Map #8.

County seat is Blairsville, 30512.

Created December 3, 1832, from original Cherokee County.

Land was first distributed in the 1832 Land Lottery.

Superior court records begin in 1860, although some earlier records exist.

Probate court records begin circa 1838.

Tax digests begin in 1849.

Major published records

> Cemetery
>
> Elliott, Dale, and C. T. Wimpey. *Cemetery Records of Union County, Georgia*. Blairsville, GA: Union County Historical Society, n.d., ca. 1989.

UPSON COUNTY. Map #69.

County seat is Thomaston, 30286.

Created December 15, 1824, from Crawford and Pike Counties.

Land was first distributed in the 1821 Land Lottery.

All records begin in 1825.

Major published records

   Cemetery

   Upson Historical Society. *The Cemeteries of Upson County, Georgia.* 2nd ed. Thomaston, GA, privately printed, 1986.

   Newspaper

   Evans, Tad. *Georgia Newspaper Clippings Upson County Extracts 1825–1889.* Savannah, GA: privately printed, 2008.

   Estate

   Georgia Society, Daughters of the American Revolution. *Wills of Upson Co., Georgia, From 1899 to 1950.* Volume 480. N.p.: privately printed, 1950–51.

   Ingmire, Frances Terry. *Upson County, Georgia: Will Abstracts 1821-1850, Minutes of Inferior Court 1825-30, Homestead Exemptions 1868.* St. Louis, MO:. privately printed, 1980.

   Nottingham, Carolyn Walker, and Evelyn Hannah. *History of Upson County, Georgia.* Vidalia, GA: Georgia Genealogical Reprints, 1969. Some early estate records are in this book.

   Local History

   Nottingham, Carolyn Walker, and Evelyn Hannah. *History of Upson County, Georgia.* Vidalia, GA: Georgia Genealogical Reprints, 1969.

WALKER COUNTY. Map #2.

County seat is LaFayette, 30728.

Created December 18, 1833, from Murray County.

Land was first distributed in the 1832 Land Lottery.

Superior court records begin in 1883.

Probate court records begin in 1883.

Tax digests begin in 1873.

Major published records

   Cemetery

   The Walker County Historical Society. *Walker County, Georgia, Cemeteries, Volume I, South Walker County.* LaFayette, GA: privately printed, 1987.

———. *Walker County Georgia Cemeteries, Volume II, North Walker County*. LaFayette, GA: privately printed, 1991.

Newspaper

Austin, Jeannette Holland. *Walker County Messenger, 1916–1921*. Riverdale, GA: n.p., n.d.

Griffith, June Brandon. *Births, Marriages, Deaths, Legal Notices, Walker County, Georgia, 1883–1904*. 6 vols. Rossville and Fort Oglethorpe, GA: privately printed, 1982–1998.

WALTON COUNTY. Map #43.

County seat is Monroe, 30655.

Created December 15, 1818, from Indian lands ceded in 1818.

Land was first distributed in the 1820 Land Lottery.

Superior court records begin in 1819.

Probate court records begin in 1819.

Tax digests begin in 1849; 1819, 1826, 1831, and 1834 also available.

In addition to the records on microfilm, the Georgia Archives has the unbound original records in Record Group 247.

Major published records

Cemetery

The Historical Society of Walton County. *In Remembrance: Cemetery Readings of Walton County, Georgia*. Monroe, GA: privately printed, 1981. (A separate typescript index to this book, entitled *Cemetery Readings Alphabetically Walton County, Georgia*, was written by Frances R. Cheney. Poway, California: privately printed, n.d., circa 1985.)

East Georgia Genealogical Society. *Walton County, Georgia Cemeteries (East)*. Winder, GA: privately printed, 2002.

East Georgia Genealogical Society. *Walton County, Georgia Cemeteries (West)*. Winder, GA: privately printed, 2002.

Local History

Sams, Anita B. *Wayfarers in Walton*. Monroe, GA: privately printed, 1967. Some tax records are included in this book.

Georgia created another earlier Walton County on December 10, 1803, in what is presently Transylvania County, NC. It never functioned as a county and was abolished in 1812. For an excellent history of this original Walton County in Georgia see Mary Jane McCrary, *Transylvania Beginnings: A History*, (Greenville, SC: Southern Historical Press, 1984): 106–132.

WARE COUNTY. Map #147.

County seat is Waycross, 31501.

Created December 15, 1824, from Appling County.

Land was first distributed in the 1820 Land Lottery.

Superior court records begin in 1874.

Probate court records begin in 1874.

Tax digests begin in 1867; 1862 also available.

Major published records

> Cemetery
>
> Walker, Laura Singleton. *History of Ware County*. Macon, GA: privately printed, 1934: 37–43.
>
> Marriage
>
> Paulk, Jessie H. *Ware County, Georgia Marriage Records Index 1874 to 1943*. Homerville, GA: Huxford Genealogical Society, 2008.
>
> Local History
>
> Walker, Laura Singleton. *History of Ware County*. Macon, GA: privately printed, 1934.

WARREN COUNTY. Map #62.

County seat is Warrenton, 30828.

Created December 19, 1793, from Wilkes, Columbia, Burke, and Richmond Counties.

Land was first distributed in the 1750s as headrights.

Superior court records begin circa 1794.

Probate court records begin in 1794.

Tax digests begin in 1849; 1794, 1798, 1801, 1805, and 1817–1822 also available.

In addition to the records on microfilm, the Georgia Archives has original estate papers, 1879–1923, in Record Group 249.

Major published records

> Cemetery
>
> Crumpton, Daniel Nathan. *Cemeteries and Genealogy Warren County, Georgia, and Immediate Vicinity, 1792–1987*. Roswell, GA: W. H. Wolfe Associates, 1987: 1–67.
>
> Land
>
> Crumpton, Daniel Nathan. *Warren County, Georgia Land Records*. Warrenton, GA: privately printed, 2002.
>
> Court
>
> Crumpton, Daniel Nathan. *Warren County, Georgia, 1793–1900: Genealogy II*. Spartanburg, SC: Reprint Co., 1993.

WASHINGTON COUNTY. Map #75.

County seat is Sandersville, 31082.

Georgia Research
Chapter III: Counties, County Records, and Local History Sources

Created February 25, 1784, from Creek Indian land ceded in 1783.

Land was first distributed in 1784 as headrights.

The original Washington County was more than 100 miles long, beginning at present-day Oconee and Oglethorpe Counties and lying southeasterly to present-day Long and Liberty Counties.

Superior court records begin in 1865.

Probate court records begin in 1843, although some earlier records exist.

Tax digests begin in 1836; 1825, 1826, 1828, and 1830 also available.

The Georgia Archives has loose original Washington County records, 1855-1952, in Record Group 250.

Major library resource is the Washington County Historical Society, Post Office Box 6088, Sandersville, GA 31082. The telephone number is 478-551-6965. Their Research Center and Old Jail Museum is located at 129 Jones St., Sandersville, GA and is open limited hours. Website: http://wacogrc.org/genealogy.html. Email: genealogyresearch@att.net.

Major published records

Cemetery

Newsom, Elizabeth P. *Washington County, Georgia, Tombstone Inscriptions.* Sandersville, GA: privately printed, 1967.

Newspaper

Births, Marriages and Deaths from the Sandersville Herald, 1873–1877. N.p., n.d. Copy at the Georgia Archives.

Evans, Tad. *Georgia Newspaper Clippings Washington County Extracts 1809–1887.* Savannah, GA: privately printed, 1998.

Evans, Tad. *Washington County, Georgia, Newspaper Clippings.* 1852–1889. 3 vols. Savannah, GA: privately printed, 1994.

Wilkins, John W. *The Central Georgian, 1852–1870.* Lufkin, TX: privately printed, no date.

Land

Dwyer, Clifford S. *Washington County, Georgia, Surveyor's Plat Book.* DeFuniak Springs, FL: privately printed, 1985.

Henry, William R. *Washington County, Georgia: Index to 1828 Tax Digest, Index to 1836 Tax Digest.* Warner Robins, GA: 1987.

Newsom, Elizabeth Pritchard. *Washington County, Georgia, 1825 Tax Digest.* Sandersville, GA: privately printed, 1968.

Warren, Mary Bondurant. *Washington County, Georgia, Land Warrants, 1784–1787.* Athens, GA: Heritage Papers, 1992.

Estate

Brantley Association of America. *Washington County Georgia Estate Records 1822–1885*. Powder Springs: GA: privately printed, 2007.

Newsom, Elizabeth Pritchard. *Washington County, Georgia, Estate Papers*. Sandersville, GA: Washington County Historical Society, 1982.

Court

Bateman, Frances, Patsy H. Hutcheson, and Elizabeth P. Newsom. *Index to Washington County, Georgia, Inferior Court Minutes, 1843–1862*. N.p., 1965.

Miscellaneous

Adolphus, Adam L., Sr. *African Americans of Washington County, Georgia: From Colonial Times Through Reconstruction*. Sandersville, GA: Washington County Historical Society, 2011.

De Lamar, Marie and Elisabeth Rothstein. *Records of Washington County, Georgia*. Baltimore: Genealogical Publishing, 1985.

Joslyn, Mauriel and Rick Joslyn. *Historical Survey of Sherman's March to the Sea and the Flight of Jefferson Davis through Washington County, Georgia*. 2 vols. Sandersville, GA: Washington County Historical Society, 2008.

Local History

Mitchell, Ella. *History of Washington County*. Greenville, SC: Southern Historical Press, 1924.

Washington County Historical Society and Mary Alice Jordan. *Cotton to Kaolin: A History Washington County, Georgia, 1784–1989*. Sandersville, GA: Washington County Historical Society, 1989.

WAYNE COUNTY. Map #130.

County seat is Jesup, 31545.

Created May 11, 1803, mostly from Indian land ceded in 1802, 1814, and 1818.

Land was first distributed in 1763 as headrights and in the 1805 and 1820 Land Lotteries.

Superior court records begin in 1810.

Probate court records begin in 1815, although some earlier records exist.

Tax digests begin in 1862; 1844 and 1853 also available.

Wayne County's boundaries have changed radically over the years. People who appear in Wayne County in some years and in other counties in other years may not have physically moved but simply were victims of county boundary changes.

Major published records

Cemetery

Jordon, Margaret Coleman. *Wayne Miscellany*. Jesup, GA: The Jesup Sentinel, 1976: 187–230.

Local History

    Jordon, Margaret Coleman. *Wayne Miscellany*. Jesup, GA: The Jesup Sentinel, 1976.

WEBSTER COUNTY. Map #104.

County seat is Preston, 31824.

Created as Kinchafoonee County on December 16, 1853, from Stewart County.

The name was changed to Webster County on February 21, 1856.

Land was first distributed in the 1827 Land Lottery.

Superior court records begin in 1860.

Probate court records begin in 1854.

Tax digests begin in 1856.

Major published records

    Cemetery

        The Weston Woman's Club. *History of Webster County, Georgia*. Roswell, GA: W. H. Wolfe Associates, 1980: 483–532.

    Local History

        The Weston Woman's Club. *History of Webster County, Georgia*. Roswell, GA: W. H. Wolfe Associates, 1980.

WHEELER COUNTY. Map #112.

County seat is Alamo, 30411.

Created November 5, 1912, from Montgomery County.

Land was first distributed in the 1807 Land Lottery.

All records begin in 1913.

The Georgia Archives has no records on microfilm of this post-1900 county, although original tax digests beginning in 1913 are available.

Major published records

    Cemetery

        Coleman, Moses M., and Lavon Stone Palmer. *Graves of Montgomery, Treutlen, and Wheeler*. Vidalia, GA: Coleman Ferrotype, n.d., ca. 1994: 339–489.

WHITE COUNTY. Map #16.

County seat is Cleveland, 30528.

Created December 22, 1857, from Habersham County.

Land was first distributed in the 1820 Land Lottery.

All records begin in 1858.

Major published records

    Cemetery

        The Northeast Georgia Regional Library. *Habersham and White Counties Cemeteries*. Roswell, GA: W. H. Wolfe Associates, 1986: 115–181.

    Local History

        Gedney, Matt. *The Story of Helen and Thereabouts*. Marietta, GA: Little Star Press, 1998.

        White County History Book Committee. *A History of White County, 1857–1980*. Cleveland, GA: White County History Book Committee, 1981.

WHITFIELD COUNTY. Map #4.

County seat is Dalton, 30720.

Created December 30, 1851, from Murray County.

Land was first distributed in the 1832 Land Lottery.

All records begin in 1852.

Major library resource is the Crown Gardens and Archives, 715 Chattanooga Ave., Dalton, GA 30722. The telephone number is (706) 278-0217. Operated by the Whitfield-Murray Historical Society.

Major published records

    Cemetery

        The Whitfield-Murray Historical Society. *Whitfield County, Georgia, Cemeteries*. Fernandina Beach, FL: Wolfe Publishing, 1998.

WILCOX COUNTY. Map #108.

County seat is Abbeville, 31001.

Created December 22, 1857, from Irwin, Dooly, and Pulaski Counties.

Land was first distributed in the 1820 Land Lottery.

Superior court records begin in 1866.

Probate court records begin in 1858.

Tax digests begin in 1872; 1863, 1868, and 1870 also available.

In addition to the records on microfilm, the Georgia Archives has the original unbound marriage records, 1871–1890s, in Record Group 256.

Major published records

    Cemetery

        McDonald, Mary Lou L., and Samuel Jordan Lawson, III. *The Passing of the Pines; A History of Wilcox County, Georgia*. Roswell, GA: W. H. Wolfe Associates, 1984: 467–518.

McDonald, Mary Lou L. *The Passing of the Pines; A History of Wilcox County, Georgia, Volume II.* Roswell, GA: W. H. Wolfe Associates, 1987: 384–394.

———. *The Passing of the Pines; A History of Wilcox County, Georgia, Volume III.* Fitzgerald, GA: Walker Printing Co., 1992: 280–282.

Newspaper

Evans, Tad. *Georgia Newspaper Clippings, Wilcox County Extracts, 1858-1905.* Savannah, GA: privately printed, 2000.

———. *Wilcox County, Georgia Newspaper Clippings.* 1898–1922. 5 vols. Savannah, GA: privately printed, 2010–2011.

Local History

McDonald, Mary Lou L. *The Passing of the Pines; A History of Wilcox County, Georgia.* 3 vols. Roswell, GA: W. H. Wolfe Associates, 1984, 1987, 1992.

WILKES COUNTY. Map #47.

County seat is Washington, 30673.

Created February 5, 1777, from what had been the ceded lands of St. Paul Parish.

Land was first distributed in 1773 as headrights.

Superior court records begin in 1784, although some earlier records exist.

Probate court records begin in 1782, although some earlier records exist.

Tax digests begin in 1783.

In addition to the records on microfilm, the Georgia Archives has original unbound records in Record Group 257, and in the Joseph M. Toomey Collection in the Private Manuscripts section. The Georgia Archives has original land court minutes for Wilkes County in Record Group 257-13-25.

Major published records

Cemetery

Newsom, F. M., and Nell H. Newsom. *Wilkes County Cemeteries and a Few From Adjoining Counties.* Washington, GA: Wilkes Publishing Co., 1970.

Newspaper

McRee, Fred W. Jr.. *Wilkes County, Georgia Deaths 1805–1925.* Dahlonega, GA: privately printed, 2009.

Poss, Faye Stone. *Wilkes County (Washington), Georgia Newspaper Abstracts 1802, 1805–1809.* Snellville, GA: privately printed, 2003.

———. *Wilkes County (Washington), Georgia Newspaper Abstracts 1810–1815 Vol. II.* Snellville, GA: privately printed, 2005.

Land

Farmer, Michal Martin. *Wilkes County, Georgia Deed Books A–VV, 1784–1806*. Dallas, TX: Farmer Genealogy Company, 1996.

Hudson, Frank Parker. *Wilkes County, Georgia Tax Records, 1785–1805*, 2 vols. Atlanta: privately printed, 1996.

Hudson, Frank Parker. *A 1790 Census for Wilkes County, Georgia Prepared from Tax Returns with Abstracts of the 1790 Tax Returns*. Spartanburg, SC: The Reprint Company, Publishers, 1980.

Estate

Brooke, Ted O. *Wilkes County, Georgia, Will Index, 1777–1921*. Cumming, GA: Briarpatch Press, 1997. This is a list of testators.

LeMaster, Mrs. Vernon L. *Abstracts of Wills 1790–1852 and Marriages 1790–1832 of Wilkes County, Georgia*. Decatur, GA: privately printed, 1959.

Smith, Sarah Quinn. *Early Georgia Wills and Settlements of Estates*. Washington, GA: privately printed, 1959.

Miscellaneous

Davidson, Grace Gillam. *Early Records of Georgia, Wilkes County*. 2 vols. Vidalia, GA: Rev. Silas Emmett Lucas, 1968. Many early Wilkes County records are published in this book. Numerous omissions are evident in these two volumes.

Davis, Robert S. *The Wilkes County Papers, 1773–1833*. Easley, SC: Southern Historical Press, 1979.

———. *Supplement to the Wilkes County Papers, 1773–1889*. Greenville, SC: Southern Historical Press, 2000.

WILKINSON COUNTY. Map #86.

County seat is Irwinton, 31042.

Created May 11, 1803, from Indian lands ceded in 1802 and 1805.

Land was first distributed in the 1805 and 1807 Land Lotteries.

Superior court records begin in 1854.

Probate Court records begin circa 1820.

Tax digests begin in 1871.

Major published records

Cemetery

Maddox, Joseph T. *Wills and Cemeteries, Wilkinson County, Georgia*. Irwinton, GA: privately printed, 1977: 367–603.

Maddox, Joseph T. *Gravestone Inscriptions and Lineages, Wilkinson County, Georgia.* Irwinton, GA: privately printed, 1980. The same cemetery records also appear in the above book.

Wilkinson County Historical Society. *Cemeteries of Wilkinson County, Georgia.* Gordon, GA: privately printed, 2010.

Newspaper

Evans, Tad. *Georgia Newspaper Clippings Wilkinson County Extracts Volume I 1809–1851 & Volume II 1852–1907.* Savannah, GA: privately printed, 2002, 2003.

Estate

Maddox, Joseph T. *Wills and Cemeteries, Wilkinson County, Georgia.* [1817–1920]. Irwinton, GA: privately printed, 1977: 1–366. Chapter one of this book contains the will abstracts.

———. *Wilkinson County, Georgia, Wills, 1817–1920: With Genealogical Information.* Irwinton, GA: privately printed, 1971

Local History

Davidson, Victor. *A History of Wilkinson County.* 1930. Reprint, Spartanburg, SC: The Reprint Co., 1978.

WORTH COUNTY. Map #137.

County seat is Sylvester, 31791.

Created December 20, 1853, from Dooly and Irwin Counties.

Land was first distributed in the 1820 and 1821 Land Lotteries.

Superior court records begin in 1892, although some earlir records exist.

Probate court records begin in 1879, although some earlier records exist.

Tax digests begin in 1874.

Major published records

Cemetery

Wells, Catherine F. *The Complete Cemetery Records of Worth County, Georgia.* Tallahassee, FL: privately printed, 1984.

Newspaper

Wells, Catherine Fussell. *Obituaries and Death Notices from the Sumner Free Trader/Worth County Local 1885–1893 Volume I.* Valdosta, GA: Wells-Gen Search, 2000.

Wells, Catherine Fussell. *Obituaries and Death Notices from the Worth County Local 1895–1902 Volume II.* Valdosta, GA: Wells-Gen Search, 2002.

Local Histories

Local histories exist for almost every Georgia county and major city, largely as a result of an act of the legislature to commemorate Georgia's bicentennial in 1933. New county histories, picture books, cemetery compilations, and publications of family sketches are being published at an accelerating rate. In addition to the specific bibliographies for Georgia only, also see P. William Filby, *A Bibliography of American County Histories* (Baltimore: Genealogical Publishing Company, 1985).

Several resources are available specifically for Georgia for use in compiling works on local histories and records. See for example:

> "Sources for Writing a Georgia County History." *Georgia Librarian* 29 (1993): 91–93.

> Walch, Timothy, ed. *Our Family, Our Town: Essays on Family and Local History Sources in the National Archives*. Washington, DC: National Archives and Records Administration, 1987.

The Georgia Archives (Record Group 44) and the Hargrett Rare Book and Manuscript Library at the University of Georgia each has 1930s compilations of historical data on Georgia counties prepared by the Works Projects Administration (WPA).

There have been "heritage" books published for many Georgia counties, containing mostly family sketches, by County Heritage, Inc.. See http://www.county-heritage.com/.

City Directories

Guides to extant city directories for the entire United States, including Georgia, may be found in:

> Research Publications. *City Directories of the United States, 1860–1901: Guide to the Microfilm Collection*. Woodbridge, CT: Research Publications, 1983.

> Spear, Dorothea N. *Bibliography of American Directories Through 1860*. Westport, CT: Greenwood Press, 1978.

The Library of Congress and many local libraries also have old telephone directories. No bibliographies or catalogs of these holdings exist. At the Library of Congress, searches are made of these directories by locality. See *Telephone and City Directories in the Library of Congress: A Finding Guide* (Washington, DC: Library of Congress, 1994). The Georgia Archives maintains a "City Directory Index" in a ring binder in its publications area, listing its holdings of city directories in all formats: book, fiche, and microfilm.

Ancestry.com has a collection of city directories that includes the Georgia cities of: Albany, Americus, Athens, Atlanta, Augusta, Brunswick, Columbus, Dalton, Dublin, Gainesville, LaGrange, Macon, Rome, Savannah, Valdosta, and Waycross.

Georgia city directories prior to 1950 are located as shown below and anyone who is aware of pre-1950 directories located in repositories other than those mentioned here is asked to notify the Georgia Genealogical Society at the address in the front of this work. Hyphenated dates indicate inclusive dates of annual directories. For example, "1868–1870" indicates a separate directory for each of the years 1868, 1869, and 1870. Consecutive dates with an ampersand (&), such as "1941&42," indicate there is only one combined directory for both years, in this case, 1941 and 1942. Also listed below are city censuses that can be used in a similar manner to city directories.

For city directories after 1950, the Central Library of the Atlanta-Fulton Public Library System and the Library of Congress have substantial collections representing many Georgia cities. City directories usually can be found in the main library of their respective cities. Some Georgia directories listed below also can be found in out-of-state repositories not included in the following list. The Georgia Archives also has many other municipal records on microfilm. The website at https://sites.google.com/site/onlinedirectorysite/ is an online historical directories website that links to all the online city directories in one place, listed by location and in date order. It also shows lists of resources of where to find offline historical directories.

Acworth/Marietta. The Georgia Room of the Marietta Central Library has 1883&84.

Adel. The Library of Congress has 1903–1980.

Albany. The central branch of the Dougherty County Public Library has 1907, 1922, 1925, 1928, 1930&31, 1934&35, 1937&38, 1939, 1941&42, 1943&44, 1946&47. The Library of Congress has 1912&13, 1922, 1922&23, 1925, 1946&47, 1949&50. The Georgia Archives has 1941&42. The National Daughters of the American Revolution Library has 1912&13, 1922, 1925.

Americus. The Lake Blackshear Regional Library has 1869, 1891&92, 1900&01, 1908&09, 1921, and telephone directories for 1939, 1949, 1950. The Library of Congress has 1916&17, 1921, 1923.

Athens. The University of Georgia's Hargrett Rare Book and Manuscript Library has 1889, 1897, 1904, 1909, 1914&15, 1916&17, 1920&21, 1923&24, 1926&27, 1931, 1935, 1937, 1938, 1940, 1942, 1947, 1949. The Athens-Clarke County Library has 1889, 1909, 1912&13, 1920&21, 1923&24, 1926&27, 1928&29, 1931, 1937, 1938, 1940, 1942, 1947, 1949. The Library of Congress has 1889 (on microfilm), 1899, 1937.

Atlanta (includes Decatur and Marietta in early years). The Atlanta History Center and the Georgia State University Library in Atlanta both have 1859, 1867, 1870–1872, 1876–1916, 1918–1945, 1947–1950. The Central Library of the Atlanta-Fulton Public Library System has 1859&60, 1867, 1870, 1871, 1876–1909 on microfilm and 1910–1916, 1918–1945, 1947–1950 in book form. The Georgia Archives has 1859&60 on microfiche; and 1859&60, 1867, 1870–1872, 1874–1935 on microfilm; and 1876, 1889, 1897, 1900, 1902, 1910, 1912–1916, 1918–1945, 1947–1950 in book form. The University of Georgia's Hargrett Rare Book and Manuscript Library has 1859, 1860, 1870, 1899, 1901, 1902, 1906, 1907, 1909, 1911–1913, 1916, 1918, 1924, 1926, 1928, 1929, 1930–1945, 1947–1950. The Georgia Historical Society has 1859. The Library of Congress has pre-1861 (on microfiche), 1861–1960 (on microfilm), 1870, 1875, 1882, 1886, 1888, 1890, 1894, 1899, 1900, 1936–1945, 1947, 1948&49, 1950. The Georgia Room at the Marietta Central Library has an Atlanta telephone directory of 1912 and an Atlanta city directory for 1929.

Augusta. The Augusta Regional Library has 1841, 1855, 1859, 1861, 1865&66, 1867, 1872, 1879, 1880, 1882, 1886, 1889, 1891, 1898, 1901–1903, 1905, 1907, 1908, 1912, 1913, 1915, 1917, 1919, 1921, 1923, 1925, 1927, 1929, 1930, 1932, 1934, 1935&36, 1937–1942, 1945, 1946, 1947&48, 1949, 1950. The University of Georgia's Hargrett Rare Book and Manuscript Library has 1865&66, 1882, 1888, 1889, 1892&93, 1910, 1925, 1940, 1946, 1947&48, 1949, 1950, in addition to 1841 in the library's DeRenne Collection. The Library of Congress has 1841–1939 (on microfilm); 1865&66, 1867, 1882, 1888, 1895&96, 1896&97, 1898, 1899, 1904, 1905, 1909, 1910, 1912–1915, 1917, 1919, 1921, 1923, 1925, 1927, 1929, 1930, 1932, 1934, 1935, 1937–1942, 1945, 1946, 1947–48, 1949, 1950. The Georgia Archives has 1841 in book form and 1841, 1859 on microfiche. The Georgia Archives also has the original and a microfilm copy of the 1852 Augusta City census, which has been published by the Augusta Genealogical Society in *Ancestoring* VII (1983), pp. 59–78 and in Volume VIII (1984) pp. 6–12. The National Daughters of the American Revolution Library has the 1921 Augusta City Directory. Also see Arthur Ray Rowland, *Index to City Directories of Augusta, Georgia, 1841–1879* (Augusta, GA: Augusta Genealogical Society, 1991), which describes each volume and its location. The Catalog of the Augusta (Georgia) City Directories, 1841–1939, describes each volume's details and location.

Brunswick. The Georgia Archives has 1890, 1892, 1898, 1901&02, 1903, 1905, 1917&18, 1921, 1923, 1925, 1930&31, 1935, 1937, and 1939 on microfilm and 1930&31, 1937 in book form. The Brunswick-Glynn County Regional Library in Brunswick has 1890, 1892, 1896, 1898, 1901&02, 1903, 1905, 1908, 1912, 1914&15, 1917&18, 1921, 1923, 1925, 1935, 1937, 1939, 1941, 1944, 1946, 1949. The University of Georgia's Hargrett Rare Book and Manuscript Library has 1890, 1930&31. The National Daughters of the American Revolution Library has 1914&15. The Library of Congress has 1914–1925, 1935–1983.

Carrollton. The West Georgia Regional Library has 1940 and 1947. The University of Georgia's Hargrett Rare Book and Manuscript Library has 1939&40.

Clarkesville. See Cornelia.

Columbus. The Columbus Public Library has 1859&60, 1873&74, 1878, 1880, 1880&81, 1884, 1891&92, 1894, 1896&97, 1900, 1902, 1904, 1906, 1908, 1912, 1914, 1916, 1918, 1921, 1923, 1925, 1927, 1928, 1931, 1934, 1936, 1937, 1939–1942, 1945–1947, 1949, 1950. The Library of Congress has 1886–1899 and 1906–1934 (on microfilm); 1886, 1889, 1894, 1898&99, 1906, 1910, 1912, 1914, 1916, 1918, 1921, 1923, 1925, 1927, 1928, 1931, 1934, 1936, 1937, 1939–1942, 1945–1947, 1949, 1950. The Georgia Archives has 1859&60 on microfiche. The University of Georgia's Hargrett Rare Book and Manuscript Library has 1923. The National Daughters of the American Revolution Library has 1908, 1921.

Cordele. The Carnegie Library in Cordele has 1914&15, 1938, 1949&50.

Cornelia/Clarkesville. The Library of Congress has 1950.

Covington. The Library of Congress has 1861–1883, according to James C. Neagles, et al., *The Library of Congress* (Salt Lake City: Ancestry Publishing, 1990): 256.

Darien. The Georgia Archives has on microfilm 1892, which is included in the 1892 Brunswick city directory.

Dalton. The Georgia Archives has 1912 in book form. The Library of Congress has 1913. The Dalton Regional Library has 1940. The National Society, Daughters of the American Revolution Library has 1912&13. The Crown Garden Archives, located at 715 Chattanooga Avenue, Dalton, Georgia 30720, and operated by the Whitfield-Murray Historical Society has 1909, 1926, 1930–1931, 1936, 1943.

Decatur (sometimes included with Atlanta directories in early years). DeKalb History Center in Decatur has Atlanta city directories, which include Decatur, beginning in 1930. The Center also has a 1915 DeKalb County tax map and a 1915 tax atlas. The Woodruff Library of Emory University and the Library of Congress have 1928&29. The Atlanta History Center has a DeKalb County directory for 1939.

Douglasville. The Georgia Archives has the 1915 census on microfilm.

Fitzgerald. The Georgia Archives has 1937&38 in book form. The Fitzgerald-Ben Hill County Library has 1937&38, 1950&51. The Library of Congress has 1920, 1950&51.

Gainesville. The Chestatee Regional Library in Gainesville has 1882, 1883, 1911&12, 1913&14, 1918, 1926, 1928&29, 1937, 1939, 1941, 1947, as well as the original 1908 Gainesville city census. The Georgia Archives has 1882&83, 1911&12, and 1918 on microfilm and 1928 in book form. The Library of Congress has 1915&16, 1917&18, 1920&21, 1925&26, 1927&28, 1939, 1942&43, 1948&49. The Georgia Room at the Marietta Central Library has 1941 (Volume 2).

Glynn County. The Library of Congress has a 1913 directory.

Griffin. The Library of Congress has 1913, 1917&18, 1921, 1927&28. The University of Georgia's Hargrett Rare Book and Manuscript Library has 1929&30. The National Daughters of the American Revolution Library has 1913&14.

LaGrange. The LaGrange Memorial Library has 1927&28, 1929, 1934, 1938, 1939, 1941, 1948, 1950. The Troup County Archives has 1912, 1927&28, 1929, 1936, 1938, 1939, 1941, 1946, 1948, 1950. The Library of Congress has 1912&13, 1921, 1946–1982.

Macon. The Georgia Archives has 1860, 1866, 1869&70, 1872, 1877, 1878, 1880, 1884, 1888, 1892, 1893, 1898&99, on microfilm. The Georgia Archives has 1878, 1909, and 1917 in book form. The Wesleyan College Library in Macon has 1908, 1909, 1911, 1912, 1915, 1917, 1918, 1920, 1922, 1924, 1925, 1941, 1942, 1945, 1946&47. The Washington Memorial Library in Macon has 1860, 1866, 1867, 1869&70, 1872, 1877, 1877&78, 1878, 1880, 1884, 1885&86, 1887, 1888&89, 1890&91, 1892, 1893&94, 1894, 1894&95, 1896&97, 1899, 1900, 1901&02, 1903–1909, 1911, 1912, 1914, 1915, 1917, 1918, 1920, 1922, 1924, 1925, 1927, 1930, 1932, 1934, 1935, 1935 (supplement), 1937, 1939, 1940, 1940 (supplement), 1941, 1942, 1943&44, 1945, 1946&47, 1948, 1949&50, 1950&51, 1952–date. The University of Georgia's Hargrett Rare Book and Manuscript Library has 1878, 1901&02, 1904, 1917, 1920, 1922, 1932, 1940, 1949, 1949&50. The Library of Congress has 1897–1935 (on microfilm), 1897, 1899, 1904–1907, 1909, 1911, 1912, 1914, 1915, 1917, 1918, 1920, 1922, 1924, 1925, 1927, 1930, 1932, 1934, 1935, 1937, 1939–1942, 1943&44, 1945, 1946&47, 1948, 1949&50, 1950&51. The National Daughters of the American Revolution Library has 1920. The Georgia Room of the Marietta Central Library has 1935.

Marietta (sometimes included with Atlanta directories in earlier years). The Georgia Room at the Marietta Central Library has 1936, 1938–39, 1941, 1944, 1947, 1947 (supplement), 1950. The Atlanta History Center has 1938, 1939, 1941, 1944, 1947, 1950. Also see Acworth.

Milledgeville. The Georgia College Library has 1938 and 1949 (supplement only) and telephone directories for 1936–1939, 1941, 1943–1948, 1950. The Georgia Archives has the original and a microfilm copy of the 1911 Milledgeville City census.

Moultrie. The Moultrie-Colquitt County Library has 1939&40, 1949&50. The Library of Congress has 1922, 1949&50. The National Daughters of the American Revolution Library has 1922.

Newnan. The Georgia Archives has 1927&28. The Carnegie Library in Newnan has 1949. The Library of Congress has 1917 and 1921.

Rome. The Sara Hightower Regional Library in Rome has 1880&81, 1883, 1888, 1895&96, 1898&99, 1904, 1913, 1919, 1922&23, 1926&27, 1929, 1931, 1934, 1936, 1938, 1942, 1947, 1950, and later. The Library of Congress has 1913, 1916, 1919, 1922, 1934, 1936, 1938, 1947, 1950. The National Daughters of the American Revolution Library has 1913. The Rome/Floyd Records Center, Rome, Georgia, has microfilm copies of 1880&81, 1883, 1888, 1898&99, 1904, 1913, 1919, 1922, 1926&27, 1929, 1931, 1934, 1936, 1938, 1940, 1942. The Georgia Room of the Marietta Central Library has 1947.

Savannah. The Georgia Historical Society in Savannah has 1848, 1858–1860, 1866, 1867, 1870, 1871, 1874, 1876–1886, 1888–1903, 1905–1928, 1930, 1932, 1934, 1936–1942, 1947, 1948, 1950. The Georgia Archives has 1848–1850, 1858–1860 on microfiche; 1866, 1867, 1870, 1871&72, 1874–1928, 1930, 1932, 1934 on microfilm and 1941 in book form, as well as a 1950 directory of Chatham County. The Chatham-Effingham-Liberty Regional Library in Savannah has 1848–1850, 1858–1860 on microfiche; 1866, 1867, 1870, 1870&71, 1874&75, 1877&78, 1879–1901 on microfilm; 1871, 1874&75, 1877, 1879 (two versions), 1880 (two versions), 1881–1898, 1900–1928, 1930, 1932, 1934, 1936–1942, 1947–1978 in book form. The University of Georgia's Hargrett Rare Book and Manuscript Library has 1867, 1871&72, 1874&75, 1877, 1877–78, 1879, 1880–1886, 1888–1918, 1928, 1930, 1934, 1937–1939, 1942, 1950. The University of Georgia's Hargrett Rare Book and Manuscript Library, DeRenne Collection, has 1848, 1849, 1852&53, 1858, 1859. The Library of Congress has 1861–1934 (on microfilm); 1876&77, 1880, 1882–1884, 1897–1900, 1904, 1907, 1917–1922, 1925, 1926, and 1950. The National Daughters of the American Revolution Library has 1919.

St. Mary's. The Georgia Archives has 1892, included in the 1892 Brunswick City Directory, on microfilm.

St. Simon's Island. The Georgia Archives has on microfilm 1892, 1898, 1903, and 1905, which are included in the Brunswick city directories for each of those years.

Thomasville. The Thomas County Historical Society has 1886, 1917&18, 1926, 1938&39, 1942&43–1950&51, and a 1946 business directory. The Georgia Archives has 1886 on microfilm and 1917&18, 1942&43, 1946&47, 1950&51 in book form. The Library of Congress has 1886, 1922, 1944&45, 1950&51.

Tifton. The Lake Blackshear Regional Library in Americus has 1939. The Library of Congress has 1949&50.

Valdosta. The South Georgia Regional Library in Valdosta has 1940, 1947, 1949. The Georgia Archives has telephone directories for 1896–1897 on microfilm. The Library of Congress has 1908&09, 1913&14, 1921, 1923, 1925, 1937, 1947, 1949.

Waycross. The Okefenokee Regional Library in Waycross has 1917&18, 1921, 1923, 1930&31, 1937&38, 1949&50. The University of Georgia's Hargrett Rare Book and Manuscript Library has 1908&09. The Library of Congress has 1908&09, 1912&13, 1914&15, 1917&18, 1921, 1923, 1925, 1939&40, 1945&46–1949&50. The National Daughters of the American Revolution Library has 1914&15.

Business Directories, Gazetteers, and Almanacs

In addition to the city directories, there have also been directories of Georgia businesses and gazetteers providing information on Georgia towns, cities, counties, businesses, professionals, and occasionally even planters.

As early as 1841, Lewis Tappen's Mercantile Agency offered for sale credit ratings of individual businesses. His company evolved into the R. G. Dun & Co., which began publishing credit ratings as the *Mercantile Agency's Reference Book* in 1859. As Dun & Bradstreet, the company still publishes credit ratings today. Because these and similar yearly compilations by its competitors were only leased to individual customers, and were collected for destruction at the end of each year, few of these compilations survive. The Library of Congress (on microfilm), the Baker Library of Harvard Business School, and the New York Public Library have the most complete collection of these works. The Atlanta History Center has these volumes for the South for at least 1891.

R.G. Dun & Company Credit Report Volumes, 1840–1895 are in the Baker Library, Harvard University, Boston MA. The collection is arranged geographically by state or territory. An online inventory to the collection is available at www.library.hbs.edu/hc/. Access to the collection is limited and permission must be obtained from the Baker Library, Harvard Business School, Boston, MA 02163. Also see:

> *International Directory of Company Histories.* 16 volumes to date. Detroit: St. James Press, 1984–.
>
> Partin, Randall D., and James D. Partin. *Georgia Trade Tokens.* N.p., 1990.

The Georgia Archives has a photostat of *Bradstreet's Commercial Reports Embracing the Bankers, Merchants, Manufacturers, and Others, in a Portion of the United States, Selected from the General Volume, Under Special Contract. Volume 83 – September, 1888.* [File II Subjects, Oversize Photostats, folder #17 "Gazetteer", POL-173]. For historical background see James D. Norris, *R. G. Dun & Co. 1841–1900* (Westport, Connecticut: Greenwood Press, 1978).

The Georgia Archives has on microfiche:

> Smith, John T. *Georgia Commercial Tax Digest and Directory.* Augusta, GA: Constitutionalist Press, 1851. A list by county of most Georgia merchants with financial worth and number of slaves for each.

The Southern Business Directory and General Commercial Advertiser. Charleston, SC: Press of Walker and James, 1854. There is a paper copy in the Central Library of the Atlanta-Fulton Public Library System. This volume may also be downloaded from Google Books.

Many early incorporations approved by the Georgia legislature are listed under a variety of headings in Volume 42 of *Official Code of Georgia* (Charlottesville, VA: Michie Co., 1982). Also see Alex M. Hitz, "Georgia's Early Laws of Incorporation," *Georgia Bar Journal* 11 (November 1948): 156–74, which includes a list of some companies incorporated before 1877. The Georgia Archives also has on microfilm corporation registrations, starting in 1908 and extending to around 1940. Fulton County was filmed separately from the other corporation registrations. The National Archives at Atlanta has the direct tax records on corporations for 1864–1872 and 1913–1917 for Georgia and for other southeastern states. Also see National Archives microcopy M667, Corporation Assessment Lists, 1909–1915. For modern corporation reports write to Corporations Division, Georgia Secretary of State, Atlanta, GA 30334.

In addition to the gazetteers and business directories listed on later pages in this work, there are also the following publications. This list is not complete. Many of the Gazetteers and Directories included in this section are available free from Google Books.

> Candler, Allen D. and Clement A. Evans. *Georgia: Comprising Sketches of Counties, Towns, Events, Institutions, and Persons.* 4 volumes. N.p.: Atlanta State Historical Association, 1906. Also known as the "*Cyclopedia of Georgia.*"
>
> Department of Agriculture. *Georgia Historical and Industrial.* Atlanta: G. W. Harrison, 1901.
>
> Derry, Joseph T. *Georgia.* Philadelphia: J. B. Lippincott, 1878.
>
> ———. *Prosperous Georgia: The Ideal Home for All Classes.* N.p., 1900.
>
> Derry, Joseph T. and R. F. Wright. *Advantages of Georgia.* Atlanta: Mutual Publishing, 1904.
>
> Henderson, J. T. *The Commonwealth of Georgia.* Atlanta: J. P. Harrison, 1884.
>
> Nesbitt, R. T. *Georgia: Her Resources and Possibilities.* Atlanta: Franklin Publishing Co., 1895.
>
> *The Georgia Annual: A Compendium of Useful Information About Georgia.* 2 editions. Atlanta: A. B. Caldwell, 1911 and 1912.
>
> White, George. *Statistics of the State of Georgia.* Savannah, GA: W. T. Williams, 1849.
>
> ———. *Historical Collections of the State of Georgia.* New York: Pudney & Russell, 1855.
>
> *Young and Company's Business and Professional Directory of the Cities and Towns of Georgia.* Atlanta: Young & Co., 1904.

Georgia almanacs for 1764 to 1900 are listed in Arthur Ray Rowland, *Georgia Almanacs* (Augusta, GA: privately printed, 1996). This work provides a checklist of almanacs from 1764–1900 believed to be related to Georgia. The entries are listed chronologically. At the end of each entry there is a location symbol based on the symbols of the National Union Catalog of the Library of Congress.

Gazetteers are geographical dictionaries or indexes[8]. There are a number of gazetteers that relate to Georgia. Adiel Sherwood published the earliest four from 1827–1860. Late 19th century editions date from 1876–1899. The information contained in each group is quite different, but both series are useful to historical research.

Sherwood Series

Adiel Sherwood (1791–1879) was a Baptist minister who came to Georgia in 1818. His work, *Gazetteer of the State of Georgia*, appeared in four editions: 1827, 1829, 1837, and 1860. Only the 1827 and 1860 editions have been reprinted and are likely to be found in libraries. Each edition contains valuable information. For example, information in the 1860 edition includes railroad histories and mileage between the towns they serviced; some data about each county and its towns; colleges and other centers of learning (he makes some comment about most of them); a list of newspapers existing in 1859, their location, and frequency of publication; some brief details about springs and other resorts; locations of cotton factories and other industries; and a list of United States post offices and their counties in Georgia. There is also some discussion of climate and the locations of minerals. The Georgia Archives has all four volumes (1827, 1829, 1837, 1860), although the 1829 edition is on microfilm only in Drawer 233, Box 25.

Late 19th Century Series

The late 19th Century group of gazetteers was not published by a single publisher. These volumes are now quite fragile, bulky, and have never been reprinted. Most libraries have a few, none have all listed below, and there is no assurance that the list below is complete.

For the most part, all of those below contain alphabetical lists of towns. Each town is described, mentioning the major industries, churches, rail lines, and banks. A list of businessmen and sometimes major farmers also is given.

Other supplemental information is listed in the foreword and some appendices, but the major value of these works is the town data.

1876–1877

> *Georgia State Directory, Volume I, 1876–1877*. Nashville, TN: Wheeler, Marshall and Bruce, 1876. Copies are located at Georgia Archives and the University of Georgia Libraries.

1879–1889

The titles vary slightly. They were published by J. H. Estill and A. E. Sholes.

> *Sholes' Georgia State Gazetteer and Business Directory for 1879 & 1880* [Volume 1]. Copies located at Atlanta History Center, Woodruff Library of Emory University, and the Georgia Archives.

---

[8] Kenneth H. Thomas Jr., formerly of the Georgia Department of Natural Resources, provided the information on gazetteers.

Sholes' Georgia State Gazetteer, Business and Planters Directory 1881–1882 (Volume 2). Copies located at Woodruff Library of Emory University and the Central Library of the Atlanta-Fulton Public Library System. Includes lists of teachers and farmers.

Georgia State Gazetteer, Business and Planter's Directory for 1883–1884 (Volume 3). Savannah: Morning News P. H., 1883. Copies located at Georgia Archives, Central Library of the Atlanta-Fulton Public Library System; and Library of Congress. Includes a list of planters and farmers.

Ibid. (Volume 4). 1886–1887. Copies located at Atlanta History Center, the Central Library of the Atlanta-Fulton Public Library System, and Woodruff Library of Emory University include a list of farmers and planters.

Ibid. (Volume 5). 1888–1889. Copies located at Georgia Archives and the Central Library of the Atlanta-Fulton Public Library System include a list of planters and farmers.

1881–1882

Georgia State Gazetteer and Business Directory, 1881–1882. Standard Directory Co.; Atlanta: J. P. Harrison and Co., 1881. Copies located at Georgia Archives and Library of Congress.

1893–1894

Southern Business Guide, Alphabetical and Classified, 1893–1894. Chicago: U.S. Central Publishing Co., 1893[?] This is southern wide and arranged within each state by occupations. Copy located at Georgia Archives.

1896

Georgia State Gazetteer and Business Directory, 1896. Atlanta: Agnew and Tierney, 1896. Copies located are at Woodruff Library of Emory University, the Central Library of the Atlanta-Fulton Public Library System, Georgia Archives, and Library of Congress. This gazetteer is slightly different from the other types, containing a valuable list of farmers, in addition to the town/city data.

1898–1899

Gazetteer and Directory of Georgia for 1898–1899. Richmond, VA: J. L. Hill Printing Co., 1898. This Volume says Fifth Edition but no others have been located. Copies located at Georgia Archives and Library of Congress.

1900–1901

Department of Agriculture, Georgia Historical and Industrial. Atlanta: Franklin Printing & Publishing Co., 1901.

Sanborn Fire Insurance Maps

The list below was compiled from a list of the Sanborn maps (and other lists) in the Map Room of the Science Library of the University of Georgia. Many of the maps from two (often overlapping) collections are on separate microfilms at the library of Georgia State University in Atlanta. The maps show individual building floor plans, streets, and other important information. Distances on these maps are usually distorted, however. The Georgia Archives also has a set of the Sanborn maps for Georgia, including pasted-on additions not found in the set at the University of Georgia. Also see:

> Hoehn, R. Philip, William S. Peterson-Hunt, and Evelyn I. Woodruff. *Union List of Sanborn Fire Insurance Maps Held by Institutions in the United States and Canada.* 2 volumes. Santa Cruz, CA: University of California, 1976. (Less complete than Ristow's work.)

> Ristow, Walter W. *Fire Insurance Maps in the Library of Congress.* Washington, DC: Library of Congress, 1981.

In the listing below, maps with pasted-on additions are shown as two dates divided by a slash (/), for example, 1924/1936. This indicates the original map of 1924 has been updated with pasted-on additions up to 1936. Years underlined indicate maps found only in the Library of Congress Collection. Years in **bold face** indicate maps found only in the University of Georgia Collection. An asterisk (*) indicates that the map is not in the collections of the Library of Congress or the Map Room of the University of Georgia Libraries but is available on microfilm from University Publications of America and was copied from the archives of the Sanborn Company.

Some other local street and building atlases and maps exist, not all by the Sanborn Company, that are not shown on this list.

Many, if not all, of the Sanborn Maps for Georgia, 1884–1922 have been digitized and are available in the Digital Library of Georgia: http://dlg.galileo.usg.edu/sanborn.

Abbeville: **1889** (1899?), 1899, 1906, 1913, 1924, 1924/1936

Acworth: 1921, 1930

Adairsville: 1916

Adel: 1903, 1908, 1913, 1924, 1924/1938

Albany: 1885, 1890, 1895, 1900, 1905, 1911, 1920 (includes Putney), 1930 (includes Putney and Radium Springs), 1930/1948 (includes Putney and Radium Springs), 1972*

Alma: 1942

Americus: 1885, 1890, 1895, 1900, 1905, 1912, 1924, 1924/1948, 1963*

Arlington: 1909, 1921, 1934, 1948*

Ashburn: 1912, 1921, 1930, 1930/1942

Athens: 1885, 1888, 1893, 1898, 1903, 1908, 1913, 1918, 1926, 1926/1950, 1967*

Atlanta (and some surrounding areas): 1886, 1892, 1895, 1899, 1911, 1917–1923 (additional sheets), **1917, 1920, 1921, 1923,** 1924, 1924/1962, 1925, 1925/1950, 1925/1962, 1931, 1931/1950, 1932, 1978*

Augusta: 1884, 1890, 1904, 1917, **1920**, 1917–1923 (additional sheets), 1923, 1923/1951, 1923/1954, 1954*, 1965*, 1970*

Georgia Research
Chapter III: Counties, County Records, and Local History Sources

Austell: <u>1923</u> (1925?), **1925**

Bainbridge: 1885, 1890, 1898, 1900, 1905, 1909, 1916, 1924, <u>1924/1963</u>, 1963*

Barnesville: <u>1885</u>, 1888, <u>1893</u>, 1898, 1903, 1908, 1913, 1924, <u>1924/1942</u>

Baxley: 1930, <u>1930/1944</u>, 1954*

Blackshear: 1885, 1895, 1903, 1908, 1913, 1924, <u>1924/1939</u>, 1947*

Blakely: 1906, 1912, 1920, 1930, <u>1930/1948</u>, 1955*

Blue Ridge: 1909, 1924, <u>1924/1938</u>, 1947*

Boston: 1898, 1903, 1909, 1916, 1924, <u>1924/1943</u>

Bowdon: 1911, 1922, 1930

Brunswick: **1885**, 1889, 1893, 1908, 1913, 1920, 1930, <u>1930/1949</u>, 1969*

Buena Vista: 1904, 1909, 1924, <u>1924/1943</u>

Buford: 1921, 1931, <u>1931/1944</u>

Bullochville: 1921

Butler: 1927

Cairo: 1912, 1924, <u>1924/1944</u>, 1956*

Calhoun: 1911, 1929, <u>1929/1948</u>

Camilla: 1885, 1890, 1895, 1900, 1906, 1913, 1921, 1934, <u>1934/1944</u>, 1952*

Canton: 1921, 1930, 1947*

Carrollton: 1885, 1890, 1895, 1900, 1905, 1911, 1922, 1930, <u>1930/1946</u>, 1960*

Cartersville: 1885, 1890, 1895, 1900, 1905, 1909, 1916, 1927, <u>1927/1945</u>, 1959*

Cave Spring: 1900, 1905, <u>1911</u>, 1923

Cedartown: 1885, 1890, 1895, 1900, 1905, 1908, 1915, 1923, <u>1932</u>, <u>1932/1945</u>, 1960*

Chickamauga: 1929, 1948*

Claxton: 1917, 1924, <u>1924/1942</u>, 1950*

Cochran: 1885, 1888, 1893, 1898, 1906, 1912, 1926, <u>1926/1943</u>

College Park: 1911 (also see Atlanta 1925)

Colquitt: 1906, 1915, 1924, <u>1924/1941</u>

Columbus: 1885, 1889, 1895, 1900, 1907, **1918, 1921, 1923**, 1918–1923 (additional sheets), 1929, <u>1929/1953</u>, 1966*

Commerce: **1895**, 1908, 1922, 1932, <u>1932/1943</u>

Conyers: 1884, <u>1890</u>, 1895, 1901, 1909, 1921, <u>1921/1945</u>

Coolidge: 1920

277

Georgia Research
Chapter III: Counties, County Records, and Local History Sources

Cordele: 1891, 1895, 1898, 1903, 1908, 1913, <u>1918</u>, <u>1926</u>, <u>1926/1948</u>, 1959*

Cornelia: 1922, **1923 (1932?), 1926**, <u>1932</u>, <u>1932/1941</u>, 1950*

Covington: 1884, <u>1890</u>, 1895, 1901, 1909, 1916, 1923, <u>1923/1948</u>, 1959*

Cuthbert: 1885, 1890, 1895, 1900, 1905, 1911, 1920, 1930, <u>1930/1943</u>

Dallas: 1895, 1900, 1905, 1911, 1923, <u>1932</u>, <u>1932/1945</u>

Dalton: 1885, 1889, 1897, 1903, 1908, 1914, 1925, <u>1941</u>, <u>1941/1950</u>, 1963*

Darien: 1885, 1890, 1895, 1908, 1920, 1940*

Dawson: 1885, 1890, 1895, 1900, 1905, 1911, 1920, <u>1930</u>, <u>1930/1943</u>

Decatur: 1911

Demorest: 1922

Doerun: 1924, 1946*

Donalsonville: 1930

Douglas: 1907, 1912, 1920, 1930, <u>1930/1946</u>, 1959*

Douglasville: 1895, 1900, 1905, 1911, 1923, <u>1923/1942</u>, 1951*

Dublin: 1895, 1898, 1903, 1908, 1913, 1920, 1930, <u>1930/1947</u>, 1962*

East Point: 1911 (also see Atlanta 1925)

Eastman: 1885, 1893, 1898, 1903, 1908, 1913, 1918, 1927, <u>1927/1944</u>

Eatonton: 1884, 1890, 1895, 1901, 1909, 1921, <u>1921/1924</u>

Edison: 1924, <u>1924/1939</u>

Elberton: 1885, 1888, 1893, 1898, 1903, 1907, 1913, 1922, 1930, <u>1930/1950</u>, 1959*

Ellijay: 1948

Fairburn: 1892, 1903, 1909, 1921, 1929, 1946*

Fayetteville: 1923, 1946*

Fitzgerald: 1898, 1903, 1908, 1915, 1921, 1928, <u>1928/1944</u>, 1960*

Flowery Branch: 1912, 1924

Forsyth: 1885, 1890, 1895, 1900, 1905, 1911, 1920, <u>1930</u>, <u>1930/1942</u>, 1950*

Fort Gaines: 1885, 1890, 1895, <u>1900</u>, <u>1905</u>, 1911, 1922, 1932

Fort Valley: **1885**, 1890, 1895, 1900, 1905, 1911, 1920, 1930, <u>1930/1948</u>, 1958*

Gainesville: 1886, 1888, 1893, 1898, 1903, 1909, 1915, 1922, 1930, <u>1930/1962</u>, <u>1936</u>, 1965*

Glovers: 1923

Good Hope: 1924

Grantville: 1921, 1930, <u>1930/1940</u>

Greensboro: 1885, 1890, 1895, 1901, 1909, 1921, 1921/1945

Greenville: 1898, 1903, 1908, 1913, 1926

Griffin: 1885, 1890, 1895, 1900, 1909, 1915, 1925, 1925/1949, 1961*

Hampton: 1890, 1895, 1900, 1905, 1911, 1923, 1923/1937

Hapeville: 1911 (also see Atlanta 1925)

Harmony Grove: 1895, 1901

Hartwell: 1901, 1908, 1917, 1924, 1924/1943

Hawkinsville: 1885, 1890, 1895, 1900, 1906, 1912, 1926, 1926/1939, 1960*

Hazlehurst: 1935

Hogansville: 1898, 1903, 1909, 1926

Jackson: 1895, 1900, 1905, 1913, 1924, 1924/1941, 1951*

Jasper: 1924

Jefferson: 1916, 1926, 1947*

Jesup: 1889, 1895, 1903, 1908, 1913, 1920, 1930, 1930/1940, 1950*

Jonesboro: 1890, 1895, 1900, 1905, 1911, 1923, 1923/1934

Juliette: 1923, 1924

Lafayette: 1928, 1928/1948

LaGrange: 1885, 1889, 1895, 1900, 1906, 1911, 1921, 1930, 1930/1950, 1960*

Lavonia: 1911, 1924, 1924/1932, 1947*

Lawrenceville: 1924, 1924/1950

Lexington: 1921, 1930

Lithonia: 1895, 1901, 1909, 1923, 1923/1932, 1946*

Louisville: 1904, 1909, 1921, 1930, 1930/1940, 1949*

Lumpkin: 1904, 1909, 1922, 1933

Macon: 1884, 1889, 1895, 1908, **1920**, 1920 (new streets), 1924, 1924/1951, 1968*, 1969*

Madison: 1885, 1890, 1895, 1901, 1909, 1921, 1921/1941, 1951*

Manchester: 1921, 1931, 1931/1940, 1947*

Marietta: 1885, 1890, 1895, 1900, 1905, 1911, 1923, 1923/1948, 1961*

Marshallville: 1922, 1933

McDonough: 1905, 1911, 1923, 1923/1936, 1947*

McRae: 1904, 1909, 1924, 1931, 1931/1939, 1949*

Meigs: 1909, 1913, 1924, 1924/1939, 1950*

Metter: 1930, <u>1930/1942</u>, 1951*

Milledgeville: 1884, 1889, 1895, 1901, 1908, 1913, 1926 (includes Hardwick and Midway), <u>1926/1949</u>, 1961*

Millen: 1917, 1927, <u>1927/1940</u>, 1947*

Monroe: 1888, 1895, 1901, 1909, 1916, 1924, <u>1924/1945</u>, 1960*

Montezuma: 1885, 1890, 1895, 1900, 1905, 1911, 1920, 1928, <u>1928/1938</u>, 1948*

Monticello: 1888, 1893, 1898, 1903, <u>1909</u>, 1921, 1931, <u>1931/1945</u>

Moultrie: 1899, 1903, 1908, 1912, 1920, 1929, <u>1929/1950</u>, 1966*

Mount Vernon: 1893, 1897, 1906, 1913, 1924

Nashville: 1930, <u>1930/1942</u>, 1951*

Newnan: 1885, 1889, 1895, 1900, 1906, 1911, 1927, <u>1927/1947</u>, 1959*

Ocilla: 1912, 1924, 1928, <u>1928/1938</u>, 1948*

Palmetto: 1885, 1890, 1900, 1909, 1924

Pelham: 1906, 1913, 1924, <u>1924/1939</u>, 1946*

Perry: 1930

Portal: 1917

Quitman: 1885, 1890, <u>1895</u>, 1900, 1905, 1912, 1921, 1930, <u>1930/1943</u>, 1950*

Reynolds: 1927

Richland: 1903, 1908, 1913, 1922, 1934

Rochelle: 1909, 1924, <u>1924/1934</u>

Rockmart: 1928, <u>1923/1945</u>

Rome: 1885, 1888, 1893, 1898, 1903, 1909, 1915, 1926, <u>1926/1950</u>, 1969*

Rossville: 1917, 1924, 1929, <u>1929/1948</u>

Roswell: <u>1911</u>, 1924, 1946*

Royston: 1924, <u>1924/1936</u>, 1947*

Sandersville: 1895, 1901, 1908, 1913, 1923, <u>1923/1938</u>, 1954*

Sasser: 1912, 1924

Savannah: 1884, 1888, 1898, 1916, **1922**, <u>1922</u> (additional sheets), <u>1916/1950</u>, 1963*, 1966*, 1973*

Shellman: 1930

Social Circle: 1899, 1904, 1909, 1924, <u>1924/1945</u>

Sparta: 1884, 1889, 1895, 1901, 1909, 1920, 1930, <u>1930/1945</u>

Statesboro: **1903** (1908?), <u>1908</u>, 1913, 1922, 1930, <u>1930/1946</u>, 1947*

Stone Mountain: 1924, <u>1924/1944</u>

Suwanee: 1923

Swainsboro: 1901, 1909, 1922, 1931, <u>1931/1949</u>

Sylvania: 1927, 1947*, 1951*

Sylvester: 1911, 1924, <u>1924/1941</u>

Talbotton: 1895, 1900, 1905, 1911, 1926

Tallapoosa: 1888, 1890, 1895, 1903, 1909, 1914, 1923, 1930, <u>1930/1939</u>, 1950*

Tennille: 1903, 1909, 1918, 1927, <u>1927/1937</u>

Thomaston: 1885, 1890, **1895**, 1900, 1905, 1911, 1921, 1930, <u>1930/1947</u>, 1962*

Thomasville: 1885, 1889, 1895, 1900, 1905, 1912, 1920, 1928, <u>1928/1950</u>, 1966*

Thomson: 1895, 1901, 1908, 1913, 1921, 1930, <u>1930/1949</u>

Tifton: 1898, 1903, 1907, 1912, 1917, 1924, <u>1924/1948</u>, 1961*

Toccoa: 1893, <u>1898</u>, 1903, 1908, 1923, 1931, <u>1931/1950</u>

Ty Ty: 1924

Unadilla: 1915, 1924, <u>1924/1940</u>

Union Point: 1930

Valdosta: 1885, 1889, 1895, 1900, 1905, 1911, 1912, 1922, 1930, <u>1930/1947</u>, 1971*

Vidalia: 1913, 1924, <u>1924/1938</u>, 1946*

Vienna: 1907, 1912, 1924, <u>1924/1943</u>

Villa Rica: 1923, 1933, <u>1933/1944</u>

Wadley: 1922, 1930

Warrenton: 1884, 1890, 1901, 1909, 1918, 1930

Washington: 1885, 1890, 1896, 1903, 1909, 1917, 1930, <u>1930/1940</u>, 1950*

Waycross: 1889, 1892, 1897, 1903, 1908, 1913, 1922, 1930, <u>1930/1947</u>, 1966*

Waynesboro: 1885, 1890, 1895, 1901, 1907, 1912, 1921, 1930, <u>1930/1937</u>, 1958*

West Point: 1885, 1890, 1895, <u>1900</u>, 1906, 1911, 1922, 1930, <u>1930/1949</u>, 1959*

Winder: 1903, 1909, 1921, 1930, 1959*

Wrightsville: 1906, 1913, 1924, <u>1924/1937</u>, 1947*

Photographs

Most major archives and libraries, and many local historical societies and libraries, have photograph collections. The Vanishing Georgia Project of the Georgia Archives has copied photographs from many Georgia counties (see list below). Included in the Georgia Archives Virtual Vault (www.GeorgiaArchives.org) are images from the Vanishing Georgia Collection, Small Print Collection, Historic Postcard Collection and World War II photos in the Lamar Q. Ball Collection. Among the other photographic holdings of the Georgia Archives is an album of railroad property along the Western & Atlantic Railroad; photographs made in the 1950s of surviving one-room school houses arranged by county; as well as the photograph archives of the Georgia Bureau of Mines, Mining and Geology, including photographs of scenery as well as mining, from 1890 to the 1940s, arranged by county (Record Group 50-2-20). Several counties including Bartow, Bibb (City of Macon), Chatham (City of Savannah), Coweta, DeKalb, Forsyth, Gwinnett, Hall (two volumes), Lowndes, Pickens, and others have published historical photograph books. Also see Gary L. Doster, *From Abbeville to Zebulon: Early Post Card Views of Georgia* (Athens: University of Georgia Press, 1991), and Doster's six books, by region, of Georgia post cards.

Sites Visited By The Vanishing Georgia Photograph Project Of The Georgia Archives

The following list provides the county and city or location within the county of the site.

Baldwin; Civilian Conservation Corps Reunion, F. D. Roosevelt State Park

Barrow; Winder

Ben Hill; Fitzgerald

Bibb; Macon

Bulloch; Statesboro

Burke; Waynesboro

Camden; St. Marys

Camden; Woodbine

Carroll; Carrollton

Chatham; Savannah

Clarke; Athens

Clayton; Forest Park

Cobb; Marietta

Coffee; Douglas

Colquitt; Moultrie

Coweta; Newnan

Decatur; Bainbridge

DeKalb; Decatur

DeKalb; Lithonia

DeKalb; Oglethorpe University

DeKalb; Stone Mountain

Dougherty; Albany

Early; Blakely

Emanuel; Swainsboro

Evans; Reidsville

Floyd; Rome

Franklin; Carnesville

Fulton; Oakland Cemetery

Fulton; East Point

Georgia Research
Chapter III: Counties, County Records, and Local History Sources

Fulton; Roswell
Glynn; Brunswick
Glynn; Jekyll Island
Gordon; Calhoun
Greene; Greensboro
Gwinnett; Buford
Gwinnett; Lawrenceville
Gwinnett; Lilburn
Habersham; Clarkesville
Hall; Gainesville
Hart; Hartwell
Houston; Perry
Jenkins; Millen
Johnson; Wrightsboro
Jones; Gray
Laurens; Dublin
Liberty; Hinesville
Lowndes; Valdosta
Lumpkin; Dahlonega
McDuffie; Thomson
Monroe; Forsyth
Murray; Chatsworth
Muscogee; Columbus
Newton; Covington

Pickens; Jasper
Polk; Cedartown
Polk; Rockmart
Pulaski; Hawkinsville
Putnam; Eatonton
Rabun; Clayton
Randolph; Cuthbert
Richmond; Augusta
Rockdale; Conyers
Seminole; Donaldsonville
Spalding; Griffin
Stephens; Toccoa
Sumter; Americus
Tattnall; Reidsville
Taylor; Reynolds
Thomas; Thomasville
Troup; LaGrange
Walton; Social Circle
Ware; Waycross
Washington; Sandersville
Whitfield; Dalton
Wilkes; Washington

Researcher Notes

CHAPTER IV
GENEALOGICAL PERIODICALS AND OTHER RESOURCES

General

Georgia has many genealogical and historical organizations which issue periodicals and separate publications. The most significant periodicals for Georgia genealogical research are listed in this chapter under "Genealogical Periodicals."

Genealogical newspaper columns are found listed in Anita Cheek Milner, *Newspaper Genealogical Column Directory*. 6th ed. (Bowie, MD: Heritage Books, Inc., 1996). Genealogical columns are often collected by local public libraries. The most popular column in Georgia is "Genealogy" by Kenneth H. Thomas, Jr. which has been published since 1977 in the Sunday *Atlanta Journal-Constitution*.

For a list of Georgia's historical societies, see James A. Overbeck, *Historical Organizations and Resources in Georgia* (Atlanta: Georgia Historical Records Advisory Board, 1996). This is updated on the Georgia Archives website at the address, http://www.sos.state.ga.us/archives. This website also provides direct links to the home pages of more than 150 historical organizations. Many of the historical organizations have newsletters or other publications useful to genealogists.

Genealogical Societies

For a list of genealogical societies, see Robert Holcomb Warnock, *Georgia Sources for Family History* (Atlanta: Georgia Genealogical Society, 1995). Only those societies that publish substantial genealogical material are included in the following periodicals list. Write to these societies for their latest list of publications. Readers should be cautioned that addresses, and particularly telephone numbers, are subject to change occasionally.

Many genealogical societies are listed on the GGS website (http://www.gagensociety.org) under "Research Tools" if more information is needed.

Genealogical Periodicals

The following are Georgia genealogical periodicals published at least biannually. Locally, the Georgia Archives in Atlanta and the Washington Memorial Library in Macon have the most complete collections of Georgia periodicals, including defunct Georgia periodicals. Periodicals no longer being published include *Douglas County, Georgia, Genealogy; Family Puzzlers; The Georgia Armchair Researcher; Georgia Genealogical Survey; The Georgia Genealogist; Georgia Pioneers; Harris County, Georgia, and Her People; Heard Heritage; They Were Here;* and *Troup County, Georgia, and Her People*.

Georgia Research
Chapter IV: Genealogical Periodicals and Other Resources

The Georgia Archives collection is listed in a ring binder titled "Periodical Collection Index" located in its periodical search room and is updated periodically. The Allen County Public Library in Ft. Wayne, Indiana, has an extensive collection of Georgia genealogical periodicals.

For a bibliography of the articles appearing throughout these periodicals, see James E. Dorsey, *Georgia Genealogy and Local History: A Bibliography* (Spartanburg, South Carolina: The Reprint Co., 1983), which has been updated in the *Georgia Historical Quarterly for 1982–1986* and in the *Georgia Genealogical Society Quarterly* for 1987–1992. The "Bibliography" series initiated by James Dorsey has been superseded by the Periodical Source Index (PERSI) (Ft. Wayne, Indiana: Allen County Public Library, 1988–1996), which is a topical index to all periodicals, including these and others nationwide. PERSI consists of an 1847–1985 index in 16 volumes and annual supplements beginning in 1986. The PERSI index was issued on CD in 1997 and a revised CD version is issued annually. The Georgia Archives has a complete and current set of the PERSI index, including the CD version. PERSI is also available online via HeritageQuest. PERSI users should note that subjects that are not geographical or a family name would usually appear under "US" in the geographic "Places" section, and some record types such as "deed" and "land" are used interchangeably.

Most of the following periodicals are topically indexed in PERSI, except as noted. The following list includes all active and defunct Georgia periodicals.

Ancestoring (1980–); Augusta Genealogical Society, P.O. Box 3743, Augusta, GA 30914-3743. No copy has been issued since 1990.

Ancestor Update (1992–); previously titled *Ancestors Unlimited* (1979–1991); Genealogical Society of Henry and Clayton counties, P.O. Box 1296, McDonough, GA 30253.

Ancestors Unlimited (1979–1991). See *Ancestor Update*.

Armchair Researcher, The (1980–1982). See *The Georgia Armchair Researcher*.

Bartow County Genealogical Society Quarterly (1992–); Bartow County Genealogical Society, P.O. Box 993, Cartersville, GA 30120-0993.

Carroll County Genealogical Quarterly (1980–); Carroll County Genealogical Society, P.O. Box 576, Carrollton, GA 30117.

Central Georgia Genealogical Society Quarterly (1979–); Central Georgia Genealogical Society, P.O. Box 2024, Warner Robins, GA 31099-2024

Chattooga County Historical Society Quarterly (1988–); Chattooga County Historical Society, P. O. Box 626, Summerville, GA 30747. This Quarterly is not topically indexed in PERSI as of 1999, although it may be included retroactively in the future.

Coweta County Genealogical Society Magazine (1982–1995); previously titled *Norma's Coweta Chatter* (1975–1981) and retitled *Coweta Courier* (1995–). See Coweta Courier.

Coweta Courier (1995–); previously titled *Coweta County Genealogical Society Magazine* (1982–1995) and *Norma's Coweta Chatter* (1975–1981); *Coweta County Genealogical Society*, P.O. Box 1014, Newnan, GA 30264.

Douglas County, Georgia, Genealogy (1978–1982); periodical by Joe Baggett, Douglasville, GA. This periodical is defunct.

Family Puzzlers (1964–1997); was published weekly by Heritage Papers, Athens, GA. The Internet address is http://www.heritagepapers.us/. Each issue of *Family Puzzlers* has a surname index and each yearly volume has a separate annual surname index. This publication is now defunct.

Family Puzzlers, The Next Generation (July, 1998–June 2001) by Amy Warren Sanders, Athens, GA. This publication is now defunct.

Family Tree (1991–); published quarterly by the Cobb County Genealogical Society, P.O. Box 1413, Marietta, GA 30061-1413.

Family Tree, The (1990–); an international genealogical bi-monthly publication by the Odom Library, P.O. Box 2828, Moultrie, GA 31776-2828. *The Family Tree* has a Scottish emphasis and distributed 76,000 copies in 1999. To subscribe write to the post office box above or call 912-985-6540.

Genealogical Gazette (1983–); published quarterly by the Southwest Georgia Genealogical Society, P.O. Box 4672, Albany, GA 31706.

Genealogy Unlimited (1985–); by Genealogy Unlimited, c/o Lillian N. McRee, 2511 Churchill Drive, Valdosta, GA 31602-2547.

Georgia Armchair Researcher, The (1983–1984); previously titled *The Armchair Researcher* (1980–1982); quarterly periodical by Joel Dixon Wells, Armchair Publications, Hampton, GA. This periodical is defunct.

Georgia Genealogical Magazine (1961–); Southern Historical Press, P.O. Box 1268, Greenville, SC, 29601. Also see Silas Emmett Lucas, *Master Index to the Georgia Genealogical Magazine Numbers 1–46, 1961–1972*, (Easley, South Carolina, n. p., 1973).

Georgia Genealogical Society Quarterly (1964–); Georgia Genealogical Society, P.O. Box 550247, Atlanta, GA 30355-2747. A paper copy is bound and available at the Georgia Archives. A topical index is by Jan McLendon, *Subject Index to 25 Years of the Georgia Genealogical Society Quarterly 1964–1989* (Atlanta, Georgia: the Society, 1990), Index available on the Georgia Genealogical Society website at www.gagensociety.org.

Georgia Genealogical Survey (1981–1982); quarterly periodical by Nancy J. Cornell, Riverdale, Georgia. This periodical is defunct.

Georgia Genealogist, The (1969–1985); was a quarterly periodical by Heritage Papers, Mrs. Mary B. Warren, editor, P.O. Box 7776, Athens, GA 30604-7776. This periodical is defunct, although back issues are available from the publisher.

Georgia Pioneers Genealogical Magazine (1964-1984); quarterly periodical by Mrs. Mary Carter, Albany, GA. This periodical is defunct.

Georgia Settlers (2000–); Quarterly periodical by East Georgia Genealogical Society, P. O. Box 117, Winder, GA 30680.

Harris County, Georgia, and Her People (1985–1987); quarterly periodical by Martha S. Anderson, Family Tree Publications, LaGrange, GA. This periodical is defunct.

Heard Heritage (1976–1983); biannual periodical by Lynda S. Eller, Lanett, AL. This periodical is defunct.

Heard and Scene, Quarterly published by Heard County Historical Society, P. O. Box 30217, Franklin, GA.

Heritage (1986–); Formerly Gwinnett Historical Society Quarterly (1978–1986), published quarterly by the Gwinnett Historical Society, P.O. Box 261, Lawrenceville, GA 30046. Website: http://www.gwinnetths.org.

Huxford Genealogical Society Magazine; Formerly Quarterly, then Huxford Genealogical Society Quarterly. Huxford Genealogical Society, P.O. Box 595, Homerville, GA 31634. The Society has published an index, which topically indexes, by state and county, all of its genealogical periodicals.

Muscogiana (1989–); quarterly periodical, presently being issued biannually, of the Muscogee Genealogical Society, P.O. Box 761, Columbus, GA 31902.

Norma's Coweta Chatter (1975–1981); retitled *Coweta County Genealogical Society Magazine* (1982–1995) and *Coweta Courier* (1995–). See *Coweta Courier*.

Northwest Georgia Historical and Genealogical Society Quarterly (1969–); Northwest Georgia Historical and Genealogical Society, P.O. Box 5063, Rome, GA 30162-5063. The Society has published a topical index to articles and photographs printed in its *Quarterly* from 1969 through 1993. Note that Vol. 23 #3 (1991) and Vol. 24 #4 (1992) of its *Quarterly* were never printed and these issue numbers were skipped.

Origins (1990–); periodical of the Thomasville Genealogical, History and Fine Arts Library, 135 North Broad Street, P. O. Box 1597, Thomasville, GA 31757. Website: http://home.rose.net/~glibrary/

Pine Barrens (1987–); quarterly periodical of the South Georgia Genealogical Society, 706 Crabapple Dr., Thomasville, GA 31757.

Southern Roots and Shoots (1985–); quarterly periodical of the Delta Genealogical Society, Rossville Public Library, 504 McFarland Ave., Rossville, GA 30741. Website: http://www.rootsweb.ancestry.com/~gadgs/.

They Were Here; Georgia Genealogical Records (1965–1971, 1976–1979); quarterly periodical by Mrs. Frances Wynd, Albany, GA. This periodical is defunct. It is now available at the Bryan-Lang Historical Library, 311 Camden Avenue, P. O. Box 715, Woodbine, GA 31569. Phone: 912-576-5841. (Camden County, GA research)

Troup County, Georgia, and Her People (1981–1988); quarterly periodical by Martha S. Anderson, Family Tree Publications, LaGrange, GA. This periodical is defunct.

Whitfield-Murray Historical Society Quarterly, (1976–83, 1988–); Formerly Murray-Whitfield County Historical Quarterly (1976–77). Quarterly periodical of the Whitfield-Murray Historical Society, P. O. Box 6180, Dalton, GA 30720-6180. Website: www.whitfield-murrayhistoricalsociety.org.

Libraries and Records Repositories

Only major libraries in Georgia with significant genealogical collections are included in this book. However, almost every local library in Georgia has genealogical holdings, if only a collection of local family histories. Every public library should have addresses of libraries, nationwide. Hours at the archives and libraries vary. Always call or write ahead before planning a visit. A complete list of Georgia libraries with addresses, telephone numbers, and collection descriptions are in Robert Holcomb Warnock, *Georgia Sources for Family History* (Atlanta, Georgia: Georgia Genealogical Society, 1995). Recent articles about major libraries that have been published in the Georgia Genealogical Society Quarterly are available on the GGS website http://www.GaGenSociety.org.

Latter-day Saints (LDS) Branch Libraries In Georgia

The Genealogical Library of the Church of Jesus Christ of Latter-day Saints (the Mormons), 50 East North Temple, Salt Lake City, Utah 84150 has microfilmed local records of genealogical value all over the world. The church makes this microfilm available to researchers (including non- Mormons) through its branch libraries. Each branch library has microfilm and microfiche of the lists of records that have been microfilmed and microfiche/microfilm of various computerized indexes to their multimillion name genealogical files. The church's holdings include the records indexed in E. Kay Kirkham, *An Index to Some of the Family Records of the Southern States* (Logan, Utah: Everton Pub., 1979). These branch libraries are staffed by volunteers, and days and hours open vary widely. Always call or write ahead. For a list of Georgia centers, please see their website at https://familysearch.org/locations.

The following public libraries also serve as a Family History Center:

Carrollton, West Georgia Regional Library, 710 Rome St., Carrollton. Phone: 770-836-6711

Chatsworth, Chatsworth-Murray County Library, 706 Old Dalton-Ellijay Rd., Chatsworth. Phone: 706-695-4200

Dawsonville, Chestatee Regional Library System, 342 Allen St., Dawsonville. Phone: 706-344-3690

Lafayette, Cherokee Regional Library, 305 South Duke St, Lafayette. Phone: 706-638-4912

Louisville, Jefferson County, GA Public Library, 306 E. Broad St., Louisville. Phone: 478-625-3751

Macon, Middle Georgia Regional Library, 1180 Washington Ave., Macon. Phone: 478-744-0800

Thomasville, Thomas County Public Library System, 201 N. Madison St., Thomasville. Phone: 229-225-5252

Washington, Bartram Trail Regional Library, 204 E. Liberty St., Washington. Phone: 706-678-7736.

Researcher Notes

INDEX

Index Notes:

1. Repository websites are not listed separately from the repository entry.
2. Please check the Contents for items of interest in addition to this index.

African-American Research, 3, 15, 52, 65, 66, 67, 68, 79, 83, 84, 93, 95, 101, 105, 106, 111, 112, 113, 116, 121, 127, 129, 157, 186, 197, 243, 261, 272

Cities

    Abbeville, 276

    Acworth, 268, 276

    Adairsville, 276

    Adel, 268, 276

    Albany, 39, 267, 268, 276

    Alma, 276

    Americus, 40, 267, 268, 276

    Arlington, 276

    Ashburn, 276

    Athens, 40, 267, 268, 276

    Atlanta, 40, 59, 60, 84, 267, 268, 276

    Augusta, 40, 59, 60, 66, 84, 95, 267, 269, 276

    Austell, 277

    Bainbridge, 277

    Barnesville, 277

    Baxley, 277

    Bethany, 136

    Blackshear, 277

    Blakely, 277

    Blue Ridge, 277

    Boston, 277

    Bowdon, 277

    Brunswick, 267, 269, 277

    Buena Vista, 277

    Buford, 277

    Bullochville, 277

    Butler, 277

    Cairo, 277

    Calhoun, 277

    Camilla, 277

    Canton, 277

    Carrollton, 269, 277

    Cartersville, 277

    Cave Spring, 277

    Cedartown, 277

    Chickamauga, 277

    Clarkesville, 269

    Claxton, 277

    Cochran, 277

    College Park, 277

    Colquitt, 277

    Columbus, 40, 60, 118, 267, 269, 277

    Commerce, 277

Conyers, 277
Coolidge, 277
Cordele, 269, 278
Cornelia, 269, 278
Covington, 269, 278
Cuthbert, 278
Dallas, 278
Dalton, 84, 267, 270, 278
Darien, 131, 137, 269, 278
Dawson, 278
Decatur, 268, 270, 278
Demorest, 278
Doerun, 278
Donalsonville, 278
Douglas, 278
Douglasville, 270, 278
Dublin, 267, 278
East Point, 278
Eastman, 278
Eatonton, 278
Ebenezer, 136
Edison, 278
Elberton, 278
Ellijay, 278
Fairburn, 278
Fayetteville, 278
Fitzgerald, 270, 278
Flowery Branch, 278
Forsyth, 278
Fort Gaines, 278
Fort Valley, 278
Frederica, 131

Gainesville, 60, 267, 270, 278
Glovers, 278
Good Hope, 278
Grantville, 278
Greensboro, 279
Greenville, 279
Griffin, 270, 279
Hampton, 279
Hapeville, 279
Hardwick, 280
Harmony Grove, 279
Hartwell, 279
Hawkinsville, 279
Hazlehurst, 279
Hogansville, 279
Jackson, 279
Jasper, 279
Jefferson, 279
Jesup, 279
Jonesboro, 279
Juliette, 279
Lafayette, 279
LaGrange, 267, 270, 279
Lavonia, 279
Lawrenceville, 279
Lexington, 279
Lithonia, 279
Louisville, 40, 279
Lumpkin, 279
Macon, 40, 59, 61, 84, 85, 118, 267, 270, 279, 282
Madison, 279

Manchester, 279

Marietta, 40, 268, 271, 279

Marshallville, 279

McDonough, 279

McRae, 279

Meigs, 279

Metter, 280

Midway, 280

Milledgeville, 40, 118, 271, 280

Millen, 280

Monroe, 280

Montezuma, 280

Monticello, 280

Moultrie, 271, 280

Mount Vernon, 280

Nashville, 280

Newnan, 271, 280

Ocilla, 280

Palmetto, 280

Pelham, 280

Perry, 280

Portal, 280

Putney, 276

Queensborough, 137

Quitman, 280

Radium Springs, 276

Reynolds, 280

Richland, 280

Rochelle, 280

Rockmart, 280

Rome, 267, 271, 280

Rossville, 280

Roswell, 280

Royston, 280

Sandersville, 280

Sasser, 280

Savannah, 20, 40, 59, 61, 66, 84, 130, 131, 153, 267, 271, 280, 282

Shellman, 280

Social Circle, 280

Sparta, 40, 280

St. Mary's, 271

St. Simon's Island, 271

Statesboro, 281

Stone Mountain, 281

Suwanee, 281

Swainsboro, 281

Sylvania, 281

Sylvester, 281

Talbotton, 281

Tallapoosa, 281

Tennille, 281

Thomaston, 281

Thomasville, 40, 271, 281

Thomson, 281

Tifton, 272, 281

Toccoa, 281

Ty Ty, 281

Unadilla, 281

Union Point, 281

Valdosta, 40, 267, 272, 281

Vidalia, 281

Vienna, 281

Villa Rica, 281

Wadley, 281

Warrenton, 281

Washington, 281

Waycross, 267, 272, 281

Waynesboro, 281

West Point, 281

Winder, 281

Wrightsville, 281

Counties

    Appling County, 66, 98, 154, 213, 237, 258

    Atkinson County, 148, 154

    Bacon County, 154, 155

    Baker County, 155, 166, 188, 227, 228

    Baldwin County, 59, 98, 112, 145, 155, 156, 157, 212, 215, 230, 239

    Banks County, 157, 158

    Barrow County, 158

    Bartow County, 73, 95, 158, 159, 169, 200, 282

    Ben Hill County, 159

    Berrien County, 148, 159, 160, 180, 217, 252

    Bibb County, 61, 66, 160, 161, 282

    Bleckley County, 161, 162

    Bourbon County, 162

    Brantley County, 162

    Brooks County, 73, 162, 163

    Bryan County, 66, 163, 164

    Bulloch County, 95, 164, 168, 191, 192, 214

    Burke County, 73, 143, 145, 153, 164, 165, 213, 214, 244, 259

    Butts County, 73, 165, 166

    Calhoun County, 73, 166

    Camden County, 62, 93, 95, 145, 153, 166, 167, 170

    Campbell County, 167, 168, 188, 197

    Candler County, 168

    Carroll County, 60, 93, 99, 167, 169, 188, 206, 208

    Cass County, 93, 158, 159, 169, 200

    Catoosa County, 73, 169, 170

    Charlton County, 162, 167, 170

    Chatham County, 20, 61, 65, 66, 76, 92, 95, 134, 136, 145, 146, 153, 163, 170, 171, 172, 271

    Chattahoochee County, 59, 172, 173

    Chattooga County, 60, 73, 173

    Cherokee County, 62, 73, 95, 99, 143, 158, 169, 173, 174, 177, 194, 195, 198, 221, 227, 231, 236, 256

    Clarke County, 59, 60, 62, 66, 73, 93, 145, 174, 175, 223, 234

    Clay County, 62, 176

    Clayton County, 60, 62, 176, 177

    Clinch County, 62, 154, 177, 178, 190, 217

    Cobb County, 62, 86, 95, 177, 178, 227, 287

    Coffee County, 62, 154, 159, 178, 179, 213

    Colquitt County, 60, 179

    Columbia County, 59, 62, 66, 95, 145, 179, 180, 224, 259

    Cook County, 180

    Coweta County, 62, 99, 167, 180, 181, 182, 208, 282, 286

Crawford County, 59, 62, 66, 93, 182, 183, 257

Crisp County, 183

Dade County, 62, 73, 183, 184

Dawson County, 62, 148, 184

Decatur County, 62, 93, 184, 185, 201, 244, 251

DeKalb County, 34, 54, 62, 167, 185, 186, 187, 197, 270, 282

Dodge County, 187

Dooly County, 62, 73, 95, 99, 183, 187, 188, 255, 263, 266

Dougherty County, 62, 188

Douglas County, 188, 189

Early County, 60, 62, 98, 155, 166, 176, 185, 189, 190, 227, 244

Echols County, 62, 190

Effingham County, 62, 136, 153, 163, 190, 244

Elbert County, 60, 62, 112, 145, 190, 191, 207, 223

Emanuel County, 62, 73, 165, 168, 191, 192, 214, 215, 252, 254

Evans County, 192

Fannin County, 62, 192, 193

Fayette County, 59, 60, 62, 73, 99, 167, 176, 185, 193, 194, 245

Floyd County, 63, 73, 173, 194, 200, 238

Forsyth County, 73, 95, 195, 227, 282

Franklin County, 59, 60, 66, 73, 93, 94, 145, 157, 174, 195, 196, 204, 207, 211, 223, 245

Fulton County, 33, 34, 54, 60, 167, 196, 197, 198, 227, 273

Gilmer County, 95, 184, 193, 198, 199, 236

Glascock County, 59, 199

Glynn County, 66, 95, 145, 153, 199, 270

Gordon County, 73, 200, 201

Grady County, 185, 201

Greene County, 66, 95, 145, 174, 201, 202, 205, 248

Gwinnett County, 54, 73, 98, 158, 185, 202, 203, 282

Habersham County, 98, 157, 203, 245, 262

Hall County, 98, 195, 204, 205, 282

Hancock County, 76, 145, 155, 205, 206, 248

Haralson County, 62, 206

Harbersham County, 73

Harris County, 66, 206, 207

Hart County, 69, 207, 208

Heard County, 208, 288

Henry County, 60, 69, 73, 87, 99, 165, 176, 185, 208, 209, 233, 243, 245

Houston County, 66, 99, 160, 182, 209, 210, 222, 236

Irwin County, 58, 62, 73, 93, 98, 159, 178, 210, 211, 220, 251, 252, 255, 263, 266

Jackson County, 60, 108, 121, 145, 158, 174, 204, 211, 212, 223

Jasper County, 93, 95, 212, 213, 233, 241

Jeff Davis County, 213

Jefferson County, 59, 60, 93, 123, 145, 211, 213, 214

Jenkins County, 214, 215

Johnson County, 68, 73, 215

Jones County, 145, 160, 215, 216

Kinchafoonee County, 216, 262

Lamar County, 216

Lanier County, 217

Laurens County, 73, 95, 215, 217, 218, 239

Lee County, 99, 218, 224, 241, 247, 251

Liberty County, 65, 95, 137, 145, 153, 218, 219, 220, 225

Lincoln County, 60, 92, 145, 219, 220

Long County, 220

Lowndes County, 159, 162, 177, 179, 190, 217, 220, 221, 282

Lumpkin County, 60, 93, 95, 122, 184, 221, 222

Macon County, 81, 222, 223, 236, 250

Madison County, 145, 223

Marion County, 93, 172, 222, 224, 244, 250

McDuffie County, 180, 224, 225

McIntosh County, 60, 66, 146, 225, 226

Meriwether County, 60, 226, 227

Miller County, 60, 227

Milton County, 73, 197, 198, 227

Mitchell County, 227, 228

Monroe County, 66, 99, 160, 165, 216, 228, 229, 238

Montgomery County, 73, 145, 187, 191, 229, 230, 249, 252, 254, 262

Morgan County, 59, 62, 66, 95, 145, 230, 231

Murray County, 73, 95, 231, 257, 263

Muscogee County, 60, 66, 99, 146, 172, 206, 224, 231, 232, 247

Newton County, 59, 73, 87, 95, 233, 243

Oconee County, 234

Oglethorpe County, 60, 66, 95, 115, 145, 223, 234, 235, 236, 248

Paulding County, 95, 236, 238

Peach County, 236

Pickens County, 94, 236, 237, 282

Pierce County, 154, 162, 237

Pike County, 62, 216, 238, 245, 257

Polk County, 62, 206, 238, 239

Pulaski County, 60, 62, 73, 145, 161, 187, 239, 263

Putnam County, 62, 145, 239, 240

Quitman County, 62, 240

Rabun County, 62, 93, 98, 240, 241, 253

Randolph County, 62, 176, 212, 240, 241, 246, 251

Richmon County, 66

Richmond County, 60, 62, 66, 95, 145, 179, 241, 242, 243, 259

Rockdale County, 87, 243

Schley County, 62, 244

Screven County, 62, 136, 164, 214, 244

Seminole County, 244, 245

Spalding County, 62, 245

Stephens County, 245, 246

Stewart County, 62, 73, 216, 240, 246, 262

Sumter County, 60, 62, 66, 244, 246, 247

Talbot County, 60, 62, 66, 247, 248, 250

Taliaferro County, 59, 60, 66, 93, 95, 248

Tattnall County, 60, 62, 66, 95, 145, 168, 192, 249, 252

Taylor County, 62, 249, 250

Telfair County, 59, 62, 73, 178, 187, 250, 251

Georgia Research

Index

Terrell County, 62, 95, 251

Thomas County, 62, 73, 162, 179, 201, 251, 252

Tift County, 252

Toombs County, 252, 253

Towns County, 62, 253, 254

Treutlen County, 254

Troup County, 33, 62, 99, 206, 208, 226, 254, 255

Turner County, 255

Twiggs County, 62, 160, 255, 256

Union County, 62, 95, 193, 253, 256

Upson County, 62, 66, 95, 257

Walker County, 73, 169, 173, 183, 257, 258

Walton County, 60, 73, 98, 158, 233, 258

Ware County, 148, 154, 170, 177, 178, 237, 258, 259

Warren County, 62, 66, 73, 95, 145, 199, 213, 224, 248, 259

Washington County, 59, 201, 205, 215, 229, 259, 260, 261

Wayne County, 98, 162, 261

Webster County, 216, 262

Wheeler County, 262

White County, 262, 263

Whitfield County, 73, 169, 263

Wilcox County, 73, 159, 255, 263, 264

Wilkes County, 27, 66, 67, 105, 111, 115, 127, 134, 144, 145, 146, 190, 219, 234, 248, 259, 264, 265

Wilkinson County, 98, 217, 250, 256, 265, 266

Worth County, 252, 255, 266

Fraternal Organizations
    Masons/Freemasons, 37
    Other, 38

Military
    Amnesty, 64
    Cherokee Disturbances, 5
    Civil War, 1, 3, 4, 5, 16, 17, 18, 29, 30, 34, 38, 40, 41, 55, 56, 60, 61, 64, 65, 66, 67, 69, 70, 71, 72, 73, 74, 75, 76, 78, 79, 80, 81, 82, 83, 84, 85, 86, 87, 88, 89, 90, 91, 92, 102, 104, 108, 143, 144, 160, 175, 180, 191, 195, 205, 209, 224, 233, 243, 252
    Compiled Service Records, 4, 61, 74, 78, 79, 80, 81, 82, 101, 103
    Indian Wars, 101
    Militia, 14, 25, 37, 62, 73, 74, 78, 100, 101, 118, 122, 134, 144, 153
    National Guard, 8, 37, 55, 61
    Pardons, 64
    Pensions, 3, 4, 48, 56, 61, 65, 69, 72, 73, 75, 76, 78, 80, 84, 87, 88, 89, 101, 102, 103, 104, 105, 111, 119, 125, 126, 127
    Philippines Insurrection, 61
    Revolutionary War, 3, 4, 5, 17, 18, 27, 35, 39, 41, 48, 68, 92, 96, 98, 104, 105, 116, 117, 118, 119, 120, 121, 123, 124, 125, 126, 127, 128, 129, 130, 138, 269, 270, 271
    State Troops, 61
    Texas Revolution, 102
    War of 1812, 3, 5, 18, 87, 96, 98, 101, 102, 103, 104, 105, 108, 121, 129
    War with Mexico, 102, 103, 105
    War with Spain, 61
    World War I, 3, 54, 55, 58, 61, 282

World War II, 3, 55, 56, 282

Native American Research, 3, 5, 6, 18, 29, 43, 93, 95, 99, 100, 101, 103, 105, 106, 107, 108, 109, 111, 113, 116, 119, 120, 125, 127, 174, 182, 189

Parishes
- Christ Church Parish, 153, 170
- St. Andrew Parish, 153, 218
- St. David Parish, 153, 199
- St. George Parish, 153, 164
- St. James Parish, 133, 153, 218
- St. John Parish, 153, 218
- St. Mary Parish, 153, 167
- St. Mathew Parish, 153, 190
- St. Patrick Parish, 153, 199
- St. Paul Parish, 153, 242, 264
- St. Philip Parish, 153, 190
- St. Thomas Parish, 153, 167

Record Types
- Adoption, 52
- Almanacs, 272, 273
- Asylum, 57
- Bankruptcy, 4
- Bible, 14, 15, 17, 47
- Biographies, 30, 71, 72
- Books, 15
- Cemetery, 15, 18, 25, 34, 42, 55, 56, 58, 78, 85, 86, 111, 138, 148, 160, 267, 282
- Census, 2, 3, 4, 5, 6, 16, 26, 30, 48, 51, 52, 58, 59, 60, 62, 68, 69, 73, 74, 83, 84, 87, 89, 92, 93, 95, 105, 106, 107, 108, 111, 113, 115, 121, 126, 129, 131, 138, 144, 145, 174, 248, 268, 269, 270, 271
- Church, 14, 16, 42, 43
- City Directories, 20, 68, 114, 267, 268, 269, 270, 271, 272
- County, 15, 48, 57, 141, 145, 148, 171
- Court, 4, 5, 6, 7, 12, 13, 14, 35, 47, 52, 57, 58, 66, 67, 68, 83, 85, 95, 109, 112, 113, 115, 117, 121, 122, 126, 141, 143, 144, 146, 147, 148, 157, 174, 214
- Death, 52, 60
- Divorce, 13, 14, 41, 144
- Estate, 34, 41, 69, 93, 111, 113, 134, 135, 141, 142, 143, 147, 148, 172, 257
- Federal, 1, 2, 15, 83, 102, 130
- Foreign, 16
- Freedmen's Bureau, 67
- Gazetteer, 25, 35, 272, 273, 274, 275
- Immigration, 6, 58, 137
- Land, 4, 26, 71, 96, 98, 102, 103, 104, 107, 108, 111, 113, 115, 116, 117, 118, 120, 124, 125, 128, 133, 134, 135, 143, 144, 147, 148, 196
- Land Lottery, 48, 95, 96, 98, 99, 100, 115, 143, 147, 233
- Marriage, 14, 41, 42, 43, 46, 52, 57, 60, 67, 69, 105, 109, 114, 135, 138, 141, 142, 143, 147, 148, 239
- Municipal, 15
- Naturalization, 5, 6, 14, 58, 62, 63, 131
- Newspaper, 14, 16, 20, 22, 29, 31, 32, 39, 40, 41, 42, 45, 46, 48, 70, 76, 78, 83, 91, 112, 113, 114, 122, 138, 148, 156, 184, 195, 221, 238, 274
- Other States, 16
- Passenger List, 3, 5, 6, 58, 114, 137
- Passport, 58, 108, 119, 120
- Photographs, 13, 25, 42, 54, 70, 75, 76, 282

Poor School, 95, 105

Postmasters, 2, 6, 114

Prison, 3, 47, 57, 74, 75, 81, 84

Private Papers, 16, 17, 34, 73, 86

Railroad, 2, 3, 58, 81, 83, 274, 282

Social Security Death Index, 51

State, 15, 116, 128, 138, 142

Tax, 3, 6, 15, 35, 57, 59, 60, 66, 95, 115, 122, 143, 144, 145, 146, 147, 148, 270, 272, 273

Vital, 52, 60, 141

Voter, 62, 63, 108, 174

Religion

Baptist, 8, 43, 44, 45, 46, 109, 181, 248, 274

Catholic, 44, 121, 171

Congregationalist, 137

Jewish, 43, 44, 129

Methodist, 43, 45, 46, 90

Moravians, 137

Presbyterian, 43, 45, 46, 109, 157

Quakers, 137

Repositories

Allen County-Fort Wayne Public Library, 9, 31, 286

Atlanta History Center, 9, 40, 61, 71, 113, 167, 168, 186, 197, 198, 221, 227, 268, 270, 271, 272, 274, 275

Atlanta-Fulton Public Library, 32, 61, 197, 268, 273, 275

Federal Depository Libraries, 7, 59

Georgia Archives, 5, 11, 12, 13, 14, 15, 16, 17, 18, 23, 25, 26, 27, 29, 30, 34, 35, 36, 38, 41, 42, 43, 44, 45, 47, 48, 52, 54, 55, 57, 58, 59, 60, 61, 62, 64, 65, 66, 67, 68, 69, 71, 73, 74, 76, 78, 80, 81, 83, 84, 85, 86, 88, 89, 92, 93, 95, 96, 98, 100, 103, 105, 106, 107, 108, 109, 111, 113, 114, 115, 117, 118, 119, 120, 121, 123, 124, 125, 127, 128, 129, 130, 133, 134, 135, 136, 138, 139, 141, 142, 143, 144, 145, 146, 148, 156, 163, 167, 171, 172, 175, 196, 242, 260, 267, 268, 269, 270, 271, 272, 273, 274, 275, 276, 282, 285, 286, 287

Georgia Historical Society, 8, 12, 19, 20, 44, 61, 71, 74, 108, 123, 130, 135, 138, 171, 172, 242, 268, 271

Hargrett Library, University of Georgia, 10, 12, 20, 29, 31, 71, 128, 130, 131, 164, 211, 215, 267, 268, 269, 270, 271, 272

Historic Preservation Division, 20

Huxford-Spear Genealogical Library, 21

Library of Congress, 7, 11, 23, 25, 26, 30, 31, 39, 41, 47, 49, 76, 83, 84, 90, 91, 112, 118, 120, 138, 172, 177, 267, 268, 269, 270, 271, 272, 273, 275, 276

National Archives at Atlanta, 2, 3, 4, 54, 57, 58, 62, 64, 66, 68, 74, 79, 85, 93, 101, 106, 108, 115, 125, 130, 273

National Archives(NARA), 1, 2, 49, 52, 55, 64, 66, 68, 78, 79, 80, 83, 84, 85, 87, 101, 102, 103, 104, 114, 125, 126

Other, 18, 35, 88

Washington Memorial Library, 22, 84, 160, 161, 253, 270, 285

Woodruff Library, Emory University, 39, 138, 186, 270, 274, 275

Southern Claims Commission, 64, 65

Websites

Ancestry.com, 5, 6, 9, 31, 48, 51, 52, 54, 58, 62, 63, 66, 67, 74, 75, 79, 80, 84, 92, 100, 111, 112, 114, 177, 267

Index

Archives.com, 48

Digital Library of Georgia, 13, 22, 26, 39, 40, 47, 48, 198, 276

Fold3, 48, 64, 66, 79, 83, 87, 125

GenealogyBank, 7, 39, 40, 66, 106, 138, 172

HeritageQuest, 9, 31, 48, 52, 58, 62, 92, 125, 144, 286

New Georgia Encyclopedia, 22, 32

Researcher Notes

Researcher Notes

www.ingramcontent.com/pod-product-compliance
Lightning Source LLC
Chambersburg PA
CBHW060310240426
43661CB00059B/2717